Ben Sidran has recorded thirty solo albums, produced recordings for artists Van Morrison, Diana Ross, Mose Allison, and Jon Hendricks, and is the music producer of the acclaimed film *Hoop Dreams*; he hosted "Jazz Alive" and "Sidran on Record" for National Public Radio and "New Visions" for VH-1 television. Sidran is the author of three previous books and holds a Ph.D. in American Studies from Sussex University.

Photo Credit: Giardini

ALSO BY BEN SIDRAN

Black Talk: How the Music of Black America Created a Radical Alternative to the Values of Western Literary Tradition

Talking Jazz: An Oral History

Ben Sidran: A Life in the Music

Music, videos, lectures, and links at:
www.bensidran.com

There Was a Fire

Jews, Music and the American Dream

Ben Sidran

BEN SIDRAN

THERE WAS A FIRE:
JEWS, MUSIC AND THE AMERICAN DREAM

Nardis Books is an imprint of Unlimited Media Ltd.

www.unlimitedmedialimited.com

Third Edition: January 2015

Book design by Planet Propaganda

For Sol Parker

Contents

In the beginning
Man created God,
So he would not be alone,
Lost, without hope,
And God became that hope,
And hope became the reason to believe
That God created man.

—BORUCH BEN ARULEB

There Was a Fire

Jews, Music and the American Dream

Ben Sidran

PREFACE

The Hebrew language is very down to earth, conversational, and immediate. The translation of the torah (the first five books of the Old Testament) that most of us are familiar with in English is, however, rendered in Old English, based on the King James translation. This tends to make the Hebrew sound stilted and lofty to us today, not at all like the language of the street and the common man that it has always been. We read *thy* and *thou*, and *begat*, and it sounds distant and from another time. It was never intended that way—the *teaching* (the literal translation of the word *torah*) was meant to be for everyone at all times, from children to grandparents, and from the most simple person to the most erudite scholar. Before blaming poor King James, however, it's important to recognize that his translation put Hebrew into what was, at the time, the everyday English spoken by the common man. Many generations later, clergymen and publishers retained the *thys* and *thous* either out of a sense of tradition, or because they felt it added a sense of important and separateness, of holiness. (The Hebrew word *kedushah*, which is translated as *holy*, literally means *separate* or *apart*.)

A contemporary translation of the torah to modern English would make it sound like it did to the ancient Hebrews who first wrote it down, would make it sound like the everyday conversations we overhear around us spoken in cities and in the country, in the mountains and in the plains, the language of all of us. It would sound more like the 20th Century American pop music that Ben Sidran writes about, and less like high opera. And this is what the American Jews who wrote this great and treasured canon were trying to achieve—to create songs that captured the new American vernacular, that reflected the way we spoke to one another, and often as not provide us with concise lessons in how to live and love.

When Jews started coming to America in the early 1900s, we had been a people without a home for two thousand years, a people in exile. We had become expert at learning the morays and vagaries of different cultures, of picking up new languages and habits. But we had not become expert at assimilating, at fitting in. Everywhere we went, we were *separate* and *apart*, and not by our own doing. As outsiders we were mistrusted. Our religion was grossly mischaracterized, slandered, and misunderstood, giving rise to hideous stories about our rituals including that Jews engaged in child sacrifice every Passover. (The irony here of course is that the historical record shows that the Jews were the first of the ancient people to condemn child sacrifice through Abraham's embracing of monotheism; this is the central point of the Akeida, the story Ben describes in his Introduction.)

The central tenet of Judaism is monotheism, that there exists a single, just God who is not capricious, and who does not show favor to those in power. This image of God was a tremendous advance from the ancient pantheistic ones who were warring with one another and whose petty jealousies always seemed to be taken out on puny humans.

Judaism's central tenet is captured in a simple prayer that every Jewish child is taught to recite, the shema. American children typically learn the Hebrew alongside a stolid

English translation full of those *thys* and *thous*, and other words we never hear anywhere else. The extraordinary thing about the shema is that it functions very much like a pop song. (Or is it that Jewish-American songwriters fashioned their songs after the shema?) It employs repetition, meter, and rhyme. It's catchy enough to stick in your head. Here for example, is how it might read in modern, conversational English, staying true to the way it sounds to native Hebrew speakers:

> Hey buddy—listen up! Our God is one God, and there is only one of him....
>
> And here's what you need to do: love God with all your heart, with all your soul and with all your strength.
>
> And these words that I'm saying to you now come right from Him. They should live inside your heart. You should teach them thoroughly to your children. You should talk about and think about these words and what they mean when you are sitting in your house, when you are walking along the roadside, when you lie down to go to sleep and when you first wake up in the morning. You should make written reminders for yourself so that you'll remember what I'm saying here and be sure that the reminders are close to your hands, and that you can see them with your eyes. You should also write these words down on the front door of your house, and on the gate that leads to your garden so that you'll remember them.

God reveals himself here to be an expert in learning theory, employing repetition, imagery, and above all, instructing us on the proper use of mnemonic devices. It's not sufficient to hear an important instruction once—we humans forget too easily. If you say "I love you" to your significant other only once in the relationship, chances are he or she will think that you don't love him or her anymore, and your relationship will not last. Here God knows that we need to rekindle ideas not just in our minds but in our hearts. That by teaching things to our children we come to believe them more ourselves. That by talking about them throughout the day with our loved ones, by writing them down, they become more tangible and more real, so that eventually they stick in our heads. Such is the power too of pop songs. Experimental evidence in cognitive science now shows us that the average person can recognize hundreds of songs, and knows the lyrics to nearly as many. "The answer, my friend, is blowin' in the wind," "God bless America, land that I love," "Well I would not give you false hope, on this strange and mournful day, but the mother and child reunion is only a motion away" are just a few of the words embedded in our consciousness through repetition, through talking about them, and through the beauty of the craftsmanship that went into them.

Like a great song, Ben's book is beautifully crafted. It is a social, cultural, musical, economic and family history of some of the great contributors to music that is distinctly

American. These songwriters managed to do what Jews for thousands of years could not—they fit in. They defined American culture and gave it back to the rest of the country, in words and music so memorable they are bonded to the American psyche. How did they do it—where did they find the inspiration, the chutzpah to pull this off? Somewhere over the rainbow, way up high...

Dan Levitin,
McGill University
Montreal, March, 2014

FOREWORD

Foreword

The Yiddish writer Isaac Bashevis Singer once remarked that there were two things he needed to be sure of before he could embark on a new literary work: first, that the story was truly worth telling, and second that he was the one best equipped for the task. Ben Sidran's *There Was a Fire* admirably satisfies both of Singer's criteria.

There has long been a need for a serious study of Jews in American popular music. The reasons seem obvious enough: by the second decade of the twentieth century Jews had come to dominate many aspects of the popular music scene. They were songwriters and publishers, film studio moguls, theater chain owners, managers, and booking agents. A couple of decades later they were also record company entrepreneurs, distributors and retail outlet operators, music journalists and critics. As musicians, performers and singers the Jewish impact has been only slightly less profound, as the cases of Al Jolson, Benny Goodman, Bob Dylan and Barbra Streisand suggest. But if it seems self-evident that the Jewish factor constituted a crucial part of the American musical equation, why has it been so studiously ignored?

The daunting nature of the task has no doubt dissuaded many previous scholars. The precise meaning of and the reasons underlying Jewish prominence are hard, indeed treacherous, to pin down. For some historians, including many Jewish ones, merely pointing out Jews' concentration in a given secular field of endeavor is problematic and risks fueling antisemitism. Did Jews act conspiratorially to control an entire industry? The notion seems preposterous, especially when we remember that many of the Jews in question – e.g., songwriters like Irving Berlin, Jerome Kern or Jerry Leiber and Mike Stoller; businessmen like Milt Gabler and Leonard Chess, or music critics like Jon Landau and Greil Marcus – while not altogether denying their Jewish origins, hardly emphasized them either. What role, one might ask, did Jewishness play in the lives, motivations and behaviors of individuals who remained religiously and communally unaffiliated or who even sought to escape such connections and associations? Given the opaque quality of their ascribed Jewish identity, how can we assign special relevance to it?

On the other hand, as Sidran rightly asks, how can we possibly understand twentieth-century American popular music without understanding Jews' profound contribution to it? Which brings me to the second of Bashevis Singer's considerations. It would be difficult to conjure up an author better equipped than Ben Sidran to trace the Jewish impact on American music. A brilliant jazz pianist and composer with many songs and albums to his credit, an academically trained scholar and the author of pioneering studies of jazz, Sidran knows the music business first hand. One reason why *There Was a Fire* is such an important book is that the author conveys an insider's awareness of the underlying if often subtle ways that Jews in the music business acknowledged and even relied upon their membership in the "tribe." Veteran record executive Bob Krasnow, who signed Sidran to his Blue Thumb label in the 1970s, was more direct than most when he confessed to a reporter, "I could work for a big company like Warner Brothers because I had all the ethnic qualities—I was white, I was Jewish, they could invite me over to their home for dinner, and I could talk to black people." For Krasnow and many others, what we might call "assimilated Jewishness" provided an opening, an admission ticket to a career in the music business.

There Was a Fire is both a popular history, admirably thorough and beautifully written, and an invaluable insider's account. Its approach is equally empirical and impressionistic, analytical and anecdotal. It covers most of the topics one would expect and a few that are surprising. The familiar Jews of Tin Pan Alley appear, but also the less well-known Jewish composers of Hollywood film music. The Brill Building crowd surrounding publisher and impresario Don Kirshner receives attention, but is fascinatingly juxtaposed with the young Jewish leaders of the Chicago blues revival of the mid-1960s, such as Paul Butterfield and Mike Bloomfield. Some of these Jews, stemming from families oriented to the world of business, found the meaning and authenticity they craved in the culture of an older generation of black blues musicians whom they came to know, learn from and support. As we would expect, the storied black-Jewish relationship looms large in Sidran's account, and he offers many fresh insights into its meaning.

Sidran rightly presents no single formula to account for what sociologists would label the remarkable Jewish "overrepresentation" in the music industry. Jews occupied too many disparate rungs – creative and crass, magical and mundane – for the phenomenon to be reduced to a single cause. Their biblical inheritance notwithstanding, Jews were not the only people in this new land with a story to tell. On the contrary, what is perhaps distinctive about the American popular music business is that it developed an astonishing capacity to absorb the stories of many of the groups who traversed the national landscape and to recast them as a kind of manufactured folk merchandise. That Jews should find themselves at the heart of this process, or often as the processors themselves, is the unique result of the encounter between their centuries-old role as mediators of cultures, classes and commodities, on the one hand, and the remarkably dynamic American capitalist and cultural environment, on the other. Despite its entrenched racial and social divisions, American cultural symbols and markers were still sufficiently malleable – and moveable – to permit a wholesale reordering of status, at least in the auditory realm of musical imagination. We get this sense in Sidran's trenchant analysis of Kern and Hammerstein's landmark 1927 musical *Show Boat*, among the first art works to treat blacks as full human beings engaged with their own individual tales and predicaments. "It was almost as if the Jews were imagining an America where everyone was marginalized," Sidran observes, "each in their own way, where everyone was an outsider with a story to tell, if only one could find the words and music to tell it." *Show Boat's* authors thereby helped to expand "the Jew within the American as well as the American within the Jew."

The ultimate source of this Jewish drive to reshape both the self and the environment is really the ground of much of modern Jewish history as a whole. Modernity for Jews meant one thing above all else: the determination to end the condition of "exile" (*galut*) and isolation that had defined Jewish political and spiritual life for close to two millennia. The Jews' insatiable appetite to participate in the larger narrative of modern life took the most diverse and contradictory forms, ranging from militant ethnic self-assertion to conscious and unconscious self-abnegation. But American popular entertainment offered, quite literally, a unique theater for the working out of these of these powerful impulses, both onstage and backstage. Whether at the level of mere playacting, as a psychological release valve from the anxieties of being a Jew in a still hostile environment, or in the conviction that entertainment—and in particular, popular music—could actually help reconfigure American life in a manner more congenial to Jewish needs and sensibilities, many Jews quickly grasped the reality that popular entertainment held a remarkable transformative power.

It is a credit to Ben Sidran that he reveals Jews' diverse uses of popular music as possessing a broad humanism in character and intent, while in no way discounting the frequently cutthroat character of "the business." Yet it is an ironic mark of the Jews' success in helping to make American culture more inclusive that this humanistic quality seems to have dwindled of late. The recent but precipitous decline of American popular music can in part be laid at the doorstep of the giant corporations that since the 1980s have gobbled up the music and regurgitated it as standardized product, as well as at the feet of the managerial class of lawyers and accountants who have abetted this process. But the loss that Sidran decries also appears to be the discordant accompaniment to Jews' fuller integration into late twentieth-century America. It is now safe, even fashionable, to be open about one's Jewishness in the business. This is a mixed blessing, to be sure. What it signifies, as Sidran makes clear, is a decline of the kind of alienation for which many Jews paid a heavy psychic price but which likewise served to animate the search for new musical forms and entrepreneurial niches. Acceptance, a kind of general receptivity to Jewish identity as normal, even attractive, and an unprecedented transparency about Jewish identity, has somehow gone hand in hand with the increasingly generic flavor of American popular music as we find it today. Sidran's surprisingly apt linkage of 1980s smooth jazz with gangster rap, on the grounds of their shared emotional vacuity, underscores the point.

Whether Jews will again play a large role in reviving the lost art of American popular music seems doubtful. Future revitalization will likely derive from other wellsprings. What Jews accomplished, however, in helping to forge the American contribution to popular music can never be effaced or forgotten. Certainly not now, thanks to Ben Sidran's remarkable book.

Jonathan Karp
State University of New York
Tel Aviv, January, 2014

INTRODUCTION: IF GOD IS A STORY, WHO IS A JEW?

What boy can forget his bar mitzvah? The excitement of being onstage. The fear of forgetting the magic song. What thirteen-year-old has not asked himself, "What am I doing here?" My bar mitzvah was just such a confection, leavened with months of tedium, iced in moments of sheer terror, and served up to a small congregation of refugees from the Pale of Settlement—car dealers, insurance salesmen, retail clothiers, and my crazy uncle Hymie. Looking out at the room that morning, I knew I was from another planet. Perhaps this was part of the greater plan; in order to be a real Jew, one had to learn the taste of alienation early. Perhaps the bar mitzvah wasn't designed for the child at all; perhaps it was designed for the man that he would one day become.

The affair was typical of those held in small American cities at the center of the twentieth century. Nothing fancy, like today's choreographed events. I also led the Friday night service and the special Musaf service following my Torah portion; apparently, in our family, it was a matter of pride to see just how long you could carry on without actually knowing what you were saying. Because while we were trained to read the Hebrew, and even to interpret the little cantillation marks above the text, we were never introduced to the *meaning* of the sounds we made; that is, I read Hebrew much as I read music, purely for the sound of it.

Actually, the whole Jewish liturgical experience was obscure. For one thing, why, on Rosh Hashanah, one of the two holiest days and the one time of the year my father regularly attended synagogue, was there a point in the service when all the children were asked to leave the sanctuary? "It's not for children," my mother would say as she shooed me out. Goofing around in the social hall, I would wonder, "What is going on in there?" This was, I supposed, just one of the many mysteries that would be revealed once I came of age.

When that happy moment finally arrived, following my bar mitzvah service, the congregation retired to the social hall for an *oneg shabbat*, to enjoy a piece of cake and a glass of sweet wine. I sat at the head of the table, next to Rabbi Cohen, who, in his most luxurious baritone, told the assembled that today I was a man. Actually, he didn't say that. He was a bit more circumspect: what he said was that I was now a full member of the community, enjoying all the benefits and obligations that came along with the honor. Unknowingly, I had signed up.

When it was over, I went home, hung up my new suit in the closet, and sat down with my jazz records; I had a pile of my father's old boogie-woogie 78s and when I listened to them—miraculously!—I felt connecting to something both serious and mysterious (everything religion was supposed to be but, for me, clearly was not). In time, I came to understand that I had a much better chance of resolving the secrets of jazz than unraveling the riddles of Judaism.

To this day it seems odd to me to take a boy just at the age of maximum social discomfort, train him for several years to make a string of incomprehensible sounds, and then have him give a little speech at the end about its meaning and significance. The whole process is designed to confuse him about the nature of meaning and significance. A feint within a feint, perhaps? Where is the magic if not in the incomprehensibility of it all? For me, and for so many others of my generation, the liturgy was just so many ancient stories, repeated week after week, year after year, stories in which I was both intimately bound up and completely left out.

Because the year of my bar mitzvah was also the year one of my friends (my best friend, actually) asked me if it was true that Jews used the blood of Christian babies in their services. (I have always wished I had had the presence of mind to tell him yes.) I understood, in the classic moment of Jewish alienation, that I was the outsider. But as an outsider, I also understood something else: I was special in a way he would never know. That in itself made me a kind of insider: the classic duality at the heart of the Jewish experience.

I began searching for jazz records. My favorite was Horace Silver's *Six Pieces of Silver*, with Blue Mitchell on trumpet; I listened to that one over and over, huddled around my little record player like an Eskimo by a fire. There was clearly something profound in this music, and I could almost comprehend its inner meanings; just one more listen, just one more . . . as if it might be possible to parse the hidden grammar of jazz, which spoke to me of the commonality of all people. Intuitively I grasped that these musicians were related to me in some essential way. When I found out that Horace and the others were black, I understood that we were all basically alike; we are all related. Black was just a color, and there was only one race: the human race.

One record led to another. I took piano lessons. Musicians of all colors and styles came into my life: Pinetop Smith ("Pinetop's Boogie"), Dave Brubeck ("The Duke"), George Shearing ("Lullaby of Birdland"), Errol Garner ("Misty"), Bud Powell ("Time Waits"), Ray Charles ("What'd I Say"). I quit piano lessons. One night, I took my suit out of the closet and went to play a dance at the local YMCA; I got paid $3 to play with a small orchestra while love-hungry teenagers dressed in their Sunday best embraced each other and slowly circled the floor. I remember the room was dark, I wore white socks, and when I came home and hung my suit back in the closet, it was *then* that I felt like a man.

By the time I arrived at college, I was playing gigs three or four nights a week and reading philosophy, history, and literature during the day. I loved the stories, and the search for a deeper meaning in the ordinary state of affairs continued to be my m.o. In a class on European intellectual history I discovered Rosa Luxemburg, who rode the age-old Hebrew directive of *tikkun olam* (to heal the world) into the heart of the revolution. In a semantics seminar, I discovered Ludwig Wittgenstein, who, in his landmark book *Philosophical Investigations*, warned against presuming that any utterance in any language has any one definable meaning. Words, he wrote, are not charged with a specific property of meaning, but rather, "the meaning of a word is its use in a sentence." I immediately wondered if this was also true for music: Was the meaning of the music likewise in its use?

I went to England, where I wrote a dissertation on the cultural implications of black music in America. My obsession with what and how music could *mean* something—part of an ongoing search for greater meaning in my own life, I suppose—continued apace. Ultimately it led me to Los Angeles, where I entered the record business, determined to stop studying the information and instead to *become* the information. I wanted to know, first-hand, what it felt like to be a practitioner of the ancient art of music in the modern world.

Flash forward forty years. I had recorded thirty solo albums, produced dozens more for other musicians, toured conscientiously, and even recorded with Blue Mitchell himself. I knew well that fortunes had been made and lost, lives saved and sacrificed, hope restored and destroyed, all, in part or in principle, through this music. Clearly, American popular music was more than just the soundtrack of our generations; it was both a river of emotion and a powerful social force. But never did I think about my own place in that ongoing rush—how or why I myself may have turned to the music for solace, meaning, and deliverance.

Then, in 1981, when my son was five years old and I was thinking that it would be nice if he had some sense of his Jewishness, I happened to pass a little synagogue on the morning of Rosh Hashanah, and, entering, experienced a small awakening. I remember particularly the congregation reading the following passage:

> The Gods we worship write their names on our faces, be sure of that
> And a person will worship something, have no doubt of that either
> One may think that tribute is paid in secret
> In the dark recesses of his or her heart, but it is not
> That which dominates imagination and thoughts will determine life and character
> Therefore, it behooves us to be careful what we are worshipping
> For what we are worshipping, we are becoming.

What was I worshipping? What was written on my face?

Too, there was the story known as the Akedah—the binding of Isaac. It is a central part of the Rosh Hashanah service in which the patriarch Abraham is instructed by God to bring his son, Isaac, to the mountain and there, with a special knife, to sacrifice him. It is a test of Abraham's faith, and it plays out in the most touching way. Abraham tells his son to walk with him (the words in the text are *Vayelchu shnayhem yachdo*, or "they went up together"), and tells him that they are going to make a sacrifice to the Lord. Isaac asks, "But where is the lamb?" and Abraham assures him the Lord will provide one. At the very last moment, with Isaac bound on the altar and Abraham raising the sacrificial knife, God finally calls out to Abraham that it was all just a test of his faith ("Just kidding"), and since Abraham passed the test he could set his son free: a man at risk, a child at risk, a life at risk. This was a voice from the past speaking about issues that are still very much at issue today.

This story also raises multiple questions. What kind of God would ask a man to kill his own son, and what kind of man would actually agree to do it? (An ordinary man, it turns out; Abraham simply went for a walk in the desert and "heard a voice" that commanded him to follow, and Abraham followed.) And what about the son? Surely Isaac knew what was going on. What was his role in this passion play? And finally: Why had I never heard this story before? The answer to this last question became instantly apparent: this was the part of the service when the children at my old synagogue had been asked to leave the room.

Now, I do not accept the literal truth of this story any more than I necessarily believe in the reality of the Exodus (the Sinai isn't such a big place; surely Moses could have found the way out in less than forty years) or even the existence of God. That is just my personal position, but the physical truth of these events doesn't seem so important to me. To me, *if God is just a story, then the story is God.* That is, we worship a narrative; and as this particular narrative has moved so much history, perhaps it is even more miraculous than if the details were to be literally true.

The Jewish narrative, beginning with Abraham's covenant with God, is at the root of contemporary Western faith and philosophy. It is not simply faith in the veracity of a deal made centuries ago by a mythical man who may or may not have been experiencing an aural hallucination. It is faith in something quite real: the commonality of all people—what I think of as *the inner Jew in us all.* Others may call it by a different name, but in principle it remains the same. For it seems to me that social justice—a radical concept five thousand years ago, when human sacrifice was the norm—is inherent in the very idea of monotheism, the existence of the one God, the same God who spoke to Abraham. For if we believe there is only one true God, who speaks directly to anyone who can hear—who can be moved by an individual's prayers, and who has made all people in his own image—then all people, having equal access to this single divine source, are equal to one another. (If A = C and B = C, then A = B.)

Hence every individual has an equal responsibility to do good and an equal obligation to do unto others as they would have others do unto them. In this way, social justice is inherent in Abraham's acceptance of the voice that spoke, just as it is an essential aspect of the Jewish narrative today. (Apparently, I *had* signed up.)

This I could understand: the power of a narrative to frame our daily lives. It was what I was living in the music business, and the biblical narratives are not that dissimilar. Consider the story of King David. It is a story straight out of today's pop mythology: The old king (Saul) is depressed, and his kingdom is coming apart. He's unable to unite his people and unsure how to defeat the Philistines at his border. Word reaches his court of a poor but magical boy out in the hinterlands whose music has the power to heal (think Johnny B. Goode). By all accounts, that boy, David—a handsome and charismatic young singer who played a proto-guitar (the lyre)—arrived at Saul's tent and was able to calm the king with his music. This same David, it is said, stepped up to fight the Philistines single-handedly, challenging Goliath and, in a very public show (like halftime at the Super Bowl), felling the giant with a single stone from his slingshot. But David's fame was fixed for all time when he wrote the Psalms, for it is believed that he is the author of most, if not all, of them, including the great Twenty-third ("The Lord is my shepherd . . ."). The Psalms were "hits" when he wrote them and are still hits today. Millions and millions of people have recited David's words over the years.

For all these reasons and more, David has been hailed as the first true "king of the Jews," and hundreds of years after his death, three wise men were following a star to a manger in Bethlehem, seeking out the Davidic heir. King David is at the root of the search for the messiah who will deliver unity and meaning to his people.

Yet David was a modern man. In the words of one biographer, "he seemed to embrace the thoroughly modern notion that nothing succeeds like success—or, when it came to satisfying his sexual appetite, the equally modern notion that nothing succeeds like excess." In fact, anticipating today's pop celebrities, he even experienced the first public "wardrobe malfunction" when his codpiece flew up, exposing his genitals, as he danced ecstatically in front of the Ark. His triumphs with women, particularly his infatuation with the great beauty Bathsheba, are legend. And though he was open and remorseful about his human failings, he embraced them in such a heartfelt and poetic manner that the people only loved him more. Today he is remembered as that brave young man who defeated Goliath and let love rule, not as the aging, self-obsessed politician that he also allegedly became. In short, not to trivialize his story but to contextualize it in modern terms, King David was the first rock star.

Like rock stars ever since, he was forgiven (even justified) by the size of his musical gift and because of his ability to bring a kind of solace and unity to the community. "If this person's music can move me so," the typical fan thinks, "he must be in touch with a higher power." If so, surely part of that particular power is just how randomly it has been distributed throughout the ages; so often a great musical gift is visited upon those whose failings (like their successes) are larger than life.

David, too, had feet of clay: he finished out his years more or less alone, living in a tent and anticipating the rule of his son, Solomon, who would one day erect the stone monument (the first temple) that David had always refused to build (preferring to remain a man of the road). His story is a template for pop stars everywhere, from its humble beginnings to the crumbling edifices at the end.

But what is of particular interest to me is that this story—like all the stories in the Bible and all the great epic poems such as *The Iliad* and *Gilgamesh*—was originally meant to be *sung*. All the stories in the Bible were once magical songs. And even though writing had been in use for hundreds, if not thousands, of years before David, the Hebrews purposely chose not to write these stories down, insisting that this proto-liturgy be passed on orally—that it be sung. Today, similarly elaborate musical histories are still being created: in Ghana, for example, where young drummers spend years learning to play their people's history on the drums; and in Australia, where Aborigines still memorize the story of their people as a song that is, among other things, a literal map of their territory.

What is this impulse for people to store their deepest hopes and dreams in song? Obviously, oral epics benefit from the fact that music and memory go together (we remember what we sing better than what we say). Yet there is something else operating here: it seems that for a story to be a living thing, it needs to be part of a social occasion. Hence the ritual, even today, for a minyan of ten men (and/or, more recently, women) to be present to hold a Jewish service; you cannot tweet a minyan or skype a *brucha* (blessing). There must be a physical gathering. And music is the best social lubricant ever devised; it is the way people come together most naturally, and perhaps most profoundly.

It is as if we are all notes in the ongoing symphony of our people. Alone, we are a mere punctuation of the silence; with others—within the context of our people, to extend Wittgenstein's point—we are music, we have meaning. In the modern world, we usually see music as an artistic endeavor ("organized noise"), but it is, and for centuries has been, much more than that: it is community in action, the human in situ. Call it, for lack of a better phrase, the inner voice of our collective self.

Music is a root of religion. Why not? With today's multiplatform technologies it is difficult to imagine an era when the only time one experienced music was live, in the moment, as it was being created. But once upon a time, and for a very long time, music put the individual at the precise moment of creation. And that is what music represented for virtually all of human history. But the creation of what?

The answer, I think, is memory. Not just that song helps people remember their own story as it is being told; this is obvious. Rather, that the act of singing replicates the original emotions of earlier people, and so, in a profound and direct way, passes on what it *felt like* in the past to be alive, as a reality, *on the pulse*. We can feel what it felt like thousands of years ago when we sing certain songs; this retained memory is not so much about the details of the narrative—the so-called "episodic memory," which in most cases is no doubt apocryphal—but the particular admixture in the neurochemical soup. Feeling is knowledge; you don't know a thing until you feel something about it; and you can't feel something until you stop, if only for a moment, trying to understand it. If only for a moment. *This* moment. Hence popular music is part and parcel of our spiritual self.

Here's a story about memory and the Jews:

Once upon a time, deep in the heart of the Pale, the great rabbi known as the Bal Shem Tov had to work a miracle to save his people. He went to a certain place in the woods, lit a little fire, and said a special prayer. And this prayer was answered and his people were saved. One generation later, his disciple had yet again to save the people. So he too went to the same special place in the woods. But by now, the way to light the little fire had been forgotten. He said, "We do not know how to light the fire anymore, but we still know the prayer." So he said the prayer, and again the people were saved. Then yet another generation later, the disciple's disciple had once more to save the people, so he in turn went to the very same place in the woods. But by now, the prayer itself had been forgotten. So he said, "We do not know how to light the fire anymore, and we no longer know the prayer, but we still know the place in the woods where it all happened. It must be sufficient." And it was; his people too were saved. Finally, one generation later, when the disciple of the disciple's disciple had to again save the people, he found they no longer knew the right place in the woods. So he said, "We do not know how to light the fire anymore; we do not know the prayer anymore. Even the place in the woods where it all happened has been forgotten. But we can still tell the story." And he did. And it was sufficient. And again the people were saved.

This story says that memory is the higher power operating in the lives of ordinary people, and sometimes, just the memory that there *was* a story is all that is required to invoke that higher power; it is the *passing on*, in the end, that is passed on. We are all connected through our shared past, and it is that connection that is sacred. The persistence and importance of music in this process is a reminder that while our mind-memory is inevitably inaccurate and obscure, our emotional memory remains profoundly relevant. Music literally keeps the past alive for us.

Consider, then, that to the extent that today's popular music contains elements of the Jewish story as transmitted down through the centuries, we are, when listening to popular songs, perhaps feeling something of the original Jewish experience. Like the flame from a single torch passed down a long line of thousands of torches, American popular music is just one of the many ways Jews have remembered themselves into existence. Why? Why should we need some external reflection of ourselves to feel that this life has meaning? Better put, why isn't it obvious that without this historical context, the human animal doesn't exist? Popular music may be trivial, but it is also essential.

Memory is the context in which we all live. It is the frame around our story, and without it, we disappear. The neurologist Oliver Sacks famously recounts the case of a man who had absolutely no memory: at every moment, he felt he had just woken up with a sense of "Aha! Now I am awake for the first time." Without a memory, he had no *context* for the cascade of present moments. "I haven't heard anything, seen anything, touched anything, smelled anything," he would say. But of course he had heard, seen, touched, and smelled many things; he just couldn't remember them. "It's like being dead," he said.

To be human, then, is to be in context. And to create one's own context (to create memory through music) is, in both the Jewish tradition and the popular mind, very close to godliness; hence the adoration known as "fandom." Popular music, even today (for better or for worse), is how we continue to create the context that tells us who we are—it literally keeps our collective memory alive. By creating this memory, popular music is not just what we know, it's how we know it.

We live on in the memories of those who follow. One's personal story follows one's life just as a stalk follows a root and a root follows a seed. The seed was planted in you; you are the expression of that which came before you and the origin of that which comes after. We are somebody's child, so we have meaning. We are somebody's parent, so we give meaning.

At the conclusion of the Rosh Hashanah service in 1981, I went up to the young woman leading it and asked if I could help with the music. Beginning that year, and every year thereafter, I played piano for the high holy days with my son sitting next to me on the bench. (We "went up together.") Year after year, there was something hauntingly familiar in songs like "Avinu Malchenu" and "Oseh Shalom" as they were being sung by the congregation. These were dark emotional streams that had passed through my youth and now seemed to reconnected me to a deeper pool: I experienced a welling in the chest, stirrings of something that had nothing to do with the narrative or the liturgy but everything to do with the music. (Although perhaps the fact that the words themselves were like music to me made this possible.)

What I remembered was the feeling of sitting next to my father in a small synagogue many years before and the sense, then, of being connected to something profoundly old—his father, his father's father, and so on—a knowing that went beyond understanding. Surrounded by old men wrapped in prayer shawls, chanting and mumbling in Hebrew, rocking to a mysterious language, raising their hand and their voice to God, with the past literally all around me, I think even then I understood that these first Jewish experiences—moments of collective entrainment and spiritual longing—were also my first jazz experiences; and, vice versa, my introduction to the world of popular music has always been part of my experience of what is spiritual in the world.

This, it turns out, is a very traditional view, both in the world of jazz and in the world of Jews, whereby melodies from popular songs are regularly adapted for spiritual singing. Since the beginning of the Diaspora, Jews have taken folk songs and popular tunes from whatever country they happened to be passing through and embedded Hebrew prayers and sentiments in them. It appears that the sacred text is quite easily conveyed on the wings of popular song; or, alternatively, that any song becomes sacred when the community sings it for a higher purpose.

Hence not a few of the melodies sung in Ashkenazi synagogues today started their lives as German drinking songs. Most modern Jewish liturgical melodies are no doubt quite different from their original Hebrew origins. But something remains. The word *talmim* (for the musical notations above the text) actually means "flavors," and that is perhaps the best way to describe what these melodies deliver to us today—a taste of what it used to feel like in the presence of the original liturgy.

Talmim are interpreted variously by Jewish communities around the world. Each community, then, becomes a community in part through how it comes to agree upon the correct melody for the prayers and texts. This idea of authentic, or "correct," melody—which, in turn, is referred to as *nusach* or "good *nusach*," meaning the community's version of "correct melody"—in the neuroscientist and musical sociologist Daniel Levitin's phrase, "contains clues . . . to the interpretation of words or passages that might otherwise be ambiguous. That is, the assignment of words to melody (and vice versa) was not arbitrary—it helped not only as an aid to memorization and recall but also to ensure the correct interpretation." Nusach is an example of how, in the Jewish tradition, not only is there music in the words, but there are words in the music. I believe that being attuned to music in this way, being able to hear *into* the music and attach it to common speech, is a key to Jewish influence in the world of popular music.

The salient fact here is that the Jewish narrative, from the beginning, was meant to be sung, to come alive in the raising of the communal voice. Music and meaning go together, and they are revealed through a community coming to an emotional consensus in song. This is exactly what a "hit song" is. If we each knew what a hit song was, we'd all write them; only the community knows, and even then it doesn't know until it hears one. Consider how democratic this process is; despite our best efforts to sell them something, it is the community that chooses the hits. We can control what they hear, but we can't force them to sing along.

Our little Jewish community too had its own nusach, and when our son came of age, we hired a tutor to prepare him for his bar mitzvah. How could I, in good faith, having experienced what I considered an alienating sham of a spiritual exercise, have led him down this path? Simple: I didn't. He chose it. It was every bit as much a part of his American experience as going to summer camp or learning to ride a bike. Clearly, his life as a Jew in America was going to be much different from my own. His bar mitzvah tutor, for example, was an accomplished blues and jazz singer, and together they integrated a lot of vocal tradition into the "magic song" he would sing on the big day.

When that day came, a bright crisp November morning in 1989, he was radiant in his new suit, recently flown in from Barney's of New York. The hip threads and their urban origin signified not only that he was born at a more affluent time than myself, but that the community into which he was born was dramatically different as well. In a matter of one generation, we had gone from Holocaust survivors to "Cool Jews." Not only had he prepared his Torah portion in a clear and confident voice, but his love of music was everywhere evident: he was his own opening act, playing piano and doing a little shtick to get the party rolling. Was it any less "spiritual" than my own more traditional bar mitzvah? To the contrary, it was wonderfully moving to see a young person literally come of age through a highly personal performance into the welcoming arms of a loving community.

For years, the members of that little community had been saying to me, as they left the synagogue after the high holy days, "You should record this music." The year following our son's bar mitzvah, I began the process by schlepping reels of tape around the country and cornering my Jewish musician friends at recording studios, saying things like, "Hey, man, I got you down for a solo on 'Avinu Malchenu.'"

What was so striking was the similarity of their responses. "I was born a Jew," said trumpet player Randy Brecker. "I mean, I'm Jewish, but I'm not religious . . ." I reassured him and the others that I felt the same way and that they should just come down and play and if after the recording they didn't like the results for any reason, we wouldn't use it. They all came, they all played, and they all left with a tape for their mother. Twenty of America's finest Jewish jazz musicians played like angels on songs they probably hadn't heard nor thought of since they were kids.

At the time, although black musicians had often recorded gospel tributes in a jazz vein, few Jews had really done jazz versions of their liturgical music. This alone seemed odd—so many Jews in the music business and yet so few showing any interest in their own music. Then one day it occurred to me that perhaps we *were* playing our own music, every day, walking a very Jewish path, and just didn't know it. How Jewish was American popular music? In what ways was it Jewish, and what were the implications of this Jewishness in American popular culture?

To answer that, one couldn't simply prepare a list of Jews in the music business. That would prove nothing except that there are many. In fact, it appeared to me that a group that at no time exceeded 2 percent of the total population (the Jews) contributed more than 80 percent of the popular music in this country. The 2 percent is accurate; the Jews have always been a small minority, not only in America but in the world. The 80 percent I made up. There is no way to quantify the vast Jewish contribution to popular music. But if one takes into account the thousands of Jewish musicians, promoters, publishers, producers, executives, writers, hustlers, *schuchlers*, vaudevillians, and downright arrivistes who have populated the U.S. music business over the past one hundred or so years, it does not seem out of line; while the 80 percent is an imaginary number, it is, like the square root of pi, an imaginary number whose significance is real.

If making this Jewish record (*Life's a Lesson)* opened up broad philosophical questions for me—who or what is a Jew, for example—it also opened up urgently practical ones. I saw to it that the record was distributed in Japan and through a company in Germany (the irony of its being distributed only by the Axis powers was not lost on me), but in the United States, as they say, I couldn't get arrested.

I had come to know most of the men who ran the record labels in the States, and as the cliché would have it, they were Jews one and all; some were even quite active in the Jewish community, proud recipients of the B'nai B'rith humanitarian award. At first, I felt confident that one of these gentlemen would see the beauty and the logic in this project and make it available through their distribution network. I sent the CD to a dozen of these top executives. To a man, they were complimentary about the music (several requested extra copies for the wife's family); they saw the beauty, but not the logic: they all turned it down. The reasons will become apparent, if not obvious.

Then, in 1992, another year had passed and another Rosh Hashanah had come around, and as usual I found myself sitting in the little synagogue with my son, playing the music. But this year, a television crew from CBS *Sunday Morning* was also there. At the time, I was producing a record for Diana Ross and another one for Mose Allison, and working on what would become the soundtrack for the film *Hoop Dreams*, and oh, by the way, I had this little Jewish album, *Life's a Lesson,* which I couldn't get distributed. The confluence of all these things—black, Jewish, pop, jazz, success, failure—attracted the attention of Charles Kuralt's producer: it was good Sunday-morning human-interest fare.

On Sunday, September 19, our little Jewish service went national on CBS television; within hours, my phone started to ring, and it didn't stop for weeks. People from all over the United States wanted to know how they could get this record. And of course they couldn't. But I promised if they left their name I'd send them an album. And so I did what, for me, was a dramatic, last-ditch move. I actually manufactured copies of an album. Up until that time, I had lived my professional life by two guiding principles: do not have boxes of CDs in your basement, and avoid the Jewish thing at all costs—only to wind up with boxes of Jewish CDs in my basement.

In time, this small part of my life expanded exponentially. The music took me deeper and deeper into the world of contemporary Jewish culture and thought, and I had many wonderful conversations with people like Velvel Pasternak, the ex-Hassid from Whitestone, who was now the biggest distributor of Judaica in America and was hocking me to record obscure music from the Belzer sect; like the Jewish Russian refugee who wanted to know how to move to the town where I lived; like the hotshot L.A. lawyer who wanted a piece of the action; and like the many ordinary folks who called from pay phones and car phones and home phones, and who, like the grandmother who called one evening in tears, just wanted to tell me that my music had reunited them with someone or something from their past.

But the conversation that really gave me pause was the one I had with an older black musician, a good friend and somebody I had been working with for a long time. When I got to the part about being unable to get distribution for *Life's a Lesson* in the United States, he became visibly agitated. Finally he said, "But, Ben, everybody knows you got to have a Jew in this business." I was taken aback; first of all, I had never heard the expression before, and second, I realized I was probably *his* Jew.

At that moment, the question of Jews, music, and the American dream became very personal. It was my story too.

But what to make of the fact that even as I write this, a young pop singer named Britney Spears, raised in the Southern Baptist Convention, is wearing a Jewish Chai around her neck? Or that the woman she famously kissed on national television, whose name is

Madonna, is a student of Jewish mysticism, or Kabbalah, and regularly lights the Sabbath candles? Who or what is a Jew in America these days, and what is Jewish about American popular music?

What follows is not the one true story—there are many true stories—but it is the one that told itself to me, and so it is the one I want to tell to you. It is an outsider's story with recurrent themes of authenticity and alienation, memory and change, struggle and social justice, all encoded in narrative and melody. These themes will provide our stepping stones as we move through the onrushing tide of American history; each chapter is a kind of soliloquy on the journey. You might feel I left out key parts of the story or dwelled too long on others, but in the end, that's the beauty of it: we live our lives by the stories we tell, and there is something deeply autobiographical, for me, in this search for the divine in American popular music.

Ben Sidran
Madison, April, 2012

WHERE HAMBURGERS COME FROM

For thousands of years, the mob was singing about God; today they're singing about girls. This shift from the sacred to the secular, a fairly recent anomaly in our history, is not totally devoid of divinity. Indeed, as noted, Jewish popular music in America is a kind of spiritual music, and it arises, both directly and indirectly, from many of the same causes that gave voice to the songs of King David more than three thousand years ago. In American popular music, you may be calling the name of the girl next door, but more often than not, you are singing about the life of the soul.

Why? Because, as Daniel Levitin writes, "what all love songs have in common is the sense of caring," and this feeling, this longing for personal connection, is not different from love in its larger sense, i.e. the need to treat others fairly, to recognize that all men and women are related. "The sweeping, selfless commitment to another person, group or idea is the most important cornerstone of a civilized society," Levitin says, and is "essential for the establishment of what we think of today as human society, what we regard as our fundamental nature." This capacity for knowing and experiencing love—for being driven by the *need* to be connected to something larger than oneself—is what has allowed, in the religious historian Karen Armstrong's phrase, for "the creation of systems of courts, justice that is meted out to all members of society equally, welfare for the poor, education." "The opposite of love," writes Levitin, "is not hate, but indifference."

And this—the connection of all people through a seemingly mundane emotion that, for lack of a better term, we call love, like our connection to and through music, like the unfathomable human need for religion—is the best part of who we are. Perhaps it is the *why* of why we are here: the desire for desire; the caring about caring.

There you have it: falling in love, the macro and the micro; a boy and a girl hold hands and in that instant the world changes and it is a brand new day. Hope, transformation, change; in a three-minute version, with an elegant melody, a couple of hooks and a good beat, it's the American popular song. How did the Jews come to play it on American soil?

There has been a Jewish presence in America since before the nation was founded. The first small boatload of Sephardic Jews washed up on America's shore in 1654, twenty-three men, women, and children who had sailed by way of Brazil to arrive, desperate and destitute, in the port of New Amsterdam. Earlier in their journey, they had been detained in Jamaica and stripped of their belongings, so when, upon disembarking, the ship's captain demanded payment for the journey, they had nothing with which to pay him. Subsequently they were thrown into debtor's prison, and the Dutch director general of New Amsterdam, Peter Stuyvesant, appealed to his employers back in Europe for permission to deny them permanent residency, but following pressure from influential Dutch Jews, they were allowed to stay in the New World. Their treatment was particularly ironic inasmuch as the original New England Puritan settlers, who had themselves landed only a few years earlier, had declared themselves the "new Israelites," with America a new Canaan, comparing their flight from England to the Exodus of the Jews from Egypt.

The first great wave of Jews to America, however—as many as sixty thousand—arrived in the 1850s, as part of the great German Jewish Reform movement. These Jews quickly became part of New York society. Their acceptance in German society had been predicated upon their abandoning a separate Jewish nationality (they were Germans first, Jews second), and they brought this willingness and ease as citizens with them to the new land. These Jews subsequently lost sons on both sides of the Civil War; the Confederate attorney general, and President Jefferson Davis's right-hand man, Judah P. Benjamin, was a Jew; the mid-nineteenth-century composer Louis Gottschalk, whose light classical pieces were popular all across the country, was a Jew, as was Julius Meyer, the interpreter for Sitting Bull in the 1870s. So Jews have been part of the American experience all along.

It has been well documented how important America has been for the Jews, a true homeland where they could finally move freely, participate openly and ultimately, become who they were, whatever that was. Some have opined that if the authors of the Bible had only known about this land beyond the sea, it, and not Palestine, would have been the "promised land." But how important have the Jews been to the formation of this land? Specifically, how did their overwhelming participation in the business of popular music create the songs that America has used to sing itself into existence? Not just how deep did their roots extend into the soil of America, but how might their Jewishness have actually *brought about* that ecology?

The main wave of Jewish immigration—those whose children and whose children's children, by and large, became the creators of American popular music—didn't occur until the 1880s. These Jews came from the Pale of Settlement, a large portion of Eastern Europe set aside by the Russian czars to contain the Jews and keep them apart from the general population. Unlike the German Jews, who had been considered citizens of the state, Jews from the Pale had been sent running by the attacks of urban mobs, some of which passed from one locale to the next via the newly built railroads. Pogroms had been part of life in the Pale for decades, with Jews murdered, their homes burned to the ground, and their businesses destroyed. For more than a century, Jews, singly and in groups, had been wandering across Eastern Europe, where they often starved, lived in hovels, and traded in rags because they were prohibited from selling new clothing.

Going back to the sixteenth century, episodes of persecution had lead to an intensification of kabbalistic study and practice among Jews in the Pale; the kabbalistic way of thinking used an elaborate symbolism to tease meaning out of a meaningless world. If their predicament made no rational sense to them, answers were sought in the obscure and the occult. By the eighteenth century, the Kabbalah's magical thinking had given rise to Hasidism, a form of orthodox Jewish worship in which music and dance produced a kind of trance state in which one could, quite literally, experience God. To achieve this state, Hasids relied on what are called *niguns*, simple vocal riffs, sung over and over again, like an ecstatic rap. Songs without the baggage of words—indeed, hooks without the baggage of songs—became the ultimate religious expression. The parallel to modern-day rap and jam band music is striking.

As all entertainers know, a great performance can turn a meaningless phrase into a religious experience. These *niguns* employed what are called *krekhts*, or breaks in the human voice, similar to the vocal cry in the African-American blues form. This parallel was not lost on the Jews when they arrived in America. Equally important was the Hasidic tradition of adapting secular songs for religious use. In many ways, Hasidic tradition looked upon converting old folk tunes as holier than creating new ones, inasmuch as they were already of this world and so became transformed through the act of prayer. And while many have searched to find the Jewish liturgical roots of popular music, it is perhaps more interesting to seek out the popular roots of Jewish liturgical music. This transformation of the profane into the sacred through the use of music is at the heart of our discussion of Jewish popular music in America.

One finds it particularly among the Jews in the Pale of Settlement, where even social life revolved around the study of Talmud, the negotiated commentaries on the Torah, the rolling horizon of Jewish life. It was an oral activity in which different points of view were encouraged and learning was done aloud, in full voice. There was chanting and the use of musical tropes to bring out the contending threads in an argument, and many arguments existed in the gray area of no resolution (they were considered *teyku*, or to be determined later, the resolution being less important than the discussion of the text). The Talmud itself pours scorn on anyone "who reads without melody and studies without a tune." The confluence of music and learning, popular song and transcendence, street life and spiritual life was vital during some of the darkest days of the Jewish experience. This secular thrust of Jewish spiritualism was actually fixed with the arrival of the "Jewish Enlightenment," or Haskala, from the Hebrew word meaning awakening or rebirth, in the early nineteenth century. The Haskala was also important in that it reinforced the Yiddish language as the primary voice of Jews from the Pale.

For Yiddish, a combination of Hebrew, German, and various local dialects, was by the nineteenth century the language of writers and thinkers all across Eastern Europe. It was fluid, informal, inventive, a true language of the streets, one in which deals were done, Talmudic points were argued, and tales were told: Yiddish was perfect for the flowing narratives and darkly humorous stories, where irony ruled the day. As Sholem Aleichem, perhaps the best-known Haskala writer, said through his character Tevye in *Fiddler on the Roof*, "I was with God's help born poor." The great Russian composer Shostakovich referred to this particular brand of *yiddishkeit* humor as "laughter through the tears," and it is an emotional quality found in Jewish music as well, where the shift from minor to major and then back to minor again has the similar effect of dark meeting light, of the sun breaking through the clouds, if only for a moment, offering hope before we are once again plunged back into the reality of existential despair.

Another (more technical) way to look at this phenomenon is that every major scale contains a minor scale within it (the exact same row of notes, starting on the sixth step) and vice versa, every minor scale harboring the major (same row of notes, starting on the third step). The concept of major versus minor, then, depends on your point of view, or, alternatively, whether music "feels" major or minor to you all depends on where you anchor the listening experience (that is, define the tonic). It is a simple demonstration of the importance of expectation and context in the creation of emotion and meaning. This minor-to-major-to-minor move will play a profound role in the development of the American popular song form.

It would be hard to overestimate the importance of Yiddish to the development of popular music in America. Yiddish was the first grammar to capture what would ultimately become a peculiarly American sensibility: it swings, it is inherently musical; Yiddish words often sound like what they mean (*shpritz, kvetch, putz*). It allowed for the constant generation and regeneration of new words (it wasn't fixed or arbitrated from above); it was tumultuous, built on dualities and dichotomies: it answered questions with other questions. Jewish learning, like much of Jewish life, became a riot of irony, double entendres, and street humor. Much as these same qualities emerged out of America's black communities, Yiddish was designed to hide the secrets of a people who spoke it in plain sight. Language came to define a way of life—who was in and who was out. In the case of Yiddish, as in the case of black American speech, it implied, for those in the know, that the roles were reversed—outside was the new inside.

Into this precarious, improvised street life came the klezmer, show-business archetypes who entertained the troops on their long journey, wanderers among the exiled. Klezmer are thought of as Jewish musicians playing essentially Jewish music, but this is not totally accurate. First of all, they played all kinds of music—songs from the temple, folk songs from the various communities through which they passed, themes from gypsy music. And secondly, klezmer were both Jews and gypsies; because each group had outsider status and was itinerant in the Pale—and because they "shared a predilection for Eastern influenced melodies and the elegiac, mournful tunes known as *doinas*"—they often impersonated each other. One of the great gypsy bands at the time really had no gypsies in it. It was all Jews. Similarly, some of the great klezmer bands had maybe one or two Jews in them.

Perhaps the most famous klezmer of the nineteenth century was a man named Michael Joseph Gusikov, a brilliant performer on an instrument known as the *shtroyfidle* (straw fiddle), a set of wooden tubes placed atop a bed of straw and played with small wooden sticks. It had a "thin and humble sound." A musical genius whose gift was so great that he performed for kings and queens, and for the gentile upper society in general, Gusikov parlayed his Jewish "otherness" into a show business asset, becoming the first "crossover" klezmer, traveling throughout Europe, from Kiev to Vienna, Krakow to Odessa, representing the new "modern primitive," the Jew as fashion statement: in Paris, his *peyes* (long sidelocks) generated a fad among Frenchwomen, who suddenly wanted the *coiffure à la Gusikov.*

Gusikov's great success reflected a brief but general respite from official anti-Semitism in Russia during the late nineteenth century. Czar Alexander II, who reigned from 1855 to 1881, had begun to liberalize the anti-Jewish laws. This had a tremendous impact on the Yiddish-speaking population; suddenly it seemed that they might begin to catch up with their brothers in the West, who were virtually citizens in Germany and France. Now, for example, Jews in Russia were allowed to study music without having to convert to Christianity, a previous requirement. In 1868, Alexander founded the St. Petersburg Conservatory with an open admission policy for Jews. In the 1870s, 60 percent of the students at the Government College of Music and Arts were Jewish. Under the czars, there had been a law that a Jew could not live in Moscow unless he or she was an artist (to entertain the rich), and so in Jewish families throughout the Pale, children were encouraged to become musicians in order to live in the great city of the czars. One such city, with a population of 140,000 Jews and growing opportunities for talented artists, was Odessa.

There, Abraham Goldfaden, a Jewish poet who had an interest in theater production, "invented" Yiddish theater. Previously, Jewish theater—entertainment performed for its own sake—didn't exist; there were only the little playlets performed by children at holidays like Chanukah and Purim. Goldfaden went out of his way to audition anybody and everybody who stopped by his studio and found ways to insert them into his performing troupe. If somebody had a nice voice, for example, but only knew a couple of Ukrainian lullabies, or perhaps had a penchant for performing but only remembered a snatch or two from their bar mitzvah service, Goldfaden signed them up. With the addition of storytellers, actors, and an orchestrator, his productions soon began to look like little musical dramas. Only a few decades later, these innovations would help launch the Broadway musical.

In the midst of this cultural flowering, a bomb went off: on Sunday, March 13, 1881, Czar Alexander II was assassinated when his carriage was attacked in the streets of St. Petersburg by several members of the People's Will movement, the predecessor to the Bolshevik revolutionaries of 1917. When it was discovered that a Jewish woman was one of the plotters, it didn't take long for new waves of violence to be launched against the Jews, new pogroms, much more vicious and widespread than in the past. In every town, once again, Jews were murdered, their houses and businesses torched. Whatever liberalizing laws had been put into place by Czar Alexander were swiftly reversed by his successors Alexander III and Nicolas II, who followed a policy designed to pressure Jews to emigrate or convert -- or else serve as scapegoats for Russia's turmoil.

Along with the wave of pogroms, a new, virulent form of anti-Semitism was born. In the past, Jews had been seen as redeemable through religious conversion (even during the

Inquisition, Jews could be saved through repentance). Now, due to a growing interest in the concept of race throughout Europe, people were beginning to see ethnic and religious differences in the population as reflecting innate or hereditary conditions. If a Jew was somehow inherently different from birth—that is, racially different from non-Jews—then conversion would do nothing to appease the anti-Semite. The only solution was the annihilation of the Jews. Taking on a veneer of science, anti-Semitism mutated beyond irrational; it became homicidal. It spread like a virus across the Continent. Czar Nicholas himself commissioned a man named Serge Nilus to unearth or invent damning proof of a Jewish conspiracy; Nilus came up with the *Protocols of the Elders of Zion*, a forged set of documents about a Jewish plan to conquer the world (which also included the "blood libel" charge, which accused Jews of using the blood of Christian babies in their services). At the same time, a French Jewish army officer named Alfred Dreyfus was falsely accused of spying in an attempt to cover up a greater military boondoggle, and crowds gathered daily outside the courtroom in Paris to scream anti-Semitic threats. Anti-Semitic political parties sprung up across Europe. By the end of the nineteenth century, the walls were closing in on European Jews. Where could they turn? To the new world.

Europeans had been traveling to America for years. The California gold rush in 1849 had attracted thousands of European emigrants, and a healthy transatlantic shipping business had developed. One of the first in the business of transporting emigrants was a man named Joel Ballin, a Jew from Hamburg. By 1881, his son Albert had taken over the company and was in a position to help the hundreds of thousands of Jews now fleeing the chaos of the Pale of Settlement. Ballin arranged relatively low-cost passage ($500 in today's cost) and set up a vast kosher city in the Hamburg dockyards where the people could await the next ship.

Emigrants traveling steerage had to provide their own food for the twelve-day crossing. It needed to be simple to prepare and uncomplicated to serve, strictly kosher, and above all cheap. Kosher meat, being salted, keeps well. When minced, it goes farther than steak. Rolled into balls and flattened into patties, it can be rapidly cooked on a hotplate and served on bread, even on a pitching ship. The dish soon became known as the Hamburger; in this way, the Jews brought America's signature meal with them when they came.

This was not the first time that food, or the lack thereof, had propelled immigration to America. In the 1840s, the great potato famine had driven many Irish to the New World. Potatoes were not indigenous to Europe but were introduced there by Christopher Columbus, who brought them back from his voyages; soon they were supporting much of Northern Europe, particularly Ireland, where the climate was favorable to their cultivation. Because potatoes were so nourishing, many Europeans abandoned their other crops, thus risking starvation if the potato crop failed, which it did when a blight struck in 1845; in Ireland alone, a million people died from starvation and more than a million emigrated, most of them to the United States.

In many ways, just as the Jews had been the outcasts of Europe, so Irish Catholics had been the "blacks" of the United Kingdom for hundreds of years. Papists in a Protestant world, a perennial underclass, the Irish were seen by many British as lazy, immoral, ignorant, and superstitious—the same clichés that were used to describe blacks in America. And when they arrived in the United States, several decades before the great wave of Jewish immigrants, the same sort of greeting was awaiting the Irish: there were anti-Catholic riots and "Paddy Makings," hanging an effigy dressed in rags with a whiskey bottle stuck in one pocket. The renowned cartoonist Thomas Nast portrayed the Irish marching in a St. Patrick's Day parade with ape faces on human bodies. The Irish dug in, particularly in New York City, where they came to control the streets of midtown Manhattan. By the mid-nineteenth century, one in four New Yorkers was of Irish descent. And it was here that the Irish theatrical innovation called "minstrelsy" took off.

Minstrelsy featured songs and skits by (mostly) white men wearing burnt cork on their faces and pretending to be "black" by falling about, clowning, and in general acting lazy, licentious, and foolish. One theory is that the Irish seized upon this concept of imitating blacks as a way of distancing themselves from black Americans. In this way they became more "white," or at least joined the white majority in ridiculing blacks. Another theory has it that because Irish men had to compete with blacks for jobs on the docks and in warehouses, minstrelsy was an outgrowth of normal economic competition. Whatever the root cause, minstrelsy turned out to be the first truly American form of entertainment, and "Daddy Rice" was its first superstar.

Thomas D. Rice was the man who started this American showbiz tradition with a single song: "Jump Jim Crow." An Irish immigrant, Rice claimed he first heard the song being sung on the streets of Cincinnati by a black man who would do a little dance and repeat the hooky chorus: "I turn about an wheel about an do jis so. An eb'ry time I turn about I jump Jim Crow." For his New York performance, Rice covered his face in burnt cork, and in so doing he invented the blackface American stage character. His "Jump Jim Crow" song was originally scheduled to be a three-minute diversion between acts of a play, but, like a form of proto-rap, complete with some hip dance moves, Rice's act drove the audience wild; they rushed the stage and wouldn't let him off, making him perform it more than twenty times that first night. It was a hit, maybe the first American "street" hit, and it can be seen as the first "cover song," a white man doing essentially black music and delivering it (crossing it over) to a white audience. It was totally unlike the sweet sentimental music being promoted at the time by Victorian women and their American counterparts. This was the literal start of that long tradition wherein whites turn black music into commercial gold.

While Rice's performance was a parody of black slang, the cork on his face was in the manner of generations of circus clowns; as far back as the sixteenth century, Italian commedia dell'arte performers wore makeup and walked that fine line between order and chaos. But the song he sang was pure Americana. For one thing, the words didn't scan as did formal English. It was American street talk; and it was black. Minstrels were the first to make (counterfeit) black music the essence of American popular culture. It is ultimately why white America has always needed rock and roll. By intent or not, T. D. Rice was the genre's first international superstar—its Elvis—and "Jump Jim Crow" was his "Hound Dog".

Rice became an overnight sensation and traveled the country doing his hit. (In the nineteenth century, before electronic media and universal distribution, it was possible to support a whole career on just one song; some would say, looking at pop stars today, it is still possible.) Ultimately, "Jump Jim Crow" was heard all over the world, as ubiquitous as a Beatles song would be a century later. For example, the U.S. ambassador to Ecuador, on arriving in the Mexican city of Merida, reported that he was greeted by a brass band playing Rice's hit.

Soon there were many imitators. With each new iteration, the parody of blacks became broader, the stereotyping more crude. In 1843, Dan Emmett and three blackface companions created the first minstrel troupe, the Virginia Minstrels, and he wrote the song "Dixie" as a walkaround for them, years before it became the battle cry of the Confederate army during the Civil War. By 1846, Edwin Pearce Christy defined the unique minstrel format that lasted for a hundred years: he expanded the shows to include a black "dandy" (named Zip Coon) and a pair of clowns who were disruptive and rude (called Tambo and Bones); every black stereotype was represented and flaunted through a barrage of jokes, fables, song-and-dance routines, and spoofs of contemporary manners. The music was basically happy ditties made to accommodate the improvised knockabout that happened on stage. It was pure show business and had no real relationship to the actual lives of either black or white Americans. (This too will find its counterpart in twentieth century pop acts such as Kiss.)

One way to think of early minstrelsy is as a kind of proto–rock and roll. It appealed primarily to young men out to have some fun, the first signs of a rebellious youth culture in the newly forming America. Even the instruments used to play the music—banjo, fiddle, tambourine, jawbone—were considered rude at the time, noise to the refined ear. That all these instruments were associated with Southern blacks lent them immense cool with the Northern whites. (Think of the Rolling Stones a hundred years later.)

During the early and mid-nineteenth century, when the country was only decades old, there was not a lot that could truly be called "American" popular culture. With few exceptions, most of what passed for popular entertainment in America had been borrowed from England, which, at the time, was in the thrall of Queen Victoria, or from other European models (for a while, the Viennese waltz was the height of risqué social conduct). Many American women, aspiring to be middle-class, took up the Victorian pastime of writing poetry, trying their best to "civilize" their husbands and sons by using books, songs, and playlets imported from across the ocean.

Of course, true American culture *is* outsider culture and is nothing like the parlor culture from Britain or the European capitals. Unlike European countries, where there was a long tradition of royalty—the ultimate insider culture—America was founded by those who left someplace to seek out a new life, who were looking for a little relief from the strictures of the past. It took most of the nineteenth century for America to break free of the European hold on its self-image, and one can easily imagine the dramatic impact minstrelsy had on this process; like rock and roll itself, it called the question of a true American identity and the role of black Americans in creating that identity.

A similar dynamic is found in the literature of Mark Twain; Huck and Jim on the raft were the perfect metaphor for the struggle taking place for America's cultural soul. Huck chose to go to hell and help Jim rather than do what he was taught by the Victorian women in his life. It was American literature cut loose from "proper grammar" (the voice of the various ladies' guilds), from polite tea-society formality. Twain's dialogue was written the way Americans really talked. The voice of America did not sound like some matronly Victorian woman. Tom and Huck and Jim spoke American slang. Basically, they spoke black talk.

There's an old Jewish saying, "When I hear what I say, then I know what I think." America needed to hear itself in order to know itself. Minstrelsy was part of this process, if badly flawed and crudely drawn. It both recognized the existence of black America and provided a venue for the new masculine personality of the American streets to surface. The problem was, it was an empty vessel, an inarticulate form without much content; it wasn't *about* anything. Minstrelsy had a new kind of timing and language; there was a rawness to it that appealed to the rock-and-roll crowd and a thread of humor that appealed to almost everybody; but there was no backstory, no narrative. That would not come into being for several decades. In the meantime, there was Stephen Foster.

Stephen Foster was born on July 4, 1826, in a little white cottage just east of Pittsburgh, and he died at age thirty-seven in a flophouse in New York City with just 38 cents in his pocket and a note reading "Dear friends and gentle hearts." In between these two mundane markers, he created a new kind of American song, one that combined black and white sensibilities and memorialized a romantic vision of the American South. His South was home to all those who longed for home, where friends and family waited faithfully for the return of the prodigal son.

Early on, Foster understood that for his songs to be widely distributed, he needed to write for the minstrel shows; his first hit, which he wrote when he was only twenty-two, was "Oh! Susanna." First performed by the Christy Minstrels in 1848, it became a kind of theme song for the forty-niners during the great California gold rush. The form of the song was so simple, the melody so *singable*, that anybody could improvise new lyrics as they made their way West. Foster himself was not well known to the public. And since at the time there was really no established song publishing business—no way to collect royalties beyond the selling of sheet music, and no way to protect unauthorized versions from being sold—the song was widely pirated. More than two dozen music publishing firms put out versions and earned tens of thousands of dollars from sheet music sales of "Oh! Susanna." But Foster received only $100 from a single firm in Cincinnati. Most people thought—and to this day, still think—that the song was a "folk song," written by no one in particular and carried on the wind.

Foster's songs were deceptively bucolic—"Jeanie with the Light Brown Hair," "Old Dog Trey," "Camptown Races," "My Old Kentucky Home"—all carefully and patiently crafted by a middle-class man in a middle-class house in northern Pennsylvania, but that invoked a simpler time in an American South (one that never actually existed) when people, regardless of race or status, were connected by the same longings, the same feelings for family and home. This universal, calming nostalgia at the center of his songs played to both blacks and whites. He was truly the first American people's composer.

Foster often instructed those who sang his songs never to mock the black folks he wrote about, but to get their audiences to feel "compassion." He was on a mission to improve the quality of Americans through the quality of the American popular song, and in this he was way ahead of his time. Instead of turning to a stilted moralistic vocabulary, as the Victorian women did, he captured the sound and rhythm of black speech—not in a cartoonish fashion, as in the minstrel shows, but in a humane way. Just the fact that he was consciously trying to make a mixed audience *feel* something together was a premonition of what American pop music would one day become. And the image of an idealized homeland, where people were equal in their feelings and their love for the everyday things (in Yiddish, this quality would be called *heimish*), deeply attracted the Jewish songwriters fleeing the pogroms of Russia several decades later.

His most popular song, "Old Folks at Home," was written in 1851. It was about a man roaming the land and missing his home, his youth, and his former happiness—typical themes for Foster and for America in transition. The main character could just as easily have been white as black. But he *spoke* black. It was a kind of slang that was created to be sung. Even the way Foster named the most famous poetic image in this, the most famous of his songs, is a good example of how he used his ear to choose his language. The image of the Swanee River, perhaps the most talked-about river since the Styx, opens "Old Folks at Home," but it is no river Foster had ever crossed. For Foster, just the sound of "swaa-neee river" created a sense of warm nights and a shared past. In reality, it was just a random name he had picked out of an atlas and abridged to fit his metric scheme. The fact is, the Suwannee is *barely* a river—it slowly works its way through western Florida to ease into the

Gulf of Mexico—but because Foster grabbed it out of a book when he needed a name that had the right *sound*, it is now the most famous river in the American South.

Years later, the Swanee River would come to represent much more than "just a sound" to the Jews of Tin Pan Alley. In the hands of Irving Berlin or George Gershwin, it would become a memory as real as any other to the Jews; not the memory of a specific place, but the memory of a memory, of a time when things were better: what was a small detail of place became a great fact of nostalgia and circumstance to the Jewish immigrants who began arriving in large numbers toward the end of the century.

The great wave of Jewish immigration at the turn of the twentieth century was unlike anything that had ever been seen before in America. In the words of one writer, "Not a family but a whole people moved." Two million Jews fled Russia for the United States between 1880 and 1920. Nearly half of them settled in New York City, which by 1910 housed 540,000 Jews on Manhattan's Lower East Side alone. This neighborhood came to contain the highest density of poverty in the world. And these people could never go back to the shtetl (not that many would want to); home was in the future, not the past. It was a modern Exodus, and most Jews brought nothing to the new land but their beliefs and their way of life. But wasn't this also the point of making no idols, of substituting prayer for sacrifice? Your ideas were all you needed. These dirt-poor mystics, hustlers, dreamers, tummlers, tailors, klezmers, doctors, *luftmenschen* (intellectuals), rabbis, and schlemiels all arrived with their beards and their Yiddish, their music and their learning—and their feel for social justice.

The rise of the garment industry in America is a great example of this Jewish predilection for democracy. Originally, Jews had learned to sew because they weren't allowed to sell new clothes in Russia; hence they learned how to repair the old clothes they were allowed to sell. This gave them a skill to practice when they hit the New World; it was hard, gritty piecework—which meant WASPs (the tautological white Anglo-Saxon Protestants) wouldn't do it—and because the Jews could do the sewing at home, in the tenements, it was a natural occupation. Fortunately for them, the sewing machine had been invented in the last decade of the nineteenth century, giving them the wherewithal to start small, stay portable, and expand, expand. Jews could often be seen at the turn of the century schlepping their sewing machines through the streets of New York's Lower East Side. A pennies business, it also provided an opportunity for the Jews to do well by doing good. Because within a few years, the Jews of New York had pioneered the world's first exact-sized, ready-to-wear clothing industry, which coincidentally had the effect of driving democracy and blurring class distinctions: suddenly, anybody could afford to look good. Perhaps they didn't set out to democratize fashion (their motives were more economically inclined), but their impulses led them there nonetheless.

From sewing to selling, it wasn't long before Jews had retail shops to distribute their clothing. From retail clothing to show business was also just a small horizontal move. Because when nickelodeons became popular—the turn-of-the-century sensation consisting of a primitive film loop shown on a small machine for a nickel—Jews put them in their clothing stores as an added attraction. Another pennies business, nickelodeons made sense to the Jews, and at the same time, the early movie business was anathema to the WASP establishment: they considered it a fad at best, a diversion for the rabble, and wanted nothing to do with such a low-class operation. Soon some Jewish shopkeepers were making more money on their nickelodeons—as much as $700 per day—than on the clothes, and they brought in more picture machines, creating the first arcades, and soon thereafter, the first cinemas. Entertainment centers!

At the time, Thomas Edison's company controlled the patents and monopolized production of nickelodeon films. The Jews, needing ever more product for their expanding cinema empire, started producing films on their own. When Edison threatened to sue them, they took their production business out to California, as far away from Edison as possible. Within twenty years, they had created Hollywood. In 1925, the top five studios in the world were all run by men who had grown up within a few hundred miles of Warsaw.

No, the Jews were not afraid of a penny or nickel business. Song publishing too was just this kind of business, from the few cents that one got selling sheet music to the few pennies that were collected from placing a song in minstrel shows. And like the film business, it too was dominated by Jews. Among the oldest and most successful Jewish publishers was M. Witmark and Sons, founded in 1886. The sons actually convinced their father that music publishing was the opportunity of the future. Julius, the youngest, had performed in a local minstrel troupe, and seen firsthand the reaction to the new popular music. Witmark became the first publisher to transform front-page news stories into best-selling songs. This sense of music made "while you wait, for any occasion" typifies the early Jewish publishing business. When Italian songs were in vogue, they wrote Italian songs. When it was Irish songs that sold, they featured Irish songs.

Many of the Jewish publishing houses that started up in New York during the last decade of the nineteenth century were run by German Jews, who had had time to survey the landscape and stake their claim. One such composer-publisher was Charles K. Harris, who submitted his first song to Witmark, but when he received a royalty check for only 85 cents, he started his own firm. Harris was the first to sell more than two million copies of a single song ("After the Ball"). But the most prolific composer of the time was Harry Von Tilzer (who changed his last name from Harry Gumm to sound more Germanic, the German Jews having more "legitimacy" at the time). In 1890, Von Tilzer hit the jackpot when his "A Bird in a Gilded Cage" sold two million copies. Another Jew, Leo Friedman, sold five million copies of "Let Me Call You Sweetheart." Gus Edwards (Gustave Edward Simon back in Germany) wrote "In My Merry Oldsmobile" and "By the Light of the Silvery Moon."

These Jews, like so many of the immigrants who came from Russia, were fiercely proud to be Americans; they wanted to assimilate, to be seen as Americans, and by and large they rejected whatever and wherever they had come from. As the Hollywood impresario Adolph Zukor remembered, "No sooner did I put my foot on American soil than I was a newborn person." And they inherently understood public taste; they *were* the audience. The sprawling Yiddish theater, the street-centered, slang-driven literature of the Haskala, the magical thinking of the wandering *luftmenschen*, all these past experiences came together to create a perfect opportunity for the Jews to manufacture and market the people's dreams. This was *their* country. But no matter how hard they tried—and they all, literally or metaphorically, shaved their beards—they remained quite obviously "other," circumcised in an uncircumcised world.

While most Jews who arrived in America around the turn of the century from the Pale were dirt poor, others were rich and powerful, important players across the world stage. They financed revolutions; they propped up monarchies. But rich or poor, all were kept outside the boundaries of normal social discourse; even the court Jews, the Rothschilds themselves, were outsiders in the end. And so, whereas other ethnicities may have disappeared into the dominant culture, become Austrians or French within a generation or two, the Jews never did. Was there something within the Jewish condition that, as Groucho Marx so famously said, didn't want to be part of any club that would have them? The good news was the bad news; always looking in from the outside, the Jews worked twice as hard to compete and, remaining isolated, wound up competing with themselves. They couldn't lose. And they couldn't win.

Leslie Fiedler, teaching "Alienation and American Identity," noted that to be an American, one is required to launch out and search for the true spirit of the place. In that sense, Jewish alienation was a kind of passport into American culture. The need to discover and create one's own identity for oneself (self-reliance and reevaluation of tradition) is the American way. Tom Sawyer and Huck Finn were doing no less. To see oneself, one needed to have a sense of context, a sense of duality; of separateness. Judaism virtually codifies this awareness and inculcates a sense of unique destiny. Indeed, as the French philosopher Jean-Paul Sartre has argued, without being "the other," the Jew of Judaism lacks definition.

Perhaps this begins to explain the Jewish fascination and identification with black America. Virtually all other immigrant groups upon arriving in America identified "up" with the WASP majority and showed little love for black Americans. The Jews, on the other hand, also identified "down," immediately gravitating toward black culture. There were obvious reasons. The first is slavery: for thousands of years, Jews at the Passover seder had repeated "this year we are slaves, next year we shall be free." And clearly, they were drawn by a minority that was more manifestly familiar with American life. In any case, no other

Caucasian minority was so willing to construct out of its own historic rejection a bridge to the African-American experience. As Lenny Bruce once said, "Negroes are all Jews."

And in America, at the turn of the twentieth century, Jews were also considered by many to be black, or perhaps "oriental," but certainly not white like the WASPs. Like the blacks, Jews were cut off from a homeland with no way back and little way forward (forward, that is, to become totally "American" in the eyes of the establishment). Unless, that is, they could redefine what it meant to be an American. Unlike the blacks, however, the Jews had a historical narrative with which to accomplish this sleight of hand. Blacks had a profound absence of narrative; theirs was an oral continuum disrupted by diaspora. The Jews, on the other hand, were a cultural continuum perpetuated precisely through the narrative of diaspora; the difference was in the story. Or, more precisely, the difference was in the constant telling and retelling of the story.

As the black Jewish writer Laurence Thomas has said,

> Both blacks and Jews have a history of having been systematically and horrendously oppressed. . . . The reality is that when a people have greatly suffered, then to that extent their suffering tends to be an eliminable part of their self-identity. . . . The problem is that the self-identity of American blacks as members of the black race is tied entirely and exclusively to their past history of suffering. By contrast, while the self-identity of Jews accords suffering a fundamental place in the Jewish experience, suffering is by no means the most central aspect of Jewish identity. There is, I believe, a rich historical narrative which is also a part of the self-identity of Jews. Nothing comparable exists for blacks.

On the one hand, Jews wanted to be Americans, totally. On the other hand, they also needed to be the "other" in order to exist as Jews. By identifying with blacks, they were able to accomplish both: Jews were guaranteed to be connected to the true American outsider experience. And by identifying with black America, Jews were guaranteed their "otherness" because of the simple fact that they could never *be* black. This was part of the beauty of the relationship. In return, as we shall see, Jews gave blacks a powerful voice and a narrative context in which to reinterpret their own history.

The Russian Jews, who arrived in New York at the precise moment when interest in race and ethnic humor was being paraded across stages everywhere, fell comfortably into the new show business. There, the Irish made fun of Germans, but they also made fun of the Irish; Jews made fun of the Irish, but they also made fun of the Jews; it was how one got along in the teeming streets of the Lower East Side. To deflect criticism, it was normal to laugh at yourself before others could do it, and if there was something one didn't understand, the reaction to make fun of it, marginalize it, was similarly normal. Laughter was a great weapon on the Lower East Side, and comic role playing was like trying on various personas to find something that might fit. One of the biggest musical hits of 1890, written by a black minstrel—yes, he put cork on his face even though he was black—was called "All Coons Look Alike to Me." His name was Ernest Hogan (he had changed his name from Reuben Croutest in order to sound Irish so that he could succeed in the world of minstrelsy!), and his song inspired a flood of so-called "coon" songs for decades to come. So here is a black man with an Irish name wearing cork on his face writing a song saying "All coons look alike to me." Obviously these were uncharted waters in regard to race and ethnicity that America was entering at the turn of the century.

It is important to caution against judging these times by today's politically correct standards, because even as "coon songs" were popular, the Jews were also participating in "best Heeb" contests, in which the audience judged who looked more like the caricature of the big-nosed avaricious Jewish refugee. At the same time, the Irish were falling down on stage pretending to be drunk. One sold what one had in order to stay alive. They were all "greenhorns," and popular theater made no pretense at art, or even culture—it was entertainment; forget your troubles, laugh at your neighbor and yourself, be a Yankee. There was no political correctness; it was chaos, cacophony, plain and simple.

At the turn of the century, New York was a pandemonium of cultures and sounds. Four out of five people on the streets were immigrants; below fourteenth street, one could walk for blocks and never hear the English language spoken. The fluidity of culture and identity began with your name. You landed at Ellis Island and had a brief encounter with an American official, who might have misspelled it, or mispronounced it, or you might have purposely changed it on the spot. Why not? You were a new man, and hadn't God changed Avram's name to Abraham to indicate that he was a new man? And then, when you managed to get past the health inspectors, you grabbed your bundle of belongings and took a brief boat ride to the island of Manhattan.

And there you were, at the beating heart of the modern world, raging on all sides: noise, filth, humor, freedom, tall buildings, crime, love, death, music, hustlers, an abundance of everything, including poverty and opportunity. There was no such thing as credit; you found somebody who knew somebody who knew somebody, flopped on the floor, and started planning your future. If you were good at recreating yourself—saying yes, in effect, to whatever came along—you might actually make a few pennies. After all, you couldn't go back to the shtetl; saying yes might mean "a little song, a little dance, a little seltzer in your pants." All music was race music: Jews wrote derogatory songs about the Cohens while blacks wrote derogatory songs about the coons. None of them were white—not the Jews, not the Irish, not the Catholics, certainly not the blacks; if you weren't WASP in America, you were just a different shade of gray. Yet you were just as American as George Washington.

The Jews threw open these psychic doors, proclaiming that our main resource was our hope, and just as everybody contained an "inner Jew," so too they now had an "inner

American" to discover. It wasn't about polemics or rhetoric so much as the sound of laughter in the backroom of a cafe. A sensual revolution; a perceptual paradigm shift; hearing an inner voice. Change how a person feels about himself and you change how he feels about everything. The street, not the synagogue, became the classroom; the girl, the opportunity, was part of the curriculum, and "making it" literally meant inventing something brand new. In the twentieth century, America would remake the world, the whole world, and popular music would remake America. It was singing in America's ear, a song about how they care about each other, about how they can change their lives, about how they are finally ready for their close-up.

We return now to that pitiful boatload of Jews who first washed up on the American shore in New Amsterdam in 1654. After they were released from debtor's prison, some went on to do quite well; their descendants became the "elite Sephardim" of New York. A girl named Emma was born in 1849 into just such a family of rich secular Jews, one of New York's "upper ten thousand." As a young girl, she was inspired, as were many at the time, to take up poetry. She had talent—Ralph Waldo Emerson and Emily Dickinson were her mentors—but her work was unremarkable. She was at home in high society but also aware of the anti-Semitism that existed—Emerson himself had questions about her "Jewishness." She strove to fit in, to be part of the great American literary experiment. Finally she seemed to come into her own creatively when she wrote a poem titled "1492" about the expulsion of the Jews from Spain. It was the first time she had looked inward through her work to examine the gulf between her own assimilated life to that whence she had come. Although she remained a secular Jew, as American as any descendant of the *Mayflower*, she was inspired to a new kind of social activism when the Russian pogroms of 1881 tossed up hundreds of thousands of Jews on the streets of New York. Walking among them on the docks, Emma saw their appalling conditions, their hope, their confusion, and recognized something of herself in them. In 1882, she arrived at her often-quoted formulation, "Until we are all free, none of us is free."

That same year, Auguste Bartholdi's enormous statue of a woman holding a book and a torch was formally given to the people of the United States on behalf of the people of France. Entitled *Liberty Enlightening the World*, it had been commissioned as a monument to a hundred years of friendship between the two countries. It wasn't shipped to America until early 1885, however, when it finally arrived in four hundred separate crates, but there was no place to put it. The money to build a pedestal needed to be raised, and much of it was being raised by collecting dimes and nickels from the people of New York City. Emma, who by this time was very much involved with Jewish refugee causes, wrote a special poem for one of the fundraisers. She called her poem "The New Colossus," and she referred to the great statue as "The Mother of Exiles," waiting with open arms for the refugees of the world. The poem took on a life of its own. When Emma died in 1887, her friends and family campaigned to have this poem affixed to the pedestal of the statue, which was finally done in 1903.

With that single act, the Statue of Liberty, originally dedicated to the memory of Franco-American friendship, became a towering symbol of hope for the outcasts of modern society. Suddenly the statue was no longer about two economic powers; it was a powerful welcome to the international outsider, a beacon of hope for the poor and disenfranchised everywhere.

> Give me your tired, your poor,
> Your huddled masses yearning to breathe free,
> The wretched refuse of your teeming shore.
> Send these, the homeless, tempest-tost to me,
> I lift my lamp beside the golden door!

Emma's poem had recast the discussion: America was now to be the homeland for all those in exile, the poorest of the poor; it was about the opportunity to change; it was about social justice. In short, it was about the Jewish narrative. No longer just a former British colony, not simply a remnant of the French or Spanish or Dutch colonial expansion, but a new America; the promised land for a people who traditionally traveled with little more than the skin on their bones and the ideas in their heads.

The story of Emma Lazarus and the Statue of Liberty can be seen as a story of assimilation; assimilation as something the Jews did to other people.

Or it could be a blazing example of how America was searching for the Jews even as the Jews were discovering America.

RAGTIME JEWS

The sensation at the Chicago World's Fair of 1893 was the world's first Ferris wheel, but the most lasting impression by far was made by a handful of piano players from Sedalia, Missouri. Sedalia, with its gambling and wide-open red-light district, employed dozens of pianists around the clock, and in Chicago, these keyboard "professors" introduced a style of playing known as "ragtime" to the world, and to another pianist who happened to be walking the runway. His name was Scott Joplin, and while he was at first dubious about this new piano style, driven by jagged rhythms and flowing harmonic improvisation, he eventually became an enthusiast and the composer of some of the most famous ragtime pieces, including "The Maple Leaf Rag" and "The Entertainer." Also at the fair that year was a man named W. C. Handy, who was also not a big fan of this new music, but who eventually took a melody he heard there on the runway and fashioned it into the "St. Louis Blues." Ragtime and the blues: two pillars of modern American music. And they are as different from each other as haute couture and ready-to-wear.

The American blues form seems to have been around since the Civil War, passed down in performance from one musician to another. It typically had a twelve-bar structure: a four-bar statement is made, repeated, then answered. And although a blues can be any number of bars long—elongated or curtailed according to the mood of the performer—all blues contain this element of statement, recapitulation, and answer. The blues is very simple. The elegance is in form following function, how easily it lends itself to simple storytelling.

Unlike spirituals, which are choral or group music and rely on a rich harmonic structure, the blues is not about harmony. It is not even so much about melody. The blues is all about the story of a person's life: this is what happened to me and I can tell my story on any notes I choose and change them if and as I like. The blues is driven by the human voice: even if it's played on a guitar, it is "vocalized." In the blues, the voice is not used with precision, as it is in most Western music; the singer does not strive for accuracy, to hit the note exactly in the center. Rather, he or she approaches the note from above or below, sliding into the tonal center, in order to test the best route to the truth. The meaning is delivered in the manner. This melismatic sliding around the note is also a central feature in Jewish cantorial singing. The two have often been compared for this reason. And finally, blues songs were written by blacks for blacks.

Ragtime, on the other hand, was primarily a show music, written down and played by musicians highly educated in Western classical technique. In the beginning, "rag" was a verb, not a noun; piano "professors" would rag a popular song, and while the introduction of player pianos made it possible for people who couldn't read music to learn to play ragtime, most could read. "Ragging" a song generally meant taking liberties with the rhythm, injecting anticipation and forward motion by focusing on the upbeats rather than the downbeats (also known as syncopation), while at the same time arpeggiating the chords and reweaving the melody throughout. It is a technically challenging and harmonically adventurous style of playing, quite the opposite of the free-form meandering of the blues. When a ragtime composition was written down, it could sell millions of copies of sheet music. So whereas the blues may have generated great feeling and sympathy, one person at a time, ragtime could and did generate huge sales, one piece of sheet music at a time. (Fifty years later, however, sales of blues recordings would humble the sales figures of ragtime songs.)

American popular music is not so much in the notes (the actual pitch) as in the shape of the notes (the timbre) and in the way the notes bump into each other. This is rhythm—the way music moves, and by extension, the way *we* move. It is accepted that music is a reflection of the times, but it is also a way the times move through us and insinuate themselves into our lives. Changes in rhythm invariably indicate deep underlying changes in society. Take for example the transition from the waltz to ragtime at the turn of the century. Waltz time, or 3/4 time, is by nature polite, formal: *one*, two, three, *one*, two, three. It starts and stops, your partner is held at arm's length, and while your feet move, your upper body remains rigid. It does not have a forward-driven pulse, in part because it is not in time with the rhythm of the human heart. The human heart beats in quarter time with a dotted-eighth, or syncopated feeling: the heart plays a march that swings. Starting with John Philip Sousa, the March King, and continuing up through Prince and beyond, American dance music has been one long parade in 4/4, common time, the people's meter.

The popularity of ragtime coincided with the growing availability of pianos. Through the industrial boom, the price of pianos was coming down even as the income of the people was going up. The piano soon became a focal point of the middle-class home. By the 1890s, in a world still without electricity, radios, films, or automobiles, pianos were the main social lubricant; every young woman of good breeding could play a bit and knew how to read music. On a Friday night, family entertainment meant sitting around and listening to your daughter play piano. Perhaps her suitor would come over and sit on the couch with the family, and after the concert they could spend some time alone on the front porch. That was entertainment in nineteenth-century America.

Manufacturers of pianos made another giant leap when they began to extend credit to consumers: pianos were the first major consumer item that could be purchased over time, the actual start of the great American credit boom. Improved manufacturing, extended credit, and increased leisure time can all be tracked in the sales of pianos—between 1890 and 1900, piano production increased five times faster than the population; between 1900 and 1910, six times faster. The peak year was 1910, when 365,000 pianos were sold in the United States and piano literacy was almost as pervasive as print literacy. Times were clearly getting better.

All those amateur piano players needed something to play: they needed sheet music. There was a huge need here that was not being serviced, and as it was a relatively new business, there was no anti-Semitism to keep the Jews out. Similarly, as it was a pennies business, there was no reason for established WASP businessmen to want in. Many of the Jewish song publishers came straight out of the needle trades and pushcarts to make music publishing a multi-million-dollar business. Joseph Stern, before he became one of the biggest music publishers, sold neckties; Edward Marx, notions and buttons; Leo Feist, corsets. There was nothing magical or mystical about the song business to them; they simply saw an economic opening and threw themselves into it. Music was made to order, ready to wear, a commodity, an opportunity. The Jewish music publishers simply applied and extended the marketing techniques they had pioneered in the garment industry, where handwork and exact sizing were winning over the average consumer.

Of course, there had been a nascent music publishing business prior to the arrival of the Jews. The most successful publisher was a man named Oliver Ditson, who specialized in choral, chamber, and religious music. From an office in Boston, Ditson used catalogs and formal notices in newspapers to alert the public to his songs. (Jews were not allowed into his firm or into any of the old-line publishers.) When Jews started their own firms, they concentrated on popular songs, marketing them in every way imaginable: they hired singers—called "boomers"—to go out on the street corners and sing their latest tunes at the top of their lungs (this was broadcasting before radio). Boomers also went backstage in theaters, corralled the stars, and slipped them some money, saying "Check out this new song, you're gonna love it" (perhaps the earliest form of payola in the music business). Jewish publishers pioneered marketing techniques that are still in use today: Ed Marx even had the idea to market a song using visuals: employing colored lantern slides, a pianist, a projectionist, and a vocalist who moved around to various locations throughout New York setting up in cabarets, vaudeville houses, and storefront nickelodeons, it was like an early form of MTV. And just for good measure, Marx also planted a "stooge" in each crowd to whip up "spontaneous" audience participation, much as companies still manipulate chart position and MTV uses a paid "host" to direct your attention to the goods.

Within a few years, Ditson was out of business and the Jewish publishers were selling, in proportion, more sheet music than Madonna ever sold CDs. Without the benefit of radio, television, a movie deal, or an advertising tie-in, a hit song from the 1890s, such as "After the Ball" or "In My Merry Oldsmobile," was familiar to 90 percent of the people in the United State within months of its release and could sell more than five million copies (roughly the equivalent of fifty million units today). This is virtually a definition of a hit in popular culture: a work in the vernacular of the times that becomes a part of the times.

Music drove the times; along with the ragtime craze came an underlying social displacement. Show business was becoming a new secular religion, and having fun (the pursuit of happiness) was the new gospel. As America approached the realization of her promise, interest in Victorianism quickly waned and her obsession with warm nights, fast cars, and young love became apparent. Just as the buzzword of the 1990s would be the "hip-hop life," implying that the music represented a whole new world view, so too the "Ragtime Life" was not just the title of a hit song but a cultural manifesto at the turn of the twentieth century. People talked about living this way; they were no longer riding on a bicycle built for two, they were taking the subway down to the Lower East Side to go slumming with the bohemians, and they were singing songs like "Everybody's Doing It" and nobody had to ask what "it" was.

The difference between what came before ragtime, which was moving the feet, and ragtime, which was shaking the ass, was enormous. Suddenly people started embracing in public, being openly physical with one another. Whereas previously, young people had needed chaperones on their dates, now they began hanging out in clubs, drinking and dancing and raising the roof. There was something visceral—something *free!*—about this exotic new life in the big city. This new music was "putting the sin back in syncopation."

Up until the turn of the century, New York had more or less been just another large American city, along with Chicago, Boston, New Orleans, St. Louis, or San Francisco, vying for bragging rights. But in the first decade of the century, New York became *the* American city for art, for commerce, and for modernism. If you weren't in New York, the only way for you to see and hear the songs and singers was to wait for the vaudeville show or the sheet music to come to your town. Before radio and recordings, there was only printed music and word of mouth. Given that the major difference in the demographic makeup of New York City between 1890 and 1920 was the arrival of two million Jews from the Pale of Settlement, one may well ask to what extent they just happened to arrive at the moment of ignition of the beating heart of the modern world and to what extent they actually brought that pulse into being.

Curiously, many of the Jews who arrived during this period were not from urban centers at all, but rather from deeply isolated rural areas in Russia, Poland, and the Balkans—yet when they landed at Ellis Island, they were somehow prepared for this emerging American modernism. As the expatriate American author Henry James observed, "Foreign as they might be, newly inducted as they might be, they were at home. Really more at home at the end of their few weeks or months or the year or two than they had ever been in their lives before." This was not necessarily true for immigrants from other places. Why might the transition have been easier or more immediate for the Jews? First of all, for Jews, identities, occupations, even physical appearance had been fluid for generations. Within one generation, names were changed, beards were removed, and children were no longer taught the Yiddish language. The goal was to become completely American, "a Yankee Doodle," as quickly as possible. In their haste, they invented a lot of it out of whole cloth. It is hard to imagine your average Protestant family from England or Germany going to such great lengths to forget their past and fit in. There was this tremendous pent-up energy among Jewish immigrants finally released from generations of arbitrary prohibition, finally free to show their stuff.

Many of this generation were smart, fast, literate, funny, open to innovation and looking for the main chance; they reveled in irony (the most modern kind of humor) and were determined to survive, to *make it*. The "longing for belonging" among perennial outsiders is a powerful force. And yet this very quality, the aching desire to be accepted, to be invisible in the crowd, guaranteed them their outsider status, because it was not shared by those already on the inside and never would be. Jews trying to fit in were seen as "on the make." Their very intense yearning to be like others is often what set them apart. It was a kind of perpetual motion machine, fueled by the impossible and driven by hope; a kind of cultural nuclear fusion device, a glowing source of achievement and frustration for the Jews. This duality too drove modernism, because modernism implied change, and for Jews, change had been their only constant, what they did best.

Breaking with the past while the future was breaking all around was a key to both American Jews and modernism. Modernism implied that something was broken and then reassembled in a new way: cubism in the world of art, for example, was a graphic representation of this process. To see the world in a new way, one had to stop seeing it in the old, very much like the experience of Moses and the old generation who were prohibited from entering the promised land: something had to end for something else to be. There is an element of Talmudism at work in this: the idea here too is that the old world is shattered and needs to be reassembled in a new way. Modernism contained just such a mandate to rotate the cube of perception around and around to arrive at new insights, to see things through the prism of concepts and ideas, hence creating and recreating reality.

Modernism swept the capitals of Europe before it reached America, and on both sides of the Atlantic, it was equated with the idea of a bohemian existence. In America, sales of popular novels such as the licentious runaway bestseller *Trilby*, a story about a love triangle of English art students in Paris in the 1890s, let the average man and woman on the street know they were not alone in their emerging desires. A new day was dawning: people understood, from the sales figures alone, that the old moral order was no longer enforceable. The result was called an "optics of pleasure," a new way for people to see life. Previous generations had viewed cities as the source of all that was evil, sinful and anathema to solid middle-class values. Now, at the century's turn, cities became places of pleasure and possibility. This perception of the urban landscape as a place where one could live a "good life" was a huge reordering of communal senses and social habits, perhaps nowhere more so than in America.

In New York, one expression of this was the new vogue for the "gentlemen's ramble," where well-to-do bons vivants from Uptown would visit the theaters around Times Square, then proceed farther downtown to Greenwich Village, winding up late at night in the bars and cafés of the Lower East Side. There, this exotic Jewish culture could be observed firsthand. For many, it was a voyage into darkness; white Anglo-Saxon Protestants were at the top of the racial ladder and African-Americans at the very bottom, and Jews too were close to the bottom and considered to be part of the "black race." But while African-Americans had been in America for generations and were part of the national confusion and guilt surrounding slavery, Jews were new, "oriental," and not undeserving of sympathy; their very presence, therefore, made black culture "safe" for the Uptown crowd. Similarly, Jews were in a unique position to contextualize black culture for other Americans as well as to present their own.

It was a time of great improvisation and social exploration. As cataloged by one rambler, the Jewish neighborhoods featured "students, journalists, scholars, advanced people, socialists, anarchists, free-thinkers, and even free lovers," a pressure cooker in which ideas about politics and art were often the pretext for men and women to fall in and out of sexual and political arrangements. The Jewish writer Gertrude Stein referred to this celebration of modern life by the young and the restless in New York at the turn of the century as "life without father," perhaps the best description of the modernist impulse. Boundaries—social, economic, ethical, spiritual, aesthetic—were no longer fixed. The term "ragtime" itself came to represent any kind of splashy, up-front, "Hey how ya doin'? Nice to see you" kind of American show tune: "Hello my baby, hello my honey, hello my ragtime gal, send me a kiss by wire. Baby, my heart's on fire." And the place where many people first heard this new musical vocabulary was in the vaudeville theaters, a new form of show business that was replacing minstrelsy and being promoted in large part by Jewish immigrants.

Coming out of the Yiddish theater tradition, vaudeville was an easy transition for many Jews, and the seemingly overnight popularity of vaudeville was matched by the remarkable hustle of Jewish entrepreneurs to mount new revues. In 1900, for example, the Shubert brothers, Lee, Sam, and J.J., acquired their first theater in New York. Within one year they had six theaters; soon they came to control thirteen vaudeville houses in Manhattan alone, and sixty others in cities across the country.

It's hard to imagine just how popular vaudeville was at the turn of the century, given our current saturation with all things designed to entertain and distract us. But at the time, vaudeville was the equivalent of television, the iPod, the Internet, and a rock concert all in one. Americans couldn't get enough of this ragtag collection of singers, dancers, spielers, animal acts, comics and contortionists, singers of heart songs from back home, and tummlers of every stripe. The idea of a national identity being represented through the arts was brand-new, and America was literally discovering itself in real time in vaudeville theaters. Show business became the new American obsession, and everybody saw themselves as having the potential to get onstage.

In fact, to many observers it appeared that vaudeville was becoming a new form of secular religion, so all-consuming was it to so many. And if show business was like a religion, everybody was welcome in the church. Vaudeville put the "pop" in popular theater. Unlike minstrelsy, it was not about black culture or Jewish culture per se: it was about everybody. Vaudeville performances could last all day, with participants appearing two or three times over the course of one show. Whole families came for the day, wandered about the theater, ate their lunch, shouted comments up to the stage. Just as in the Yiddish theater back in Odessa, the audience became part of the show. Everybody gawked at everybody else; this was true American multiculturalism. Long before there was political correctness, there were solidarity and relief from the anxiety of modern life—let's call it *fun*—in identifying down to the street rather than up to the Victorian parlor.

By 1905, vaudeville had displaced the professional minstrel show and had become more than a fun day out; it was a communal learning experience for many immigrants. Vaudeville bred a certain familiarity; it was a ground-level example of tolerance, creating a context wherein each new greenhorn could see himself in the crowd; it taught the notion of American consensus; it was communal learning at its best. So it is not surprising that for some Jewish immigrants, conditioned by the Yiddish theater and the chaos of the *cheders*, the vaudeville stage replaced the synagogue. The great Jewish lyricist Yip Harburg remembers, "On many a Saturday, my father packed me up and told my mother we were going to *shul* to hear a *maggid* but somehow we always arrived at the Thalia Theater." For men of Harburg's father's generation, the vaudeville theater was a connection to his Yiddish past. But for children like Yip, who learned about America by sitting in the dark and reveling in the vernacular, vaudeville was an opening into a whole new future: the evolving American language, the rhythm, swing, and humor of life on the streets.

How important was this new language, this secular religion, to the formation of the American character? In every era we know ourselves by the language we speak, not only because these words are running through our heads all day long but because this grammar is the rhythm defining the tempo of our life. If music actually conveys literal and emotional meaning, affects *how* we think, not just *what* we think, then a communal stage proved very powerful. The music itself was talking. It is interesting to note that modern popular songs have generally been written music first, with the lyricist using the melody to generate the words. The melody itself often tells the story, even down to the phonemes of the language employed. Implicit in this arrangement is that music means something in and of itself, and this is exactly the point of "good *nusach*." Through generations of Jewish cantors—with one man singing the story of the people so that the entire congregation could experience the catharsis—the connection of music and meaning was highly developed in the Jewish culture.

Coincidentally, at the turn of the century, there was a great resurgence of interest in cantorial music in America. Liturgical singers like Boris Thomashefsky, a huge celebrity back in Russia, became famous all over again in America. The essence of the cantorial tradition was not about the specific notes or modes that were employed but about the emotional meaning of the notes, the words *in* the music. Just so, during the twentieth century, many of the important changes in American speech were not happening at the level of grammar or language but at the level of sound itself. In music, the movement of the notes is the grammar, but the *sound* of the notes—this is something that goes much deeper, to the very meaning and existence of community.

Think of the sound on the streets—Times Square or Delancey—at the turn of the century; the vast majority of people on those streets were Jews from the Pale. "It is no coincidence that theater and synagogue shared more than just the patrons," writes one historian. "Virtually every major composer who wrote for the Yiddish theater had studied as a *meshroyer*—an apprentice cantor or *khazn*—and knowingly employed modes and scales used in the time-honored cantorial tradition, cementing an instant familiarity between audience and song." In New York, most of the patrons of vaudeville theaters were Jews.

One such patron was Israel Baline, born in Russia in 1888, the son of a cantor. He claimed to have no memories of his early childhood except one: lying on a blanket by the side of a road watching the Cossacks burn his family's house to the ground. The family arrived in New York shortly thereafter and settled on Cherry Street in one of the worst neighborhoods of the Lower East Side, or "Jewtown" as it was then called. At age seven he went to public school, where his teacher told his parents, "He just dreams and sings to himself." His family, he remembered, "spoke only Yiddish and we were conspicuous for our 'Jew clothes.'" He sang with his father in synagogue. "I suppose it was singing in *shul* that gave me my musical background," he later said. "It was in my blood." In 1901, just after his bar mitzvah, his father died, and the following year, ashamed that his sisters were bringing in money and he wasn't, he quit school and moved out of the house. He was, he said, "sick with a sense of his own worthlessness." For several years, he lived in a string of flophouses, a young boy on his own in a concrete jungle.

Just nine years out of Russia, with English as a second language, he found himself scrounging for a living on the streets of New York. He turned to the only thing he knew: singing. In 1902, at age fourteen, he got a job as a "boomer" for Harry Von Tilzer, singing Von Tilzer's latest compositions on street corners, in pool halls, wherever crowds gathered. Von Tilzer could not read or write music but had composed hundred of songs, including hits like "I Want a Girl Just like the Girl That Married Dear Old Dad," and "coon songs" such as "Alexander, Don't You Love Your Baby No More?" Perhaps Von Tilzer's success gave the young Izzy Baline the sense that he could do it too.

He hung out in Chinatown for several years, the roughest part of the Lower East Side, plugging songs. Eventually he got a job as a singing waiter, working the 8 p.m. to 6 a.m. shift at a dance-hall-cum-saloon known as the Pelham Cafe, a seedy place that catered to the "gentlemen's rambles" passing through Chinatown. Word was that the well-known Jewish gangster Monk Eastman would hang out at the Pelham, which attracted a lot of folks from Uptown who were interested in slumming with big-time exotics. Upstairs at the Pelham was a brothel run by a woman known as Chinatown Gerty, who charged tourists a small fee to watch her smoke opium.

"Once you start singing, you start thinking of writing songs," Baline said later. "It's as simple as that." Together with the club's pianist, he wrote a song called "Marie from Sunny Italy" and had it published by Joseph Stern. This first song was followed by many others, including "Sadie Salome Go Home," about a young Jewish girl dancing in a burlesque hall, and "Cohen Owes Me $97," about an avaricious Jew on his deathbed. Like the "coon songs" and various ethnic parodies of the era, these songs were attempts to capitalize on passing fashions. He didn't write for the art of it: he wrote songs to try to make money. If Italian tunes were in vogue, he wrote Italian; if Irish, then he wrote Irish.

Although he eventually learned to play the piano (using only the black keys), he always used musical secretaries throughout his career, singing the melodies to them and guiding them to the harmony he was hearing in his head. He boasted that his lack of musical education was an asset. "In my ignorance of the laws of music," he said, "I have often broken all laws, and the result was an original twist. In popular songs, a comparative ignorance of music is an advantage, also, in that my vocabulary being somewhat limited through lack of education, it follows that my lyrics are simple." It was a formula to be repeated by many others throughout the century.

He was not necessarily writing the way *he* talked but rather the way he heard people on the street talk. He was "slanging" (slang being a kind of verbal swing, the rhythm of the street itself). In his big hit, "Alexander's Ragtime Band," for example, he used the phrase "Ain't you goin'?" He had knowingly dropped the final *g* and used "ain't" to reach a wider audience. Over and again, with songs like "Blue Skies" and "Cheek to Cheek," he demonstrated he was more than capable of writing in "standard English." But as H. L. Mencken once observed, "Nobody ever went broke underestimating the intelligence of the American public." In his hands, slang was a deliberate disguise or pretense, artifice interested in creating a new mass culture, and, at the turn of the century, America was just discovering its appetite for the fast food of popular song.

Eventually, he stopped cowriting with others and began working with "arrangers," piano players to whom he would sing the melody, turning out a new song every day. With continued success, he officially changed his name from Baline to Berlin and began to dress in suits and ties, creating a tailored persona for himself. Only nineteen years old, just five years after moving out of the family apartment and onto the streets, Irving Berlin became not just a legitimate American songwriter but a role model for many future songwriters: a man who could neither read nor write music, but who spoke the people's English.

Berlin was well aware that every hit song needed a hook—he once described the right word as a "spear" or a "punch"—and that slanging the language was a good way to achieve this. One of the main purposes of using slang in songs—as true at the turn of the century as it is today in the language of rap music—is to shock those who cling to old sensibilities. Using the street language of the time rather than parlor politesse was part of the ongoing assault on

Victorianism, a sign of an emerging purely American identity. The same rough crowd that haunted the vaudeville houses was beginning to dictate the language of popular songs.

Prior to this, the apogee of songwriting had been the works of W. S. Gilbert and Arthur Sullivan for the British Savoy opera company. Their lyrics, brilliant and written in classic iambic pentameter (the rhythm of the monarchy), were widely admired by the emerging Jewish songwriters, and many tried to copy its wit and range:

> Here is a first rate opportunity
> To get married with impunity
> And indulge in the felicity
> Of unbounded domesticity.
> You shall be quickly personified
> Congenially matrimonified
> By a doctor of divinity
> Who resides in this vicinity . . .

Very clever, like poetry itself, with words clearly written before music; one might well wonder what the advantage was of putting music to it at all. It was relatively easy to write verse after verse this way, without having to worry about the emotional demands of a more profound melody line. In Gilbert and Sullivan's work, the melodic often seemed like an afterthought: there was little need for connection between the words (the story line) and the music. Similarly, there was very little connection between the narrative premise of the songs and the lives of the ordinary people listening to the performance. How many in the audience had any familiarity with the military generals and flouncing royalty that often made up the music's subject matter? This is exactly the kind of songwriting that Berlin rejected. He referred to it as something foreign to America. "They [other American songwriters] write imitation European music which doesn't mean anything," he said. "Ignorant as I am, from their standpoints, I'm doing something they all refuse to do: I'm writing American music."

He was right, and he was not alone working on a purely American style of composition. It's just that most of these alternatives were from the African-American culture, and white America, since the death of Stephen Foster and prior to the arrival of the Jews from the Pale, was not inclined to listen to actual black music. It was the emergence of Jewish popular songwriters that brought Foster's work back to life. In addition, there were other, more contemporary black models. By 1902, Ernest Hogan, the composer who wrote the hit song "All Coons Look Alike to Me," was working with composer James Reese Europe on the musical comedy *Smart Set*, an elaborate production billed as "the greatest Negro show ever seen." It was perhaps the first taste white audiences in America had had of a genuine black musical experience, but few whites saw the production. Hogan died in 1909; by then, he and Reese Europe had helped launch an American dance craze using uniquely American rhythms that one would never find in the cotillions and waltzes: dances with names like the turkey trot, the grizzly bear, the chicken scratch, the lame duck, the humpback rag, the bunny hug, the ostrich, the fox trot, and many others, some highly sexual, where people actually pressed their bodies together on the dance floor. It was scandalous, and everybody was doing it. American composers scrambled to keep up with the demand.

By 1910, Berlin was drawing from all these black sources. His big breakthrough, however, came in 1911 with the song "Alexander's Ragtime Band." At the time, ragtime itself was rather old hat, and Berlin had tried several times previously to hitch his wagon to the star of this new music, with no success. Every time popular fashion shifted, he gave it another shot with corny songs like "That Opera Rag," "Sweet Marie, Make a Rag-a-Time Dance with Me" and even "Yiddle on Your Fiddle Play Some Ragtime." He had no idea what ragtime actually was; as he was not a musician, the subtleties of syncopation were lost on him. But being a sophisticated student of the streets, he also knew that ragtime was a lot more than a musical idiom: it was a buzzword for modernism, for freedom, and young Americans—his peers—were enthralled with the *idea* of ragtime as much as by the music itself.

His inner ear was unfailing, and he understood that there was something in ragtime music that was connected to contemporary American speech. If you listen to the well-known four-note musical figure that introduces the chorus of "Alexander's Ragtime Band," it's there: the chromatic phrase starting on the "and" of the third beat with a triplet feel—"Come on and hear!"—is straight out of the way that American English swings and in its own way suggests the ragtime idiom. (It is also somewhat similar to the opening chromaticism that Berlin would use in his song "White Christmas," which has often been considered a great part of that song's success.) Berlin's gift was in understanding that American English was a very specific form of English, and that like ragtime, it too swings. His melodies were driven by this symbiosis of words and music. "Syncopation," he said simply, "is the soul of every American."

Berlin's description of how he wrote "Alexander's Ragtime Band" is similarly revealing. "First," he said, "it starts with 'come on and hear, come on and hear!' an invitation to come, to join in, to hear the singer and his song. The idea of *inviting* every receptive auditor within shouting distance became part of the happy ruction, an idea pounded in again and again throughout the song in various ways; it was the secret of the song's tremendous success." From his point of view, the song was a call to community. What he doesn't say, but was well aware of, was that the name "Alexander" was itself a kind of call to community, a code word for a black man acting educated or "uppity," just as it had been used in Von Tilzer's "Alexander, Don't You Love Your Baby No More?" years earlier, and this association with "coon songs" was also a big part of the song's success. Similarly, Berlin included a reference to the Stephen Foster hit ("If you want to hear that 'Swanee River' played in ragtime") and appealed to the budding nationalism of Americans following the turn of the century ("They can play a bugle call like you never heard before / So natural that you wanna go to war"). All these lyrical hooks captured the popular mind.

Finally, it is important to note that the song wasn't a rag at all—musically speaking, it had virtually nothing to do with the music that emerged from Sedalia in the 1890s—but was actually a straight-ahead march. It was Berlin's language that delivered the swing, and he used "ragtime" as a code word for "getting loose," so everybody understood that this was a party song. Berlin didn't belabor the issue:

> Ain't you goin', ain't you goin',
> To the leaderman, ragged meter man,
> Grandstand, brass band,
> Ain't you comin' along?

By 1911, Berlin had discovered that one could rag a song by syncopating its words without syncopating its music, by shifting to the weaker beat and forgetting correct grammar, relying instead on how people on the street actually talked (the ongoing rush of the colloquial). In America, then, we can propose that while blacks initially provided rhythmic swing to the music, the Jews, because of their familiarity with and empathy for a heightened populism, provided the lyrical or grammatical swing, a form of American English that the dominant (white) culture could easily accept. It is not so much that the Jews dressed up black American speech; rather, they translated it into the American mother tongue in a way that could be understood and appreciated by the average man on the street. They didn't make it "safe" so much as they made it both personal and universal.

Berlin had finally nailed his method of operation: "Three-fourths of that quality which brings success to popular songs is the phrasing," he said. "I make a study of it—ease, naturalness, every-day-ness—and it is my first consideration when I start on lyrics. Easy to sing, easy to say, easy to remember and applicable to everyday events." A friend recalled, "I sometimes used to sit beside Irving at his tiny piano and listen while he composed. He would go over and over a lyric until it seemed perfect to my ears. Then he'd scrap the whole thing and begin over again. When I asked Irving what was wrong, he invariably said, 'It isn't *simple* enough.'" He might just as well have said, "It didn't swing."

Stephen Foster, whose songs were still being sung fifty years after the composer's death, was Berlin's hero. "These things I am writing," he said, "are only for the brief career of the vaudeville stage. They will be a hit for a week or two [but] folks are still singing 'Swanee River' and 'My Old Kentucky Home'; it's something to be known like Stephen Foster." He hung a portrait of Foster on the wall behind his desk to remind himself of his mission. And he was not alone in idolizing the success and populism of Foster's music; many Jewish songwriters not only longed for the national acceptance of his timeless melodies, but recognized in Foster's idealization of the South something that captured both their own nostalgia and a truly American ideal. In time, Jewish composers made the South into America's honorary homeland, a place of pastoral elegance and, strangely, one devoid of race problems.

For the Jews, the South wasn't so much a place but a premise: the concept of home, the idea of belonging somewhere. They substituted the Swanee River for something that they had been missing for generations: a homeland. A few years after Berlin wrote his hit about the "Swanee River played in ragtime," George Gershwin and Irving Caesar wrote the song "Swanee," another huge hit, and it was only after they had made enough money from it to travel to the South that they discovered the river itself was just a muddy creek. There were many others: "Shine On Harvest Moon" was written by Dora Goldberg and Harry Von Tilzer, who had never experienced a harvest on the streets of Manhattan; "Rock-a-Bye Your Baby with a Dixie Melody" was written by Jean Schwartz, Sam Lewis and Joe Young (all Jews), and none of them had ever been south of Brooklyn; "Waiting for the Robert E. Lee" was written by L. Wolfe Gilbert about a spot "way down on the levee, in old Alabammy," but having been born in Russia, Gilbert had never been to Alabama and so had no idea there were no levees there; Gus Kahn (born Koblenz) wrote "Carolina in the Morning" (than which nothing could be finer). The list goes on and on. The Jews were re-contextualizing America with their own inner desires, using the South to channel their dreams.

On some level, all songwriting is about channeling dreams. Even the most "objective" writers like Berlin, who claimed they were only doing it for the money, can't avoid reaching into their own subconscious for subject matter, or an emotional premise, or perhaps just some raw material. Similarly, songwriting is also channeling mass dreams (think Jung's collective unconscious). This is not to say it was done on purpose; simply that the music-first grammar the Jewish writers favored naturally led to a particular style of storytelling through song, and that story tended to humanize all that it touched.

Take for example the case of Albert Von Tilzer, younger brother of Berlin's first employer, Harry. Albert too was an instinctive composer—that is, he had no formal training but wrote songs for all occasions. In 1908, to help the Jewish immigrants make their transition to America, the New York Yiddish newspaper *The Jewish Daily Forward* ran a series of articles explaining the game of baseball. Von Tilzer, who had never been to a baseball game in his life, read the articles and decided to write a song about the game. The name of the song he wrote was "Take Me Out to the Ballgame." And if you think about the lyrics, it's a dream about a man who wants to go, who wants to belong to the masses, who wants to participate. It's a song looking for a community, and he says, "I don't care if I never get back." This isn't just about baseball. It's about discovering America. And although it's not a complete song—that is, the form is truncated into two brief eight-bar phrases—it *is* a complete sentiment.

"Take Me Out to the Ballgame" is about a dream, a very Jewish dream that came to speak for all Americans; like the mythical South, the ballgame was a place from which no one was excluded and in which everyone was safe. For Jews, this was key. Yes, they wanted desperately to succeed, but they didn't want to take over America (as anti-Semites have long claimed). In fact it was just the opposite. They wanted to create a crowd in which to hide, a mass culture, a vox populi, a country where they could feel safe. Many years later, Dick Cavett would ask Woody Allen why he was so hesitant to leave New York City, and Woody's response was something along the lines of "Among all these people, what could happen to me?" He was more threatened by the quiet of the countryside, by standing out, than by disappearing into the crowd. Hence Berlin's dictum "The mob is never wrong," and the strange duality at the heart of the Jewish American experience: their "inauthenticity" as outsiders becomes the core of their American "authenticity." Everybody wanted to "come on along!"

"Alexander's Ragtime Band" took off across the country as performers took it to vaudeville houses everywhere. Berlin's publisher, Ted Snyder, hired seventy-five "boomers" to work the song on the streets; Al Jolson, who was working in Lew Dockstader's minstrel show (the premier East Coast troupe), delivered it nightly with emotional bravura. In 1911, more than a million copies of the sheet music were sold. The following year, another million. Then it crossed the ocean and became a huge hit in England and on the Continent, where America, following its victory in the Spanish-American War, was for the first time being taken seriously as a nation. The song was associated with the American "can do" spirit, and Irving Berlin became the "king of ragtime." Some people, aware that the song had nothing to do with actual ragtime music and sensing it was so much more advanced than his previous efforts, started spreading a rumor that the song hadn't actually been written by Berlin at all but by "a little black boy" he kept in the closet. As ridiculous as the rumor was, it persisted to the point where Berlin had to defend himself on several occasions.

What Berlin *had* done, for the first time since Stephen Foster, was accurately capture something of the black American experience, on a vast commercial scale and in a way that whites, both in America and around the world, could understand and empathize with. That is, he did not attempt to "steal" black rhythm or appropriate black speech; rather, he wrote in (and thus helped create) American slang and let the "blackness" of the narrative sell itself. It is important to remember that this was during a transitional period when black culture was both suspect and diffuse; it was only a few years since the disaster of Reconstruction, wherein African-Americans in the South were victimized by Jim Crow laws, and only a few years prior to the formation of the great black neighborhoods like Harlem and the possibility of a black "renaissance." Berlin helped make black culture part of popular American culture in an authentic way. The key word here is "authenticity," for it would be a guiding concept as Americans emerged into the modern world. The quest for an authentic American language was on, and Berlin was there at the starting line.

Black grammar collided with Yiddish irony, the deconstruction of old words met with snatches of sound to form new words; the explosion of language in America was unlike anything that had come before. In Europe, one's status and social class were immediately obvious in one's accent; in America, the classless society dictated that the language too was without class; there was no right or wrong way, only ways that swung and those that didn't, and it was evolving on a minute-by-minute basis. And if white people taught African slaves how to speak English, it was equally true that Africans helped teach everyone how to speak *American.*

1910 to 1916 was a time of rapid transition in America. Many of the principles that had held the old order together were coming unraveled. The year 1913, for example, saw the first large exhibition of modern art in the United States; held at a large hall on Lexington Avenue, the Armory Show featured artists such as Matisse, Picasso, Braque, Kandinsky, Brancusi, and Marcel Duchamp. There, mixed in with realistic paintings in the classical style, were hundreds of works of cubism, fauvism, and expressionism. The exhibit provoked huge demonstrations unprecedented in the world of painting. In particular, Marcel Duchamp's *Nude Descending a Staircase* was actually attacked by a mob that considered the canvas to be offensive. At the same time, parallel events could be seen in the worlds of science—where Einstein's theories were destroying old paradigms of the physical universe—and social theory, where Emil Durkheim's theories of collective consciousness were similarly altering the way people viewed community. At root, modernism was a dramatic shift in one's thought process, perhaps best described as the shift from literalism to abstraction; it was a new "temper of mind that enriched whatever it approached." And it was relentless.

Quite understandably, this new mentality made people insecure, as what had long been fixed suddenly became fluid. People whose culture could deal with chaos, who were flexible, and who, psychologically speaking, had a bag packed at all times, could do well in the new America. Those who were rigid could easily get passed over or passed by. This tension between the old and new orders was only exacerbated by the expanding war in Europe. Most Americans wanted nothing to do with it; for some, it was exactly what they had worked so hard to escape. And yet if America was to become a real world power, it could not ignore what was happening across the sea. One consequence was that outright escapism became a popular spectator sport, and it arrived in a uniquely American format: the Broadway musical.

Broadway musical theater had been around for some time when, in 1907, the European hit musical *The Merry Widow* was staged at the New Amsterdam Theater in New York. For some reason, this light confection by Hungarian composer Franz Lehár caused a sensation. Having first opened in Vienna in 1905, within two years it had spawned more than nine hundred productions worldwide, the equivalent of Andrew Lloyd Weber's *Cats* a century later. (Coincidentally, both Leo Stein and Viktor Léon, the librettists of *The Merry Widow,* were Jews.) After *The Merry Widow*, one could not simply bring a thrown-together musical revue to Broadway. One needed a narrative arc of some sort, regardless of how thin or far-fetched. This arc was the justification for Broadway music to be taken "seriously," while the music of Tin Pan Alley tended to be considered trivial. Subsequently, there was a new legitimacy attributed to Broadway productions that attracted both educated composers and a well-to-do clientèle. If vaudeville was entertainment for the masses, Broadway was entertainment for the black-tie crowd.

At the time, a series of pale imitations of *The Merry Widow* were staged, all with story lines based on European themes and mostly built around the waltz. It was the last stand of the old order, and it didn't last long. In 1914, the producer Charles Dillingham, using Irving Berlin's music, broke with the tradition of waltz-based productions and launched what he called "the first all-American Broadway musical." Called *Watch Your Step,* and clearly influenced by the musical productions developed by Ernest Hogan and James Reese Europe, it was billed as "The First All-Syncopated Musical." Berlin did away with the usual violins and brought in horns and modern percussion instruments. (*Smart Set* had done this in 1902, but since it had been staged in New Jersey and not on Broadway, Dillingham's hyperbole stuck.) *Watch Your Step* became the big hit of the season. In less than seven years, Berlin had made the transition from the Pelham Cafe to the legitimate theater.

In a way, *The Merry Widow* was the last waltz for America. Just as American popular songs no longer employed the 3/4 time signature, henceforth Broadway music would primarily be written in 4/4, the time signature of the march, the human heart, and all the new dances. But the composer who established 4/4 as Broadway's underlying beat was not Irving Berlin: it was Jerome Kern.

Jerome Kern, a Jew from New York, was an Anglophile, and at first, his songs sounded much like their European counterparts. He was drawn, as were many writers at the time, to the Viennese light operas and to Gilbert and Sullivan. As a composer, Kern was interested in long form, not pop songs, and he initially went to England in 1903 because that's where musical theater was happening. When he returned to America, he began thinking about a new kind of musical theater that was prototypically American: instead of themes about kings and queens and gods and fairies, it would need to be believable, about real people. He and a few other Jewish composers started contemplating what they called "the New York Opera." Its primary requirement would be that both the music and the dialogue would move the action forward (to be known as a "through-composed" production). In the Viennese and British models, there was generally a thin narrative line to accommodate some snappy dialogue, but there was no developed "book," or backstory, to the production.

The American musical, which is so familiar to us today, innovated this idea of a two-hour musical experience premised on a dramatic narrative. To have the story support the music was a very Jewish concept, and it was no coincidence that it found a warm reception in American theaters during the first decades of the twentieth century: during this period, Jews made up more than half of the New York theatergoing audience. Having been prepared by the Yiddish theater, Jews often used the theater as a fundraising opportunity, organizing groups to attend in the name of a social cause. So not only were the Jewish composers writing most of the music, but they were writing it for an overwhelmingly Jewish audience. We owe Broadway to the Jews.

Kern's music first appeared on the American stage in 1904, in the British-based farce *Mr. Wix of Wickham*, and for the next decade he continued to supply extra tunes to various shows. Called "interpolating," it was common practice for publishers to place new songs in productions already up and running, songs that, for the most part, sounded as if they might be European imports. Some speculated that this was intentional, a kind of protest against the "slangy speech" of Tin Pan Alley songs, to keep the serious theater at arm's length from the streets. More likely, Kern wrote to fit what the productions demanded. But, in 1914, for the production *The Girl from Utah*, Kern wrote what has been called "the single most influential song in the history of the American musical." It was called "They Didn't Believe Me," and upon first hearing it, the composer Richard Rodgers said that he realized it was a new day for musical theater in this country. Similarly, a young George Gershwin, who first heard "They Didn't Believe Me" at a wedding, decided on the spot that he wanted to write for the Broadway stage.

What made this song so influential? First, the production for which it was written was launched at the beginning of World War I, and its producer had asked Kern for a song that wasn't as lighthearted as his previous material; he needed something that captured the spirit of the times. Hence Kern was given license to reach deeper into his emotional stores for the *meaning* of the music. Second, as the production was to be based on an American theme, the language too had to fit the subject; it had to "swing." This did not imply syncopation so much as using the way people actually spoke. The melody, for example, required the singer to use a colloquial contraction ("and I'm certainly *gonna* tell them"), which at the time seemed quite bold in the world of musical theater. It was important because it was conversational, it was then considered *democratic*. The melody too was democratic; Kern wrote his songs in a narrow range so that the average person could sing them. It implied that now in the American theater, we were going to have actors who could sing (the better to move the story forward), rather than singers who were usually bad actors. It placed the narrative front and center.

Yet Kern still wrote from the head down; a native speaker, he understood the language, and his songs are unfailingly elegant in nature ("Smoke Gets in Your Eyes," "All the Things You Are," "The Way You Look Tonight," "Yesterdays"). Berlin, however, wrote from the feet up; he *spoke* the language. His songs are remarkably diverse, reflecting the many aspects of the American experience and united only in the fact that their language invariably sounds like the way people actually talked. A partial list includes "Anything You Can Do (I Can Do

Better)," "The Best Thing for You," "The Girl That I Marry," "I've Got My Love to Keep Me Warm," "Let's Face the Music and Dance," "Puttin' On the Ritz," "The Song Is Ended (but the Melody Lingers On)," "Steppin' Out with My Baby," and "There's No Business like Show Business." One can see from Berlin's song titles alone that he was obsessed with the secular religion of show business—"puttin' on the ritz," "no business like show business," "face the music," and so on—and throughout his career, he continued referencing the music from within the music itself, inviting the people to "come on and hear." The result of his oeuvre was to make songwriting itself more important.

Even his songs with overtly Christian themes, such as "White Christmas" and "Easter Parade," had so much *yiddishkeit*, downhome street smarts, that the author Philip Roth, in his essay "Operation Shylock," was moved to comment, "The two holidays that celebrate the divinity of Christ—the divinity that's the very heart of the Jewish rejection of Christianity—and what does Irving Berlin do? Easter he turns into a fashion show and Christmas into a holiday about snow." But it isn't just about snow; "White Christmas" is also a song about loss, of longing for something that isn't there. Berlin didn't do it from the point of view of a Jew; he did it as an American. As his biographer, Laurence Bergreen, wrote, "Patriotism was Irving Berlin's true religion. It evoked the same emotional response in him that conventional religion summoned in others; it was his rock." Berlin often responded to questions about his Jewishness by saying he was an American songwriter, not a Jewish one, and that the two had nothing to do with each other. Yet we can see, with the advantage of hindsight, that there is little distinction between the two for Berlin; despite his most fervent denials, his Americanism retained many aspects of his Jewishness, and vice versa. Indeed, claiming that being Jewish had nothing to do with his success might have been the most Jewish thing he could have said. And the most American.

Unlike Kern, Berlin was not a long-form writer; his forte was the hit song, not the Broadway production, which required a much more sophisticated, one might say "educated," approach to storytelling. He was the master of the three-minute form, the "single" in today's parlance; and whereas Kern went on to define and expand the possibilities of the American musical theater, writing songs of great harmonic beauty and narrative elegance, Berlin kept writing hits, song after song, that captured the actual moment in time with great humanity, rather than humanizing the fictitious moments of a musical theater.

Perhaps this was the reason that Kern, when asked to comment on the significance of Irving Berlin's work, responded, "Irving Berlin has no place in American music. He *is* American music." To which the *New York Times* music critic Stephen Holden referred on the occasion of Berlin's ninety-ninth birthday: "The quality that Jerome Kern recognized as the essence of Irving Berlin is a faith in the American vernacular so profound that today the composer's best-known songs seem indivisible from the country's history and self-image . . . The best of it is a simple, exquisitely crafted street song whose diction feels so natural that one scarcely notices the craft . . . And his greatest melodies have a similar directness. For all of their innovation, they seem to flow straight out of the rhythms and inflections of everyday speech." The genius of Berlin was that, rather than play with the forms of language (as writers since Gilbert and Sullivan had done), Berlin wrote from the *sound* of language, its shape and swing. His language was not just "music first"; it was music, plain and simple.

And then suddenly, technology opened a new door for Berlin and the others: recordings. Technically, recordings had been around since 1877, when Edison invented the process of recording on wax cylinders, but the innovation of the 78 rpm flat shellac disc started the recording revolution. At first, these recordings were mostly used for spoken word and children's recordings, but as the technological problems were sorted out, recordings became more than a fad or a document of something curious or nostalgic: recordings became the experience of music itself. The man who invented the flat disc recording device, which he named the Gramophone, was Emil Berliner, a German Jew, who also invented the microphone several decades later, making every aspect of modern recording possible. Ultimately, Berliner's inventions would become classic examples of how this technology fundamentally altered the tradition that it was intended to preserve.

Gradually, people needed to own the recording in order to experience the song. Records turned entertainment and sentiment into a commodity that could be packaged and marketed, enjoyed wherever and whenever one liked. Prior to the invention of recording, enjoying music depended on where and when it happened; not only was the music being presented, but the moment in which it was created was being experienced. With recordings, one could in essence tie a string around the emotional package and pass it around to any number of people in any number of places at any time. Of course some things were gained and many other things were lost. What had been a pleasant homemade experience for a few people, with a friend at the center, became a mass marketing opportunity, with a professional entertainer doing the work. Hence, the document of the experience became the actual experience itself—that is, the experience was turned into a product that could be controlled and commodified. Selling lifestyle is one of the things that the American popular song does best.

At the time, nobody could have imagined that the record business would ultimately swallow up every other aspect of the music business; in fact, many songwriters of the day were worried that recordings would only hurt sales of sheet music, diminishing their main source of income. Of course, just the opposite was the case: recordings ultimately generated new fortunes for songwriters.

The earliest record companies, such as Columbia, Victor, and Edison, originally saw the recording business as a way to sell ethnic music back to the various groups that were arriving daily on ships to America: sell German songs to the Germans, Irish songs to the Irish; it was a way of packaging and commodifying nostalgia. This too had its cultural impact in that it helped erase what ethnomusicologists refer to as "regional variation," the differences that exist in music from one community to the next. With the advent of recording, the recorded version became *the* version, and alternative versions (from other regions) often disappeared without leaving a trace. Recordings homogenized the music even as they preserved it. At the same time, local performers who were lucky enough to be recorded could influence thousands of others thousands of miles away.

A classic example of technology's impact was the experience of the Original Dixieland Jazz Band, a group of white musicians from New Orleans who managed to make their way to New York City in 1917 and record for Victor. Their music, long on brassy sounds, barnyard noises, and casual ensemble work, became known everywhere as the "first recording of American jazz." Meanwhile, back in New Orleans, other superior, mostly black musicians were making musical history nightly. Only the world wouldn't know about them for several years, and even then, the real story behind America's only native art form had to compete with an incorrect historical record. Why was the music of the ODJB the first to be recorded? Because when approached in 1916 to go to New York and record for the Victor Talking Machine Company, trumpet player Freddie Keppard and the Original Creole Orchestra—skeptical of the whole recording process and not wanting to have their music "stolen"—turned the offer down. Instead of being stolen, it simply became lost.

In addition, the phonograph, by its very nature, altered aspects of the music. Primitive recording technology picked up the brassy sounds of the trumpet and the goofy barnyard sounds of crude percussion instruments much better than it could possibly represent the more dynamic ranges of the piano, bass, saxophone, or violin. Add to this the surface noise—the pops and scratches and interminable hissing of the shellac discs—that almost drowned out everything that wasn't physically positioned right next to the recording "horn." The technology favored some voices too, like Enrico Caruso's, who fared much better than other softer, more intimate voices. By definition, what sounded better was recorded more often. So singers who belted out the songs did well, while those who would be considered "crooners" had to wait until Berliner's invention of the microphone several years later. Until then, the sound of Louis Armstrong's horn, minus much of its richness and humor, would be identified with jazz.

Not that Armstrong's horn wasn't a great representation of American popular music. In fact, Armstrong's sound and career are prototypically American, more than most people realize. As a small child, desperately poor and trying to make his way on the streets alone—his father was missing and his mother was often unavailable—Louis was reduced to collecting discarded potatoes and selling them to New Orleans restaurants for a few pennies when he was discovered by a family of immigrant Jews from Lithuania, the Karnofskys. In many ways, they saved his life and laid down the conditions for his great musical success.

The Karnofskys began by paying the boy a few pennies to help them on their junk wagon. The young Louis would deliver buckets of coal to customers and blow on a little tin horn to attract attention. The family often worked the streets of Storyville, the red-light district that was the birthplace of New Orleans jazz, where the brothels employed ragtime piano players or small orchestras and there were "spasm bands" on many corners playing a new kind of improvised music on harmonicas, fiddles, brass, drums, whistles, cowbells, and bizarre homemade instruments.

But more important than the few pennies the Karnofskys were able to pay Louis, or the music he heard on the streets while traveling with them, was the love and affection he received from the family. After work, the young boy would join the Karnofskys for dinner, and he would remember those meals for the rest of his life. "I was only seven years old," he wrote, "but I could see the ungodly treatment that the white folks were handing the poor Jewish family whom I worked for. . . . I learned a lot from them about how to live. I began to feel like *I* had a future." The Karnofskys gave him that future: "They could see that I had music in my soul," he said. "They really wanted me to be something in life. And music was it. Appreciating my every effort."

There is a well-known story about how Louis Armstrong received his first trumpet, like the holy grail of jazz. Received wisdom has him being placed in the Colored Waifs Home and there receiving the instrument to play in the school band. Like much of New Orleans jazz history, this story is apocryphal. Armstrong's actual first horn, too, came from the Jews. "One day," he recalled,

> when I was on the wagon with Morris Karnofsky we were in Rampart and Perdido streets and we passed a pawn shop which had in its window an old beat up B-flat cornet. It only cost five dollars. Morris advanced me the money . . . and I put aside fifty cents each week from my small pay . . . boy was I a happy kid. Morris cleaned my little cornet with some brass polish and he requested me to play a tune on it. Although I could not play a good tune, Morris applauded me just the same which made me feel very good. After blowing it for a while I realized I could play "Home Sweet Home" . . . from then on, I was a mess and tooting away. I kept that horn for a long time.

And finally, along with the horn, the Jews gave Armstrong a wellspring of feeling from which he could draw throughout the rest of his life. Specifically, it came from the singing he did every night at bedtime in the Karnofsky home. After supper, he and the others would sing Russian lullabies as they rocked their baby to sleep. "We all sang together until the little baby would doze off," he remembered. "When I reached the age of eleven, I began to realize it was the Jewish family who instilled in me singing from the heart."

By 1918, the year the United States entered World War I, Armstrong was on his way to becoming an important figure in New Orleans music, a young man playing in jazz bands with his heroes. In a few years he would find his way to Chicago, then to New York, and ultimately to the rest of the world. By 1918, Irving Berlin had enlisted in the Army and was writing a little patriotic song called "God Bless America," which he wouldn't release for another couple of decades because he felt insecure about it. "It was just a little sticky," he would say; "I couldn't visualize soldiers marching to it. So I laid it aside and tried other things." He needn't have worried about the patriotic impact of his music: the sense of a unique destiny that all Americans shared came, in part, from the music of Irving Berlin. When he wrote a song about a bugle call that made you want to go to war, people went. And, interestingly enough, according to the War Records Bureau report of 1919, the most frequent last name to appear among enlistees in World War I was Cohen.

The Jewish experience is, and has always been, a dynamic one; it can only be understood in the context of the time and place of its circumstance. Just as the patriarch Abraham can only be understood in the context of pagan religions, Moses in terms of the Egyptians, the Bal Shem Tov in terms of the Pale of Settlement, and Irving Berlin in terms of America at the turn of the century, the future of Jews in America can only be understood by the historic coming together of Jews and African-Americans beginning at the turn of the twentieth century. Simply put, American popular music is the direct result of where, when, and how the Beat met the Book.

THE NEW YORK OPERA

THE NEW YORK OPERA

Following their victory in World War I, Americans woke to discover they were now major players on the world stage. Those returning from overseas, particularly black and Jewish soldiers who had seen the world and defended their country in the "war to end all wars," brought a new self-esteem back home with them. No longer a stepchild of European culture, the American identity was a thing of great interest to the rest of the world, and so to Americans as well. The rapid industrialization that had been used to gear up for the war was rapidly being converted to produce a multiplicity of new consumer products. The rise of popular culture in America during the 1920s reflects this new hunger for understanding who we are through what we consume.

With rising affluence and new technologies, Americans fell into a swoon of modernism and new media, sophistication and sex. Everybody came to the party; there were multicultural gatherings and interracial hangs for every taste, true social interaction between races and cultures, not just slapstick vaudeville parodies. Whipped up by the media into a froth known as the "Jazz Age"—more to use the highly charged word "jazz" than to reference the music itself—Americans faced a bright new world full of optimism and opportunity. But in the end it was a dream, dreamed mostly by the children of immigrants just a few short years out of the Russian Pale, turned loose in an urban environment.

Popular culture not only reflected people's dreams back to them, but more often than not invented those dreams in the first place. The media—radio, recordings, films, even photos and print advertisements—glowed with a vision of what modern life could be. And with the new recording and broadcasting technologies, people finally could *feel* what this future was all about as well as hear it, at home or hundreds of miles away; the music was being captured with reasonable fidelity, allowing the truth of the music to live "on the pulse" of the listener. As technology became more transparent, affording the qualities of sound safe passage, the music felt more visceral, more important; and *feeling* is what the Jazz Age was all about.

The emerging popular culture was a big part of the national discussion about who we were going to be, a way for anybody, coast to coast, to join in and vote with their feet. They went and bought movie tickets, or phonograph records. The "American identity," as opposed to the immigrant identity, was being created on the spot and the images being projected were remarkably consistent in their theme: previously, one was an extension of one's family and class; now the mandate for Americans was to discover, to invent, to become *oneself*. There was a great effort, particularly among Jews in America, to be *somebody*: a composer, a gangster, a businessmen, a writer, an identity of your own design. Descent was no longer destiny; regardless of race or class, every man or woman might be one lucky break away from frame and fortune. In the midst of this social free-for-all, role models were desperately needed; it was well and good to know who you no longer were, but who you were going to be—that was the question. People looked to the growing popular culture for answers, and those who were driving or channeling this culture became even more important to the shape of the American character.

On August 10, 1920, Mamie Smith, a young black singer who had been kicking around the vaudeville circuit for years, walked into a New York studio and recorded a song called "Crazy Blues." It was a hot and sticky day outside and even hotter in the recording studio, without air conditioning or even fans—strict silence was required for the brief recording experience. (These recordings were like musical snapshots, short versions of something that the band might play for twenty or thirty minutes in the nightclubs.) Within weeks, "Crazy Blues" had become a sensation across the nation; it went on to sell more than two million copies, 75,000 copies in Harlem alone in just one month; at $1 per copy, this represented a full day's wages for a lot of folks. What was so special about this recording that people would swap eight hours of hard labor for it?

First, whereas the "St. Louis Blues" and others like it had been songs *about* the blues, "Crazy Blues" was much more raw, made by and for a black audience who knew the difference. It was an authentic, classic twelve-bar blues, plain and simple, and it became an actual phenomenon: word hit the street immediately that here was a black artist singing a contemporary black song and you could buy it and bring it home. People wanted to own a piece of the action. This was the dawning of the era of "race records," when all the major labels would establish a separate catalog for "the Race," a term African-Americans themselves used to denote their peers. Mamie Smith's "Crazy Blues" forced American corporations, perhaps for the first time, to take black Americans seriously as consumers, a potent market force.

"Crazy Blues" also signified a sea change in the life cycle of a popular song: for the first time, the recorded version vastly outsold the sheet music. Okeh, the record company that released it, could barely press enough copies to satisfy demand. As such, the recording stands as a signpost in American popular culture for that moment when sales of "units" overtook sales of tickets, and the virtual experience—recordings, time-shifted and space-shifted so that anybody could listen where and when they wanted—became the most common ("authentic") way to experience popular music. The success of this release set off a mini recording boom, with many companies scrambling to record women singing the blues; Bessie Smith, Ma Rainey, Ida Cox, Ethel Waters, Sippie Wallace, Victoria Spivey, Alberta Hunter, Chippie Hill, and many other blues singers owed a lot to Smith's impassioned recording. The document (the recording) had dramatically altered the culture. The media age had arrived.

There was good reason why the recording of the song outsold the sheet music: it was impossible to capture the essence of black music on a piece of paper. Unlike Western classical music, which is about precision, repetition, and notation, there is no way to experience the impact of black music without actually being there, either in person or virtually, through the media. Sheet music could never suffice. But where, exactly, was "there"? Was it at the time and place where the song was being sung? Or was it at the time and place where the recording was being played? And what was gained and what was lost in this trade-off? Was the recording an actual representation of the musical moment as it happened, or was it something entirely other, something new and in its own way quite different from the song and the singer? Recordings opened up a vast world of possibility for performers and audiences alike, and at the same time, a can of worms regarding what in fact was the situation on the ground versus that in the virtual world of popular culture.

What was being celebrated in houses around the country as people listened to the recording of "Crazy Blues" was undoubtedly a pale copy of what actually happened in the recording studio on that hot August afternoon, as if the sound was coming to the folks at home through a long tube. In fact, the sound did come through a tube: the acoustic horn through which it was recorded in the studio, with all the musicians and the singer positioned in a circle so that the musical balance could be approximated. All things considered, the sound really was quite wonderful. Not the sound of the instruments or the voice—they are thin and distant; no, the sound of the record itself, of the artifact; though it lacks fidelity, it is full of passion. That passion is what's being celebrated; recordings capture passion as well as sound. In a way, "Crazy Blues" was the culture singing about itself, celebrating being here, in the modern moment. It was both more and less than what it appeared to be: bad fidelity and a great sound, a group of modern musicians in a room sounding thin and faraway, and a piece of wax that seduced the listener with its vitality and portability.

So here we have the pattern for American popular culture for years to come: the actual need for role modeling at the center of a virtual experience; the kernel of truth at the heart of artifice. In the age of electronic media the search for the authentic experience will become central, as without this grain of sand, the oyster gives up no pearls. Artifice pure and simple is not popular culture; popular culture is a response to a real need, or it is the need itself. In this way, it can often be like a dog chasing its tail; but the movement must be actual. It must reflect a living desire in the hearts and minds of the populace. Inasmuch as the 1920s saw the rise of advertising, marketing, recording, broadcasting—the whole range of indigenous pop-culture conduits, touting everything from high art to low blues, from flagpole sitting to operatic posturing—virtually every kind of media event we know of today was in place by the end of the 1920s; the Internet is merely the latest flowering of this push toward the virtual. So if Americans are all about the search for authenticity within the virtual experience, what is it to become an "authentic" American; what is the authentic American experience?

The man who played piano on Mamie Smith's "Crazy Blues" was Willie "the Lion" Smith; he was just twenty-three and this was his first recording. Like many young men, he had gone to Europe to fight in the Great War—where his bravery in combat earned him the

"Lion" sobriquet—and on his return, he became one of the main innovators of a style of piano playing known as "stride." Stride was an outgrowth of ragtime, a two-fisted approach to the instrument that was improvised, technically challenging, and above all mercilessly swinging. "The Lion" was equally at home playing flowery classical pieces, but the blues and what was starting to be called "jazz" were what he was best known for. A man of many facets, Willie "the Lion" Smith was an African-American musical innovator who also just happened to be a self-identified Jew and a cantor in a Harlem synagogue. (Years later, he would say, "People can't seem to realize I have a Jewish soul and belong to that faith.") His churchgoing mother had tried to steer him toward holy music, and his father, a long-gone Jewish rake, had left him with a powerful curiosity: he learned to swing the church hymns and to read Hebrew and speak Yiddish fluently. His story tells us that authenticity in America can be a curious thing, the result of happenstance and self-invention, and that for Jews and blacks alike, self-invention in America is an ongoing process: the act of *becoming* is itself the root of their American authenticity. "The Lion," said Duke Ellington, "was a myth that you actually saw come alive."

Ultimately, Smith and the other stride pianists had a major influence on George Gershwin, who in turn influenced the whole musical world. Born Jacob Gershovitz in Brooklyn in 1898, Gershwin began playing piano at age twelve, when he sat down at an old upright that had been purchased for his older brother Ira and, without having had any lessons, began to play, with both hands, a popular song of the day. Given that the only thing he had played up to that point had been hooky from school, his parents recognized his gift and found him a serious music teacher. When he wasn't practicing piano or listening to music, he remained an indifferent student at school and preferred running on the streets of New York, where he heard all the musical styles of the day and immersed himself in the aural chaos of big city commerce. Later, he would say it was the sound of America that he wanted to capture with his music. His family moved often—he grew up in nearly thirty different apartments from Harlem to Coney Island, but mostly in the Jewish ghetto around Grand Street—and it was no surprise when, at age fifteen, he quit school and went to work as a professional musician, the youngest songplugger on Tin Pan Alley.

His first job was at Remick & Co., pushing songs on vaudeville performers, musicians, dancers, anyone who dropped by the office. His playing was obviously an asset to the company; the lyricist Irving Caesar was not the only professional composer who stopped by Remick's just to listen to him play. Caesar remembers, "His rhythms had the impact of a sledgehammer, and his harmonies were years ahead of his time." While Gershwin spent his days demonstrating popular hits, he was intrigued with all aspects of the music business; he even considered composing for the Yiddish theater. His father had taken him to hear Abraham Goldfaden at the National Theater on Second Avenue and had introduced him to the great Yiddish entertainer Boris Thomashefsky. Boris quickly agreed to introduce the boy to Sholom Secunda, an established composer of such Yiddish classics as "Bei Mir Bist

Du Schön" (later popularized for American audiences by Sammy Cahn). Upon meeting the boy, however, Secunda declined to work with him, saying Gershwin was too young, too inexperienced, and "too much American, too little Jew." In this way, he liberated the young Gershwin more than he could have possibly known, for, as one wag put it, breaking into Yiddish theater was like "breaking into prison." Yiddish music, based on specific modes, is a restrictive compositional form, a universe unto itself, whereas the blues, which Gershwin adapted as an underlying motif, is based on certain alterations of traditional scales and is an approach that can be applied to compositions across the board. For years, when Gershwin would meet Secunda on the streets of New York, he would thank the Yiddish composer for not hiring him.

Gershwin continued to write pop songs, achieved modest success, and eventually quit his job at Remick's "to be closer to production music, the kind Jerome Kern was writing." (He was only seventeen at the time.) During this period, he also applied to be Irving Berlin's musical secretary. Hearing him play, and recognizing the size of his talent, Berlin also refused to work with him, saying, "Stick to writing your own songs, kid." It was obvious to him that the young genius would never be content to play second fiddle to a self-taught composer of popular songs like Berlin. Too American for the Jews, too advanced for Tin Pan Alley, Gershwin was being told who he wasn't; but who *was* he? He too required role models.

By 1920, he was one of New York's finest pianists and was spending time up in Harlem, where some of the city's greatest stride pianists—Willie "the Lion," James P. Johnson, Lucky Roberts—were starting to talk about him as "this very talented ofay piano player who could perform their most difficult tricks." Harlem at the time was not just another neighborhood; it was exploding with creative energy and original music. As recently as the turn of the century, it had been a sleepy white suburban community. In 1904, when the city built the Lennox Avenue subway line up to Harlem to deliver more wealthy whites into the beautiful new brownstones there, it was assumed that the neighborhood would be a wealthy white enclave. But for various reasons, the boom never materialized. Instead, between 1920 and 1930, more than a hundred thousand whites left Harlem and more than a hundred thousand blacks arrived. In 1890, only one in seventy people in Manhattan had been African-American; but by 1930, it was one in nine. Harlem gave blacks, for the first time, a sense of their own cultural and numerical strength. The "Harlem Renaissance" was one result, with black intellectuals, writers, poets, painters, philosophers, and musicians all discovering one another, exchanging views, generating a vibrant nightlife, and turning Harlem into *the* place for cultural excitement. It was being advertised as "the Nightclub Capital of the World," and white New Yorkers were going up to Harlem regularly, trying to fit in: one sign was that tanning of the skin, shunned during the Victorian era, suddenly became fashionable.

More than two hundred nightclubs opened in Harlem during the twenties, featuring the most beautiful dancers and talented musicians in the world. But while these clubs all employed black waiters and waitresses, dancers and musicians, most were initially out of bounds to black customers, as social integration was officially off the table, even in New York City. But when the sun went down, Harlem was for all intents and purposes integrated, and nightclubs there were the first venues where black and white musicians could discover and learn from each other. At the time, "jazz" wasn't even a common word, and if it was, it was a verb. The music that was being played was so new it didn't really have a name. It was just American popular music, being invented on the spot, and the people who played it were like a small family. Gershwin could often be found at black parties in Harlem. Unlike many of the fun seekers who went there, however, he was not slumming: he was going to school or to synagogue, but in any case he was going to discover himself.

Just as crime and vice had powered the musical explosions in Sedalia and New Orleans, it similarly fanned the creative fires up in Harlem. Where there is nightlife, cash changes hands, and where there is a lot of cash, there are gangsters. But if crime was once again the fuel for innovation in a black community, this time it was being driven by Jewish gangsters as well, who were turning Prohibition into the marketing opportunity of the young century. The clubs were often owned and operated by Jewish mobsters, such as Bernard Levy, who opened the famous Cotton Club at 142nd Street and Lexington Avenue, the musical home for Duke Ellington's orchestra. Even the Savoy Ballroom, where the Lindy hop was popularized, Connie's Inn (owned by Connie Innerman) and the famed Apollo Theater itself (operated by the Schiffman family) had Jewish owners.

In some ways, these "tough Jews" were a natural reaction to the Jewish experience in the Russian pogroms. Meyer Lansky, perhaps the most famous Jewish gangster of the twentieth century, came to the Lower East Side in 1911 from Grodno, Poland, and he remembered that back in the old country, "One man held a meeting in my grandfather's house. 'Jews,' he shouted, 'why do you just stand around like stupid sheep and let them come and kill you, steal your money, kill your sons and rape your daughters? Aren't you ashamed? You must stand up and fight!' I remembered those words when I fought back at the Irish as a boy on the East Side. They were like flaming arrows in my head."

When Jews began arriving in New York, they found themselves dealing with a virulent form of anti-Semitism often disguised as social theory. One respected writer described them this way: "Ignorance, prejudice, stubborn refusal to yield to American ideas, religious habits and requirements, clannishness and hatred and distrust of Christians; these combine to hinder any device for raising the condition of the poor of the great Jewish district . . . these people are the worst element in the entire make-up of New York City . . . human parasites." It wasn't just the tough Irish street gangs they were fighting but an insidious global prejudice as well.

Hence some Jews fought back by making a science out of crime. One particular Jewish mob from Brooklyn took on the name "Murder Incorporated." They were fearless, merciless, and highly organized, and they arranged contract killing as a kind of service industry. Another Jew from Brooklyn named Arnold Rothstein actually brought the organization to organized crime. Before he arrived on the scene, crime in New York was more or less a matter of street thugs killing each other. Rothstein raised crime to a kind of economic art by making it appear legitimate, at least on paper. All the crime families, including those of the Italian mob, were schooled in the ways of modern crime by Rothstein. And it was Rothstein who showed both Joseph Kennedy (President John Kennedy's father) and the Jewish scion Samuel Bronfman, of the Seagram fortune, how to turn bootlegging into a multi-million-dollar business.

The fathers of these Jewish gangsters were typically hardworking, small-time merchants, peddlers, or tailors; there had been no family tradition of crime in the Jewish community. Unlike the Italian gangsters, who would recruit kids on street corners to ensure the next generation of the "family," the Jews never recruited. They still saw themselves as "good Jews" and separated what they did in the world to stay alive—the life of the body—from what they believed in—the life of the soul. They went to synagogue on the high holy days and sent their children to the best schools. For them, crime was not a way out of the system; it was a way into the system. This was a major difference between the Jewish gangsters and their Italian counterparts: while the Italians spent lavishly, proud of using their money to stand out, the Jews by and large lived modestly, using their wealth to fit in.

Ironically, Prohibition polished the image of these gangsters inasmuch as the Eighteenth Amendment to the Constitution drove the crime wave deeper into the heart of middle America; it served to legitimize the criminals and to criminalize those who were legitimate. Prohibition was one of the last vestiges of the Victorian era, based on a tea-party morality and a spinsterish distaste for physical pleasure. It is ironic that in the United States, the only country in the world where "the pursuit of happiness" is guaranteed in writing and where there is by definition a separation between sin and crime—crime is punishable by law, sin is between you and your God—there remains a puritan antipathy to pleasure. Hedonism in America is often an equal and opposite reaction to the ongoing pressure to conform to this puritanism. In the 1920s, with the economy booming and the average citizen feeling freer than ever before, people wanted to celebrate: Prohibition merely created a huge underground economy that fueled the party and gave the average American a taste for a walk on the wild side.

In New York, as elsewhere, Prohibition was a farce. Called "the noble experiment" by President Hoover, the amendment that outlawed the manufacture, sale, or transportation of intoxicating liquors had been passed by a quick one-sided vote after a short debate in Congress; nobody wanted to be perceived as being in favor of hedonism. And yet even Jimmy Walker, New York's mayor who became known, for obvious reasons, as "the

Nightclub Mayor," ignored the law. He spent most evenings in the city's party dens in the company of Ziegfeld Follies girls. When reproached for the high salary he was pulling in and the short hours he was putting in, he said, "That's cheap; think what it would cost if I worked full time."

By 1923, enforcement was practically abandoned, and even though the law itself remained in place for another ten years, in New York City alone the number of illegal speakeasies, dives, and drugstores where alcohol was sold was somewhere between thirty-two thousand and a hundred thousand; nobody knew for sure. The thrill of visiting these clubs, descending some funky stairs to a room where scantily clad women danced to jazz music and the races could mix freely, drew thousands of upright citizens to Harlem nightly. There, tucked in among the bootleggers and entertainers, the show types and street types, polite society learned to talk the talk and walk the walk of American modernism, the vocabulary of gangsters and musicians. These were the role models, the inventors of American slang, the providers of cultural currency. Now the city's middle-class and moneyed elites were "outsiders" too. They didn't see themselves as criminals; they were just out on a Friday night. But because they were subject to being treated as criminals, they were forced to line up on either the side of the criminals or the side of the law. Thus, Prohibition was not only a failure as a social experiment, and impossible to enforce, but a radicalizing element in American popular culture: never before had so many law-abiding citizens been redefined, en masse, as social outsiders.

In the context of the two million recently arrived Jews who had for generations defined themselves in the same way, as professional "people in exile," this psychological shift was profound: suddenly being on the outside was in, and Jewish composers, as outsiders, were now able to speak to and for a greater section of the populace, with more clarity than ever before. This underlying synergy between Jewish tradition and the American experience—brought on in part by Prohibition—helps explain how, during the early part of the century, a small cultural minority managed to midwife such a vast popular culture: down started to look like up to a lot of folks.

Musically speaking, the decade of the 1920s marked the birth of the "Great American Songbook." Many of the compositions of the era are still being approached by pop stars trying to gain a foothold in middle-aged longevity and by young students trying to feel their way toward legitimacy. What is it about this music that made it so defining for the American identity? First, it came from a time and a place where there was little disconnect between what would become art and what was commerce, a time when, in the words of Ann Douglass, "artistic achievement and mass distribution were not yet in conflict but worked together and invigorated one another." Today, the "art" aspect of popular music is mostly a matter of style or just a new way to use the technology—for example, the *sound* of the music, or the way it arrives, as opposed to the actual notes, might be considered part of the artistic credential—but in 1920s, the words, the harmonies, the melodies, the orchestrations, the musical forms, the technology itself, everything that was happening was happening for the first time. It had not only a freshness about it but a plain, unvarnished sense of self-respect; it was what it was, and that was why it was both popular and important. It was authentic.

In America, it often seems that everything must be commodified in order to be understood—in F. Scott Fitzgerald's phrase, "Culture follows money." Take for example the introduction of radio. In 1922, there were five hundred stations; by 1925, the number had doubled to more than a thousand. In 1923, a total of 200,000 radios were manufactured; by 1925, more than five million. And although radio existed elsewhere around the world, there was a big difference in the way it was integrated into the American economy: elsewhere, the development of radio was paid for by the government and through fees levied on those who owned radio sets; in America it was paid for by advertising; the selling of time. Time itself became commodified, and advertising became part of the entertainment.

In the 1920s, stars began singing and dancing for products, and products made stars out of singers and dancers. Products brought you programming. It was the dawning of the age of public relations—the calculated enhancement of a personal image with a view to selling a product. In America, being a "star" seemed universally attainable, a common dream, just as becoming President was theoretically open to all, and the middle class became the ideal launching pad for one's success; it proved one's connection to the common man. As portrayed in the movies and on Broadway, the American hero was invariably a regular guy who got his break; on the radio, he was your friendly pitchman who made you feel at home. But the product wasn't just the toothpaste or the cigarette. Advertising and marketing created a more general need in people, a free-floating want. People didn't necessarily know *what* they needed, only *that* they needed; and so advertising simultaneously created a sense of loss, or absence, in people's lives and then proposed to fill it. In America, buying and selling often takes the place of feeling, and beginning in the twenties, popular music became a way to sell feeling to the middle-class consumer.

Of course the most celebrated of human feeling is love, both in its mundane sense and in its spiritual incarnation, and that is what the Great American Songbook is all about. Tied to the Jewish belief in social justice and the common man, there was a proclivity for love, not just for your fellow man but for your fellow woman too. Take for example the songs of Richard Rodgers: "Manhattan," "There's a Small Hotel," "Blue Moon," "You Are Too Beautiful," "Mountain Greenery," "Thou Swell," "With a Song in My Heart," "Little Girl Blue," "My Romance," "The Lady Is a Tramp," "My Funny Valentine," "Spring Is Here," "It Never Entered My Mind." They all speak to the growing need for intimacy in the face of urban facelessness; to feel something personal, authentic in the midst of a new, nerve-racking urban world. The 1920s was the decade when for the first time the majority of Americans lived in cities rather than on farms or in small towns, and they were experiencing for the first time the chaos and distractions we now take for granted. New York City was the world leader: by the late 1920s, there were so many automobiles in New York City that they outnumbered all the automobiles in Europe put together. Writer Edna St. Vincent Millay, viewing the situation, said New York was so loud "you could see the noise." Holding on to your emotional center became a visceral need.

In the midst of this modern maelstrom, Jewish songwriters were saying, "We can still find meaning if we can find each other; we might get the blues, but we can put on our dancing shoes and turn this jungle into an isle of joy." It's the American love song—as opposed to any other national anthem: a song as much about place as it is about people, about both character and culture. And while this modern love song spoke of a new sexual freedom for both women and men, seeing your own life as somehow exotic, full of extraordinary opportunity—one "break" away from success—it also spoke of a new kind of permanence, a modern edifice against the winds of past, present, and future. The modern struggle was given meaning only by the simple and profound love between a man and a woman. The American love song is the middle way: intimate love in a public space. The middle-class blues was born.

And like the lyrics, the melodies upon which these sentiments were carried were vastly superior to those of just a few years before; the harmony, through the use of altered chords to create a sense of richness and density (that perhaps mirrored the texture of urban life), was similarly more sophisticated. The "Jewish move," the shift from major to minor, which harmonically called into question the concept of key (or tonic) and gave a place for traditional Jewish modes to cavort with the flatted "blue notes" of Harlem, created a context for the shifting ground of modernism; when you were comfortable in both places at once (the joy of sadness, the blues that "hurts so nice"), you were experiencing the dilemma at the same time that you were feeling its resolution. The Jewish move in popular music is what, to this day, makes American popular song so identifiable; where and how the major meets the minor seems always to resonate in the American experience.

This move is found in so many compositions by Jewish song writers that it prompted Cole Porter, who was not Jewish but memorialized the harmonic move in his lyrics to the song "Every Time We Say Goodbye" ("There's no love song finer, but how strange the change from major to minor"), to say that in order to become successful in the music business, one had to first learn how to "write Jewish." We have seen this "Jewish move" before in the Jewish Talmudic tradition, where contrary positions can be held simultaneously. But now, in American popular song, the major/minor relationship seemed to suggest the intricacies of modern life in a way that could be understood, or *felt,* by one and all. Lovers of the Great American Songbook are addicted to this emotional spice: it creates the delicious aftertaste that signals the recognition of life's complexities. It too is a token of the "middle way," the reconciliation of apparent opposites.

The twentieth-century American dream is this dream of the middle way, lived somewhere between the luxury of the rich and the desperation of the poor, a new normalcy, a "leisure class," where lives were reflected not just in the sentiments of song lyrics and melodies but in the sound of the music itself. By 1920, the phonograph had taken the place of the piano as the "must have" entertainment center of the middle-class home. Films were wildly popular too, but they were still silent until the end of the decade, while the radio and recordings were "live," or at least they captured life in a much more immediate way. Along with the rise of the middle class as cultural consumers came a new aesthetic, between "high art" and "low art"—call it "popular art," because it was dependent on the masses for its tone, character, and conception and could not have existed without the new media technology. From the beginning, American "popular art" has had a flash to it, a louche, upscale, off-the-shoulder class. It hints at a higher style in a way that accommodates both social issues and the dreams of the average man on the street; it is witty yet down to earth, offhand yet highly literate, romantic yet has its feet firmly planted on the urban street corner. Whose dream was that? A small, specific group of urban Jews and their pals, many who hung out with blacks and gangsters up in Harlem during the 1920s; composers who for the most part grew up within a few blocks of one another at the turn of the century: George and Ira Gershwin, Lorenz Hart, Oscar Hammerstein, Howard Dietz, Harry Ruby, Irving Caesar, Jay Gorney, Yip Harburg, Richard Rodgers, and Arthur Schwartz, to name a few.

Through radio broadcasts and Broadway musicals, from nightclubs and dance halls to parlor rooms and drugstores, the music they created informed the locals how others around the country were *feeling* (and acting, and falling in love, and getting "the blues"). The new middle-class aesthetic was not just about money but about aspirations and culture. Of course, this territory had been well trodden by Jews in the past. Even when they were living as complete outsiders, among the poorest of the poor, they were literate, they had a love for impassioned vocal music of various pedigree, they attended the popular theater and interpolated the popular music of the day into their own liturgy. Many years later, in the 1950s, the composer Gunther Schuller proposed the idea of a "third stream" in American music. For Schuller, the first stream was Western classical music; the second stream was jazz; the third stream would be where the two met, a uniquely American perspective. In the 1920s, these Jews anticipated Schuller by thirty-five years, only in their construct, instead of the term "third stream," they used the term Jerome Kern was so fond of: "the New York Opera."

The New York Opera can be seen as both a musical proposition and a social condition, a term for a middle way between highbrow and popular music and a metaphor for finding one's identity, living the American dream of tuxedos and hot dogs. We can find it in the music and lives of the many creative people who during the 1920s provided the role models for contemporary archetypes. And in every case, achieving the "middle way" in America involved coming to terms with African-American culture. In examples that range from the sublime to the subsumed, there would have been no American middle way, no New York Opera, without the cultural pas de deux of the black and the Jew.

George Gershwin, for example, had his first big commercial success as a young man with the song "Swanee," but he still felt the need for something more. His hit had come in 1920, when the lyricist Irving Caesar suggested that they write a song together; they were discussing it while riding on a bus up to Gershwin's house, and by the time the bus stopped at his corner, they had the song sketched out. This is so often the story of a hit song; it happens fast, almost in a thrown-away manner. "Swanee" hitched its star to the Berlin formula of recalling an idealized South and getting the great Jewish blackface performer Al Jolson to deliver it on stage. But Gershwin, who had been motivated by Jerome Kern's earlier work, had greater ambitions. Although he continued to write popular songs with his brother Ira—George wrote only the music while Ira provided the lyrics—he similarly continued to develop his interest in long-form instrumental music. His goal was to participate in the creation of this New York Opera, to capture the vast sweep of the country in a way that had never been done before and to make it accessible to the masses. "I am one of those who honestly believe that the majority has much better taste and understanding, not only of music but of any of the arts, than it is credited with having," he said. "It is not the few knowing ones whose opinions make any work of art great, it is the judgment of the great mass that finally decides."

Very much like Berlin's "the mob is never wrong," Gershwin did not believe that there was necessarily a great distinction between his popular songs (commercial work) and his concert works. To him, the process of creation was the same in both cases. "It's just as difficult to write popular music as it is to write serious music," he reported. "I use as much energy in writing popular music as I do the other kind. And in 1924, he got the opportunity to prove his point. He was only twenty-five years old when the orchestra leader Paul Whiteman, whose stated goal was to "make a lady out of jazz," asked Gershwin to write an instrumental piano opus that combined the sophistication of a classical concerto with the raw passion of jazz. The result was *Rhapsody in Blue*.

Rhapsody in Blue was performed on February 12, 1924, at New York's Aeolian Hall, with Whiteman and Gershwin appearing in tuxes and spats. Whiteman's announced goal for the concert was to answer the question "What is American music?" and, always a showman as much as a bandleader, he had a gold-plated jury present, including Western classical musicians Jascha Heifetz, Fritz Kreisler, and Sergei Rachmaninoff, to help "decide." Also in attendance, at the invitation of Gershwin, was Willy "the Lion" Smith. The presentation was divided into sections, and Whiteman led off with his version of "jazz," for which his band wore funny hats (few people at this time, including Whiteman, had any idea what "jazz" was really about). Even before his last piece was performed, people were heading for the door, into the snow on West Forty-third Street. But when, out of nowhere, they heard the immortal wail of the clarinet that opens Gershwin's *Rhapsody in Blue*, the final piece of the evening, the crowd stopped in their tracks, listened, and returned to their seats en masse. One writer present remembered the moment as "electrifying" and went on to say, "I ought to be slightly drunk to be able to describe it properly for it was the music of intoxication. As I listened it seemed that the whole of new America was blossoming before me!" The rest is history.

Only twenty-five years old and known chiefly as the author of a few popular hits and some show tunes, Gershwin had brought something unprecedented to the American concert hall. It was not the dumbing-down of Western classical music, as many had feared, nor was it the prettification of jazz, which had more or less been Whiteman's intention; rather, *Rhapsody in Blue* was an entirely new animal: concert hall music with street roots, rhapsodic dance music with classical structure, swooning popular themes expanded with delirious harmonies and hard-driving rhythms integrated into sweeping themes of American musical history. Gershwin had personally bridged the widest of cultural gaps and was now standing with one foot in the European concert hall and the other in the Cotton Club. It was to music "very much what Lindbergh's flight across the Atlantic was to transportation," said the music scholar Robert Kimball. At the end of the evening, both Rachmaninoff and Willy "the Lion" were on their feet cheering.

The *Rhapsody* had been written very quickly, in only three weeks, so there was not a lot of time for premeditation or manipulation. (Reportedly, Gershwin had lost track of time and only upon seeing an announcement for the concert in the newspaper realized that he needed to get down to work.) In fact, as performed on opening night, one long section of the *Rhapsody* was completely improvised by Gershwin at the piano, with the instructions to the conductor reading simply "Wait for the nod." Hence the piece represented an authentic musical snapshot of who Gershwin was at the time. For a start, he, like Berlin before him, regularly answered questions about the Jewish influence in his work by saying he was an American, a "modern romantic" who wrote American music: "My people are American. My time is today." His stated intention was to create "a musical kaleidoscope of America—of our vast melting pot . . . our blues, our metropolitan madness." Being a Jew, he reported, was not a conscious part of his equation.

The rest of the world added it up a little differently. An article about Gershwin in *Time* magazine opened with the line "A young Jew last week went about the business of packing a suitcase. . . ." Similarly, critics searching his music for Jewishisms often pointed to the clarinet opening of the *Rhapsody* as direct evidence: it was several articulated notes on the instrument that morphed into a great rising glissando, a cry that has a defining quality to it, unlike almost any other musical phrase of the era. The opening of the piece is like an audio logo for 1920s modernism, and it has been compared to a Jewish cantor on the high holy days begging for the souls of his people, or to the *krecht*, the break in the voice, in popular Yiddish music. Much as the opening notes of Gershwin's song "It Ain't Necessarily So" have been compared to the opening notes of the well-known Jewish prayer the *barchu*, the clarinet opening of the *Rhapsody* is seen as an example of Gershwin's penchant for encoding Jewish prayer in his music.

However, the simple fact is that Gershwin didn't write it that way. The original score of *Rhapsody in Blue* opened with a well-articulated seventeen-note run up the scale that the clarinet was supposed to play. The clarinetist, an excellent musician named Ross Gorman, came up with the famous musical smear during rehearsals, apparently as a parody of a musician named Ted Lewis. Lewis was a notoriously inept Jewish clarinetist who played these kinds of quasi-klezmer *schmears* to elicit sympathy from the audience, and he was quite successful at the time both on recordings and in concert. As the musician Eddie Condon once said, "[Lewis] made the clarinet talk and usually it said, 'Please put me back in my case.'" Gorman had inserted the phrase as a way to entertain the other musicians who were a bit down in the mouth about having to wear funny hats in order to play jazz. It was musical joke to entertain the troops. It wasn't until the final rehearsal that Gershwin heard Gorman's opening glissando, and he liked it so much that he kept it in.

First-generation Jews like Gershwin were not only who they were—inescapably Jewish—but also who they chose to be. Obviously, they were both Jews and Americans, but by redefining their lives as American lives, they subsumed their sense of Jewishness into their American identity; even as they were reinventing themselves as Americans, they were expanding what it meant to be a Jew. This is why the notion of authenticity becomes so interesting in discussing the Jewish roots of American popular music. The question comes down to whether there is a difference between denying the impact of one's Jewishness and absorbing it into one's Americanness.

Clearly the answer is yes. Irving Berlin, a victim of virulent anti-Semitism, a native Yiddish speaker, the son of a cantor, might well be seen as disingenuous when saying his Jewishness had nothing to do with his music; Gershwin, on the other hand, born in America, raised on the streets of New York, was essentially stating a fact: to him, there was no distinction between being an American and being a Jew in America. Which speaks both to the opportunity of America and the nature of Judaism. Along with the other composers and lyricists in the "class of '95," those first-generation American Jews from Manhattan, Gershwin was in the process of inventing the American within himself along Jewish lines. It was a process that, although invisible, happened in plain sight.

A famous story recalls Oscar Hammerstein, the lyricist, and Jerome Kern working on a musical based on the life of Marco Polo. Hammerstein allegedly said to Kern, "Well, here's a story laid in China about an Italian and told by an Irishman. What kind of music are you going to write?" And Kern answered, "It'll be good Jewish music, of course." This is not to say that during the 1920s, anti-Semitism was on the decline in America; quite the opposite. The Ku Klux Klan was riding high: you see it in the movie *Birth of a Nation* and in college yearbooks of the era, when the Klan was a respected social organization on campuses across the country. At Harvard, for example, Jews were being berated for "instilling a spirit of competition" by trying to demonstrate academic superiority over their non-Jewish counterparts; in 1923, there were anti-"kike" posters at NYU and the call to "make NYU a white man's college." And when in 1924, the Congress passed the Johnson-Reed Act enacting steep quotas for non-Nordic European immigrants, it effectively put an end to the arrival of European Jews altogether. No, if Gershwin and the others were feeling no distinction between being Jewish and being American, it came at a substantial cost. That is, it was an act of intention; of self-invention; of changing the external reality to fit the internal dream. In America, how one lives defines who one is. In societies where one's station was more or less fixed (as in the European monarchies), this might be futile; in America, it was the passing lane on the cultural freeway.

In the process of inventing themselves, Gershwin and his compatriots were fortunate to be part of the first generation of Americans to experience the rising self-reflection industry (some would call it the self-absorption industry); they witnessed the introduction of recording devices, inexpensive cameras, IQ tests, sex education, birth control clinics, opinion polls, and syndicated gossip columnists, everything geared toward a kind of triumph of personal space. Perhaps to keep the process in perspective, or to keep it at a distance, they began to use irony—saying one thing and meaning another—as a major part of modern slang and contemporary song lyrics. The use of irony functioned as a way to recognize a fellow insider, another traveler on the new open road, and a way to screen out others; it contributed to the power of many of the popular songs: "You say either and I say either . . . let's call the whole thing off."

Of course irony had long been an integral aspect of Yiddish culture, a way of dispensing with politesse and getting to the heart of the matter. The great Jewish writer Saul Bellow once described Jewish language as "The jabbing interchange of ironies, the intimate vulgarities, the blend of sardonic and sentimental. That was Yiddish speech. Nothing was what it seemed. If your mother called you an angel, that meant you were a devil. If she said your hands were clean, it meant that your hands were filthy." Humor was turned inward and released as self-definition.

The Jazz Age generation was possibly the most theatrical generation in American history. In New York, where the theater was virtually a Jewish monopoly, everybody was stage-obsessed. In 1926 there were seventy theaters in New York, and 264 plays were being produced. It would be impossible today to imagine just how all-encompassing and crucial to one's self-image the theater song became; both the inside and the outside of the person was seen as mutable, and the notion that one could—and should—create one's own persona was an obsession. This too became part of the new American authenticity; adrift in an age of unlimited possibility, awash in the reflection of new media and rising prosperity, what was left but to script your own second act?

With this great desire to reinvent oneself, an even wider cultural gap opened between parents and children (perhaps wider than at any other time in our history, with the possible exception of the 1960s). In a way, the 1920s was a dream about America; to the children of immigrants, everything was new and possible; for their parents, the world had gone mad. For those not invested in the past, it was a great opportunity; yet didn't one owe one's very life to the family that had struggled to bring you to this new place? How to incorporate both past and present, to reconcile these apparent opposites: ultimately, this became a central theme in the narrative of the popular song. In American popular song, the upright man is not necessarily the virtuous man but rather the one who maintains his balance among opposing forces.

The tension was well captured in Gershwin's 1924 song "Fascinating Rhythm." Like many of his other hits, and the hits of the day, it was originally written for a Broadway musical (in this case, *Lady Be Good*). "Fascinating Rhythm" is particularly interesting in the way it uses a conflicting time feel, a seven-against-eight phrase in the melody generating an off-balance sensation that lands on its feet at the end of the fourth bar. Before this resolution, there's a sense of weightlessness, which one suspects must have been thrilling as a reflection of modern life. While George Gershwin was quite proud of having invented this musical device, his brother Ira, who had become his principal lyricist, was initially flummoxed because he had to find lyrics that would scan. He is the one who came up with the title "Fascinating Rhythm," and the lyrics that went with it:

> Fascinating rhythm, you got me on the go
> Fascinating rhythm, I'm all a-quiver
> What a mess you're making, the neighbors want to know
> Why I'm always shaking, just like a flivver.

Even as Gershwin's music captured the feeling of shifting reality on the streets of New York, he was extending the fine line between commercialism and art. His use of a balanced through-line—a melody that could be developed, redeveloped, and resolved—anchored all his writing, whether he was composing a three-minute pop song or a thirty-minute concerto. To him, it was all the same, a matter of "design."

"With a melody [a pop song] one can take in the design in one look," he said. "With a larger composition, like a concerto, it is necessary to take it piece by piece and construct it so much longer. . . . But regardless of the kind of music a composer is writing, it must have a definite line of progression."

This idea that regardless of the form, popular music must have harmonic, melodic, and, in the case of musical theater, narrative coherence and development brought the American popular song into a new realm. It demanded much more sophistication not only from the composer and lyricist but from the listener as well. Ira Gershwin, with deadpan understatement, described the process of becoming a modern lyricist: "Given a fondness of music, a feeling for rhyme, a sense of whimsy and humor, an eye for the balanced sentence, an ear for the current phrase and the ability to imagine oneself a performer, trying to put over the number in progress. . . . Given all of this," he said, "I would still say it takes four or five years collaborating with a knowledgeable composer to become a well-rounded lyrist." It was assumed that the audience for this new popular music was articulate, literate, middle-class, and on the way up; between the high culture of opera and the knockabout of mass culture, a new, educated, lyrics-conscious audience was emerging.

Songwriting was progressing quickly, from being something that just anybody off the boat could throw together to a serious art form. Yet it was an art that unashamedly incorporated some of the conventions that had arrived off the boat, particularly those of Irving Berlin. Gershwin's use of repetition, for example (to Berlin, the "spear" or the "point"), was finely honed and became part of the underlying appeal of his melodies. One hears it in songs like "A Foggy Day," where the first three notes ("A foggy") and again the melody of the words "I viewed the (future)" and "The British (Museum)" are repeated. It's a device that in Gershwin's hands was a subtle place of rest from which the music could take off, part of the tension and release. He wasn't so much concerned with syncopation (the dotted-eighth feeling) as he was with rhythmic innovation (as seen in "Fascinating Rhythm"). At the same time, Gershwin showed a greater concern with harmony than any of the era's other composers. To this day, his compositions remain favorites among jazz musicians because of their harmonic elegance. The song "Somebody Loves Me" is another good example: its appeal lies in the facts that, first, there are few chords, and they last half a measure each, so there is plenty of room for an improviser to explore, and second, the melody is graced with an out-of-key whole note in the fourth measure ("I wonder *who*") that provides the ear candy, a kind of aural ginger, that sets up a diminished route for improvisation. It's the same musical device he uses in "The Man I Love," which also made good use of the ritual shift from major to minor. These are all thirty-two-bar A-A-B-A songs, a form that Gershwin virtually established as the model for the Great American Songbook.

For the musical improviser, nothing can compete with a Gershwin song. Even "I Got Rhythm," perhaps his most banal harmonic structure, rests on a subtle use of harmonic give-and-take; while the verses express the natural progression of major to minor and then minor back to major (I-VI-II-V, favored by pop songwriters ever since), the bridge is essentially in four key centers at once, each leading to the other. This structure creates a harmonic flow moving the ear away from the tonic and then returning it naturally for another cycle; improvising on the form can be exhilarating, like following a particularly interesting path in the woods. Today the expression "rhythm changes" is universally understood by jazz musicians the world over. In fact, so many tunes have been written by jazz musicians on Gershwin's basic chord changes that the jazz pianist Roger Kellaway once remarked, "Sometimes when we actually are playing 'I Got Rhythm,' it sounds to me like it's based on 'I Got Rhythm.'" To jazz musicians, "I Got Rhythm" is like a folksong—it's always been there, kind of like "Oh! Susanna." Gershwin is the jazz musician's Stephen Foster.

If the "Gershwin tune" was a recognizable entity, an innately modern intact universe, it is partly because of the advent of the electronic microphone. Berliner's invention totally changed the way we disseminate information, delivering Gershwin's music to anyone with a radio or phonograph. Owing to a dispute at the time between radio stations and song publishers, who feared that this new technology would stifle sheet music sales, all music heard on the radio in the early 1920s was live; if you heard Gertrude Lawrence sing her hit version of Gershwin's "Someone to Watch over Me," she was actually there in the studio. By the end of the decade, Bing Crosby and Fred Astaire were not only bringing Gershwin's music into homes across the country but were quite literally insinuating it into the ears of listeners. The whispered vocal was the result; it was called "crooning." With the electronic microphone, one's success was tied to one's ability to project subtle emotions in an intimate way, and Gershwin's offhand, sophisticated songs were perfect vehicles for this new aesthetic. A Gershwin song differed dramatically from the raw, emotional plaints that had been written for vaudeville performers, who shouted to reach the back rows; the crooners had listeners leaning into the song, focused on their voices, their literal breath, instead of their bodies.

Tangentially, this effect helped make popular music more palatable to mainstream America; for example, it helped mitigate the perceived sexuality attributed to blacks and Jews because even if the song was about sex, it was cast in the elegance of separate beds and satin sheets. By definition, the technology required that composers begin writing a different kind of music: it not only helped deliver the new aesthetic—music that was both sophisticated and popular—but created a necessity for it.

This new aesthetic relied on harmonic and melodic sophistication and on the continued reinvention of American English. Just as Gershwin claimed the musical high ground for the masses, writers everywhere—from novelists like F. Scott Fitzgerald and Ernest Hemingway to popular journalists like H. L. Mencken and Ben Hecht to lyricists like Lorenz Hart and Yip Harburg—were rejuvenating the language from the bottom up. How did one talk on the street? What was the greeting they gave you when you walked into Lindy's, the all-night Jewish deli in Times Square, famous for its cheesecake and for the Jewish entertainers and gangsters who hung out there? Lindy's was a kind of clubhouse where you might find both Irving Berlin and Arnold Rothstein having coffee; it was the place where Damon Runyon went to learn how Sky Masterson and his pals should talk in the musical *Guys and Dolls*, a major incubator for the new American slang, where playing with language was the norm and the argot of entertainers and criminals mixed as the two congregated. From this one corner in Times Square, the vernacular trickled down to folks around the country.

Ira Gershwin was incensed when people referred to his song "'SWonderful" as "It's Wonderful"; he was very well aware of the "correct way" to say it but that was not what he intended to say. The name of the song was "'SWonderful," and he was very proud of the fact that he used it because this was how modern people spoke: they used colloquial contractions (like the impermissible "ain't"), and it was an original device, on his part, to insinuate this into a song, one that would never occur in "serious" culture. By using it, he was not only recognizing the importance and strength of America's mass culture, but he was sending a message: like slanging itself, this new music was an assault on the old elite. To be this free with the language was to own it; to own the language was to own the world.

In Jewish tradition, words are magical things and language is more than communication; it's self-revelation. Jews discover themselves in what they say and how they say it. "At school," Saul Bellow once wrote about growing up in Chicago during the 1920s, "we, the sons and daughters of European immigrants, were taught to write grammatically. Knowing the rules filled you with pride." Yet he "deeply felt the constraints of 'correct' English . . . and excess of corrections caused shrinking . . . [I] had been waiting for an appropriate language. By that language, and only that language, could I be redeemed." Redemption? Redemption from what? "The challenge was to emerge intact from the grip of these would-be dominators. To extract the secret of their powers from them while eluding their control became my singular interest. If I had any game it was this independence game. Perhaps it was not so much an interest as it was a spiritual exercise. I recognized that I did not have to do the will of others."

Redemption from the past was in the freedom to invent yourself through your own language. In America, you were free to be who you were, but first you needed to discover it. For Jews, the process often began with knowing how to express it. "In the opening sentence [of *The Adventures of Augie March*, Bellow's breakthrough novel], I don't say that I am an American Jew," wrote Bellow, "I simply declare that I am an American. My eldest brother was the first to point out the advantages of this. America offered to free us from the control of the family and of the Jewish community."

What is interesting here is how the Jewish institutions (family, community) are framed as the walls of a cultural ghetto, an embarrassment, a dead end, while at the same time the traditions (social justice, a sense of duty, a drive to change the self) were being embraced wholeheartedly. It's almost as if the *how* of the message became more important than the *what*; I can't hear you if you speak the old language; you must learn to speak the new language. The traditions remained intact; it was the delivery system that was being rejected. Bellow was not alone in feeling that the old religion was out of date. In Chicago, during the 1920s, there were many other young men wandering the streets in search of the main chance: the Jew in America was in a heated search for the American in the Jew.

No one was more assiduous, more frenzied, more resourceful in this process than a young Chicago musician named Milton "Mezz" Mezzrow. Mezz was not a great musician, although he did play the clarinet professionally; he was not an artist of influence, although he did influence many artists, by providing the wherewithal for them to change their perspective: Mezz was a marijuana dealer. Not just *a* marijuana dealer: *the* marijuana dealer. His clients included the great Louis Armstrong, and in the end, on the streets of both Chicago and New York, his fame was such that marijuana itself was known as "mezz." It would be a mistake, however, to dismiss Mezz as just some dope pusher or wannabe jazzer; he was emblematic of much more than that.

Mezzrow was born into an upper-middle-class Jewish family on Chicago's Northwest Side in 1899. They were solid citizens and expected the same from him. But at an early age, he felt the pull of the streets: they were "like a magnet to me. . . . There was something in the air that whispered of big doings you wouldn't want to miss," he wrote. The streets of Chicago in the early days of the century were like a new kind of Wild West. "The sidewalks were always jammed, gamblers and racketeers, dressed sharp as a tack, strutted by with the diamond stickpins, chicks you heard stories about would tip up and down the avenue real cool, the cops toured the neighborhood in big Cadillacs filled with shotguns. Anything and everything could happen on the Northwest Side and usually did." So his first move was rejection of the old way. He knew who he wasn't.

Like children in big cities everywhere at the time, he had to fight to gain respect. "It took just a whispered 'kike' or 'Jew bastard' from a member of some rival Polish or Irish gang and fists were flying." Mezz describes a great potential energy on the scene, which, like Bellow, he attributed to the need for a new way to express himself and describe the life around him. "At fifteen," he writes, "I was all jammed up full of energy, restless as a Mexican jumping bean. Something was all puffed up in me, but I couldn't dig what it was or give it a name. I felt I wanted to jump out of my skin . . . I was maneuvering for a new language that would make me shout out loud and romp on to glory. What I needed was the vocabulary." In his case, however, that vocabulary was a musical one. "I was feeling my way to music like a baby fights its way into talk."

What is interesting here is that he was not a musician at this point, and yet the music spoke to him so clearly that everything else was drowned out. In 1913, at age twelve, he and some pals took off and rode the rails. They disembarked in Cape Girardeau, Missouri, dirty and dark-skinned, and went into a drugstore. They sat down at the counter but the waiter ignored them; finally the owner came over and said, "We don't serve niggers in here." On the American racial scale, Jews were blacks; the boys were thrown out. "In small towns we hit after that, whenever we saw a sign saying, 'Nigger don't let the sun shine on your head,' we knew that meant us too, although we didn't know why." Before he became a teenager, he had already experienced the call of the music and the identification with black culture.

At age sixteen, Mezzrow went to prison for auto theft, where the pieces began to fall into place. There, for the first time, he heard the blues and met black musicians. The cell blocks were segregated. "Night after night we'd lie on the corn-husk mattresses in our cells listening to the blues drifting over from the Negro side of the block . . . those few simple riffs opened my eyes to the Negro's philosophy more than any fat sociology textbook ever could. They cheered me up right away and made me feel wonderful towards those guys." Upon release from prison, he decided, "I not only loved those colored boys, but I was one of them—I felt closer to them than I felt to the whites... They were right for kicking me out of that beanery in Cape Girardeau. I belonged on the other side of the track. By the time I reached home, I knew. . . . I was going to learn their music and play it for the rest of my days. I was going to be a musician, a Negro musician, hipping the world about the blues."

Mezz was a special case of a special case. Many young Jewish would-be musicians in Chicago were struggling to gain access to the musical vocabulary bubbling up from New Orleans. Most were practicing their instruments rather than stealing cars, but nonetheless, as Bellow has noted, "There was a great demand for images or models of rough-and-ready frontier types. . . . In a country of immigrants, there was a singular need for prototypes, especially among the young." But very early on, Mezz went way beyond the search for role models; he sought to transform himself thoroughly, from the inside out: to be the outsider he was. He may also be seen as an extreme example of Chicago style music education.

"Few of these white Chicago musicians reasoned their ways to jazz," writes William Kenney. "Rather, they were drawn to visceral, nonverbal forms of personal expressiveness as teenagers. Their shared devotion to jazz functioned as a religious faith, providing a new form of sectarian cohesion and an idealistic scale of values. Jazz, as Neil Leonard has explained, often acted in this manner as a religion for many who had been cast adrift in the maze of urban America." As an eighteen-year-old, the Jewish pianist Art Hodes (he was born in Russia and came to Chicago as a boy) remembers, "Our mistress was music, we worshipped her as a god. In the morning, when we'd start in on the Victrola, till late at night, when we were exhausted and had to sleep, we had but one desire—to play, to play better this minute than we had the last, to hear something played that would knock us out."

Chicago style: fast and loose, down and dirty, but with a broad intellectual framework. "First to knock, first to enter." For if jazz was a big part of the new vocabulary, the city was also something of a literary center during the 1920s: Theodore Dreiser, Sherwood Anderson, Willa Cather, Edgar Lee Masters, Carl Sandburg, Vachel Lindsay, all came to Chicago to study or to write for the newspapers or the ad agencies. High school students read Mencken's *American Mercury*. Mezzrow and his fellow musicians from the Austin High neighborhood were avid readers, and according to one of them, Max Kaminsky, they were "on a genius kick."

The genius kick: to live on both sides of the tracks at once, to understand and to experience it all, from the bottom to the top. This is the embodiment of the "middle way," the emergence of a new popular art. Bored by school, turned off by organized religion, constantly at odds with old-world parents who had no sense of the new American popular culture, like Studs Lonigan and his friends, the young Chicago musicians searched for adventure in the defiance of middle-class respectability; they ran in gangs, fighting, stealing, smoking, and discovering the forbidden pleasures of the street life. They wanted desperately to create a new life without regard to their parents' past, but at the same time, inherent in that desire was the Jewish tradition of personal change: the conflation of street life and the life of the intellectual, one of the oldest moves in the Jewish playbook. Jazz was a great secret language for the insider's insider: "We could roam around a town for weeks without digging another human who even knew what we were talking about."

The great migration of blacks to Chicago had begun in 1916, and by 1920 more than 65,000 African-Americans had arrived from Louisiana, Mississippi, Alabama, Arkansas, and Texas, helping to trigger the city's Jazz Age. During and after World War I, "the Stroll," the name given to the black district of South State Street, became the center of Chicago's nightlife. In a twenty-block "vice district," there were 500 saloons, 1,000 "concert halls," 15 gambling houses, 56 poolrooms, and 500 bordellos. Eventually, as the black population grew on the South Side, "the Stroll" moved farther south. There, stores remained open twenty-four hours a day and at night the sidewalks were jammed with people. When poet Langston Hughes visited Chicago's Stroll in 1918, he said, "Midnight was like day." Some South Siders, after a hard day at their jobs, went directly to bed so that they could arise at 2 a.m., get dressed in their best clothes, and hit the Stroll. The trumpet player Joe "King" Oliver was among them; arriving from New Orleans in 1919, he left the eighteen-year-old Louis Armstrong to take over his band back home and joined the Original Creole Jazz Band on Chicago's South Side. Not long thereafter, he was leading his own band on the Stroll and had sent word down to Louis to come up north and join him.

Armstrong arrived in Chicago in 1923 to work with Oliver at the Lincoln Gardens, and during this period almost single-handedly invented the role of the soloist in modern jazz, the lone voice that emerged from group improvisation to extend and amplify the direction of the proceedings. Prior to 1923, jazz was played by ensembles with no soloing per se, just breaks of a bar or two. Armstrong virtually invented the solo form. His playing had an innate drama to it, and each musical outing transcribed a unique arc that commented upon and gave greater meaning to the music.

On first hearing Louis Armstrong, Max Kaminsky remembered, "I felt as if I had stared into the sun's eye. All I could think of doing was to run away and hide till the blindness left me. Above all—above all the electrifying tone, the magnificence of his ideas and the rightness of his harmonic sense, his superb technique, his power and ease, his hotness and intensity, his complete mastery of his horn—above all this, he had the swing. No one knew what swing was until Louis came along." Technically, the way Armstrong achieved this effect was by treating eighth-note phrases as though they were written in triplets, but emotionally what Armstrong did was like adding an extra dimension to the time spectrum; swing is the way the future unfolds in the present, and triplet phrasing opened that door.

In New Orleans, jazz had been woven into the social fabric of the community, the picnics, funerals, and celebrations. It was a casual occupation. In Chicago, playing jazz was part of the commerce of a great city, the "commodification of art," a profession performed by men wearing tuxedos. Armstrong brought musical grandeur to a form that had been, in the musician Danny Barker's phrase, dominated by "ham fat" players. Sharp clothing was a form of show business advertising, as well as a strike against certain racial stereotypes. In Chicago, jazz musicians became the new role models, symbolizing urban style and pride. Similarly, Chicago jazz players began including more Tin Pan Alley, thirty-two-bar popular songs in their sets, a nod in the direction of Broadway and the importance of New York's Jewish culture: in Chicago, blues and ragtime met the popular song nightly, and in time, the differences between these forms diminished. For jazz was not a style of playing: it was an approach to playing, and as such it became an approach to living one's life. The young white musicians who were in the thrall of Louis Armstrong held him up as a kind of prophet, imitating how he dressed, walked, and lived.

Chicago, like New York, was also wide open during Prohibition. Big Bill Thompson, the city's mayor, openly protected the speakeasies, and if Eliot Ness and the feds closed a club, Thompson usually had it reopened within days. The threat of police raids became part of the excitement of nightlife there, adding drama to the music scene. Crossing the threshold of the club was a rite of passage for the young. Going to hear Armstrong at the Gardens, one passed through a dark and winding hallway, feeling the excitement mount as the music grew louder, emerging into a room of sound and lights—like being reborn into a new world.

"As the door opened, the trumpets, King and Louis, one or both, soared above everything else. The whole joint was rocking. Tables, chairs, walls, people moved with the rhythm. It was dark, smoky, gin-smelling. People in the balcony leaned over and their drinks spilled on the customers below. . . . Oliver and Louis would roll on and on, piling up choruses, with the rhythm section building the beat until the whole thing got inside your head and blew your brains out. . . . " The white kids were completely hypnotized by the music. "The music poured into us," said musician Eddie Condon, "like daylight running down a dark hole."

If New York City was the home of the popular song, of Broadway and Tin Pan Alley, Chicago was the home of improvised jazz music. It became a mecca for musicians who wanted to learn the New Orleans approach, and at the same time it fueled a dance craze among the young. They were no longer content to sit passively and watch some vaudeville musicians, singers, and dancers perform their acts onstage; they wanted to become the stars of the show themselves. By the 1920s, social dancing in Chicago had become more popular than going to the movies, and as many as 86,000 youngsters a night thronged hundreds of obscure clubs and dance halls. They did new "tough" dances, full-contact grinding to the slow blues. In an attempt to stop this physicality and sexual intimacy in public, city moralists ordered the musicians to speed up the tempo of the music; within twenty-four hours, every orchestra in town had doubled the tempo of its songs, which only drove the kids wilder and gave Chicago jazz a new sound and a new cachet. New Orleans musicians, transplanted to Chicago, were like the rock and roll musicians of their day—they played "loud and wrong" and the kids loved it—and the roots of the 1930s jitterbug craze, with kids doing physically challenging dances to big band swing, can be traced back in part to this misguided Chicago ordinance.

This was the social milieu in which Mezz and the others grew up, and their drive for a new language appeared to expand exponentially on the day in 1926 when Mezz got his hands on an advance copy of Louis Armstrong's recording of "Heebie Jeebies." This single recording is considered a jazz milestone because it marks the first time Louis was heard "scat singing," a style of vocalizing based on instrumental playing. Jazz instrumentalists are normally distinguished by their "vocalized tone," clearly reminiscent of the human voice, and, similarly jazz singers are often influenced by instrumentalists. This musical quid pro quo has driven jazz improvisation well beyond the boundaries of Western harmonic theory. Ultimately, like American speech itself, innovations in jazz come from the sound of the music more than the strict harmonic grammar of the notes being played. In its purest form, scat singing is the way musicians communicate with one another off the page; it is their shorthand, a way of expressing the essence of a melody or a musical thought. It has long been thought that its origins go back to that moment in the recording studio when Armstrong dropped the lyric sheet to "Heebie Jeebies" and had to make up something to sing for the rest of the chorus. According to legend, Armstrong then started singing, "I got the heebies, I mean the jeebies," and launched into a vocal improvisation that sounded just like his horn playing.

"This recording started a vast musical craze," Mezzrow wrote, "all the hi-de-ho and vo-de-o-do and boop-boop-a-doo began sprouting up around the country. For months after you would hear cats greeting each other with Louis' riffs when they met around town. Louis' recording almost drove the English language out of the Windy City for good."

If Mezz had only known the true backstory about Armstrong's scat singing, he might have had to reconsider many things; or perhaps it would only have accelerated his trajectory of choice. For the truth was, as Armstrong told his friend Cab Calloway years later, the source of his scat singing, which he claims first occurred to him as a child on the streets of New Orleans, was something he got "from the Jews rockin'." He was referring to the davening that he had heard back in the Karnofskys' kitchen when they were praying before mealtime. "But Louis never talked about this in public because he feared people would assume he was making fun of Jews praying, which wasn't his intention at all." Scat singing had its roots in both the Jews and the blues.

By 1927, because of the notoriety of Al Capone, the feds were starting to crack down hard on the Chicago nightclub scene. Laws were reinterpreted to include not only places where alcohol was being sold but also "places where people carrying liquor congregate." Speakeasies that only provided setups—glasses, ice, and water—for those who carried liquor onto the premises in a hip flask were now being prosecuted. (These clubs could well have been the origin of the term "I'm hip," meaning somebody who was a jazz fanatic and went to hear the music with a flask hidden in his hip pocket.) Capone's operation, which controlled the places where jazz musicians played, had been good to both Oliver and Armstrong. In fact, Armstrong once referred to the notorious gangster as "a nice little cute fat boy." Now, with the heat on Capone and many Chicago clubs no longer able to support show-style bands, King Oliver left on his first national tour, winding up in New York City at the Savoy Ballroom. Armstrong followed soon after.

National touring was a relatively new phenomenon for musicians in the 1920s, made possible in part by the aggressive action of Chicago's MCA booking agency. Started by Jules Stein in 1922, MCA eventually blossomed into one of the largest media operations in America, a billion-dollar force in mass entertainment including all aspects of booking, recording, and distribution, and Stein himself became one of the most feared men in Hollywood. He is credited as the first man to convince musicians that they could make more money by traveling from town to town than by sitting in one city for prolonged periods of time when in 1924 he put the Coon-Sanders Orchestra on the road for five weeks. The tour was a smash and many other bands subsequently signed on. When Armstrong followed Oliver to New York, Mezz and the other Chicago musicians followed Armstrong. By the end of the decade, the club scene in Chicago was reduced to occasional small bars where individual piano players held forth, pioneering in the style known as "boogie-woogie" in which one musician, using a driving left hand and flashy fingering in the right, kept the crowds dancing through the long Midwestern night.

In New York, Mezz moved up to Harlem, married a black woman, had a family, and claimed that even his skin was growing darker by the day. He lived his life from then on as a man of color, a member of "the race," spending most of his days on the New York Stroll, between 131st and 132nd streets and Seventh Avenue, beneath a well-known meeting spot, the Tree of Hope—selling pot. Known as "the Reefer King," or "Poppa Mezz," he felt he had finally found a home: "I did become a kind of link between the races there," he said. "My education was completed . . . and I became a Negro."

Why should we consider the eccentric, quirky life of Mezz Mezzrow so extraordinary when clearly it was tangential, not only to the evolution of jazz but to the greater flow of Jewish history? There were certainly other young Jewish jazz musicians in Chicago during the 1920s with superior musical facility; why not focus on the career of Bud Freeman, for example, a saxophonist whose playing influenced Benny Goodman and virtually every jazz clarinetist since? Why focus on Mezzrow rather than on some other, more "serious" member of the Jewish music fraternity? Quite simply because Mezz may well be the prototype for what author Norman Mailer dubbed the "white Negro." To have moved to Harlem in the 1920s, to what Jack Kerouac called the "Great American Negro Sidewalk of the World," to have reinvented himself as a black man *in fact*, to have lived the life from the street up, he helped demonstrate the possibilities to those who came after: Jack Kerouac, Allen Ginsberg, Neal Cassady, and John Clellon Holmes. Mezzrow was thus a key author and player in that living drama of self-revelation, the New York Opera. His search influenced and inspired not only the Beat generation, but through them the so-called counterculture of the 1960s. Before Mezz, it was assumed that color was culture; after Mezz, one had to allow the possibility that it was the other way around: culture was color.

In the cases of George Gershwin and Mezz Mezzrow, we see two very different approaches to integrating the Jewish drive for self-invention with the authenticity of the black American experience. In both cases, the notion of a "middle way" between high culture and street culture, between popular art and a more intellectualized form, is obvious. Color, of course, is an accident of birth, but culture can be a choice, an active invention, a dream fulfilled. By 1927, living this dream, participating in the New York Opera, was an ongoing process across the country, as evidenced in two of the greatest popular productions of the day. And as in the examples of Gershwin and Mezzrow, we find two very different solutions, two very different answers to the question of cultural authenticity—so different, in fact, that in terms of our media history they mark the end of one era and the beginning of another. Ironically, the first of the two, the film *The Jazz Singer*, featured the latest technology even as it looked backward into a cloudy past, while the latter, the Broadway musical *Show Boat*, captured everything that was forward-looking about the evolving black-Jewish relationship.

Based on Samson Raphaelson's short story, "The Day of Atonement," *The Jazz Singer* tells the story of a fifth-generation cantor's son who yearns to sing in vaudeville while his father demands he serve the synagogue. The film is centered on the Yom Kippur holiday, the holiest day of the Jewish year, and our hero, Jakie Rabinowitz (aka Jack Robin) is torn between filling in for his ailing father to sing the Kol Nidre (the most important prayer, begging God for forgiveness) and putting on blackface to mug in a local cabaret (and thus act out the modern "American dream" wherein blacking up was synonymous with participating in show business). When it premiered on October 6, 1927, right after the conclusion of Yom Kippur itself, *The Jazz Singer* gained fame as the first talking picture. It was actually more like the first singing picture, as most of the dialogue was still silent, but the songs of Irving Berlin, as sung by Jolson, were a revelation to theatergoers because, for the first time, the people on the screen actually appeared to have voices.

The plot tells of the struggle between an old-world father and his modern son, a typical conflict of the era. (The young Jack Robin tells his strict, religious father, "This is a different time. This is a different era. This is my life. I live my life the way I see fit.") The acting was overwrought, with greatly exaggerated expressions and eye rolling from the performers, as if they were still on a vaudeville stage trying to project to the cheap seats. Jolson's famous blackface performance of the song "Mammy," a key moment that is supposed to reveal his dedication to family, comes across as a kind of cartoon moment, a miming of actual emotions. But the real failing of the film was in its relationship to the music. Music is emotion, and our hero, Jack, is supposed to be captured by the emotion of the new American moment. He is a man whose internal struggle was driven by both the music of the past and that of the present. And yet what we see and hear in the film is music that is almost an afterthought, incidental to the action and irrelevant to the plot. What did Berlin's "Blue Skies" have to do with the plot? Nothing, really; it was simply interpolated into the script, as many of Berlin's earlier songs had been interpolated into vaudeville productions.

Stylistically, the film was remarkably out of date, even for the time it was made. It captured an immigrant aesthetic, as well it should have; it was the result of Hollywood Jews trying to work out who they were and where they came from. And Irving Berlin, although the most successful songwriter at the time, was not a man with a highly developed social conscience nor much patience for the Jewish question in America. One suspects that the film's success came not because of but in spite of its music, in part because it was ballyhooed as the first "talking picture" and in part because its resonance was not dependent on whether Jolson was believable as a cantor or a minstrel—clearly he was not—but because the film told the story of a man torn by the process of becoming an authentic American, an anguish that was very real for many Americans.

"But neither an antebellum Mammy nor a yidishe mama," wrote the American scholar of Jewish history Michael Alexander, "would recognize the jazz singer as her own. He is neither Jewish nor African-American, neither from the Russian Pale nor from Dixie. He is located nowhere but in his own imagination"—and, one might add, in the imagination of the Hollywood Jews. If the film purports to ask the question "How can we become authentic Americans and yet retain our cultural identity?" the answer appears to be "Just keep acting." In the end, the film is hard to forget but wildly forgettable, more important as a concept than convincing as an experience: an out-of-touch polemic with what was, for the day, cutting-edge technology as a dodge. While the production captures a historical truth, it delivers it in such an old-fashioned grammar that it would be clear to any of the new "outsiders" that it was a complete lie.

Show Boat, on the other hand, was quite a different story. Of the 264 shows that opened on Broadway that year, it remains the best remembered. Indeed, it changed the form of the Broadway musical forever. With a huge cast dancing, singing, acting, and pushing a monumental story forward, a story about an America as mighty as the Mississippi River and as heartbreaking as a slave family parted, *Show Boat* was a new kind of Broadway production. It is the example most often cited of the "through-composed" or "integrated" Broadway musical, a richly articulated emotional story carried along by exposition through the music itself. We can see its influence in virtually all the great musical productions of the century, whether *Oklahoma!*, *My Fair Lady*, or *West Side Story*; it was a model for the New York Opera that the Jewish composers had been seeking.

Whereas Berlin was interested in hits and Gershwin was in thrall to pianistic tradition, Jerome Kern was essentially a dramatist in music. His genius lays in understanding that if used properly, music can deliver the sentiment and backstory of the narrative much more effectively and substantially than any amount of exposition. Prior to *Show Boat*, suddenly, the action would stop and the hero might wander off to sing about . . . well, about anything he liked. And then, after the song, the action would resume. The song wasn't necessarily integrated into the story. Following *Show Boat*, American popular song and drama became very much the same thing. Kern and his lyricist Oscar Hammerstein "came from nowhere in an era when silly musicals with silly books were the rule. You wrote the book around what your best songs were and hoped it would make sense. Not only did Kern and Hammerstein not do that, but they tried to embed the songs into the characters and the story. Kern had leitmotifs that wove in and out; when you hear the underscoring, you can tell what the scene's about." In *Show Boat*, the music moved the story forward and the story made the music somehow more important. And both—the music and the story—*emerged* from the characters on the stage. This was what the "integrated musical" or "through-composed" music meant: compositions that carried the character and action.

Show Boat had six hit songs, including "Make Believe," "Can't Help Lovin' Dat Man," "You Are Love," "Why Do I Love You?" "Bill," and "Ol' Man River." Paul Robeson, one of the great African-American singers, said about "Ol' Man River," "Musically it is a complete miracle, the creation of a tone of the Negro spiritual by an alien to the Negro's traditions." Robeson asserted he could prove such a claim by "singing it between two spirituals and there is not a false note. There is no change in the emotional response of the audience." How was it possible for Kern and Hammerstein to so faithfully channel the sentiment of this vast cohort of authentic American outsiders? Perhaps because they too were living suspended between two cultures—high culture and popular culture—between Europe and America, between being insiders and outsiders, experiencing the classic Jewish tension, reframed now as all-American angst.

The story of *Show Boat* tells about life on the Mississippi from the 1880s to the 1920s, a forty-year period of transition as America moved from its rural roots to urbanization, from folk art to a commercialized popular culture. It captured a great sweep of human history with a fully integrated cast; we see American lives come and go, people get on and off the boat, but the great river itself (a metaphor for America) just keeps rolling along. There is a traditional love story as well, about a woman who loves the wrong man, and so the production reveals both the macro and the micro of the American experience. But the show's staging was novel in many ways. Normally, Broadway musicals open with a big production number that ties together all the musical themes of the evening in a way, the composer hopes, that will leave the audience humming. *Show Boat* opens with a song recalling that men live and die but the river goes on; this alone was revolutionary. Further, by producing a Broadway musical in which black chorus members do not have to act like "darkies," where the theme of social justice is right out front as the curtain goes up, the play was completely unprecedented. From the first bar of music, the score affirmed that African-Americans are just as much a part of events as their white counterparts, if not more so; they were real Americans, essential to telling the story of the boat on the river. One might ask "Why did this even need to be stated?" but that would be a question from the perspective of today. At the time, the inclusion of the most marginalized Americans into the body politic was revolutionary.

Show Boat is a classic example of how Jews helped make black culture understandable and acceptable to white America by giving it a greater historical and cultural context: African-Americans were no longer seen as just the children of slavery—which must have been profoundly difficult for WASP America to deal with only seventy-five years after emancipation—but as children of diaspora who had earned their place as true Americans; in a sense, role models. It was almost as if the Jews were imagining an America where everyone was marginalized, each in their own way, where everyone was an outsider with a story to tell, if only one could find the words and music to tell it. In this way, the Jews of Broadway didn't need to cease being outsiders, they simply created a crowd of outsiders among whom to live. They expanded the Jew within the American as well as the American within the Jew.

For all of its being hailed as a realistic take on black America, however, *Show Boat* described a life that never was, neither its world of inclusivity nor the bucolic Southern life it portrays. It was a dream (of social justice) within a dream (the mythical Stephen Foster South), a work of pure Jewish imagination that in time became part of the reality on the ground. This is how the world of popular culture works—slowly, imperceptibly; a creative product doesn't have to be real in order to be true or to have the impact of a real event. It *is* a real event, just not the event as advertised. Like the "good old days," or the life on the river that Kern and Hammerstein dreamed up, it never was, but over time it became true. The popular media—films, broadcasting, recordings—made it very difficult to tell the document from the documenting process, the actual thing from the shadow on the cave wall. In terms of marketing, Madison Avenue in the 1920s began selling the sizzle rather than the steak, and people were lining up for the best tables. (The emperor's new chef always gets good reviews.) What was true? What was a dream?

Perhaps that was the big question on the morning of October 24, 1929. Known as "Black Thursday," that was the day that the fat lady finally sang in New York, not in some nightclub but on the floor of the New York Stock Exchange, a raw, searing blues that still resonates today. A selloff of stocks triggered a panic by investors that grew by the hour, and within weeks, America was entering the frozen throes of the Great Depression, a "chastening of the nation's soul," which brought to an end the frivolity and unfettered possibilities of the Jazz Age. Money became hard to find; people could no longer afford to go out and see Broadway shows or buy records. Virtually all the Broadway composers moved to Hollywood, where they set up a proxy New York encampment in the sun. There, films were still being produced by the hundreds (the ten-cent price of a movie ticket remained affordable to the masses), and the most popular films became escapist extravaganzas, absurdist comedies, or gritty gangster flicks, each in its own way providing some respite from the newspaper image of folks ducking dust storms or selling apples on the street corner. As record sales hit an all-time low, the major labels shut down their specialized divisions, or "race catalogs," in favor of the tried and true. Radio became even more important: it was free. And Jewish pop songwriters continued to produce those rare moments of clarity and social resonance. Only now people were desperately singing a new kind of hit: "Brother, Can You Spare a Dime?"

OVER THE RAINBOW

Superman was a Jew from Cleveland. On the outside, a mild-mannered, myopic reporter, infatuated with a gorgeous shiksa; on the inside, a man of infinite strength, able to escape gravity, use the latest technology (X-ray vision!), and, most important, to think, to strategize, to save the community through a combination of virtue, intelligence, and, when needed, the occasional miracle. And yet he never got the girl. Every young boy wanted to know why Clark Kent didn't simply tell Lois Lane who he really was. Apparently something bad would happen if he revealed his true nature; perhaps he would lose his powers? Why else maintain the charade? Or was it that he was doomed to hide behind the façade of his ordinariness because he wanted to be loved for his connection to the common man rather than for his uncommon qualities? Jewish, Jewish, Jewish.

Superman was the invention of Jerry Siegel and Joe Shuster, two Jewish classmates at Cleveland's Glenville High School. Using an idea formulated by the German philosopher Friedrich Nietzsche—a "superman" of intellect and willpower (an image the Nazis would soon corrupt into the Aryan ideal)—the "man of steel" originally had a heart of gold: he was the ultimate *mensch*. "The creative breakthrough didn't occur until Siegel conceived of his brainchild as being the sole survivor of a doomed planet called Krypton," writes one observer, "a cosmic refugee who can never return home. With his alien address and miraculous abilities, Superman is the ultimate immigrant and Earth's heaven-sent redeemer." Of course he was a Jew.

If Siegel and Shuster fantasized a powerful alien presence within their own ordinary lives, they also presumed a crowd of ordinary citizens just waiting to be saved. Superman needed to have the crowd in order to be super; Clark Kent needed the crowd in which to hide, in which to be ordinary. In dream theory, one would say Siegel and Shuster were both the man of steel and the crowd that was being saved. In the end, Superman was famous and yet remained unknown and unknowable, not unlike today's pop stars, who bring together the masses under the pretense of their mutual commonality, wanting to be loved for "who they really are," yet who they really are is constantly being driven by the eye of the media. Superman, in the end, always flew off alone.

The question for the second-generation American Jew was exactly this: how to fit into the new world and at the same time have the new world accept them for who they really were. And, in fact, who were they? In the 1930s, there was a growing sense of unease about the Jews, both within and without the Jewish community. Superman made his debut in this period of economic catastrophe that was often blamed on the Jews. Partly because of the growing interest in race in America, Jews were singled out as being different, secretive, and, by extension, a threat to American values. Henry Ford's *Dearborn Independent* kept up a drumbeat of attacks on Jews as destabilizing to America's youth, and Father Charles Edward Coughlin, a Roman Catholic priest from Michigan, held forth weekly on his national radio broadcast, spewing colorful, virulent anti-Semitism that more than 40 million Americans listened to regularly. In his speeches, Coughlin blamed the Jews for causing the Great Depression and once linked himself with Adolf Hitler, giving the Nazi salute at a rally and telling the crowd, "When we get through with the Jews in America, they'll think the treatment they received in Germany was nothing." This from a well-respected conservative cleric.

At the same time, one of the most popular programs on the radio was *The Goldbergs* (perhaps the first radio sitcom), which chronicled the life of a struggling Jewish family in the Bronx. Americans of every culture and class fell in love with warm-hearted, level-headed Molly Goldberg; she was forthright, self-effacing, and funny all at the same time, as she leaned out the window of her imaginary tenement building and invited you into her home. The creation of Gertrude Berg, an educated producer-actress-writer who affected a Yiddish accent on the air, this show too was heard by millions of people coast to coast, and its star was the second most admired woman in America, right after Eleanor Roosevelt. Berg has been called "the Oprah of her day," and by the mid-1930s, radio was already bringing traditional outsiders into the intimacy of American homes.

Historically, America has had this kind of love-hate relationship with the Jews; Jewish students continued to be subjected to restrictive quotas at major universities, Jewish instructors remained rare, and at American corporations, Jewish employees were often nonexistent. The underlying question of whether or not Jews were a separate race weighed heavily on Jews and non-Jews alike. Jews themselves were not certain, and the pseudoscientific "discipline" of eugenics, which had sprung up in the 1920s, often lent credence to those seeking to explain Judaism not as a process but as a thing in itself: a separate race. For many Americans, Jews might as well have been from the planet Krypton.

Eugenics was "the study of, or belief in, the possibility of improving the qualities of the human species by such means as discouraging reproduction by persons having genetic defects or presumed to have inheritable undesirable traits (negative eugenics) or encouraging reproduction by persons presumed to have inheritable desirable traits (positive eugenics)." Although for a time this "science" was embraced by an array of prominent social thinkers, including Margaret Sanger, H. G. Wells, George Bernard Shaw, and Winston Churchill, its most infamous proponent was of course Adolf Hitler, who praised and incorporated eugenic ideas in *Mein Kampf*. In 1933, Hitler began his campaign to ostracize the Jews from Germany based on these theories: Jews were banned from normal workplaces, schools, and businesses and were hunted everywhere for trumped-up infractions. On March 21, 1933, for example, Nazis broke into the home of the scientist Albert Einstein and ransacked his belongings, allegedly searching for weapons. In America too, during the 1930s, being Jewish was perceived as a growing liability that many Jews attempted to conceal or ameliorate, and the discussion of race was on everyone's mind. Eugenics was just one iteration of that discussion.

While some Jews made the move to disappear into the culture, assuming they could physically "pass," others made the move to restructure the culture itself; both ends of the spectrum met in the middle, and every Jewish life in America on some level walked this razor's edge. If disappearing into the culture was the goal, it was done in the name of being an "American"; Hollywood, for example, turned its back on overt Jewish themes (such as *The Jazz Singer*) or Jewishisms in general. If reforming the culture was the goal, it was done most often in the name of the African-Americans. As early as 1900, *The Jewish Daily Forward* decried what it called the "bloody pogroms against the Negroes." In 1927, when Carl Laemmle, the Jewish owner of Universal Studios, presented a film version of *Uncle Tom's Cabin*, the Yiddish press reported "the most profound joy grows in the hearts of the Jewish people because to the present day we cannot forget our own slavery in Egypt," and by 1931, when the famed Jewish attorney Samuel Leibowitz defended the Scottsboro Boys (nine African-American youngsters falsely accused of raping two white women), there were claims that Jews intended to overthrow the white power structure and use blacks as "the shock troops of the revolution," the implication being that Jews were self-identified blacks.

However, Hitler's rise in Germany began raising warning flags in America about the ultimate danger of using racial definitions, and many Jews begin speaking of "culture" as a category distinct from biology and referring to themselves as an "ethnic group" rather than a "race." The Columbia University anthropologist Franz Boas was one who struggled to articulate this difference, followed by Isaac Berkson, whose *Theories of Americanization* asserted that Jews were racially identical to other white Americans and distinct only in their culture. This, they hoped, would begin to harmonize American and Jewish identities. By 1934, Rabbi Mordecai Kaplan, the founder of Reconstructionist Judaism in America, led a much wider rejection of a Jewish "racial" identity and, like the followers of Moses Mendelssohn in Germany almost a century earlier, abandoned much of Jewish orthodoxy. Jews in America could be Americans first and foremost and still remain Jews. Yet most Jews continued to feel a special sensitivity to the dangers of racism in all its manifestations.

In 1930, even George Gershwin, the most "American" of Jews, began to address the greater themes of injustice and political hypocrisy in his music. Along with his brother, Ira, he produced three overtly political musical satires—*Strike Up the Band* (1930), *Of Thee I Sing* (1933), and *Let Them Eat Cake* (1933)—each of which expressed their liberalism and their sense of the absurdity in the whole political discussion. But it was the landmark "folk opera" *Porgy and Bess* on which Gershwin hung his heart and expressed his greater yearnings for black and Jewish Americans, a yearning that went deeper than politics, into the heart of social justice and simple dignity.

Although he did not officially begin work on *Porgy and Bess* until 1932, he had some of the pieces in hand as early as 1929. They came from his attempt to write a musical built on a play called *The Dybbuk*, based on an old Yiddish folk tale. It is the story of a young man who pursues the mysteries of the Kabbalah without caution, then dies, but his soul remains in limbo; the plot focuses on the trials of this lost spirit. Gershwin's early notebook for

The Dybbuk included Hasidic dances and Yiddish folk tunes, but his plans to compose the score ended when the rights to produce the play could not be secured. Still, he had some of the themes in mind, and several reappeared later in his score for *Porgy and Bess*.

It is interesting to note how easily Gershwin was able to transfer these themes, designed to express a trapped Jewish spirit in Europe, into the soundtrack for a poor black peddler in America. The melody of "Summertime," for example, one of Gershwin's most enduring, was originally intended as the opening aria for *The Dybbuk*. It contains the classic "Jewish move"—the song's verses are set in a minor key but resolve each time to a major release (the familiar "hush little baby" refrain)—and it has been remarked often that the song establishes a mood somewhere between the cantorial and the blues. Gershwin insisted *Porgy and Bess* was a new animal: an American "folk opera," not just a musical about the disenfranchised but in some sense by the disenfranchised as well; it was as if the development of a new musical form could transfer new ownership of the subject matter. The implication was that the transition from a racial definition of Jews in America to one of culture also meant that being black was not simply about a person's skin color but rather about a person's culture.

Porgy and Bess is set in a small fishing village in South Carolina where Porgy, a crippled man living in the shantytown of Catfish Row, has fallen in love with Bess, a beautiful but disreputable woman. As the action unfolds, it reveals the story of the power of love to make ordinary people do extraordinary things, both good and evil. Acted out in a small neighborhood of African-Americans who lived a private racial life in the midst of a white civilization, *Porgy and Bess* tells the story of a real person, a black man named Samuel Smalls who traveled the streets of Charleston, South Carolina, in a small cart fashioned from a wooden soapbox drawn by a goat. "To Smalls," wrote DuBois Heyward, the book's author, "I make acknowledgement of my obligation. From contemplation of his real and deeply moving tragedy sprang Porgy." Gershwin would endow Heyward's Porgy with a "mythic immortality," and this new American "folk opera" would become the harbinger of other great works, such as Leonard Bernstein's *West Side Story*, wherein the lives of common men and women are seen straight on, without the usual artifice of show business.

"*Porgy and Bess* is a folk tale," Gershwin said. "Its people naturally would sing folk music. When I first began work on the music I decided against the use of traditional folk material because I wanted the music to be all of one piece. Therefore, I wrote my own spirituals and folksongs. But they are still folk music and therefore, being in operatic form, *Porgy and Bess* becomes a folk opera."

Of course none of this was literally true. The story was not a folk tale, it was written by Heyward, a white man, and Gershwin's music was not, nor could it ever be, folk music per se. But as audiences ever since have recognized, the overall production did have an undeniable sense of *veritas* about it; there was something very real about its folk roots. Whatever Gershwin brought from his own background translated seamlessly from Eastern

Europe to Catfish Row. On the surface, these two worlds shared very little—not language, not traditions, not geography. But they were both "saturated in and sanctified by music." Heyward's book, like the original staging of *The Dybbuk*, "flows on a stream of song and chant, the open-voiced thanks and lament of a devout people who have long been isolated from modern ways." It was the music itself that cut like a knife across time and space, joining diverse cultures and distant geographies. Todd Duncan, the first actor to play Porgy, said as much. He was trained on the "legitimate" stage (as opposed to Broadway) and, as he was teaching at Howard University at the time, initially felt that "show music" was beneath him. Then he met Gershwin around a piano, and as he later reported, "I just thought I was in heaven. These beautiful melodies in this new idiom, it was something I had never heard. I just couldn't get enough of it. When he ended with 'I'm on My Way' I was crying. I was weeping."

What Gershwin was calling folk music might just as well have been called "new American pop," as he had found a new way to translate the essence of a simple rural voice through a sophisticated urban filter. American pop music has always relied on just such counterposed forces for its freshness and effect.

At the same time in America, another musical stream, the black gospel tradition, was emerging. During the early 1930s, there was a major blossoming of black church music all across the country. The term "spiritual music," with its connotations of old-time plantation worship, was being replaced with the term "gospel music," suggesting a broader reference and a wider urban representation. The pioneer of gospel was Thomas Dorsey, a man who began his career as blues singer "Georgia Tom" but who then gave up secular music for the sacred. Between 1932 and 1935, exactly the years when Gershwin was composing the score for *Porgy and Bess*, gospel music swept through the growing urban black communities, and Dorsey, along with singer Mahalia Jackson, was its avatar, touring the country nonstop. Particularly in the South (in South Carolina, for example, where Gershwin went to research his characters) there was little difference between the audience reaction to this new sacred music and to popular music, or, as Ray Charles once explained, "The blues is just the same as gospel, except you're saying 'baby' instead of 'Jesus.'" Ultimately, the conventions of gospel music helped shape the idioms of both country music and rhythm and blues; in America, gospel is part of the popular canon, and Gershwin had a hand in putting it there.

To begin composing the music for *Porgy*, Gershwin had moved to a small island off the South Carolina coast named Folly Island. There, in a rented cottage with a screened-in porch and an old upright piano, Gershwin found himself both in a completely foreign environment and totally at home. He attended the black prayer meetings at the local church, where there were no musical instruments and the congregation accompanied itself with "a complicated rhythmic pattern beaten out by feet and hands." This was called "shouting," and one night Gershwin joined in the shout and "stole the show from their champion shouter."

Gershwin had immersed himself in a world of spiritual music and popular narrative and, as he wrote his friend Emily Paley, "we go around with practically nothing on . . . eat out at night gazing at the stars, smoking our pipes. . . . and discuss our two favorite subjects, Hitler's Germany and God's women."

There it is: the questions of race and women, tied together through the issues of personal and social survival. Composing *Porgy and Bess* had moved Gershwin into an interesting spiritual realm; according to his first biographer, he "never quite ceased to wonder at the miracle that he had been its composer, he never stopped loving each and every bar, never wavered in the conviction that he had produced a work of art." In the fall of 1935, *Porgy and Bess* opened in New York City, where it closed after only 124 performances, a commercial failure. It would be many years before the original investors received their money back. Gershwin, convinced he had done his best work and despondent about the future of Broadway, packed up again, and this time he moved to Los Angeles, renting a large Spanish-style house in Beverly Hills with his brother, Ira. There he became part of a small community of Jewish refugees from New York's music business that included Eddie Cantor, Richard Rodgers, Sigmund Romberg, Irving Berlin, Jerome Kern, Harold Arlen, and Yip Harburg. He took up painting, played tennis, and became active in anti-Nazi meetings.

Like many others, Gershwin was increasingly concerned about events in Europe, and he wrote that at the dinners and parties, along with good friends and sparkling conversation, there were "depressing moments, too, when talk of Hitler and his gang creeps into the conversation. For some reason or other, the feeling out here is more acute than in the East." Perhaps it was because Hollywood's Jewish community, often living in the grand style of show business, felt more exposed on the West Coast: for them it was not so easy to blend into the crowd, nor was there really a crowd for them into which to blend. So they hid in other ways. The heads of the film studios—like the Warner brothers, Louis B. Mayer, and Sam Goldwyn—actively, if silently, stopped representing Jews on the big screen. No more *Jazz Singer*, no more Jewish angst. In the 1930s, the Hollywood films were all about "American types," rarely ethnics, and virtually never Jews, even though (or rather because) the majority of Hollywood creatives—the musicians, writers, directors—were mostly Jews.

Too, Hollywood's social world was highly stratified, with the studio owners at the top and the rest of the talent spread out underneath them. Studio owners, often compared to paternal figures, rarely socialized with their creative "children." Directors and starlets would be at the parties of songwriters and scriptwriters, but the reverse was not always true—songwriters would rarely be invited: they were above the line, work for hire, paid when they delivered the songs, and except for ASCAP money, their work was out of their control. In Los Angeles, composers were just journeymen, the common laborers of the industry, not in the social mix. On the East Coast, they had been the main event, at the heart of the culture. So for Gershwin, who was used to the New York system in which composers and talent were the stars, life in California was particularly isolating. He felt like the hired help.

It was not that Hollywood wasn't interested in the musical side of things. To the contrary, following the introduction of sound in 1929, the film studios immediately grasped the importance of music in their product and moved swiftly to secure a steady supply. Following the stock market crash of 1929, Tin Pan Alley was essentially on the auction block, and many publishing companies sold out to the big studios. MGM bought Robbins Music; Warner Bros. bought M. Witmark and Sons as well as Dreyfus, T. B. Harms, and New World Music. This gave film studios access to vast catalogs of music, which they could use as they liked, and to songwriters, who increasingly worked under contract to studios rather than music publishers. Tin Pan Alley, which for years had regarded itself as the keeper of the American dream, was now just another cog in the gears of the dream machine. Hollywood was quite aware of the importance of music; they were simply not impressed with the importance of the musicians. As Gershwin himself said, "I had to live for this, that Sam Goldwyn should say to me 'Why don't you write hits like Irving Berlin?'"

With the introduction of sound, studios initially used public domain pieces of classical music to prop up their films, often seemingly at random. But as narratives became more sophisticated and both the acting and plot lines more interior, techniques for integrating music advanced rapidly. The advent of "underscoring"—using music specifically created to guide the viewer's expectations—opened up a whole new world of emotional reinforcement to the films. Underscoring was the brainchild of the Jewish composer Max Steiner (he eventually wrote the score for *Gone with the Wind*), who in 1932 convinced producer David O. Selznick that original music, designed for the specifics of the narrative, would improve his product. Further, he also pushed for the use of underscoring behind dialogue. (Selznick, fearing that audiences would wonder where the music was coming from, was at first dubious, but he was ultimately persuaded.) The first film Steiner scored—*Symphony of Six Million*, about New York families—used melodies from "Kol Nidre," "Eli Eli," and several other Jewish themes. Steiner's innovative approach swept up audiences and pointed the way for all future movie music. By the end of the decade, underscoring had become a serious art, with original music occupying as much screen time as the stars themselves. In many cases, it would not be an exaggeration to say that underscoring—as developed by Steiner and his European compatriots Bernard Herrmann, Elmer Bernstein, Leonard Rosenman, Alex North, and others—helped make stars of the actors, as it so skillfully guided the audience's sympathies during scenes big and small.

In addition to underscoring, the world of music in films was expanded through the invention of the playback system, a method of recording songs before the action was actually filmed. The creation of the (Jewish) director Mark Sandrich, playback solved a serious technical problem for filmmakers. Prior to the use of playback, musical numbers required the actual musicians to be playing just out of camera range and the actors to sing along in real time. Obviously, this limited both the camera angles and the ability of intimate dialog to be recorded. With playback, orchestrations could be carefully crafted in a sound studio, along with the actor's vocal, and during filming the actor could pretend to sing. This "lip synching" not only made it possible for professional singers to replace (often without credit) vocally challenged actors, but freed up camera movement and location: now musical scenes could be filmed anywhere, inside or outside, from any angle. By the end of the decade, underscored music and large production numbers were a major part of what Hollywood was offering. And, according to the composer Hugo Friedhofer, a member of the Hollywood music establishment at the time, more than 60 percent of the major film composers were Jews.

Among this distinguished list of Jewish film composers, none was more ubiquitous than Carl Stalling, who wrote the music for the Warner Bros. cartoons and in so doing inadvertently influenced the musical education of several generations of young Americans. Cartoon music was a wild amalgam of strange instruments (the marimba always accompanied a walk up the stairs) executing rapid-fire transitions, a collage that created a kind of magical discontinuity; like the cartoons themselves, the music made its own sense in a very modern, Dadaesque way. Much like the comedies of the Marx brothers, which also had a logic all their own, cartoons generally punched holes in the façade of the status quo. Indeed, there are many similarities between the sly asides of Bugs Bunny and those of Groucho Marx, and there is no doubt that cartoons led America's youth down the path of questioning authority later in life. This fearless art of deflation comes to its modern fruition in Mel Brooks's hit film/musical *The Producers*; surrealism became a more serious social critique as the society itself became more surreal.

At the same time, these Jewish roots of the Hollywood music were well hidden and well guarded. Take, for example, the case of Sholom Secunda, who told the young George Gershwin that he was "too American" for the Yiddish theater. In 1932, he composed the song "Bei Mir Bist Du Schön" (To Me You Are Beautiful), one of the biggest crossover hits in the history of American pop music. It was originally written for a Yiddish musical comedy called (loosely translated) *You Could Live but They Don't Let You*; a centerpiece of the show, it never failed to bring the audience to its feet. During the show's run, Secunda sold ten thousand copies of the sheet music in the lobby of the theater—a huge number considering the size of the audiences—and when the show closed in 1933, he moved on to something else. Then, in 1935, two Jewish composers, Sammy Cahn and Saul Chaplin, happened to be at Harlem's Apollo Theater when two black performers sang "Bei Mir Bist Du Schön"—in Yiddish!—and again, it brought the house down. Cahn and Chaplin decided to write new words for it in English.

That same year, 1935, Secunda headed to California to break into the film business. Perhaps he was aware that the studio heads were all Jews and hoped they would look kindly on his work. However, as the Hollywood studio heads were actively avoiding overt references to or portrayals of Jews onscreen, Secunda couldn't have picked a worse time to pitch the West Coast moguls. There was no way these men would risk unmasking themselves to aid any composer, actor, or writer who exuded Secunda's kind of Jewishness; it was what they had come to California to escape. At Warner Bros., the musical director Leo Forbstein and the actor Eddie Cantor both proclaimed "Bei Mir Bist Du Schön" to be "too Jewish." Secunda, deflated, returned to New York and to the Yiddish theater. So when he was approached about selling the publishing rights to the song, he figured it had achieved its maximum potential and accepted an offer of $30. In November 1937, the song was recorded by the Andrews Sisters with Cahn's English lyrics; it was a smash hit by Christmas.

The song went on to be recorded numerous times, becoming "a kind of anthem of acceptance for second generation Jews," who saw, in boxing, Barney Ross; in baseball, Hank Greenberg; and in music, Benny Goodman, "a sign that Jews could make it in the mainstream world." It even started a short-lived fad of Yiddish-inflected jazz tunes, including Cab Calloway's "A Bee Gezindt" (Live and Be Well). The Warner brothers, in their paranoia, were clearly behind the national curve. They had not understood that the discussion of Jews in America was moving away from the subject of race to that of culture; whereas race was somehow closed and immutable, something to be ducked or denied, "culture" was fluid and open to all, and many Americans were enjoying this "Jewishness."

In 1936, George Gershwin began acting in bizarre ways; he dropped his food on the table, dribbled water as he tried to drink, stumbled on the stairs, complained of severe headaches. Ira's wife, Leonore, was repelled by her brother-in-law's strange behavior, mistakenly believing it to be his neurotic reaction to the poor treatment he was receiving in Hollywood. She forced him to move out of the house and into the home of his friend Yip Harburg next door. In July 1937, George Gershwin died at the age of thirty-eight of a brain tumor. His last composition, which his brother Ira titled "Our Love Is Here to Stay" following George's death, is—like his beloved *Porgy and Bess*—about love great and small: "In time the Rockies may crumble, Gibraltar may tumble, they're only made of clay, but our love is here to stay."

The death of George Gershwin was both a shock to the music community and the end of an era. There was a kind of symmetry, if not poetry, in the fact that Gershwin died in the home of Yip Harburg—a symbolic passing of the torch, as Harburg, more than any other songwriter of his time, had grasped that the essence of the "Jewish question" in America was basically, and for the foreseeable future, about culture—social justice, human dignity—not race. In a way, race had become an emotional red herring; since the turn of the century, with the first great migrations of blacks from the rural South to the industrial North, there had been "race" riots, which were more often about class competition than "eugenics." Nationwide, more than four million white workers walked off their jobs in 1919 to protest black immigration from the South, which had flooded the industrial North with cheap labor. Between April and October, twenty-five U.S. cities were affected, with thirty-eight dead in Chicago alone. So while race and class have always been linked, in America—where money is power—race is ultimately *about* class. That is, class trumps race when and where people from diverse backgrounds come together. For example, Todd Duncan, the college-educated African-American who first delivered Gershwin's Porgy to the world, was essentially of the same economic class as the composer, and therefore the two were able to forge a close personal relationship, with Gershwin insisting that Duncan was more Jewish than he and Duncan countering that Gershwin was more Negro than he. Culture—a parallel aesthetic, understanding and worldview—made this bonding possible.

In 1933, when Franklin D. Roosevelt was inaugurated, fifteen million were unemployed in the country and six million on relief; many had lost their homes and had settled in shacks built of tin and cardboard ("Hoovervilles"). Yet most still considered themselves to be, if only culturally, part of middle America (the middle class) even though their money was gone. Of all the Jewish songwriters, Yip Harburg best understood this disconnect brought on by the Depression: for years after graduating from college, he too had given up his dream of being a songwriter to become a businessman, making a small fortune only to lose it all during the crash of 1929.

Harburg was born Isidore Hochberg to immigrant Russian Jewish parents on New York's Lower East Side, part of the astonishing concentration of musical talent to come out of the New York "class of '96," the group that included the Gershwins, Lorenz Hart, Oscar Hammerstein, Howard Dietz, Harry Ruby, and Irving Caesar, augmented by Alan Jay Lerner, Dorothy Fields, and Frank Loesser. Unlike the others, however, Harburg's family was so poor that middle-class America must have seemed like a distant world. As a child, Yip had no bed; instead, he slept on chairs that he and his sister would push together each evening, learning, "the chill of poverty which never leaves your bones." In a way, he had to raise his parents. "The street, not the home, was your life," he recalled. "Your parents spoke Yiddish. That alone made you a displaced kid. The older generation of men and women brought their Russian and Jewish culture with them. They spoke no English. Parents were very proud of children who spoke English and could interpret for them. This put parents in an inferior position." Harburg's whole family struggled to survive, working in the garment industry as many as sixteen hours a day. It was fertile ground for what Irving Howe called "Jewish socialism," a working-class radicalism with roots in Jewish orthodox culture and nurtured by daily reading of *The Jewish Daily Forward.*

Early on, Yip's dream was to deliver his family from poverty. "Every immigrant family," he said, "knew that education would improve their lives. I was aware. I empathized with my father in his sweatshop, my mother at her washing and making hairnets for a living on the Lower East Side. I always had hope that someday they would be liberated. It became part of my chemistry—to free them from drudgery." At the same time, he saw himself as a kind of avenger for the downtrodden, a closet Clark Kent: "I am a rebel by birth. I contest anything that is unjust, that causes suffering in humanity. . . . I don't think I could live with myself if I weren't honest about that."

Although the family was orthodox, what little faith Yip may have had in religion was dashed the day his older brother Max died of cancer. Yip was only fifteen, and his brother, twelve years his senior, a physicist and mathematician, was his hero. The tragedy left him firmly agnostic: he found a substitute for the synagogue in the theater, spending any money he could gather to sit in the dark of the cheap seats, watching and listening, absorbing the songs of Irving Berlin and the inherent theatricality of the Yiddish culture. He loved the writing of W. S. Gilbert, and he was shocked one day at school when the kid sitting next to him informed him there was music to go along with the words. The kid was Ira Gershwin, who invited him back to his apartment, where, to Harburg's amazement, there was an actual Victrola and recordings of Gilbert and Sullivan. Upon hearing his favorite Gilbert lines set to music, he reported, "I was dumbfounded, staggered. Gilbert and Sullivan tied Ira to me for life." But unlike Ira, who dropped out of City College of New York in 1916 to work on his songwriting, Yip did not have the option of following his dream. He remained in school, and upon graduation he became a businessman.

His first job was with the Swift Company, which sent him to Uruguay, where he made enough money to send some home for his family. On returning in 1920, he took the money he had saved and started an electrical appliance business; his hope was to build it up, sell it, and use the money to become a songwriter. It was the boom period of the twenties.

"For seven years we went up and up and were worth about a quarter of a million by 1929." And then, of course, came the crash, and Harburg was ruined. He was, however, perspicacious enough to see it as a blessing: the Depression had delivered him from his own best efforts and returned him to himself; in a larger sense, he was redeemed. "Heaven was ahead of me, and that beautiful depression of 1929 came along and knocked the hell out of my business. I found myself broke and personally in debt for about fifty thousand dollars . . . all I had left was my pencil. . . . When I found I could sell a song or a poem, I became me. I became alive . . . when I lost my possessions, I found my creativity. I felt I was being born for the first time."

In 1929, when Yip began writing lyrics, the theater song, or "book" lyric that we associate with the Broadway musical was still very new. Ira Gershwin had only begun writing with his brother, George, a few years earlier, and the lyricist Lorenz Hart had just scored on Broadway with the composer Richard Rodgers a year after that. Both Ira Gershwin and Larry Hart were in the vanguard of this new kind of lyric writing. Unlike the old Tin Pan Alley songwriters, who were often grammatically illiterate, Gershwin and Hart were born speaking American English, had been college educated, and were lifelong fans of the wit and wisdom of popular writers such as Franklin P. Adams. Adams had a column in the *New York World* called "The Conning Tower" that acted as a finishing school for a generation of American writers and humorists. (Adams discovered, among others, George S. Kaufman, Robert Benchley, and Dorothy Parker, who said of Adams, "He raised me from a couplet.") The Adams columns "synthesized a mastery of the city with a mastery of language. They offered a way to combine street smarts with book learning." This combination would come to define not only the Great American Songbook but Jewish life in general during the 1930s.

Once again Ira became Yip's mentor, lending him money to get back on his feet and introducing him to the composer Jay Gorney. The two began writing songs for Broadway reviews; the shows were flops, but Harburg was learning an important lesson: in the American "book" song (unlike the British light musical of his childhood hero Gilbert), the lyricist can go only as far and as deep as the song's composer has gone. That is, "internal rhyme is often a function of melodic or even harmonic variation; metaphor, of the mood of the music; and narrative thrust, of the unfolding of the music." Part of Harburg's genius was to hear the meaning in the notes, and so, like Gershwin and Hart, he always set the lyric after the music was composed.

His ability to hear new meaning in music was sharply honed by 1932, when he and Gorney wrote a song, for a show called *Americana*, about "the Forgotten Man." Harburg had noticed that on every corner one passed, some poor guy who would greet you with the plea, "Brother, can you spare a dime?" and he thought that would be a great title for a song. Gorney had written a melody that was reminiscent of an old Jewish folk song, something that was immediately seductive to Harburg. This narrative theme was very close to his heart.

"I grew up when America had a dream," he said, "and its people a hope . . . in 1930 the dream collapsed. The system fell apart. This was a good country on its way to greatness . . . what happened? We were baffled." It was this baffled man who sang "Brother, Can You Spare a Dime?"

> They used to tell me I was building a dream, and so I followed the mob,
> When there was earth to plow, or guns to bear, I was always there right on the job.
> They used to tell me I was building a dream, with peace and glory ahead,
> Why should I be standing in line, just waiting for bread?
>
> Once I built a railroad, I made it run, made it race against time.
> Once I built a railroad; now it's done. Brother, can you spare a dime?
> Once I built a tower, up to the sun, brick, and rivet, and lime;
> Once I built a tower, now it's done. Brother, can you spare a dime?
>
> Say, don't you remember, they called me Al; it was Al all the time.
> Say, don't you remember, I'm your pal? Brother, can you spare a dime?

The first socially conscious American soul song, "Brother, Can You Spare a Dime?" became an enormous hit, as well as the predecessor to hundreds of future songs, including Marvin Gaye's "What's Going On" and many other "social conscience" songs of the 1960s and 1970s. The year *Americana* opened (1932), nearly 25 percent of the American workforce was unemployed. Gorney's melody was simple, romantic, and ethnically rooted; Harburg's lyric was written in the everyday vernacular of the displaced worker, but it spoke from the perspective of somebody well versed in the global forces that caused the displacement. Much as Bob Dylan's songs would do thirty years later, Harburg's lyrics stunned the crowd. He had imposed a greater awareness on an audience and an industry, one that had previously assumed that show business and social consciousness were incompatible. Harburg's baffled protagonist might well be the model for Paul Simon's equally baffled protagonist in the song, "Call Me Al," wondering why his life was so hard even though he himself was so "soft in the middle." Harburg was years ahead of the curve, the one true socialist among the great Broadway lyricists, and before the curve finally caught up with him, he would not only provide some of the most insightful musical imagery in American popular music, but would be blacklisted during the McCarthy era for his trouble.

Perhaps it was inevitable. As Harburg said many years later, "Songs have been the not-so-secret weapon behind every fight for freedom, every struggle against injustice and bigotry: 'The Marseillaise,' 'The Battle Hymn of the Republic,' 'We Shall Overcome,' and many more. . . . Songs are the pulse of a nation's heart. A fever chart of its health. Are we at peace? Are we in trouble? Are we floundering? Do we feel beautiful? Do we feel ugly? . . . listen to our songs . . . the lyricist, like any artist, cannot be neutral. He should be committed to the side of humanity." Nowhere is the conflation of popular music, social justice, and the Jewish tradition of *tikkun* more clearly articulated than in Harburg's anthem for the Great Depression. The song was written, he recalled, while he "couldn't stop crying . . . I write with what they call in Yiddish *gederim*—it means the very vitals of your being."

However, it wasn't until he began writing with the composer Harold Arlen that Harburg really came into his own. Like Gershwin, Arlen was a first-rate piano player, educated in the growing jazz tradition and steeped in both Hebrew and black music; his was a uniquely "American approach" for which Harburg had a great affinity. "I had never heard that kind of music before," he said. "A great song requires a great melody that comes right out of the heart and brain of the composer . . . the composer has to more or less feed you. Feeding him an idea, a title, is fine, but usually if you give him a complete, immutable lyric first, he'll start underscoring and usually a banal melody results . . . a great composer brings out the best in a lyricist." Arlen and Harburg wrote a series of elegant, sophisticated songs that were hard-bitten and grounded in real life, although ultimately their musical masterpiece would adorn one of Hollywood's greatest fantasies.

Their first song as a team was "It's Only a Paper Moon," written for a Broadway show called *The Great Magoo*, about a barker in a Coney Island joint, a man disillusioned with the world who had finally fallen in love. Harburg's lyric hinges on a dramatic departure from previous romantic Tin Pan Alley images of show business (such as Irving Berlin's "There's No Business like Show Business"). In Harburg's vision the world of show business is "as phony as it can be," but "it wouldn't be make believe if you belonged to me." That is, simple human relationships trump the show-business hype, and real life is more interesting than that cheap "paper moon." Written in the depths of the Depression, when escapist fare was all the rage in films and music, this sentiment was, in its own way, as radical as that expressed in "Brother, Can You Spare a Dime?"

But these lyrics exist only because they were first inspired by Arlen's music. "Paper Moon" opens with a dramatic octave leap in the first two notes of the first bar; for most singers, it's a musical gesture akin to leaping off a cliff. Like so many of Arlen's innovations, it owes its existence to the fact that he was an improviser, not a tunesmith, and wrote his songs from the inside out (or from the keyboard up). That is, he let the melodies dictate the forms rather than try to stuff all his musical ideas into what was by then the standard thirty-two-bar format; it was the earmark of somebody secure in his ability to hear the inner direction the music wanted to take. He was writing from some deep inner faith. Ira Gershwin remembers Arlen at this time as having "an almost supernatural belief in inspiration."

Born Chaim Arluch in Buffalo, New York, Harold Arlen too was the son of a cantor. He claimed his father, Samuel, was "the most delicious improviser I ever heard," and he recalled an incident from his youth when he and his father were listening to a new Louis Armstrong recording and Samuel became agitated and demanded to know where the trumpet player had gotten a particular phrase he was playing. Chaim explained it was a not uncommon "riff," but his father maintained it was exactly something he himself had improvised during a recent service at the synagogue. Harold often repeated that he heard a lot of Louis Armstrong in his father's cantillation. A musical prodigy who sang in his father's choir and a pianist who developed a style built on a strong, flowing melodic line, by age fifteen Chaim had dropped out of school to play professionally. Dance bands were flourishing, and roadhouses that provided a dance floor and illicit alcohol were popping up on back roads everywhere, spurred on by the rising sales of automobiles. Arlen's band, the Buffalodians, hoped to branch out to be a "territory band," maybe even get to New York, do radio broadcasts and go national. The band didn't make it, but Chaim Arluch did: in 1925, at age twenty, he moved to Manhattan and changed his name to Harold Arlen.

The world of dance bands was a loose confederation of musicians and gigs. The first dance bands were based on the New Orleans "hot bands," using piano, bass, drums, guitar (or banjo), saxophone (or clarinet), trombone, and trumpet. Some of the larger

New Orleans bands, such as King Oliver's and Louis Armstrong's, as well as some territory bands, like McKinney's Cotton Pickers and Benny Moten's organization, expanded their size and were loved as "dance bands" but rarely played formal section arrangements; that is, while they attracted many dancers, both black and white, they did not expand their musical framework. They were like today's "jam bands," loud and swinging, but at times they would feature an extended ballad or medium-tempo number to accommodate slow dancers in the crowd. These musical aggregations relied on informal "head" arrangements, fluid, flexible, and expandable to suit the evening's mood. With increased volume, increased tempos, and increased alcohol consumption, a night out at a roadhouse or at the Roseland Ballroom in New York during the late 1920s must have felt like going to a rock concert in the sixties or a hip-hop event in the nineties: the music was loud and improvised and aimed at the young.

However, with the addition of more literate "book" songs (written for Broadway and Hollywood films) and the increasingly elegant venues at hotels and dance halls around the country, many of these bands expanded by organizing the horns into sections (reeds, brass, and others) and became slick, upscale traveling units. The more successful bands arrived in town in a brand-new bus, the musicians sporting sharp clothes, playing hot new arrangements of the latest popular songs, and introducing a string of good-looking girl and boy singers to deliver the romantic hits. These new dance bands were professionally marketed, booked, and broadcast, twelve-to-twenty-piece units that employed the full range of saxophones, brass, and occasionally strings. While each band had its own cachet, all featured hot soloists and a "name" out front: in the 1930s, the bandleaders were the pop stars. It was a time—the first, last, and only?—when popular music and cutting-edge jazz were one and the same.

In New York, Arlen met the great black bandleader Fletcher Henderson, one of the first to utilize this new style of section writing. Impressed with the twenty-one-year-old kid's orchestrations, Henderson asked Arlen to create some arrangements for his band. It was high praise for the young man from Buffalo; Henderson's smooth, carefully arranged sound was a huge draw and an influence on all the swing bands of the era. Henderson occasionally arranged music for Broadway, and playing piano at rehearsal for the dancers was one of Arlen's favorite pastimes. One day he was fooling around with a riff to keep the dancers interested, and he stumbled on something catchy. Songwriter Harry Warren heard it and immediately introduced him to Ted Koehler, a lyricist, who added some words. The result was the song "Get Happy," and when it went to number one on the charts in 1930, all the doors in New York opened for Arlen. But unlike other writers who headed to Broadway at the first sign of success, Arlen took his success up to Harlem, becoming the in-house composer for the Cotton Club revues. He loved spending his time uptown, listening to Duke Ellington, James P. Johnson, and Fats Waller at Connie's Inn, Small's Paradise, and the Cotton Club, where all the vaudeville and Broadway show musicians hung out. After the shows, there were many after-hours clubs in Harlem where musicians jammed and Harold was in heaven. One can imagine this slick young Jewish kid fresh out of Buffalo hanging out in Harlem, befriending the great jazz musicians, sitting in, seeing the women in their ermines and pearls.

Arlen was drawn to jazz from the beginning, years before he seriously studied the show music of Irving Berlin, Jerome Kern, and George Gershwin, although he was well aware of their songs and had done arrangements of them for the band. The music historian Alec Wilder finds Arlen unique in that unlike his contemporaries, he remained hip-deep in jazz ("one of the few writers I can think of who have any emotional kinship with the jazz musician and his bittersweet, witty, lonely, intense world"). The harmonic structure of "Get Happy," for example, is all about the II-V-I chord progression (as in Gershwin's "I Got Rhythm"), but then Arlen shifts the progression up an interval of a fourth for the second A section. It's a musician's move, an improviser's move; indeed, it was created by a jazz musician improvising for dancers. (Gershwin himself once congratulated Arlen on the song's innovative structure.)

Perhaps this allegiance to the jazz life is what made Arlen such a favorite up in Harlem. Some referred to his approach as "color-drenched." Harburg later noted that "Harold is a very, very melancholy person. Behind every song Harold writes is a great sadness and melancholy. Even his happy songs. You take a rousing song like 'Get Happy.' Sing it slowly. Examine it. It's *painful.*" It was, Harburg continued, at the heart of Arlen's style, an overwhelming dramatic feel that went beyond mere songwriting; it was a quality that moved audiences—to tears or to laughter—beyond the realm of the ordinary pop song. The list of compositions Arlen crafted over the years reads like the greatest "only the lonely" moments in American music: "Blues in the Night," "The Man That Got Away," "Come Rain or Come Shine," "One for My Baby (and One More for the Road)," "Ill Wind," "Last Night When We Were Young," and the mother of them all, "Stormy Weather."

At the Cotton Club, his songs were generally conceived and written for specific entertainers, and even though the shows were plotless revues, the thought that went into them was similar to that of a Broadway show. For the *Cotton Club Parade of 1933* Arlen was writing a blues for Cab Calloway to sing, but Calloway left the show before Arlen could present him with the song. He was replaced by Duke Ellington, who had no vocalist in his band. However, the singer Ethel Waters was back in town and although her career had been fading—she had spent two years in Chicago working for Al Capone, which froze her out of many New York venues on her return—she was now back, at liberty and loose ends. Within months, "Stormy Weather" (the song Arlen had been working on) had become her vehicle, not just an enormous commercial hit but a signature song that captured her blue mood in a way no explanation could.

"Singing that song at the Cotton Club," she said, "I was telling things I couldn't frame in words. I was singing the story of my misery and confusion, of the misunderstandings in my life I couldn't straighten out, the story of wrongs and outrages done to me by people I had loved and trusted." On opening night, April 6, 1933, the audience demanded she sing the song twelve times in a row. Like most of Arlen's compositions, the song had an unusual structure, extending the standard thirty-two bars to thirty-four and opening with an odd three-bar phrase, rather than more expected two; the second A section (the repeat of the verse) had an additional two bars tagged on, ten altogether instead of eight. When questioned by Alec Wilder about the unusual structure, Arlen said, "I didn't count the measures till it was all over. That was all I had to say and the way I had to say it. George Gershwin brought it up and I didn't know it. He said, 'You know, you didn't repeat a phrase in the first eight bars?' And I never gave it a thought."

Throughout his career, Arlen broke many of the accepted rules of song form—such as skipping the standard musical repeats in "Stormy Weather" because "it wasn't necessary" to the melody—and in the tradition of his father's cantorial style, he allowed his songs to stretch and breathe by building in extra measures where he felt they were needed. It was considered revolutionary at the time, and indeed it would be unusual even today. Yet his songs are among the most popular of the period. Interestingly, Arlen never spoke of hits: "He talked only of good songs. He simply didn't equate quality with sales . . . he loved the creative act for its excitement and fulfillment."

By December 1933, the era of the Cotton Club and the Harlem speakeasy was over. Prohibition had ended and alcohol was for sale legally all over town; without the sin, there was hardly any point in the fashionistas from the Upper East Side making the trip farther uptown. Even the star performers, including Ellington and Calloway, were playing downtown. It was then that Harburg persuaded Arlen to leave New York and move to California. It was clear that the combination of Harburg's social conscience and Arlen's faith in the unexpected musical solution would create something special in Hollywood. Only time would tell just how special.

In Los Angeles, Arlen and Harburg moved into a house together and got jobs writing for films. By 1934 they had become members in good standing of the elite fraternity of theater songwriters. It was a community that held its members to high standards. "I write for my peers," Harburg said. "In fact, our tribe of songsmiths always wrote for our peers . . . we got together every week, usually at the Gershwins . . . we'd hang around George's piano, playing our latest songs to see how they went over with the boys."

If the laid-back West Coast culture provided no hard edge on which they could hone their skills, the small community of New York Jews used each other. Yip and Ira would get together regularly to trade rhymes and page through dictionaries to find clever new ways of expressing themselves; they were, in their own way, as competitive as rappers in Los Angeles today. Home movies from the collections of Harold Arlen and George Gershwin during this period indicate that "the boys" included more than just their fellow songwriters, Harry Warren, Ted Koehler, Richard Rodgers, Sigmund Romberg, Irving Berlin, Jerome

Kern, and Jay Gorney; this creative mélange welcomed the musicians Oscar Levant, Arnold Schoenberg, Eddie Cantor, and Harpo Marx, as well as the writers Irving Shaw, Lillian Hellman, Moss Hart, and Dashiell Hammett. Thus did an enclave of creative refugees from New York weather the economic storm, playing tennis, taking up painting, trading stories, and churning out a few great works of art amid the (mostly) bland Hollywood fare.

Whereas the boom years of the late twenties had seen more than forty Broadway musicals produced in a season, the bust years of the early thirties saw the number cut to roughly a dozen. But in Hollywood, the production of musicals remained fairly constant, particularly after Warner Bros. released *42nd Street* in 1933, which helped revive the genre. Songwriters traded in their prestige and autonomy for the income. It was a deal with the devil, and many never recovered. Like the others, Arlen and Harburg longed to return to New York, and when Harburg's idea for an antiwar musical was accepted by the Shuberts, the two booked train tickets east. Before leaving for Manhattan, they called on their ailing neighbor George Gershwin. When it was clear things weren't working out for him at the home he shared with his brother, Ira, they offered him the keys to their place. On July 4, 1937, Arlen, his wife, and Harburg boarded a train for New York City. One week later, on July 11, Gershwin died at Cedars of Lebanon Hospital.

With Hollywood musicals pandering to the lowest common denominator and Broadway musicals searching for any denominator at all, the heartbeat of American popular music fell once again into the hands of the "third coast" organizations, the managers, bookers, publishers, promoters, and gangsters back in Chicago. At the same time, the jazz music and musicians that came out of that city were ever more reliant on the songs of Harold Arlen, George Gershwin, and all the others for their character, tone, and popularity. Without the standards at the heart of the repertoire, jazz could never have achieved the vast popularity it did in the 1930s. The best songs, the ones jazz improvisers favored, were the standards written for Broadway and the movies (the "book" songs), and the fact that they were already well known to the public made it possible for the average person to follow along and admire the advanced improvisations of the jazz musicians. Just as jazz had influenced the composers of the Great American Songbook, so now jazz was being sustained *by* the Great American Songbook. It was another example of the symbiosis that has made American popular music so resilient.

Similarly, the popular jazz music of the "swing era" relied on both black and white innovations. Contrary to popular myth and received wisdom, jazz was not and never has been a strictly black form; it is an American music, and during the 1930s, the cross-fertilization between blacks and whites was everywhere and inestimable. Louis Armstrong, for one, cheerfully listed (white) trumpet player Bunny Berigan as his favorite, and even though the races (and the musicians) often occupied two different worlds, the music was a world unto itself. There, black and white skin color was subsumed into who could play and

OVER THE RAINBOW

who could not. Ultimately, American music either has no color or it is all colors, as the bright white light before the prism of society refracts it into separate bands.

The New Grove Dictionary of Jazz states that "it cannot be emphasized too much that jazz music was seen initially by the mass American audience as dance music." The beginning of the swing era is often dated to the night of Benny Goodman's extraordinary success at the Palomar Ballroom in Los Angeles: October 31, 1935. Of course, in the preceding years, there were thousands of places for dancers to hear the big bands, and hundreds of big bands performing across America. What was notable about Goodman's band, and the others during the swing era, was the combination of skilled arrangers, virtuoso musicians, and a new beat that came out of Chicago in the years prior. As rhythm always presages social change in America, the smooth four beats to the bar of the swing bands (like the well-lubricated pistons of an Oldsmobile V8) made dancing to jazz a respectable middle-class activity, as opposed to the raucous grinding that had passed for dancing a decade earlier. But it was the "jitterbugs"—the legions of young people who went wild at swing concerts and invented the new dances that the media loved to photograph—that delivered enough cachet to attract still more media, which attracted still bigger crowds.

Benny Goodman, the son of Jewish refugees from Poland, was just a boy of sixteen when he was hired by drummer Ben Pollack to join his band in 1925. Pollack himself, born in Chicago to a wealthy Jewish family, was among the first of the Chicagoans to make a name for himself with his own big band, which featured gifted young soloists including a trombonist named Glenn Miller—who, like Goodman, would go on to become one of the most important bandleaders of the swing era—as well as both Jack Teagarden and Jimmy McPartland. Pollack's band was built on the inspiration of these soloists, with informal head arrangements (casual riffs generated by the various sections) rather than formal orchestrations. When Goodman, McPartland, or Teagarden was featured, each played as long as he wanted to, with the rest of the orchestra playing rhythm behind the solo. "When they were tired, we'd end the piece with a riff and that was it," remembered one member of the band. The technique anticipated the looseness and freedom of the Count Basie band by a decade. Sometimes called the "Father of Swing," Pollack deserved the title not just because he was the leader of one of the earliest swing bands but also because, as a drummer, he personally helped invent the new swing beat that propelled the big bands to great commercial success. He is one of the men who invented the groove that has been passed down to us today, from swing to rhythm and blues, from rock to funk, making American popular music unique in the world.

His memory of how the swing style came about is fascinating in its revelation of the often mundane roots of musical innovation. Up to this point, jazz drumming had involved a lot of fancy stickwork on small instruments like woodblocks, cymbals, and the occasional tom-tom, in part because the "group" concept of arranged "section" music was in its infancy, and in part because in early acoustic recording sessions, drummers had to avoid hitting anything too large or too hard for fear of knocking the delicate cutting stylus out of its groove.

"One night," Pollack remembers, "a master of ceremonies complained that all the 'fancy stuff' was throwing off one of the variety acts. So I just played rhythm, and the guys were so amazed with the easy way they could swing, they wanted more drumming like it. So I discovered the secret of solid drumming, that is, to feed rather than overshadow—to send the other guys rather than play a million different beats."

Pollack's innovation, which became known as "the Chicago beat"—four equally demarcated steady beats to a bar—was embraced by blacks as well as whites. It would be the hallmark of the Count Basie band a decade later, and it was already in place in New York by the time Louis Armstrong arrived to play with Fletcher Henderson's big band. Pollack's invention was actually made possible by yet an earlier innovation of another Jewish Chicago drummer, Victor Berton (born Victor Cohen), who was older than Pollack and had actually played with the March King, John Philip Sousa. He came on the scene back when the drummer's top cymbal was suspended on a leather thong and mounted atop the bass drums. One could use it for the occasional accent or "splash" but not for keeping steady time. Berton devised a vertical rod on which the cymbal could fit and fixed it in place with a nut so that the drummer could swing a steady beat. In addition, in a burst of inspiration, he mounted two small cymbals together facing each other on a vertical rod and connected them with a spring device. Using a foot pedal, he could whack them together on after beats, providing a rhythmic counterbalance to the heavy first and third beats marked by the bass drums, a kind of "boom chick" effect. The device, which he called a sock cymbal, eventually developed into the modern high hat. Both the swinging top cymbal and the high hat have been front and center on virtually every popular recording in the past seventy years, from jazz to blues, pop to country.

As the economy tightened, the Ben Pollack band eventually moved to New York City, where they got work playing for Broadway shows. The trumpet player Red Nichols, also from Chicago, hired Benny Goodman and Glenn Miller to play in the pit orchestra. By the early thirties, Goodman had become well established in New York. As the musician-historian James Maher remembered, "The thing about Benny that was so great was that it was kind of an explosion in a way. He showed up on the scene, completely unknown as far as we were concerned. We knew Ellington, we knew all the other big names, and here was this kid nobody had ever heard of. And overnight, this guy walks into the American parlor with jazz by the scruff of its neck. And all of a sudden, jazz which was almost a cult music has become American popular music. And that's what Goodman did."

The actual details of Goodman's rise to fame are a bit more interesting. In the summer of 1934, Goodman was leading a band at the Billy Rose Music Hall, a huge restaurant on Broadway run by a promoter of that name but in fact backed by the mob, which featured vaudevillians and dancers. Goodman had no band when he booked the job, so he was always scrambling, first to throw a band together, then to get a "book" together. He had no arrangements, and in fact had no idea how to conduct an orchestra, but he knew all the musicians in New York and, so the story goes, whenever he would run into one of them on the street, day or night, he would implore them, "Hey, you got any arrangements I can use?" Within a couple of months, the band became quite good. Then Billy Rose went off to Europe to discover new acts, and while he was gone, the real owners of the club (the mob) decided that it was all over for both Goodman and Rose. By chance, however, on the last night of the Billy Rose engagement, a man came in from an advertising agency and heard Benny, and he invited him to audition for an extraordinary thing that nobody had ever tried—a three-hour radio show made entirely of music.

Goodman won the audition, and the *Let's Dance* radio show soon made him famous across the country. One night, Benny was talking with his friend, the singer Mildred Bailey, and Mildred said, "Benny, the band sounds just great. One problem—it sounds like everybody else. Just sounds like a good band. You've got to have a personal identity." And out of the blue she said to him, "Why don't you get a Harlem book?" Record producer John Hammond, who was part of the historic conversation, contacted Fletcher Henderson to write the arrangements for Goodman. The combination of Goodman and Henderson changed the history of jazz, both for their marvelous original compositions and because Henderson began focusing on arrangements of popular tunes rather than just original swing things.

These were songs, according to Maher,

> that we all knew, that we whistled, that we sang in the shower generally and had a lot of fun with. So that this was our language. It was not an esoteric language being played by six guys in a cellar somewhere. This was popular music. And as far as I'm concerned, song is the windchime of memory and these were our songs. They were part of the daily ordinary and this I think is what took Benny over the gap, out of jazz, into the American parlor. He arrived with "Blue Skies." Well we knew "Blue Skies." I mean everybody knew Irving Berlin so that we were home free. This is our guy.

Goodman's version of "Blue Skies" was actually a big enough hit on the radio that Irving Berlin himself came out to hear the band. Notoriously unhappy with anybody who messed around with his melodies, Berlin told Goodman after the performance, "That was the most incredible playing I've ever heard. . . . *Never* do it again!"

Goodman is also famous for being one of the first white band leaders to hire black musicians, again through the influence of Hammond, who steered him toward guitarist Charlie Christian, vibraphonist Lionel Hampton, and pianist Teddy Wilson. Black and white musicians had been playing together in recording studios for a long time, but when Goodman put Teddy Wilson right in the middle of the stage, it generated a lot of controversy. The combination of these unique players and Henderson's arrangements made the Goodman orchestra something special. Henderson's arrangements of popular songs, like "Honeysuckle Rose," "Night and Day," "Crazy Rhythm," and "Tangerine," combined with originals like "King Porter Stomp" and "Superman," helped to create the identity of not only the Goodman band in particular, but also the swing style in general.

Despite everything, the Goodman orchestra's first national tour in 1935 was not particularly well received. In retrospect, the reason was obvious: his appearance on the *Let's Dance* radio broadcasts occurred too late at night late for high school and college students on the East Coast, who were more apt to like hot jazz music but needed to be up early for school, and the band was met with still more ambivalence as it traveled throughout the Midwest. The Goodman tour was largely unsuccessful until it hit the West Coast. There, the three-hour time difference had enabled many of the kids to tune in to his broadcasts, and when the Goodman band arrived at the Palomar Ballroom they were greeted by hundreds of adoring fans. What was to have been the end of the road for the Benny Goodman big band suddenly became the beginning of a new journey for American popular music: that night, October 31, 1935, when the band launched into a hot Fletcher Henderson arrangement, the crowd rushed the bandstand, cheering and dancing. It was a reaction that would be repeated thousands of times all across the country.

With the headlines talking about the success of the Benny Goodman big band in California, magazines like *Down Beat* and *Metronome* began to print more articles about the new swing music. Soon live radio remotes featuring swing bands popped up coast to coast as nearly all the major hotels in large cities had a "wire," a line installed for broadcast transmission. Jukeboxes were blaring swing, kids were dancing to it, record jockeys were spinning it: the big band era had arrived. And Benny Goodman, a myopic Jewish bar mitzvah bocher from Chicago, was its Elvis.

Coast to coast, at the same moment, everybody in America, blacks and whites, ordinary folks and music fans alike could check out the new music on the radio. It was a unique national moment, a cultural coming together around fully integrated, artistically challenging arrangements of current pop tunes. Even the legendary Count Basie remembers, "No matter where we were every Saturday night, we'd have to hear Benny Goodman. . . . That was a wonderful band . . . a listening thrill." Ironically, some of these same arrangements had done nothing for the Henderson band when they first played them a few years before, but this has often been the case: a black arrangement in the hands of a white band has often been the key to opening doors in America's music business. On the other hand, a decade or so later, Dizzy Gillespie would report that the advanced idiom of bebop, led by Gillespie and saxophonist Charlie Parker, was supported essentially by white college kids, and that the modern music had been a bridge too far for much of the black nightclub audience, where bands needed to play more rhythm and blues to keep their audiences happy. Integration worked both ways.

After Goodman's dramatic success, many other musicians who had been working as sidemen started their own bands. It was a race to the booking agents as bands led by the Dorsey brothers, Glenn Miller, Bunny Berigan, Lionel Hampton, Harry James, and Gene Krupa hit the road. Count Basie's band—also discovered by John Hammond on a live radio broadcast—came to New York from Kansas City. Radio was the great equalizer; you couldn't see what color the musicians were, so race became even less significant to the listening audience. Radio created a magical public place where everybody was having fun together and the "theater of the mind" was expanding nightly.

By 1935, an estimated 23 million homes had radios, with a total audience of 91 million. This was the "Golden Age of Radio," when comedies and dramas such as *The Shadow*, *Amos & Andy*, *Fibber McGee and Molly*, and *The Lone Ranger* were at the peak of their popularity. Advances in recording technology, and in particular microphones, were changing the way Americans could hear both recorded music and radio broadcasts. These new pieces of hardware captured subtle nuances for the first time and made for better live broadcasts as well as recordings. Advances in the actual discs too were being made in the 1930s; a new vinyl resin had replaced shellac to create quieter records, and lacquer-coated aluminum discs came into use in the recording process. The result was not only a quieter surface but also, for the first time, a disc that could be played back in the studio so musicians and engineers could hear what the music sounded like and make adjustments on the spot. These advances had a major part in the spread and success of big band music. Recordings played on the air could now sound almost as good as live broadcasts.

Both the musicians' union and the record companies initially opposed playing records on the radio, fearing that people would stop paying for what they could get for free, but gradually they relented, and local programs, without the resources to hire live musicians, began resorting to "disc jockeys" to spin the latest new releases. The most famous was Al Jarvis from Los Angeles, whose *Make Believe Ballroom* format was taken up across the country. It soon became obvious that playing records on the radio only increased both the musicians' popularity and the sales of recordings.

Then, in 1933, the Wurlitzer Company introduced the jukebox. It became hugely popular, virtually ubiquitous. By 1936, you could find one wherever people gathered to listen to music or dance. By 1939 there were a quarter of a million of them in speakeasies, ice cream parlors, even drugstores from coast to coast. Mostly, people were listening to big band swing music; the jukebox was at least part of the reason that record sales began to show a tremendous increase toward the end of the decade. It was also a new point of entry for the crime syndicates into the music business, and they quickly came to control the manufacture and placement of jukeboxes. This in turn ultimately affected what music was stocked and even how long the songs lasted: arrangements got shorter so that kids would have to put more nickels into the machine. Many times, artists were told to speed things up in the recording studio. Soon songs were restricted to three minutes, then two minutes and forty-five seconds. By the end of the decade, many jukeboxes were set to cut off at two and a half minutes—the needle would just lift off the record—so that the kids would have to put in more coins to keep dancing.

Like all musical fads in America, swing music was spread by high school and college kids. Any new piece of social commentary was cause for a new song: in New York a dance known as the Lindy hop (named after Charles Lindbergh's famous transatlantic flight) sprang up at the Savoy Ballroom and swept the nation. During tough economic times, a big band could still draw hundreds (sometimes thousands) of young dancers who not only got a sense of their own strength in numbers but drove still more musicians out on the road to service their demand. By the mid-1930s, Jules Stein and Chicago's MCA agency controlled as many as 80 percent of the country's most popular bands and booked virtually all of the big-band venues. "The one man," said noted bandleader Guy Lombardo, "who probably more than any other solidified the business and hastened the era of the Big Bands was Jules Stein. He had started his Music Corporation of America in Chicago and to that city gravitated bands from all over the country, seeking the buildup and engagements they would get if MCA took them in the fold." Not surprisingly, Stein's control, like the spread of jukeboxes, was facilitated by his connection with the Chicago mob (run by his pal Al Capone), and by the fact that Stein had James C. Petrillo, the president of the musicians' union, in his pocket. Petrillo allowed MCA to develop radio shows and book the talent for the shows, giving Stein a virtual lock on the development of the swing era. Stein's biggest star throughout the decade, however, was not swing's Elvis—Benny Goodman—but another Jewish clarinet player. His name was Artie Shaw, and his story, more than any other, is the story of the Jewish crisis of identity in America during the 1930s.

Born Arthur Arshawsky on New York's Lower East Side in 1910, the future Artie Shaw moved with his family to New Haven, Connecticut, when he was seven years old. It was there that his life changed dramatically.

"I learned," he said, "what it means to be a Jew." In Manhattan, his family was just another immigrant family on the block; in New Haven, he felt like "a curious kind of undesirable alien. . . . I had no idea what 'kike' or 'sheeny' meant, or 'Christ-killer'; I did sense quite unmistakably that these terms were designed to hurt, to give pain and humiliation. So that at the age of eight, I became introverted, slightly withdrawn. . . . I drew into a little shell, a coat of armor of outer toughness." In other words, from the moment he realized that being a Jew made him different from others, he suddenly became very different from himself.

"From that moment on," he recalled,

> I was no longer the same kid I had been before. Not only not the same kid, but changed in a certain, specific way, in a way that I don't believe could possibly have occurred otherwise. This one lesson had more to do with shaping the course and direction of my entire life than any other single thing that has happened to be, before or since. I had to resign myself to the truth: for no reason and through no choice of my own, I was a Jew, whatever that meant, and a Jew I would remain until the day I died.

What was the life-changing event that confronted him with this ultimate source of injustice? On his first day of school in New Haven, when he said his last name, some of the kids laughed. Later that same day, out on the playground with the other kids, he spotted a line of ants going in and out of an anthill. Having never seen ants before in New York, he called the other kids over and excitedly pointed out his "discovery." Of course, having grown up with ants, the other kids ridiculed him, and they started calling him "Columbus Arshawsky."

"To me, it was horrible, unendurable, unbelievable. I could not accept it. I was shattered." That day he realized "there was something terribly wrong with me, that I was 'different' from other kids, a strange kind of creature called 'Jew.'" That's it. Ants. Discovering ants changed his life. What is interesting is that in his autobiography, Shaw leaps from the incident with the ants to the Holocaust in two paragraphs. In the end, being a Jew is a matter of many things large and small; it's not the size of the affront, it's the size of the news and what one does with it. Shaw turned it inward.

His father was an immigrant who spoke mostly Yiddish and ran a clothing business, which he eventually lost. In New Haven, the contrast between his father and all the other fathers was dramatic. "He was a foreigner, a Jew, he spoke with a heavy accent which seemed shameful . . . my fear and shame of my father made me feel guilty, which made me fearful and hateful of myself. This being impossible to live with, I had to transform it, transfer it outside myself, project it onto him. Which intensified my self-hatred." When his father eventually deserted the family, Arthur felt like a double outcast: outcast as a Jew and outcast within the Jewish community, because Jewish men just didn't abandon their families.

Throughout his life, he himself remained confounded that a shy introverted Jewish kid named Arthur Arshawsky should wind up "in a vortex of exhibitionism . . . a sort of weird, jazz-band-leading, clarinet-tooting, jitterbug-surrounded Symbol of American Youth during an entertainment era characterized by the term 'Swing,'" a publicized symbol called Artie Shaw, which was nothing but a label for a commodity, nothing more than a brand name, rather than the commodity itself. He had achieved the ultimate alienation from his original self.

He remembers as a boy searching for some way "out of" his life and determining that he needed four things: money, success, fame, and happiness. He said he chose the weapon that appeared to hold the best chance to accomplish his goals in a hurry: a saxophone. At age thirteen (in 1923), he played hooky from school and went to a vaudeville show.

"I saw an act accompanied by a small orchestra," he remembered, "which sat right up there on the stage—unlike the regular pit band. These stage musicians were something. . . . The clincher came when, along toward the middle of the act, one of the musicians, all dressed up in a blue-and-white striped blazer, came down to the footlights, knelt down on one knee (looking sharp as a tack and rakish as all get-out) and played a tune named 'Dreamy Melody' on a shiny gold saxophone." One can sense his feeling of hope, of possibility, of escape in that single image of a jazz musician.

At fourteen he got his hands on a C melody saxophone and won a five-dollar prize; amazed that money could be earned so easily, he decided to make music his career. He spent long hours listening to recordings on an old phonograph. He practiced "like a madman." By the time he was fifteen, he was getting little gigs with local bands. The matter of Jewishness kept troubling him, so he decided to skirt it. Not, however, without a good deal of guilt. In fact, "I carried this guilt around inside of myself for a great many years," he said, "until it eventually began to permeate everything that happened to me in such a way as to make it impossible for me to enjoy whatever success I was later to achieve."

His was a dramatic sense of internal exile, not unlike the dislocation that his father had experienced or a parallel to what was going on in Europe at the same time, but on a microscopic scale. He changed his name. "Why remain Arthur Arshawsky? Why not change it to a shorter name? I never allowed myself to think about the basic reason I wanted to change it: that I was ashamed of my name; I was ashamed of being a Jew."

"In those days," Amos Oz quotes the chilling memory of his aunt, "all the Poles were drunk on Polishness, the Ukrainians were drunk on Ukrainianness, not to mention the Germans, the Czechs, all of them, even the Slovaks, the Lithuanians and the Latvians and there was no place for us in that carnival, we didn't belong and we weren't wanted. . . . We had a terrible sense of modesty. We were buried under a mountain of shame and fear." Oz recalls his aunt's unfettered emotional release upon emigrating to Israel:

> I can't describe how all at once the joy rose up in my throat; suddenly all I wanted to do was shout and sing. This is mine! All mine! It really is all mine! It's a funny thing, I'd never experienced such a strong feeling before in my life, of belonging, of ownership, if you know what I mean, not in our house, our orchard, the flour mill, never. Never in my life, either before that morning or after it, have I know that kind of joy: at long last this would be my home, at long last here I'd be able to draw my curtains and forget about the neighbors and do exactly as I pleased. Here I didn't need to be on my

> best behavior the whole time, I didn't need have to be shy because of anyone, I didn't have to try to make a good impression on the Gentiles.

For Jews, home was always defined in context of what the gentile was thinking.

Artie Shaw didn't look Jewish so he decided to pass into gentile society. He hooked up with a bunch of musicians a little older than himself and started traveling with them. Soon he discovered several were anti-Semites. He never revealed to them that he was Jewish. "For the time I stayed with them," he said, "I was a gentile . . . I lived with them as one, my name was as Anglo-Saxon as any one of theirs, and in the end, I almost came to believe I *was* one. . . . There was always an underlying sense of guilt."

He traveled, hidden within himself. He moved to Cleveland (where two Jewish nebbishes his own age named Jerry Siegel and Joe Shuster were inventing their own escape route); he stayed three years, met a girl, fell in love, then left her behind to go to California. He was running toward something and running away from it at the same time. Like Amos Oz, he was searching for a sense of return, of release, of belonging.

The year was 1929. On the way to California, he stopped in Chicago. It was there, through the influence of players such as Bud Freeman and Frank Teschemacher, that he began to understand the potential offered to him by jazz. One night, at 4 a.m. at one of the marathon dance contests, Teschemacher revealed to him the secrets of jazz improvisation. "He had this odd style of playing," Shaw said of Teschemacher,

> even while he'd be reaching out for something in his deliberately fumbling way, some phrase you couldn't quite see the beginning or end of (or, for that matter, the reason for in the first place), there was an assurance about everything he did that made you see that he himself *knew* where he was going all the time. And by the time he got there, you began to see it yourself, for in its own grotesque way it made a kind of musical sense, but something extremely personal and intimate to himself, something so subtle that it could never possibly have had a lot of communicative meaning to anyone but another musician, and at that only to a jazz musician who was pretty "hep" to what was going on.

Jazz was a world of insiders, open only to those who could step out of the mundane world, who could use this music to discover themselves in real time—a perfect solution for the alienated young man from New Haven.

And then he heard Louis Armstrong play live at the Sunset Cafe. "You cannot imagine how radical he was to all of us," he said. "Revolutionary. He defined not only how you play a trumpet solo but how you play a solo on any instrument. Had Louis Armstrong never lived, I suppose there would be a jazz, but it would be very different." Before he even got to California, then, Shaw was a changed man; he believed that jazz music—in its open-ended opportunities for invention, for self-discovery, for changing an aspect of the world—could be his way out.

Shaw eventually worked his way back to New York. By the time he arrived, only twenty years old, he had switched to clarinet and become one of the world's greatest practitioners on the instrument. It was said that whereas Benny Goodman was a technician, Shaw was a genius. One observer wrote, "Shaw's shading, tone and phrasing were singular, and unlike any other, before or since. Listening to Shaw, one can imagine that one is hearing not an instrument so much as an alien human voice. No clarinet player has ever created such an aura of command on the instrument."

Life in New York was disrupted one day when he got the news that his father had died. Despondent that he had not been there, even more racked with guilt than usual, he got into his car and went for a drive through the streets of Manhattan. And then the unthinkable happened: by accident, he struck and killed a man crossing the street.

His whole life was pulled out from under him. He was thrown into a funk that he couldn't get out of. He couldn't play any more. He wandered the streets. "I used to feel like a man standing outside a house looking in through the window at a gathering of people dancing, laughing, talking, and I would get a sense of the warmth inside, but where I stood it would be cold and dark and I would shiver and shudder inside my skin. No matter what I did I couldn't find a way to break through the sheet of glass that separated me from the life on the other side." Shaw recalled "furtive excursions into the twilight world of New York's dim dark recesses." "At length," he remembered, "I found my way to Harlem. . . . There I found temporary haven, a place to light for a while. Also, I found a friend."

The friend was none other than Willie "the Lion" Smith. The Lion was a complete original, and, from a harmonic standpoint, far ahead of most of his contemporaries. Sitting in with the pianist gave Shaw "the one thing I needed to fill in the emptiness of my life at that time, a sense of *belonging*, a feeling of being *accepted*." Just like Mezz Mezzrow before him, Shaw found himself reborn in black America. "I was actually living the life of a Negro musician," Shaw said, "adopting Negro values and attitudes, and accepting the Negro out-group point of view not only about music but life in general. In fact, on the few occasions when I was forced to realize I was a white man, I used to wish I could actually *be* a Negro."

He eventually was tried and found not guilty of manslaughter in the accident. Still, he felt deeply culpable, perhaps more so than if he had been found guilty. "I felt trapped, helpless, bitter, desperate, enraged, like a wild animal in a snare, ready to gnaw off its own leg to gain freedom." He enrolled at Columbia University to study literature, history, and philosophy, to expand his knowledge of the world, to escape from his current situation, perhaps in some way to reach out to his father. "I began to live two separate and completely different kinds of lives. One had to do with the music I played, through which I continued to pay the rent. The other, and this was for me by far the more important life, had to do with a thing called learning."

Coincidentally, in the summer of 1935, a concert was being staged at the Imperial Theater to explore the hot new music called swing. Approached to participate along with a bunch of bigger names, Artie decided to do something different. At the time, he was getting together with a string quartet and playing some of the Mozart quintets for clarinet. He liked the sound of clarinet and strings, so he wrote something for that sound in the jazz idiom. It was the first time such a concert had ever been given in New York City. Up to then, jazz had always been regarded as a functional music, good enough to dance to but not to be taken seriously. Here was this revolutionary concept : that swing music—a popular American idiom—was something to be *listened to*. Artie had a slot in between a pair of big bands. His performance proved to be a sensation, in part because it was such a quiet contrast to the loud ensembles that preceded it, and in part because the audience was mostly insiders in the music business, just the crowd who could (and did) make Shaw well known. By the next year, 1936, he was leading his own big band. It was then that he made a choice that would affect him almost as much as that colony of ants: he started to figure out how to make a hit record.

As he would remember, "The thing that each of these hit records had, it seemed to me, was a crystal-clear transparency. Not only in the recording, but in the arranging as well. You could hear every single last instrument on the record. The arrangement itself was simple; as a result even a lay listener could see all the way though the surface of the music right down to the bottom. As when you look into a clear pool of water and see the sand at the very bottom of the pool. And from there on, that's what I tried to get every arrangement to sound like." It was the formula of Irving Berlin—keep the music simple—and it was the shortcut to acceptance by the masses.

In 1938, Shaw signed a recording deal with RCA. The first record was a high-powered version of the song "Indian Love Call" with Tony Pastor on vocal. Everybody around RCA thought it was a hit. On the other side, he put a nice little Cole Porter tune that had died a fast death after a brief appearance on Broadway in a flop musical called *Jubilee*. "I had just happened to like it so I insisted on recording it at this first session. In spite of the recording manager, who thought it was a complete waste of time." It was called "Begin the Beguine," and it, not "Indian Love Call," became a monster hit.

This was his big commercial break. His income shot to $30,000 per week, and he was transformed into something entirely different from the guy he had been. It took him several years to realize what had happened; being a big name was a full-time job. "People began to point at me in the street, ask for my autograph, stare at me, and do all the nonsensical things people generally do with those they themselves have put up onto the curious pedestal erected for these oddities, these freaks, these public 'personalities' who have achieved success." It went on for months. At one point, during an appearance in the Fox Theater in Philadelphia, he was informed that on the first day of the week's engagement, there had been such a drop in attendance at the Philadelphia schools that the

Board of Education lodged a formal complaint with the police. After the first show, when he tried to leave his dressing room and go outside for a breath of air, he found the whole street packed with kids. Traffic was completely halted, and mounted police were trying to keep order.

He was making a fortune. He found he couldn't adjust to all the fame and money. He understood that the only thing that made him worth all that money was the publicity. It had little to do with him as a person or the actual music he was playing. He started to ask himself, "Whatever happened to being a musician? What's music got to do with all this stuff?" He was trapped again, disappearing into that place where appearance meets reality. "I believe I was about as utterly miserable as a fellow can possibly be and still stay on this side of suicide." By 1939, he had called the jitterbugs in his audience "morons" in the press. He had written articles in the music press condemning the entire music business.

The problem with looking at commercial music as art, he wrote, is that

> Popular music has little or nothing to do with musical values at all. It's fundamentally functional—just one more form of entertainment—and the music is only incidental. A man who makes his living leading a dance band hasn't too much time to concern himself with musical values. His main problem has to be whether the dancers are able to dance to his music. If so, good . . . but basically, it has nothing to do with musical values. And if a man happens to be the kind of guy who wants to play real music, he's likely to get into serious trouble. Far more so than the man who regards music as a strictly business matter and goes about it in a businesslike way and unemotionally and detachedly gives his customers what they let him know they want.

Then, in November of that year, during an engagement at the Hotel Pennsylvania in New York, he simply left the bandstand, went back to his room, packed his bags, and disappeared. He turned up in Mexico. He said that he had felt like "a sideshow freak, gaped at and stared at and pawed at by thousands of 'fans' wherever I went . . . and he just couldn't take it anymore." *The New York Times*, reporting on his hasty departure, said, "Any commentary that might occur to us would be lost in our sense of admiration at the Shakespearian sweep of Mr. Shaw's exodus; the kind of spectacularly irreverent farewell to his work and former associates that even the timidest soul must occasionally dream of, a beautifully incautious burning of all his bridges behind him."

But he hadn't burned all his bridges. In fact, he became even more famous for quitting the music business in such a grand manner and at the top of his game. He stayed in Mexico for a while, living near Acapulco, where one day he heard a song called "Frenesi." In a move of impassioned ambivalence, he returned to the states and recorded it with a thirty-two-piece orchestra, and it became his second major hit. This time he seemed to surrender to the success, and he moved to Hollywood, where he married a string of glamorous women, including the movie stars Lana Turner and Ava Gardner—eight wives in all. Why did this shy, introspective, troubled man return to show business, the one activity he knew he despised? In his autobiography, he asks himself the same question, and his answer is both tragic and perceptive: "for the very reason that show business is one of the best ways he can find to prove to himself that he is what he believes he is: unworthy, undesirable, unacceptable."

"I think he enjoyed the attention he got from disdaining fame even more than he did the fame itself," said his friend Gene Lees. "It was as if quitting the business had become his life's work." Not wanting to belong to a club that will have you is one thing; hitting yourself over the head with that club nightly is quite another. Shaw often claimed that he did not set out to be a public figure, that he really wanted to become a writer and studio work was just his way of financing his studies. Another close friend, however, speculated that "Artie was ashamed of being a clarinet player. He wanted to be a writer because he thought it was a higher art. Artie didn't want to write; he wanted to *be* a writer." Perhaps, at root, Shaw, like the good Jewish boy he was before moving to New Haven, simply wanted to make his father proud of him; he wanted to be an intellectual.

In Shaw's experience, it is clear that the otherness of the Jew need not be on the cosmic or historical scale—sometimes it is as small as a colony of ants—but otherness drives the Jewish identity nonetheless. By definition, perhaps, anybody who turns to show business is escaping from something. Even people with great talent don't succeed unless they have the overpowering need to succeed, and Shaw made it big; it was disingenuous for him to claim he wasn't driven by fame and public acceptance. Music may be an escape, but the music business is a destination. To enter this world—the world where music becomes a commodity and the musician himself is bought and sold—is to trade everything for a home in the popular world: to be one of the masses. By definition, that's what stardom is, and the drive for stardom is never casual: even Bob Dylan must stand naked sometime.

Shaw started out at age seven feeling like a failure and a freak and then, millions of dollars and a few short years later, became a success and felt like an even bigger freak. He waited his whole life to tell the people who finally accepted him to go to hell, a hollow victory inasmuch as he never liked them anyway. He spent his life trying to be loved by the wrong people, thus guaranteeing his status as an alien, and although a lot of misery came with it, it was ultimately a kind of success.

Shaw himself took the last word on the subject: "I prefer to invert the old phrase, 'if you're so smart, why ain't you rich?' and make it, 'If you're so wise, why ain't you poor?'" It was a statement of ultimate alienation from both the American public and the American dream. In the end, Artie Shaw was an alien in his own country, his own culture, and his own body.

So who was a Jew during those times of spreading poverty and creeping anti-Semitism? One interpretation could be found in the comic book hero from Cleveland, Superman, a nebbish on the outside but a keeper of the common man on the inside and a mensch to boot. Shaw was Superman's mirror image, a hero on the outside, but inside, a crippled self-conscious Jew, guarded and alone. In the midst of the Great Depression, with poverty spreading at home and terror spreading across Europe, fantasy was often easier to process than reality.

A case in point: in 1937, just as Hitler was gathering his forces, the Walt Disney company released *Snow White*, a feature-length cartoon fantasy; it became wildly successful, and some of the songs from the cartoon ("Whistle While You Work," "Some Day My Prince Will Come") made it on the radio charts. All of Hollywood was abuzz about the profit potential in full-length fantasies, especially ones that catered to the full demographic spectrum, from kids to grandparents. The search was on, and for the Metro-Goldwyn-Mayer studio, the answer lay in a curious book by L. Frank Baum called *The Wizard of Oz.* But it was Yip Harburg who took this little opus from straight-out fantasy to allegory, from a children's cautionary tale to a morality play for all ages. In the end, *The Wizard of Oz* proclaimed that home was not some far-off place but a quality within yourself, and the goal of life was to accept who you are and what you have. In Harburg's cosmology, "There's no place like home!" was more than a geographical longing; it was an affirmation that being a Jew in America meant, once and for all, that one was obligated to come out of hiding, to accept the real world and build on it rather than bury one's head in the sands of time. Philosophically, it was the ultimate refutation to Shaw's attempt at self-definition.

Harburg literally put the rainbow in *The Wizard of Oz* (it did not exist in Baum's original text) to frame the question of facing life head-on. "Eugene O'Neill took five hours to say in *The Iceman Cometh* that man cannot live without illusions," Harburg said. "My own belief is that man cannot live with them." In and amid the clever songwriting ("The Lollipop Guild," "Ding-Dong the Witch Is Dead," "If I Only Had a Brain") are dozens of reminders that we are responsible for our own soul even as we are obligated to look after one another. Take, for example, the penultimate scene, in which the Wizard hands out awards to the intrepid band that slew the wicked witch. To the Cowardly Lion he gives a medal to represent courage; to the Tin Man, a testimonial to his large-heartedness; to the Scarecrow, a diploma for a Doctorate of Thinkology to signify graduation from advanced study. "I devised the satiric and cynical idea of the Wizard handing out symbols," Harburg said, "because I was so aware of our lives being the images of things rather than the things themselves." He seems to be asking, in the modern world, how one maintains the delicate balance between knowledge and faith. In the context of Baum's little rural fantasy, Harburg had gone Talmudic.

The Wizard with his fake awards tells us that we already have everything we need within us, that we are both the problem and the solution. What does the wizard hand out?

Recognition of caring and compassion—and isn't this what Dorothy and her brave little band have had all along? Throughout their adventure, each of them is dependent on the others, all connected through their hopes and fears, a unity against the evils of a world that often makes no sense. Theirs is not just a wild hope or a casual belief in goodness, but the courage to enter the darkest woods together, to *lek lekah*, to actually go, perhaps not in spite of their frailty but because of it. Harburg's greatest invention was clothing this universal yet very Jewish message in a story about a little girl from Kansas, where the ratio of Jews to gentiles was approximately zero.

Yip suggested, very early on, that the picture needed a fully integrated score. That is, song and dance, far from interrupting the plot (as was common practice), would actually be the medium through which plot unfolded and character was delineated. It was a daring proposal. In 1938, only a handful of musicals on Broadway, chiefly the Kern-Hammerstein *Show Boat* and the Gershwin *Of Thee I Sing* political trilogy, as well as a few films, had taken this form.

"I loved the idea of having the freedom to do lyrics that were not just songs but *scenes*," he said. The central forty-five minutes of the film, in which Dorothy and Toto land in Oz, are introduced to the Munchkins, and then follow the yellow brick road, is one long musical exposition. Music not only tells the story but lends a kind of believable magic to the proceedings. Yip's inclination became inevitable as in time it fell to him to pull the story together. As usual, there had been numerous rewrites of the script, and ultimately Yip had become the de facto editor as well as the lyricist. Handed the assignment, he told Arthur Freed, the producer charged with piloting the project through the studio, "Give me time and let me think the thing out musically and lyrically. Let me write a score for the thing that will tell the story and then we will hang some of the best scenes on that score." Remarkably, Freed went along with Harburg, in part because it was obvious that *The Wizard of Oz* was a new kind of animal and nobody had gone down that particular yellow brick road before. Ultimately, the film owes its unity to Freed's decision to let Yip take control of the story and tell it through the music.

The story of the song "Over the Rainbow" itself reveals a great deal about the Hollywood process that Harburg and Arlen survived. Their contract was for fourteen weeks, and they were on their fourteenth week and still hadn't written what they considered the film's key song. Arlen had been agonizing over the song for weeks. Then one day, while driving down Sunset Boulevard with his wife behind the wheel, he asked her to pull over and, right there in front of Schwab's drugstore, he took out a pencil and paper and wrote down the beginning of the melody we all know today. By late that evening he had completed the music for "Over the Rainbow." The song still had no title. He excitedly called Harburg to tell him the good news, and even though it was midnight, Harburg came over immediately. At first, Harburg thought the song was too grand for the character. Arlen played it, Yip later recalled, "with such symphonic sweep and bravura that my first reaction was, 'Oh, no, not for little Dorothy!'" They decided to play it for Ira Gershwin and have him decide. Gershwin listened, then told Arlen to play it less operatically, and suddenly Yip "heard it" in a new way—as a poignant ballad that mixed simple, childlike imagery with a deep-blue feeling of longing.

It took several days for Harburg to come up with the rainbow image and the simple words that told the story of a young girl longing for a better place, but from there a narrative emerged that seemed to have been there all along. Harburg then wrote the dialogue leading into the scene, setting up the song as both a seamless expression of a young girl's alienation and a brilliant filmic transition from black-and-white to color. It was Harburg's rainbow image, after all, that gave the producers the idea of having the first part of the movie in black-and-white so that when Dorothy is picked up by the tornado and deposited "over the rainbow," she arrives in a Technicolor Munchkinland. Finally, Judy Garland (née Gumm, great-niece of Harry and Albert Von Tilzer) delivered the song with such feeling that it became the dramatic hinge of the whole film.

Only the studio didn't think so. Some in the front office felt it created too slow a moment too soon in the film. Others thought it was too depressing, too odd, to see a "love song" being sung in a barnyard to a dog. Still others thought the big octave leap at the beginning of the song ("some . . . *where*") made it unsingable. Subsequently, when the film was first screened, unannounced and unbeknownst to Harburg and Arlen, the song and the scene had been cut from the film. They were dumbfounded.

"Harold and I just went crazy," said Harburg. "We knew this was the ballad of the show; this is the number we were depending on. We went to the front office; we went to the back office; we pleaded, we cried, we tore our hair out. Harold ran to *shul*! There wasn't a god around who could help us. Finally Arthur Freed went to Louis B. Mayer and pleaded with him . . . L. B. Mayer was very kind to Arthur Freed and said, 'Let the boys have the damned song. Get it back in the picture; it can't hurt.' So the song went back in the picture and of course you know what happened." What happened was that when the film was released the following year, the song won the Academy Award.

The year was 1939; Hitler had just invaded Poland, and the film *Gone with the Wind*, depicting the ravages of war, was the biggest draw at the box office. Roosevelt vowed to keep America out of the war, but the world was spinning faster than he could control, and people needed something more than fantasy—they needed hope, they needed something to believe in. Ultimately, this is what popular music is and what it does. Searching for common footing, Americans found it in a little song that had been written back in 1919. Back then, its author felt that it wasn't good enough and had put it back in his "trunk" for later. The song was "God Bless America," and its author, Irving Berlin, gave it to a popular radio singer named Kate Smith to perform during her Armistice Day broadcast. The vast reach and immediacy of network radio, combined with the emotional turmoil of both the Depression and the war in Europe, propelled the song directly into the national psyche; a few months after Smith sang it, the song was sung at both the Democratic and Republican conventions. If Congress hadn't voted a few years earlier to make "The Star-Spangled Banner" the U.S. national anthem, "God Bless America" would surely be America's anthem today. It is by far the most singable, patriotic, and hopeful musical vision of America to date. It would also be a kind of poetic justice if a Jewish immigrant had authored the national anthem, not about war but about plenitude, not about greed but about gratitude. The song told Americans why they had "nothing to fear but fear itself."

"God Bless America" might well be the last page of the penultimate chapter of the Great American Songbook. And although many more good songs would be written in the years to come, those composed during the first four decades of the twentieth century—by Berlin, Kern, Gershwin, Arlen, Rodgers, and their many contemporaries—continue to define American popular music and indeed popular music around the world. This "songbook" set the bar and defined the way we know ourselves as a people.

"Those people, their use of language shaped our use of language," said the composer Alan Bergman. Then, casting a jaundiced eye on today's media spokespersons, he said, "If you want to know what's wrong with the grammar of the television news writers and announcers [today], listen to the songs *they* grew up on."

STRANGE FRUIT

Barney Josephson, a Jewish immigrant from Latvia, had been thinking about opening a nightclub in New York for some time, both to make money and create a convivial scene. As a shoe salesman living in Trenton, New Jersey (until the Depression shut the family business down), he had become a jazz fan on his sales trips to New York, where he regularly caught Duke Ellington at the Cotton Club.

"One thing that bugged me about the Cotton Club," he said, "was that blacks were limited to the back one-third of the club, behind columns and partitions. It infuriated me that even in their own ghetto they had to take this . . . I wanted a club where blacks and whites worked together behind the footlights and sat together out front." When Josephson opened the Cafe Society in Greenwich Village in 1938, it was known as one of the first nightclubs in a white neighborhood to welcome customers of all races.

He was further offended by "the mugs, the gangster-looking people with policies of clipping and padding checks" who, it appeared to him, ran most nightclubs. "Why can't the nightclub business be legitimate, like shoes?" he asked his ex-partner in the shoe business (and coincidentally an active member of the Communist Party), his older brother, Leon. Josephson borrowed a few thousand dollars to open his club and gathered neighborhood artists to paint murals on the walls. "I told them," Barney said, "I was going to open a political cabaret with jazz—a satire on the upper classes. You guys paint anything you want." His music adviser and talent scout was John Hammond, who, having discovered Billie Holiday, encouraged her to work at Josephson's club for much of its initial year.

Cafe Society ("The wrong place for the right people") was not alone in its atmosphere or intention. In 1936, several years prior to Josephson's club, a Jewish immigrant from Lithuania named Max Gordon had opened a New York joint called the Village Vanguard, a tiny underground hole in the wall on Seventh Avenue South. It eventually became the most famous jazz club in the world, but in its early freewheeling bohemian phase, it was a room where anything went: poets like Maxwell Bodenheim performed alongside the classical baritone Guilherme Mascato; a Jewish singer-comedian named Judy Holliday and the black folk singer Josh White both worked the room often; and satirical revues featuring Betty Comden and Adolph Green were a regular offering. Like Josephson, Gordon found the typical nightclub owner anathema and "never even wanted to look like one." He dressed modestly and always negotiated fairly with the talent.

"He loved jazz; he was a beautiful man," said musician Milt Jackson. "Because of that, [the club] was intimate. He treated musicians honestly and was always there to hear us play." These rooms, the Cafe Society and the Village Vanguard, were intimate, honest, *heimish* spaces, cultural living rooms in the best sense, and very different from the flashy gangster-driven venues uptown. They had a basic authenticity about them: they were on a human scale, not pretending to be larger than life.

The Village Vanguard would go on to become so celebrated that a Japanese investor once offered to purchase the space for a million dollars with the intent of taking it apart brick by brick and reassembling it in Tokyo (it was, after all, just a hole in the ground with some modest furnishings). The Cafe Society, on the other hand, faded into history without leaving much of a trace. And yet what happened there moved a lot of history, maybe more history than all the glitzy stage shows of that year put together.

It all began with a simple meeting at the club one cold February afternoon in 1939, attended by Josephson, singer Billie Holiday, and two Jews on a mission: Abel Meeropol and Milt Gabler. That day, Holiday and the others were meeting to discuss her recording a particular song—not just any song, but a song with a tremendous political agenda, an antilynching anthem couched in popular-front politics called "Strange Fruit." Meeropol, a teacher at DeWitt Clinton High School in New York with a Harvard education and a socialist bent, had written the song and originally published it as a poem entitled "Bitter Fruit." Shortly thereafter, Meeropol began to lobby Holiday to record it. She had the perfect black voice to deliver the message.

The lyrics to "Strange Fruit" sketch a highly graphic portrait of race in America:

> Southern trees bear strange fruit,
> Blood on the leaves and blood at the root.

Whereas the previous generation of Jewish song writers had imagined a bucolic South as a stand-in for their own lost roots, Meeropol represented black Americans in a more realistic fashion: his "pastoral scene of the gallant south" included

> Black bodies swinging in the southern breeze,
> Strange fruit hanging from the poplar trees.

Meeropol touched some very deep and painful roots with his song, just as writers like Marvin Gaye would do decades later with songs like "What's Going On." Billie herself was apolitical, and initially, wary about doing such a highly charged piece of material, she turned Meeropol down. After much cajoling she agreed, and, getting strong public support for the material, eventually presented it to the A&R people at Columbia Records. They (including John Hammond) promptly rejected it as far too controversial.

But Meeropol had spoken with Milt Gabler, an enterprising young music fan who had recently started his own record label, Commodore Records. At the meeting on that February afternoon, Gabler, only twenty-seven years old, offered to record the song for Commodore. Two months later (April 20, 1939), Holiday recorded "Strange Fruit," and Gabler's label had its first major hit. It was the perfect marriage of art, commerce, and social conscience.

The song itself was instantly controversial. Within months of its release, it was banned at radio stations all across the country, which only increased its notoriety, and in 1940, its author was called in front of a committee searching for Communists in the New York City Teachers' Union to defend it (apparently its antilynching sentiment set off an all-points alert). From the start, people assumed that Billie had written the song, and she did little to dispel the idea, or, alternatively, claimed that the song had been written specifically for her. (It was in fact written a full year before she and Meeropol met.) Many anthologies of Negro songwriters have included the name Abel Meeropol (aka Lewis Allan) on their lists. Musical patrilineage aside, the song itself became such a powerful symbol of black consciousness that after Billie died in 1959, singers such as Nina Simone and Carmen McRae carried the song forward into the social protest and freedom movements of the 1960s. In many ways, the song helped start those movements: for years, the NAACP used it to raise consciousness and funds; in the 1960s, Angela Davis, the minister of education for the Black Panthers, used it as a model for her own musical polemics; and it is still being performed today in rap and activist contexts.

Pete Seeger, talking about the power of music, said, "A short song can have as much impression on a listener as reading a whole novel. The song is a triumph of oversimplification, you can hear it often and not tire of it. Sometimes singing a song can be a reaffirmation of a feeling"—and sometimes it can be a way to literally recreate the original feeling. In the year 2000, *Time* magazine picked "Strange Fruit" as "the song of the century."

Abel Meeropol's name went on to become even more controversial in the 1950s when he adopted two children, Michael and Robert Rosenberg, the sons of Ethel and Julius Rosenberg, who were arrested and executed for espionage in 1953. The boys were just seven and three years old when they were introduced to the songwriter by the great African-American philosopher W.E.B. Du Bois; subsequently they and the composer of the "song of the century" slowly faded into the history books. Milt Gabler, on the other hand, although virtually unknown outside the music industry, went on to change the face of popular music by presiding over the birth of what has become known as "rock and roll." Ironically, it was around the same time that Abel adopted the Rosenberg children that Gabler's work dropped its own strange fruit, but by then the two men were living in very different worlds.

Milt Gabler got his start in the music business working at his family's appliance store on East Forty-second Street, across from the Commodore Hotel. The store sold radios and radios played throughout the day in the store, the better to sell them; Milt, who had discovered jazz as a teenager, put a loudspeaker through the transom of the front door to lure passersby. When people began asking about the music that was playing, Milt persuaded his father to put in a line of records. Coincidentally, at the same time, the major record labels such as Columbia and RCA were cutting out their jazz and "race" music and were more than happy to sell their stock to Milt. At the bottom of the Depression, Milt was also able to sell jazz classics from Paramount, Gennett, and Okeh, and when the Okeh label was finally discontinued in 1935, Gabler bought most of the inventory for a dime a disc. In time, Milt went into the manufacturing business, leasing selected masters for release under his own imprint, "United Hot Clubs of America." The UHCA label is credited with being the first real indie record label in the country (even though the "hot clubs" in question existed only in Milt's mind). Next, Milt began selling records through the mail (the first known mail order operation in the record industry), and he became so successful that the labels stopped licensing the sides to him altogether. And so, in January 1938, he began recording his own jazz music on the new Commodore label.

Four months later, Billie Holiday's "Strange Fruit" would put Commodore on the map. Milt's nephew, the comedian Billy Crystal, remembers Commodore as more than just a jazz label. The record store out of which it was run became a kind of combination library, museum, and hangout for like-minded jazz fans. It was "jam-packed with exciting material, photos. It was always crowded with people who knew what they were coming for." Although the whole family worked at the store, it wasn't about the money either, he remembers. It was about something more important, something captured by the release of "Strange Fruit."

"When I think about the courage it took to make this record," recalls Crystal, "this wasn't about making a hit. This wasn't about capitalism. This was about humanism. This is about civil rights. . . . Here was this plump little Jewish guy who saw the truth in those lyrics. And after everyone said they didn't want to record it—including John Hammond—Milt said 'Let's do it.' So that's part of his character—do what's right for people, we're all the same and music makes us more equal." Milt Gabler was also the first man to print the names of the musicians on the labels and liner notes, giving credit to the people who actually played the music. He was by nature, an egalitarian.

"A recording is a living thing" was Gabler's watchword, and the Commodore experience would galvanize a whole generation of record men who would in turn shape the music business for generations to come. Among the fans who hung out at Gabler's store and revered its proprietor were Alfred Lion, George Avakian, Bob Theil, John Hammond, and a kid from the Bronx named Jerry Wexler. After business hours, Milt would lock the doors to the store and the real party would begin. "We were a new cult of record collectors," remembers Wexler, "relentless in pursuit of our Grail. . . . Musically, even metaphysically, I was learning lessons about timing and patience. The marvel and mystery of great jazz was becoming clear—the point where relaxation and stimulation, cool and hot, meld together." (It may or may not be relevant to note that at the same time, Wexler was discovering marijuana, and "it was no ordinary stick, but one rolled by Mezz Mezzrow himself. Mezz's joints were rolled with a perfect six-corner tuck. Just as Picasso signed his name on the lower right side of his canvases, the hexagonal fold was Mezz's signature, known wherever jazz was played.")

Gabler extended his musical reach by organizing jam sessions, integrated parties open to the public, that introduced a generation of New York kids to "hot jazz," improvised small band music that was both modern and magical. These sessions were held at the

Central Plaza, a large room where young kids would come to dance to Dixieland, or at Jimmy Ryan's place, where, as Wexler remembers, "the music was the thing, and when a musician was building a solo, you never heard a sound from the audience. You could feel them listening. The place was always packed and for sixty-five cents you'd hear Jack Teagarden, Sidney Bechet, Joe Sullivan, or the ethereal Billie Holiday singing 'Fine and Mellow,' weaving a spell over the smoky Sunday afternoon."

Because he was a master at finding and reissuing obscure jazz records, Gabler was hired in 1942 by Decca Records to oversee their reissue program, quickly moving up the ranks to become head of Artist and Repertoire. That meant, in effect, he was now able to produce the artists he loved for one of the major record companies, one with its own "franchise" record stores. These were "authorized" retail outlets that sold only product from the major labels, not the small independent ones. Gabler's productions were now available everywhere records were sold.

Decca was something of a newcomer: the third major label (after Columbia and RCA Victor), launched in 1934 by Jack Kapp, a Jewish entrepreneur from Chicago, who focused on inexpensive pop records. Decca was known for their 35-cent record prices (as opposed to the 75 cents Columbia and RCA charged). At the time, jukeboxes consumed 13 million records a year, and, with an eye on that business, Kapp began signing performers no one had ever heard of, including Ella Fitzgerald, Jimmy Dorsey, Woody Herman, and Glenn Miller. But Decca did not have the money that Columbia and RCA Victor did, so they were forced to do everything on the cheap.

"They had to buy used equipment, and some of the wax they put on it looked like it had been reused about eighty times," said musician Woody Herman. "We used to cut the masters on this heavy machine, wheel them in boxes and every time you finished one tune, they had to go out for a fresh batch. It was all pretty basic. Some of the other companies were going ahead and developing, particularly RCA and Columbia, with all their massive appliances and scientists and people on their staffs working on sound and everything. We were just trying to make a record that wasn't warped before it was pressed. Jimmy Dorsey used to say, 'For God's sake, when are you going to put the hole in the middle?' They were always off center." In fact, it was believed that Decca records intentionally had more surface noise or "hiss" because Kapp didn't trust radio (why give the music away for free?) and purposely made his records noisier to keep them off the air.

Nonetheless, Decca managed to put together a string of successful pop artists, led by singer Bing Crosby, and became a major player in the record business during the forties. When Gabler joined the company, they picked up much of his Commodore talent roster, including Billie Holiday, Eddie Heywood, and Eddie Condon. At Decca, Gabler was able to record Louis Armstrong with Ella Fitzgerald and venture into pop productions by Peggy Lee and the Ink Spots. But in terms of his historical impact on popular music, his most important work of the period was with a singer / saxophone player named Louis Jordan.

With songs like "Saturday Night Fish Fry," "Caldonia," and "Choo Choo Ch'Boogie," Gabler began to invent the meld of music that, a decade later, would drive the rhythm of rock and roll. This was small format music, groups consisting of a guitar (the electric guitar had just been invented), piano, bass, drums, and a horn or two. The grooves were protean shuffles (dotted eighth notes recalling the left hand of boogie-woogie piano players), with a walking bass and horn shout choruses (à la Count Basie's big band arrangements). Jordan's swinging approach to the alto saxophone was a perfect complement to his smoky voice and his sly, streetwise lyrics.

In the early 1940s, this music was hard to label: they called it jazz, jump music, swing, blues, or race music. Call it what you wanted, it was adult music made for a primarily black working-class audience, and what sold in black communities would soon make its way into the consciousness of white teenagers everywhere. Nobody liked the term "race music" any longer, but it would be several years before Jerry Wexler, working for *Billboard* magazine in 1949, would coin the now classic label "rhythm and blues" for this amalgam of black idioms.

Wexler's renaming the music was very important: it brought respect and credibility to this music. Even though "race" wasn't equated with racism, it definitely was a repositioning of an "outcast" music in the music business. After Wexler renamed it, it was taken seriously by the trade publications, and once *Cashbox* and *Billboard* start taking it seriously, then the companies began to take it seriously as well. And as the companies started investing a little more money and promoting artists who had never been promoted before, suddenly one started hearing these songs on the radio. So Jerry Wexler's renaming of the idiom was no small thing.

Unlike rock and roll a decade later, this music was not toned down or prettied up for young people. The subject matter was drinking and sex: Amos Milburn's "Bad, Bad Whiskey," Joe Liggins' "Pink Champagne," and Stick McGhee's "Drinkin' Wine Spo-Dee-O-Dee" are only a few examples. Also, as opposed to rock music, which would be a rehash of urban precedent and country aesthetics, this music was clearly from the black side of the big city. Other popular black groups at the time, like the Ink Spots and the Mills Brothers, may have had a black sound, but they sang essentially white songs. Not Jordan. His songs were all about partying in the hood, and his supertight sextet would be the model for mean and lean rhythm machines in the future, from Ray Charles to James Brown. Gabler well understood the pleasure principle that often floats black popular music; like Cab Calloway before him, Jordan was a swinging witness to hardworking black folks "having a ball." As he sang in "Saturday Night Fish Fry," "You don't have to pay the usual admission / If you're a cook or a waiter or a good musician." His was the first small group, black or white, to sell out theaters and make it to the top of the charts.

It's not difficult to trace the effect of World War II on this revolution in small group music. The United States officially joined the war on December 7, 1941, following the attack on Pearl Harbor by the Japanese, but had contributed massive amounts of aid and supplies through the Lend-Lease program earlier that spring. During the period before the U.S. declaration of war, German U-boats had sunk several American ships. And while there was still not enough public outcry to go to war with Nazi Germany, there was a global sense of foreboding. In response, one could often find a kind of head-in-the-sand response in the pop culture. Silly songs like "Three Little Fishes" or "Beer Barrel Polka," along with dreamy ballads like "If I Didn't Care" by the Ink Spots, were featured on the 1939 Hit Parade; but as the country moved closer to war, topical items like "Boogie Woogie Bugle Boy" by the Andrews Sisters showed up on the pop charts. Interestingly, the smash hit of 1940, "In the Mood" by the Glenn Miller Orchestra, with its walking bass, side-stick backbeat, and twelve-bar structure, was a taste of the music to come (if the cross stick had been a snare hit, it would have been a Louis Jordan shuffle). As the war approached, big bands still held sway and jitterbugs were still dancing; the bandleader was still the star of the show, while the singers, whether Frank Sinatra or Helen Merrill, sat quietly off to the side waiting for their featured moment. The war years gradually changed all that; after the war, the big band era was over, the singer was the star, and the whole country was in love with the new small band format.

The demise of the big bands can be traced to the military draft, which reduced the pool of musicians dramatically. And the dancing audience too was gradually being thinned out as most of the boys were sent overseas to fight and many of the girls went to work in the factories to pick up the slack. Too, gasoline rationing made it difficult for bands to tour, while a shortage of shellac, now diverted to the war effort, limited the production of records. Then, on August 1, 1942, the musicians' union, led by James C. Petrillo, drove the final nail into the big-band coffin, calling a strike against the record companies and banning recordings by any union musician, except for V-Discs, which were sent overseas to entertain the troops.

Singers, however, were still free to record during this period, and so companies began to focus on them, at first with a capella records, then finding vocal stars. Hence Petrillo inadvertently helped usher in the era of the pop vocalist. Frank Sinatra was a case in point. He had left the Tommy Dorsey Orchestra in 1942 and signed with Columbia in 1943. And while he was not allowed to record any new sides with instrumental backing, his fame was such—due to his appearances on radio (*Your Hit Parade*) and the stage—that he persuaded Columbia to hire Alec Wilder as arranger and conductor for several sessions with an all-vocal group called the Bobby Tucker Singers; these songs went on to become bestsellers.

Some critics see the defining moment in the shift from big bands to singers as Sinatra's performance with Benny Goodman's orchestra at the Paramount Theater in New York on December 30, 1942. "Sinatra was third-billed on the program and although he was America's most popular singer, Goodman had never heard of him. Goodman announced him and the audience roared and shrieked for five minutes. Goodman's response was, 'What the hell was that?' Once Sinatra started to sing, the audience continued to shriek during every song. As one saxophone player said, 'When Frank hit that screaming bunch of kids, the big bands just went right into the background.'"

When the musicians' union strike ended on September 18, 1943, vocalists dominated popular music. Still, this transition was gradual, and popular music appeared to be pretty much as it always had been, driven by great songs from Broadway musicals and the movies; the Rodgers and Hammerstein musical *Oklahoma!* of 1943 generated several hit songs. Considered to be a breakthrough—it won a Pulitzer Prize for its unprecedented unity of story, music, and choreography—its original cast album on Decca marked the first time a Broadway production was brought into the recording studio, and two of the songs, "Oklahoma!" and "Oh, What a Beautiful Mornin'," reached numbers one and two on the pop music charts.

The war didn't end until 1945, but 1944 was a harbinger of things to come. That year, Louis Jordan broke through with his novelty song "G.I. Jive" to arrive on the pop charts, where his name stayed for the rest of the decade. Authentic black music, made by and for black audiences, was gradually infiltrating the American consciousness. A brief survey of the pop charts in 1945, the year the troops came home, reveals that along with Broadway fare like "The Soliloquy from the Musical *Carousel*," Hollywood themes like "Laura" (from the movie of the same name), and heart-wrenchers such as "You'll Never Walk Alone" from Frank Sinatra, there were more than a few flat-out jumpers: "The Honeydripper" by Joe Liggins, "Caldonia" from Louis Jordan, "Tippin' In" by Erskine Hawkins, "Somebody's Gotta Go" by Cootie Williams, and "Who Threw the Whiskey in the Well?" from Lucky Millinder. Clearly the times were changing.

The new music that contained elements of jazz, boogie-woogie, blues, and swing was spearheaded by small independent record companies that often existed in one-room offices. While the scarcity of shellac guaranteed the majors would only spend big budgets in state-of-the-art studios to record their most popular white acts, the demand from black buyers for black records was so great that over the next decade, it generated dozens of these little companies. Some specialized in jazz, others in folk or blues, while still others built their catalogs on this new hybrid, "rhythm and blues." And virtually all of them were owned and operated by Jews.

Their names are now legend in the record business: Hy Weiss of Old Town Records; Art Rupe of Specialty; Syd Nathan of King; Lew Chudd of Imperial; Morris Levy of Roulette; Phil and Leonard Chess of Chess; Herman Lubinsky of Savoy; Bess Berman of Apollo; Moe Asch of Folkways; Alfred Lion of Blue Note; Bob Weinstock of Prestige; Orrin Keepnews of Riverside; Al Green at National; the Bihari Brothers at Modern; Jerry Wexler; at Atlantic, and, of course, Milt Gabler at Commodore and Decca. Some of these companies remained mom-and-pop shops until they were finally bought out or crashed, others grew exponentially and ultimately did the buying (or crashing). Some were run by idealists, dedicated fans of the music, like Blue Note's Alfred Lion; Blue Note grew to become the most important jazz label in the world. Others, like Alfred Green of National Records (who had hits with Big Joe Turner and the Ravens, a vocal group that was the archetype for the great doo-wop groups of the fifties), were simply out to score what they could: Green was an ex-con who was in the toilet seat business and realized that the same plastic injection molding process used to make cheap toilet seats could also be used to make cheap plastic 78 rpm records.

But whatever their motivation, these men and women had something in common: they were inventing a business and a music from scratch. In many ways, it was like the garment industry earlier in the century brought up to date by new technology, with Jews responding to new demands, doing piecework of a different sort. Their overwhelming numbers and the diversity of their intentions seems to speak of something other than mere coincidence.

"How well I remember those labels and the grizzled infighters who owned them," wrote Jerry Wexler. "Imperial (Lew Chudd), Specialty (Art Rupe), Old Town (Hymie Weiss), Herald/Ember (Al Silver), Chess (the brothers Chess), and on and on into the night—memorable logos, all. I am reminded of the tribes of the Sinai desert—the Hittites, the Moabites, the Midianites, the Amorites. Gone, perished, vanished from the face of the earth. Only one survived—the Hebrews." Even Wexler, who was there at the time and survived with the Atlantic Records tribe, felt something inherently and historically Jewish underlying the environment.

On the one hand, Jews were simply trying, as usual, to make a living in an area where the WASPs didn't want a piece of the action. And there was plenty of action there for the taking. So opportunity was again the main driving wheel for Jews entering the ranks of independent record companies. On the other hand, there was a kind of historical affinity operating here: blacks and Jews had been sharing the same neighborhoods for decades. Whereas other ethnic groups had been uncomfortable in the black neighborhoods, Jews were not, and they had often moved in, living side by side with their African-American neighbors, running small grocery stores, clothing emporiums, or bars. Perhaps because Jews had a long history in Eastern Europe of trading among peoples of different backgrounds, they did not resent living in the ghetto in order to make their living. As early as 1911, the *Forward* noted that the typical Jewish grocer in Atlanta lived in the black section, segregated from the white population. Over and again throughout the twentieth century we find examples of Jewish entrepreneurs hanging out at black bars and record shops to find out what music was being requested, and then going out and manufacturing it. And they were tireless: "We used to bring twenty different bands in, said producer Hy Weiss. "Start recording at seven at night and stop at six in the morning. Just keep cutting."

To ramp up the war effort, the government had used posters, editorials, advertisements, every means possible to let the American people know that "we" were all in this boat together, that Uncle Sam wanted "us" to join the fight. People of all colors and classes took up the call, went overseas, and laid down their lives. And if the Jewish cause was not foremost in the minds of Americans as they entered the war, after 1946, when the depths of the Holocaust began to be revealed to the world, Jews took on a kind of symbolic martyrdom that all Americans had survived together. There was a new sense of community, or at least a communal impulse in America, and blacks and Jews shared high social expectations. In the new postwar America, surely they would find acceptance for who they were; there was an outpouring of hope, an authentic affinity operating between blacks and Jews.

We see this affinity and drive for authenticity in virtually all of the men who started the indie record labels, those who did it for love as well as for money. Take for example one of the greatest independent labels of them all, Atlantic Records, founded in 1947 by a Jew named Herb Abrahamson, a true-blue music fan who took a loan of $10,000 from his dentist and joined forces with the son of the Turkish ambassador to the United States, Ahmet Ertegun. Ertegun and his brother Neshui spent their youth in the Washington, D.C., area, much of it in the record store of Waxie Maxie Silverman; it was there they discovered the great black music of their day and began their famous record collection, totaling more than twenty-five thousand titles. Even before starting their own record label, they were motivated to merge their business acumen with their passion; their first foray into the business was a concert they presented at the Jewish Community Center featuring Sidney Bechet and Joe Turner.

Within a few years, Atlantic Records had enlisted the services of Jerry Wexler, then a young reviewer at *Billboard* magazine, to be their A&R man, and by 1953 he had helped the label catch the unique tide of what was to become rock and roll; starting with Ray Charles and continuing for decades, Atlantic was extraordinarily adept at straddling the racial divide and making music that both ends of the spectrum could not only accept but love.

Wexler himself was clear about the why and wherefore of his methods: "I found myself inspired by the artists who, through an unlikely happenstance, I was actually producing. I was in awe of those people . . . and although I was presumably their overseer, they were my instructors. These were the artists who made my career and changed my life, infusing the business blues with a joy transcending all earthly matters." For Atlantic, it was all about the quality of the music and the honest representation of the artist.

On the other hand, we can also find this intense representation of authentic artists in the careers of the men mostly driven by the money. Take for example Hymie Weiss, a rough-and-tumble guy from the Bronx who claims he invented "the fifty-dollar handshake" (a common form of payola). He began his career in 1947 as a bouncer at the White

Rose Saloon at Third Avenue and Thirty-fourth Street: "My job was throwing out whiskey heads from nine-thirty in the morning to six o'clock at night, and between six and six-thirty I washed the floor." He graduated to a job as a salesman for an independent record label called Exclusive, a purveyor of strictly black music. He found himself in a world where the legitimate record stores (franchise stores) wouldn't let him in the front door to pitch his product.

"At that time," he recalled, "you couldn't go into an accredited record shop [to sell them records]. An accredited record shop wouldn't let an independent through the door. Those were authorized shops. [They] only sold three labels: RCA, Columbia and Decca. Later they would sell Capitol too. But they never sold black records. Never." However, there was big business in the black neighborhoods for the records he was promoting. "At that time a regular record shop—for instance Rays up in Harlem—would order five thousand, ten thousand copies of Johnny Moore's latest 78s. You would sell fifty thousand records to like seven stores. Then when you walked downtown [to the franchise stores], they wouldn't even let you in."

It was the musical equivalent of the western frontier. Distributors could be found selling titles they didn't even own; everybody was hustling everybody; it was strictly a tribal, handshake business. Nobody sued anybody else; everybody scratched each other's back. Conflicts among label owners were usually resolved with a few phone calls, because even though they were competitive, there was a shared sense of enterprise. Weiss moved from Exclusive to the Modern label; from Modern to Apollo; from Apollo to start his own operation, Old Town Records (named because of some free letterhead he got from his brother who worked for the Old Town Ribbon & Carbon company). Jewish companies all.

"The whole nucleus of the independent business was black music, black buyers," said Weiss. "If we had to crack against RCA Victor we couldn't do it. Your four labels had the pop market locked. Capitol, Columbia, RCA Victor, Decca. So if you're there and you can't fight the opponent, you find another thing that he's not doing. Come when there was no shellac, the only records they [the major labels] stayed in was the pop field. They gave up the country field, which they moved into when the war ended. But they never moved back into the rhythm-and-blues field. Prior to the war, all the rhythm-and-blues was on Victor and Columbia. But when the war ended, and all these little labels had come along, 1945, '46, '47, and they grabbed off the new rhythm-and-blues artists. And the old guys were old guys. And they never were able to get back into the rhythm-and-blues field. And things changed."

What is more intriguing than the obvious delight Weiss and his contemporaries took in hustling each other is a phrase that he and many others often repeated to establish their true credentials as record men: "I might not know anything else," he said, "but I could always *hear* a record." That is, he felt he had an innate ability to hear what the buyers of this music wanted; he could hear a hit before it was a hit. He had a sense of pride, of participation, as if it was the most important thing in the world: he might as well have said, "I can feel what the people feel—I am of the community." He knew something about the music and the people because he was them and his intuition (his inner hearing) led him on. This characteristic is shared by virtually everybody in the record business: as Bob Krasnow, who eventually became the CEO of Elektra Records, one of the largest operations in the world, once said, "Everybody in this business thinks they're an artist. Even the guy in the accounting department has an opinion on the song and whether there's enough bass on the track." It remains the same to this day, after generations of record executives like Mo Ostin and Walter Yetnikoff and Bob Krasnow have come and gone, Jewish businessmen all, but above all, proud of their ability to hear a song. It is the ultimate badge of communal confidence, of their own authenticity.

So one could say that starting in the forties, Jews and the blacks were communicating on a deeper level—they could *hear* each other—and because it was happening in bars and lunch counters and record stores, it was discounted or dismissed as just "street life." But it was exactly *because* it was "just" street life that it became profoundly important. Because eventually, these men shaped popular music around the world, and the qualities of that music in turn set off a new kind of street life everywhere. (Today, you can go to the farthest corners of the globe, from Tasmania to Timbuktu, and hear local teenagers rapping as if they were standing on a street corner in the Bronx.)

Another small but profound example of this extraordinary synergy can be found in the legendary Apollo Theater of Harlem. Since opening in 1934, the Apollo has exerted an enormous influence on popular culture the world over because the thousands of entertainers who made it there went on to become world famous in swing, bebop, rhythm and blues, modern jazz, gospel, soul, funk, and blues. The Apollo had a reputation for showcasing the latest black music, for being on top of the newest trends, and it represented a cultural living room for the most discerning African-American audiences, a place where people felt comfortable enough to let their hair down. Hence the audience at the Apollo was known as the toughest crowd in show business; if they liked you, they loved you; if they didn't like you, chances are you would not even finish your act.

Playing the Apollo, said Sammy Davis, Jr., "was like playing the Copa [a notorious mob operation]. You didn't go into the Copa lightweight: they'd break your legs. But at the Apollo they'd break your heart." From its inception, the Apollo Theater was run by a Jewish family, the Schiffmans, who also prided themselves on the ability to "hear" the music of the street. And this, too, goes to the question of authenticity.

By the forties, the music business had been drifting further and further from its street origins. How authentic was Irving Berlin writing "White Christmas" in 1943? Or Johnny Marks writing "Rudolph the Red-Nosed Reindeer"; or Sammy Cahn and Jule Styne writing "Let It Snow, Let It Snow, Let It Snow," or Jay Livingston and Ray Evans writing "Silver

Bells," or Mel Tormé writing "The Christmas Song" ("Chestnuts roasting on an open fire")? Jews one and all, turning out songs—great songs—but music as *fashion*, each one a kind of musical Hallmark card depicting a different fantasy of the "holiday season." By the mid-1940s, then, it was like a big coming-out party for Jews; they aided and abetted black music, for better and for worse, but always for *real*. Without them it simply would not have happened. There was something ground-level about these guys in the indie music business, as well as in the music they went after.

The indie record business was invented by one-of-a-kind individuals. Compared with today, record sales were relatively insignificant; sheet music and live performances still accounted for the real revenue. Radio as a mass marketing tool for selling music wouldn't emerge until the fifties. Unlike the record business insiders of recent years—lawyers and accountants all, who try on opinions the way some people try on shirts, finding something that sort of fits or something that's fashionable for the moment—these independent label guys were outsiders, traveling salesmen, each with his own story to tell. They were in show business, alienated from the normal nine-to-five business world. There was something louche, disrespectable, about their world: for one thing, business wasn't conducted in boardrooms, it was conducted at joints like Lindy's, where the comedians took the first table on the left and the promo guys had the second one. This was swinging, hustling, party time, *big fun*. These guys were crude but street smart; they had style, color, lingo, the look: they wore smooth felt hats, double-breasted gabardine suits, big knotted hand-painted ties, ultrasheer rayon socks, always a smile and a story or joke to tell. They were selling themselves. They were part of the narrative.

Occasionally the business itself resembled a street fight, with folks stealing from each other and alliances forming and shifting, and if there were both good guys and bad guys, it was simply further evidence that the question of blacks and Jews working together had moved beyond the polemics of identification—i.e., whether their common self-interest was a result of political or economic conditions and whether it fell within the bounds of statistical methods—to a point where they were literally in bed together. For that's what the record business was, a family affair built around the music. The business relationship between blacks and Jews has always been contentious, in part because of the intensity of this affair, and in part because, when the dust cleared, it seemed the Jews usually wound up holding the assets and the blacks were left holding the keys to a lot of Cadillacs. Hy Weiss himself said, "The Negro is responsible for a lotta white folk making a lotta money." But of course the white folks had invested all the money, at a time when there were virtually no returns; it was still a business, and if it had been a WASP business, people would still have had a lot of trouble getting paid.

So when Jewish record execs are criticized for not paying royalties to black artists—giving them advances instead—it should be recognized that they normally didn't pay royalties to *anybody*, black or white, Jewish or gentile (it was a very democratic system this way).

And if there was a kind of paternalism built into this system, it was a two-way street; artists often came to record executives for extracurricular help, and there was general conflation of personal and professional relationships on all sides.

"They used to come to you whenever they had a problem," said Phil Chess in defense of his bookkeeping practices. "If one had his wife having a baby in one hospital and his old lady in another, they come to you to pay the bills so his lady wouldn't know. They did it almost like a family coming to a father, getting money. It would be an advance royalty. That's what you gave them . . . people forget." One must be careful not to blame the messenger for the message here; in 1942, even Bing Crosby wore blackface in the hit movie *Holiday Inn* (in which he sang Irving Berlin's immortal "White Christmas"), and paternalism was still very much a part of the show business infrastructure.

But the real creative artists in the record business, as in Hollywood, were the bookkeepers. The indie record men were not hiding behind lawyers and their creative clauses as they do today. Back then, "contracts didn't mean nothin'," said musician Ike Turner. "We would play for anybody who gave us twenty-five dollars." It was not a world of iPods and Internet downloads; it was a world of boxes of 78s in the trunk of an old Chevrolet driven by a hardworking promotion man (often the owner of the company) roaring through the Tennessee night on his way to Memphis to give the DJ at WLAC radio a "fifty-dollar handshake." At the time, virtually nobody thought that this strange outsiders' music would make a lot of money—neither then nor in the future—nor even be around much longer. Rock and roll hadn't been invented yet, and this music, call it what you want to—jazz, blues, swing, jump, jive and wail—was something few legitimate businessmen wanted any part of.

In the end, this period of small record labels was not so much about money; there wasn't big money for the indies until much later. And what profit came in was generally plowed back into the business; one had to spend money to grow and had to grow to stay alive. So while the subject of Jewish exploitation of black artists becomes contentious during the 1940s, and while there is no denying that exploitation existed, it is important to remember that at the time, this music, for everybody involved, even the pure at heart, was a highly marginal business. Its subject was money, not skin color, and in America, what often appears to be race-based is in the end reduced to issues of class: black exploitation by Jews was a fact, but so was black exploitation by blacks and Jewish exploitation by Jews; that is, in the "hustle," everybody was looking for the main chance. This is not to apologize for or to excuse bad behavior wherever it existed, but fair is fair: Who could defend everything that goes on in just about any average American family today? And the indie record business was just such an extended family. What may be more significant than the fact that some Jewish record company operators treated the musicians and their work as "made for hire" is that by the 1940s, the Jews in the business were documenting a lot of great music. Even the bad guys promoted good music.

Consider the extreme case of Joe Glaser, who ran nightclubs for Al Capone back in Chicago in the twenties. Before he got into music, Glaser had been eking out an existence as a pimp and quasi-hoodlum, spending much of his time and energy trying to avoid prosecution and jail for arrests stemming from his interest in young girls. When he became a personal manager and booking agent, he became, in Max Gordon's phrase, "the most obscene, the most outrageous and the toughest agent I ever bought an act from." George Avakian, Louis Armstrong's producer at Columbia Records in the thirties, said, "Joe was a professional tough guy. He put on a very tough front. He believed in being pretty abrupt with people because that's the way he got things done. He was coarse. He talked very rapidly and he didn't want to listen very much to anyone else's ideas." George Wein, the contemporary jazz promoter, recalls that "Joe Glaser had this wonderful ability to lie with total impunity . . . [he] didn't care what he said . . . he'd say anything he wanted to say." And these were people who *admired* Glaser.

Another was Louis Armstrong. "I always admired Mr. Glaser from the first day I started working for him," Louis wrote in 1943, thinking back to the twenties. "He just impressed me different than the other bosses I've worked for. He seemed to understand colored people so much. And he was wonderful to his whole show and band. He would give us nice presents." Glaser became Louis's manager in 1935, when they had both fallen on hard times. Louis didn't care if Glaser was a pimp, bootlegger, or racketeer. He had grown up among people like Joe. Louis was to say, "He was a crude sonofabitch but he loved me and my music."

The first thing Glaser did was get Louis out of his exclusive recording deal with Columbia (which was doing nothing for his career) and sign him to Decca, where Armstrong, working with Milt Gabler, began recording some of the best-selling music of his career. Similarly, the vibraphonist Lionel Hampton petitioned Glaser to represent him, and he too went on to career heights. Summing up Glaser's impact, Jerry Wexler put it this way: "He was a fucking gangster, a bad man. But without him they [Armstrong and Hampton] never would have scaled the heights." So in the end, it was obviously possible—and in the music business, often probable—that good things could come from the efforts of bad people. Or, as one *New York Times* reporter put it, "It is an essential paradox of the vernacular arts in America that creative expression can be the byproduct of venality and greed as often as it is of lofty esthetic impulses."

In the process, these Jews preserved the roots of black American culture—not just a white version of black music (although sometimes they did that too), but specifically the music that came from the black neighborhoods. These small independent labels were responsible for preserving a huge spectrum of American music, everything from Thelonious Monk to McKinley Morganfield (aka Muddy Waters), and in the process they helped elevate American street life to the realm of high art. And not just the manufacturing and marketing of this music was in Jewish hands; for example, the modern jazz idiom called "bebop" (after an onomatopoetic phrase that the trumpet player Dizzy Gillespie once sang) was difficult for many jazz fans to comprehend. But Jewish writers such as Leonard Feather, Nat Hentoff, Dan Morgenstern, Ira Gitler, and Nat Shapiro took up its cause, explaining to the average fan just why this new music was important, while Symphony Sid Torin, the famous New York jazz disc jockey—whose signature deep voice and late-night delivery attracted thousands of listeners to jazz, many of whom thought he was black—similarly championed its cause.

Jewish promoters, too, covered the panoply of personality types; some, like Morris Levy, the acknowledged model for the Jewish gangster Hyman Roth in the *Godfather* films, were tied to the mob. Levy was a boyhood friend of Vincent Gigante, the powerful mob figure who played crazy by walking around "Little Italy" in a bathrobe and slippers to avoid prosecution, and ultimately he became the most infamous Jewish gangster in the record business. He started out in the nightclub business at sixteen years of age, setting up darkrooms in the clubs and selling photos to patrons on the spot, before there was Polaroid film. Through this all-cash operation, he wound up not only connected to the crime world but the owner of a club on Broadway called the Ubangy Room. There, in 1948, Symphony Sid Torin and Monte Kay (a Jewish manager of jazz talent) started organizing regular bebop concerts. "We put in bebop on a Monday night, there was a line up the block." Soon the club was featuring Dexter Gordon, Charlie Parker, Miles Davis, and all the most adventurous jazzmen of the day. Renamed the Royal Roost, it was the first all-bebop club in the city. In 1949, Levy and Kay opened up Birdland, perhaps the most famous jazz club of the era and the incubator for much of the small group jazz that followed.

But for every Jewish tough guy like Morris Levy there was someone like Norman Granz, the Jewish promoter who invented the "Jazz at the Philharmonic" format, running jazz shows fifty-one weeks a year and bringing real class to the music by presenting distinguished artists such as Ella Fitzgerald, Oscar Peterson, and Count Basie on concert stages around the world. Granz banned discrimination for his musicians wherever they traveled: "He made you feel like you had accomplished something in your life," said the trumpet player Harry "Sweets" Edison. Indeed, as Dizzy Gillespie once pointed out, without the white college audiences, bebop (a high point of creative black expression) couldn't have survived into the 1950s. And, one ventures to say from personal and anecdotal experience, a large percentage of those white college kids listening to modern jazz were Jews.

Following the war, small independent record companies began popping up all across the United States, devoted to every kind of music one can imagine—Slavic music (the Balkan Record Company of Berwyn, Illinois), polkas (the Cuca Record Company of Sauk City, Wisconsin), country (Sink and Stove Records of Bristol, Tennessee)—a constellation of local and regional operations that were generally underfinanced and overoptimistic. Most of them disappeared within a few years as their ethnic demographic base dwindled or their money ran out, but in the case of rhythm-and-blues music (which had been abandoned by the big three record labels), there were plenty of fans with money to sustain real growth. This music had a huge indigenous following because it was made for working-class blacks, not white teenagers, and large numbers of African-Americans had migrated to northern cities during the war to take defense jobs. In each of these cities, there was likely to be an indie record company pumping out local dance music, jazz, hot blues, and boogie-woogie. These companies were similarly responsible for discovering much of the local talent that was eventually plucked by the majors and blossomed into the modern jazz and teen rock of the 1950s. Because the indies were forced by economics to develop and sell what they found in their own back yards, and aided by advances in technology—the development of reel-to-reel magnetic recording tape and the introduction of 33 1/3 and 45 rpm microgroove records made of vinyl, not shellac—these indies kicked off what has become known as "the Golden Age of Recording."

As with all gold rushes, it started with a lot of people getting their hands dirty and ended with a few survivors getting rich. The world of the indies was both mostly Jewish (by 1948, the word was that Yiddish was the second language of the record business) and wildly improvised. The men who started these companies were usually the producer, talent scout, marketing department, sales force, and booking agency all rolled into one. Eventually, through lucky breaks and hit records, some indie labels grew into major corporations. Of course a hit record could also put a small company out of business just as fast, because while one had to pay the pressing plant and other costs up front, the distributors and retail stores were notoriously slow to pay. So unless your company had a quick follow-up hit by the artist, or perhaps a hit from another artist that the distributors and store owners wanted, your first hit could well be the last record you ever released. But being small had its advantages too; no shareholders breathing down your back or looking over the books, and the ability to react quickly to even the hint of a possible trend. The survivors tell an interesting tale of hustle, fortune, avarice, and the ever-important ability to "hear" a record.

This affinity for popular taste is reflected in the fact that for most of the men who started the indie record business, running a label was the next logical step from an earlier job, such as a jukebox operator, record distributor, or owner of a nightclub or record shop. They had been handling the product, they knew what the audience liked; why not produce it? For the most part, they saw themselves as "record men," not "music men"—this was a business, and music was the product. Syd Nathan of King Records, located in Cleveland, Ohio, is a good example. He started in a record store and went on to launch the careers of James Brown, Hank Ballard, and many other R&B greats, more than five hundred hit singles in a cross-section of musical genres. Unlike Milt Gabler, who also started out in the retail business, Nathan was not particularly interested in the music or the musicians, although he, too, was proud of his ability to "hear" a hit single or to jump in and help write one as well.

Syd Nathan was born in Cincinnati on April 27, 1904, a myopic, asthmatic kid who quit school in the ninth grade. During the Depression he tried many things: drummer in a local speakeasy, pawnshop clerk, jewelry salesman, amusement park concessionaire and wrestling promoter, among other things. Eventually, he opened a small record shop in a poor neighborhood. It was here that he first thought of starting a record company to target the hillbilly market. The first records on the King label appeared in 1943 and were aimed at providing country music records to whites who'd relocated to the Midwest from Appalachia. After the war, he discovered that the rhythm-and-blues market was wide open.

"We saw a need," he said. "Why should we go into all those towns and only sell to the hillbilly accounts? Why can't we sell a few more while we're there? So we got in the race business." Cleveland's proximity to both Nashville (the home of country music) and Detroit (with its large black population) worked well for King.

His first R&B release was "The Honeydripper" by Bull Moose Jackson in 1945. Two years later he had a hit with Jackson's "I Know Who Threw the Whiskey in the Well," an answer to Lucky Millinder's 1944 hit "Who Threw the Whiskey?" Then in 1949, he had two more big R&B successes, Jackson's "Why Don't You Haul Off and Love Me?" and Wynonie Harris's "Bloodshot Eyes," both of which were originally aimed at the country market. Nathan wasn't trying to cross this music over from country to R&B so much as trying to get maximum return on his copyrights, but in the process he was cross-pollinating the two worlds, thereby laying the groundwork for the musical hybrid known as rock and roll.

Looking at his remarkable track record might lead one to think that he was a fan of the blues or a particularly perspicacious follower of race music, but one can discover, in a rare interview recorded in the late 1960s, that this was not the case: "I go on the assumption that nothing is any good; the percentage is one out of twenty-five. Let me see the sales ninety days after they been out and I'll tell you if it was good or not. That's how much of a goddamn genius I am. There are no geniuses."

For Syd Nathan, "good" music was music that sold, and "hearing" a song meant counting the revenues after its release. And yet this man admired James Brown and personally shepherded his career well into the 1960s. One would not be wrong to conclude that the age of the indies and the impending universe of rock and roll was a dramatic departure from what had come before; if the Broadway and Hollywood writers were coming from a point of view of romance and a heightened literacy, these indie Jews were all about business: they put the gold in the Golden Age of recording.

"The record business is not a freak business," Nathan said. "It's the same as being in the coffin business. Or a funeral parlor. Your expenses cannot exceed your income. You got to have low, low expenses. And brother, if you don't believe that people in business are tight with their money, you don't know anything about business." What is ironic, of course, is that the music he recorded and sold is perhaps the most good-time, get-down-and-party, salacious dance music ("Work with Me Annie" by Hank Ballard, "Sex Machine" by James Brown) that America ever produced; the "coffin business," indeed.

Indie record companies and the down-and-dirty small groups they recorded continued to pop up everywhere across the country, mining local veins of talent even as the big bands waned: in the space of just a few weeks during December 1946, eight of the country's most popular big bands, including those of Tommy Dorsey and Benny Goodman, broke up, and although some later re-formed, the big band era was clearly over. This was a sea change in the industry, and the indie Jews were there to navigate the rocky shoals.

In Chicago, two Jewish brothers were clearly on board. By 1911, Chicago had the second-largest Jewish population in the country, and by 1926 it was the third-largest in the world. The vast majority of Jews there had come from Eastern Europe, creating on Chicago's South Side, in an area surrounding the intersection of Halsted and Maxwell streets, their own shtetl of densely packed wooden tenement houses. At the same time there was a parallel black migration to Chicago of roughly 60,000 African-Americans who came immediately after World War I, and another 125,000 who arrived by 1930 to take jobs in the stockyards, railyards and packinghouses. They too moved to the South Side, to the area surrounding the famous "Stroll."

Yasef Czyz (Chess) came to Chicago in 1922, established himself as a carpenter, and then sent for his family back in Motele, Poland. His two sons, Phil and Leonard, arrived in the United States in the fall of 1928. Chicago was a revelation to them. There was running water in the apartment, even a bathroom and a kitchen. For a change, no one in the family had to sleep on top of the oven in the winter, and there was strange fruit: the boys had never before seen a banana or an orange. When the Depression forced Joe out of the carpentry business, he melted down some old candelabra to sell as scrap metal; by 1935, he had a junk shop on Wabash Avenue, a white neighborhood with a sizable Jewish population that bordered on an expanding black neighborhood.

Eventually Leonard left his father's junk business and bought a liquor store in the middle of the black community. Just down the block from the Savoy Ballroom and the Regal Theater, his Cut Rate Liquor store was a natural hangout for musicians. Leonard put in a jukebox, and soon locals were holding informal jam sessions in the store. It was only a short hop from there to opening a bar called the Macomba Lounge. At the time, Chicago was experiencing another wave of black migration from the South—between 1940 and 1950 the city's black population increased 77 percent, from 278,000 to 492,000—and many of these new arrivals were sustained in part by keeping some of the traditions from home intact. As a result of the recent invention of the solid-body electric guitar, and, some would say, the background noise of the urban environment, rural blues musicians were starting to go electric and were moving indoors from the street corners to the clubs. Nonetheless, the music they played was still rough around the edges and at its heart, nowhere near as sophisticated as the urban blues of Louis Jordan or Amos Milburn; it was plugged in and raw, straight from the cotton fields of Mississippi to the slaughterhouses of Chicago.

The music at the Macomba Lounge was just such good-time rocking blues, featuring guitar, harmonica, bass, and drums, reflecting the tastes of a rural population banging up against the honky-tonk streets of Chicago (the electrified harmonica more or less replaced the saxophone in the Chicago blues lineup). Phil and Leonard's first language had been Yiddish, and they fell easily into black street slang; subsequently, their accent, coming as it did from two widely divergent street cultures, was hard to place. The locals themselves were not sure: occasionally, a customer would ask, "Is you black or is you white?" This intimacy with the black culture occurred at the same time black radio was becoming a presence in Chicago; the moment was "a marriage of commerce and culture."

When a friend of Phil's started a record label called Aristocrat, Leonard wanted in and recorded one of the acts that played at his club. Soon, he was on the road, taking his first sales trip to Pittsburgh in a Buick loaded with one hundred copies of his latest record. There, he walked into a hardware store in a black neighborhood that also sold records and put the disc on the owner's turntable. "You got a hit record there," the owner said. "How many would you buy?" asked Leonard. "One hundred," said the owner. From that point on, the Chess brothers were in the business of recording black artists. Virtually everybody thought Leonard was black before they met him because that's the way he talked. "You talked to him on the phone," said Paul Gayton, "you didn't know he was white, because he was around black people all his life."

One of the first recordings on Chess Records was by guitar player McKinley Morganfield (aka Muddy Waters). Muddy had been born in Mississippi on a cotton plantation and had recently come north to Chicago. Together, Muddy and Leonard became the foundation of Chess Records, and the company was built on this convergence of outsiders, the Jewish immigrant from Poland and the black migrant from a cotton plantation in Mississippi. Waters would later say that his friendship with Leonard was one of the things he was most proud of.

"Here was a guy who had blind faith," said Waters of Leonard, "He didn't believe in my blues but he believed in me as a person when we started out. I got a big kick out of proving myself to him as a performer . . . and out of the fact that we became more than business associates, real intimate friends." Their personal affinity was built in part on the fact that the trip Muddy Waters took from Mississippi to Chicago was not unlike Leonard's trip from Poland to New York, only in Muddy's case, the train took the place of the boat and the train station took the place of Ellis Island. At bottom, these two men had much in common.

The records the Chess brothers made had an authenticity to them that couldn't be denied; they had a sound that communicated as much about life on the streets of Chicago as any newspaper could. When one heard the voice of Howlin' Wolf or the driving rhythm of Bo Diddley's guitar or the wail of Little Walter's harmonica on a Chess record, it was like being wrapped in the very social fabric of Chicago's black experience. Yet there was a kind of ease and familiarity about it, reflecting the *heimish*ness of its creation: the Chess brothers made their living *in* the black community, not just *from* it. Although they were not necessarily fans of the blues (they were businessmen, above all), they considered much of the talent like family; Willie Dixon came by whenever he wanted, and Leonard's eight-year-old son Marshall called Muddy Waters "Grandpa."

This music was much less sophisticated than the urban jump blues of Louis Jordan, and that's probably the reason it ultimately became so attractive to young white kids around the world; they were not particularly sophisticated listeners, certainly not as sophisticated as the urban black population of the time. It was, after all, the Muddy Waters recording "Catfish Blues" aka "Rolling Stone" that inspired a young Mick Jagger in England to name his band after the song and to make the Chess recording studio in Chicago one of his first stops on coming to America. There was a connection to something real, something basic in this music that was in short supply in the lives of white teenagers during the fifties, and it wasn't something that you could learn in school. What is interesting is how the music of black America had to *devolve* before it reached large numbers of white kids: the more sophisticated music of Louis Jordan was popular among the working black population but hardly penetrated the white market, while the music of rural blacks that had morphed into the electric blues when it hit Chicago immediately lit up the imaginations of a young white audience.

Take for example the song "Rocket 88" by singer Jackie Brenston, released on Chess in 1951. In many ways, it was similar to the urban jump blues that came before it, but instead of horn riffs, it featured the guitar. Listening to the record today, one hears many of the same conventions used to define protean rock and roll: the bass is really loud, the piano is playing a strict eighth-note rocking pattern, the drummer's backbeat is exaggerated and relentless, and there is virtually no melodic aspect to the lyrics being delivered by the singer, nor are the lyrics particularly important; but there is an undeniably charismatic *sound* to his voice and feel to the groove. In short, Chess was making records that stressed the *sound* and *feel* of the music rather than the details of the production or the sophistication of the lyrics or the delivery. It had to do with a new atmosphere rising in postwar America, in which rawness stood for freedom among young whites.

This idea, that a record label could have an identifiable *sound*, was something new. It may have been due in part to the fact that these indies were cranking out records quickly, often using "house rhythm sections," that is, a stable of musicians who appeared on most of its releases. For them, the sound of the label might be coincidental, the result of working quickly with a limited roster. Too, each small label was shooting for its own demographic niche, for whom the sound was a distinguishing feature; in time, the *sound* became what labels were selling as much as the artist or the song. Occasionally, however, the identifying sound of the label was something carefully thought out, and then, it was often the key to the label's longevity.

There is no better example of this than Blue Note Records, a label that in many ways was the diametric opposite of the Chess experience. Blue Note was the quintessential artist's label, run by a fan who documented the art music of the era, but it too survived on its founder's ability to "hear" into the heart of what would be popular music. It was created in 1939 by Alfred Lion, a German Jew who in 1925, as a boy back in Berlin, happened to stumble upon some American jazz musicians.

"I used to go skating, roller skating," he recalled, "and one day I went there with my skates and they told me there was no skating today. They had a band there and I saw a poster on the wall and it said 'Sam Wooding and His Chocolate Dandies' and I didn't know anything about it but it looked strange to me, different you know. And I went in. And there was Sam Wooding. It was the first time I saw colored musicians. I heard the music and I was flabbergasted, it was something brand new but it registered with me right away. It was the beat, and it got into my boots." Five years later, he began making business trips to New York, and he started collecting records. He was a regular at Milt Gabler's Commodore Records store, known to all the aficionados who hung out there, and in 1938, he immigrated to New York permanently. Within one year, he had established his own record label, stressing certain aesthetic principles that were revolutionary in the jazz recording business.

What motivated him to get involved in the business was attending the famous "Spirituals to Swing" concert at Carnegie Hall in the winter of 1938, where he heard the boogie-woogie piano playing of Albert Ammons and Meade Lux Lewis. They were not being recorded at the time, and it seemed like an opportunity to the young fan from Berlin. On the sixth of January 1939, Lion booked a New York recording studio, purchased a fifth of rye whiskey and a fifth of bourbon, and went in to document the first Blue Note recording session.

His next session featured soprano saxophonist Sidney Bechet's recording of "Summertime," which became the label's first big seller, hailed for its smoky, laid-back feeling. The session was held late at night, after Bechet's regular gig, which contributed to the haunted ambience of the recording. At the time, it was more common for labels to record during the day, when it was more convenient for the studio, but the success of this particular session started a tradition at Blue Note of recording at night, during the musicians' normal business hours. Lion continued to record traditional jazz groups until 1946, when he became taken with the modernism of bebop. By 1944, saxophonist Charlie Parker and his compatriot Dizzy Gillespie had stepped out of the Billy Eckstine big band and had started to record for Herman Lubinsky's Savoy label. This music was modern, adventurous, and self-assertive, and Lion immediately recognized it as the future of jazz. He subsequently began focusing on cutting-edge jazz, eventually recording many of the greats, including the pianists Thelonious Monk and Bud Powell.

Along with bearing the standard for this radical, essentially black-inspired form of improvised music (some would come to call it "America's only native art form"), Lion dramatically changed the way the music was packaged and presented to the public. For one thing, he used designs by modernists like Paul Bacon, Gil Melle, and John Hermansader in the cardboard cover art. Blue Note records became thought of as complete works of art, and they won many design awards. And for the first time, the package also featured full photographic images of the musicians on the cover; today it is commonplace, but that was the first time a black jazz musician had ever been featured on the cover of his own recording.

At first, bebop was a small movement within the larger jazz community, and there was a lot of back-and-forth between the modernists and the stalwarts of swing. In fact, as in all jazz music, the one followed naturally from the other, and in retrospect, there is a smooth line of transition from the jump blues of Louis Jordan, who essentially played a kind of proto-bebop, and Charlie Parker's "Now Is the Time," which itself became the template for the million-seller pop song "Do the Hucklebuck." In fact, this one song may itself be a kind of Rosetta Stone in the transition from jazz to R&B and on to rock and roll. "The Hucklebuck" was recorded by saxophonist Paul Williams in 1949 on Savoy (Parker's own label!), and it went to number one on the R&B charts for fourteen weeks. Parker's "Now Is the Time" was a romping twelve-bar blues with a light touch and a gloriously artistic solo, while Williams's version, built around the sound of a furiously honking saxophone, helped start a trend in R&B that evolved into rock and roll. Williams, a jazz musician from Detroit, where Herman Lubinsky of Savoy heard him and sent Teddy Reig in to produce him, remembers that Reig told him to *honk*: "He kept telling me not to play a whole lot of notes. He kept saying 'Honk! Honk! Honk!'" Whereas jazz was indigenous, captured music, rock and roll was *produced* music, manufactured by men angling for hits.

Still, there was a moment in time when both jazz and R&B musicians carried water from the same well. Jazzmen had grown up playing dance music and they continued to do so; Lionel Hampton's "Flying Home" or Lester Young's "Up and At 'Em" would not have been out of place at the Macomba Lounge. Similarly, one could easily trace a path from boogie-woogie and stride pianists like Willie "the Lion" Smith and Albert Ammons to Thelonious Monk, or from modern blues singers like Charles Brown to both Nat "King" Cole (a jazzman down to his socks) and Ray Charles (who set a new standard for soul music in the fifties). Jazz was simply continuing to cross-pollinate popular music—it would take several decades for jazz to cross a bridge too far, lose its dance roots, and become a kind of classical or art music. But from the forties through the sixties, Lion was there to document this rare cultural universe, curating in real time a music that was both dance music and art music.

What was most impressive was the care he took in doing so. Unlike most other small labels, Blue Note allowed its artists to rehearse before they recorded, making the final result much more coherent and balanced. Lion was willing to invest this time and money to create a better product. But equally important, Lion knew what he was listening for. There was a *sound* that he had in mind. Noted engineer Rudy Van Gelder, who recorded virtually all the early Blue Note sessions as well as sessions for other jazz labels such as Bob Weinstock's Prestige label, said that Lion "was unique at that time in that he had an idea; he pre-visualized or pre-auralized his records. He knew what he wanted before he came to the studio. He had a good idea what a record should sound like, what he wanted it to sound like." It was, continued Van Gelder, a function of who the artist was in the real world: "I'm talking about jazz, where it's an expression of a musician's personality and his own sound, and he's recognizable and he's unique, and you can identify him just as easily as I can recognize your voice or your face when I see you."

In the words of drummer Art Blakey, Alfred "had a black soul" and was "listening for the *black sound.*" And while the music varied and the audiences were diverse, this meticulous search for an authentic black sound was not unique to New York's Blue Note label. One could find it everywhere, even on the West Coast, where Art Rupe's Specialty Records of Los Angeles was pioneering the black sound in another idiom.

Born Arthur Goldberg, Art Rupe started his label recording urban jump blues, transitioning through gospel music to become one of the quintessential rock and roll companies, with Little Richard, Lloyd Price, and Sam Cooke on board. Rupe was both scientifically inclined and emotionally involved in black music, having discovered gospel music as a young boy growing up across the street from a black Baptist church. He had arrived in Hollywood from the Midwest in 1939; at the time, one could parlay an investment of a few hundred dollars into a recording and hit the streets to see if it would sell, and that's what he did. Taking $200, he went down to Central Avenue, the main stem of black L.A., and bought all the "race records" of the day to determine why some were hits and others were not.

"I made an analysis of what went to a record, technically, musically, etcetera," he said. "And I established a set of rules or principles which I felt would enable me to make commercial records. Some of this music moved me so much it brought tears to my eyes."

In his research, he had discovered a lot of hit records had the word "boogie" in the title. Also, that jukebox operators acted as wholesalers for "race records." Thus "Boogie #1" became the first release on Rupe's new Juke Box label by the Sepia Tones. It managed to sell almost 70,000 copies. He then recorded Roosevelt Sykes and Roy Milton. Rupe was totally into the details.

"It wasn't only the technology [that made this possible]; it was the arrangements . . . we spent a lot of time in rehearsal, we worked out the harmonies to make it sound big and full. I had studied records . . . I did it with a stop watch." Roy Milton's records had "the big beat" in part because he was not only the singer but the drummer, so his vocal mic picked up his drum kit, creating the big bottom end that later became the watchword to rock and roll. His "R. M. Blues" was similarly a hit.

Recalling his love for black church music as a boy, Rupe eventually became the foremost recorder of gospel quartets, the Pilgrim Travelers and the Soul Stirrers, whose lead singers were future R&B stars Sam Cooke and Johnny Taylor, not to mention the Chosen Gospel Singers, which featured Lou Rawls. And he began applying his taste for gospel to secular black popular music, particularly on sides by a young piano player named Richard Pennyman (aka Little Richard), who helped usher in the rock revolution. And while he was a stickler for details, Rupe always favored feeling over technique, often urging his artists to do another take "with a little more soul this time." To this day, Specialty records are constantly being reissued and continue to sound "fresh" because they captured something real: the sound of a living culture.

Little Richard's "Tutti Frutti" on Rupe's label was a huge seller, and it might have been the first true "rock and roll" smash hit had it not been preceded by a few months by Bill Haley's "Rock Around the Clock," the undisputed breakthrough "rock and roll" record (the term "rock and roll" was coined by a Jewish DJ from Cleveland named Alan Freed to avoid using the terms "race" or "rhythm and blues"). It is doubtful that "Tutti Frutti" would have gotten as far as it did if Haley had not first broken down the door at radio. After all, Haley was a clean-cut white man with a modest hairdo, singing about a party, while Little Richard was a black man with a slick pompadour, pounding on a piano and screaming in a wild falsetto about something that sounded suspiciously like sex.

Haley's song "Rock Around the Clock" broke all barriers; it was a hybrid of country and western and rhythm and blues, indigenous black and white forms seamlessly stitched together, tailor-made for a teenage audience. And the man who did the stitching was none other than Milt Gabler. "All the tricks I used with Louis Jordan, I used with Bill Haley," he would later say. "The only difference was the way we did the rhythm. On Jordan, we used a perfectly balanced rhythm section from the Swing era . . . but Bill had the heavy backbeat."

Once again, a shift in rhythm had presaged a shift in the social climate. By tweaking the smooth rhythm from the old Louis Jordan shuffles into something a bit more relentless, less sophisticated, and a little wilder to satisfy the growing angst in white teenage America—and by cranking up the reverb on the vocal to add a kind of haunting otherworldly effect—Gabler had set off a revolution. The song was included in the movie *Blackboard Jungle*, about a troubled high school in New York City, and both the film and the music caused a national sensation. Kids left the movie theaters emotionally supercharged and rioted in the streets, breaking windows and acting out as never before. The rush of feelings released by the movie and the song had been building for years, and subsequently the subject of "juvenile delinquency" became a hot topic everywhere. The more publicity and outrage it generated, the more the entertainment industry began selling juvenile delinquency as a kind of product to the teenage market. The film and record businesses turned juvenile delinquency into a dream and an industry.

Hence Gabler was not only present at the birth of this industry, but he helped deliver the baby. How it happened is an interesting story of circumstance, opportunity, and technology. On April 12, 1954, the New Jersey hillbilly band Bill Haley and the Comets arrived late for their first recording session for Decca because their ferryboat had run aground on a sandbank in the Delaware River. They were in the studio ostensibly to record a song called "Thirteen Women," a catchy R&B-flavored tune that Gabler liked. With time running short he wanted to cancel the session, but Haley persuaded him they could put an arrangement together quickly. Gabler agreed and said that if there was any studio time left the guys could also do their "clock song," as he called it. After six takes, Gabler was finally happy with "Thirteen Women." But it was now after four o'clock and the studio was only booked until 5 p.m. Haley and the Comets would only have time for two takes of their other song. At 4:30 p.m. they launched into "Rock Around the Clock." When they listened to the playback, the Comets sounded great, but they had completely drowned out Bill's voice, so Gabler requested another take, but this time he ordered the Comets' microphones be turned off, so only Haley's vocal was recorded. With time running out, Milt Gabler called an end to the session. The following day he had the engineers synchronize the two tapes and produced the final version of the record that would eventually sell more than 25 million copies (and still counting).

Milt Gabler did not merely record a song that became a hit; he *made a hit record.* The first take was captured in the studio; the second take was similarly captured; but when the two takes were combined, the result was something *manufactured*, a new third element that did not exist in the real world. The act of combining the two separate takes into the one hit version was a dramatic example—if not the first, quite possibly the most prominent—of the art of using technology to create a false acoustic reality that in turn altered the real world itself. For that is what modern recordings have become: the sound they contain, more often than not, does not exist "in nature," and so they suggest a different world, at times a better world, but certainly an alternative to the mundane world. In this simple act are the seeds of hope for change, of a better future. And, most important, the result of this act could be packaged and sold. One could say that "Rock Around the Clock" was the tipping point, the moment when the record business began shifting from the commerce of art to the art of commerce.

UP ON THE ROOF

By the early fifties, Americans were experiencing an environment where anything was possible and traditional roles were fading fast: who you were was in tremendous flux and generally seen as an agglomeration of what you owned, your "consumer choices." One can track in the rise of the advertising industry during the period an attempt to ease Americans through this thorny process: advertising purported to tell you not only who you were but what you needed to purchase in order to maintain that identity (in a twist, perhaps, on the currently popular philosophy "Define the job and become the person who does it," this was "Define the person and buy the products that support it"). The commodification of experience was well under way.

On Jewish Broadway, too, the subject of assimilation (how and where one fit in) was being turned over and reexamined. Many of the productions of the period (*Babes in Arms, South Pacific, The King and I, Oklahoma!*) tell a story about inclusiveness, about a community where one has "to be carefully taught" to hate, a liberal society in which a simple love story represents the possibility of Jewish assimilation into the American mainstream. When in May 1954 the Supreme Court struck down the separate but equal "standard" for schools (specifically for blacks in the South) in the landmark *Brown v. Board of Education* case, saying it was inherently unequal, technically, from that moment forward, there were no more American hyphenates. Everybody was part of the mix.

On the other hand, the great postwar Red Scare, with its anti-Semitic overtones, drove many Jews further underground; to this day, it is still not fully understood how many lives were destroyed by the HUAC (House Un-American Activities Committee) witch hunt, nor to what extent McCarthyism permanently changed the political landscape, not just for Jews but for all progressives. Simultaneously, the full horror of the Holocaust was only gradually coming to light, and German atrocities undermined the confidence of any Jew who would assume that assimilation was an end in itself: just knowing that this systematic killing of Jews had happened in the most "civilized" corner of the Western world, and that it had been happening for years, rendered futile the thought of absolute security. One result was a kind of mass denial; the news erected a great wall between American Jews and what should have been for them "the central event of their time," the destruction of European Jewry. "Nobody in America seriously took this on," reported one observer at the time, "and only a few Jews elsewhere. . . . All parties are passing the buck and every honest conscience feels the disgrace of it."

Understandably, while Jews were optimistic about becoming full-fledged members of the American family, they were not particularly eager to step into the public eye as Jews; in the move to erase the hyphen in their Jewish-American experience, they often sought to fade into the crowd, to go forward by stepping into the background. A great many Jews were "passing" for Americans as presented by the media. It does not take a great leap of imagination to connect the growing awareness of Nazi horrors to the growing number of Jewish children undergoing rhinoplasty. One need look no further than Tony Curtis (born

Bernard Schwartz) to discover a closeted Jew maintaining a modern WASP hero image. Similarly, the original premise for the Broadway musical *West Side Story*, as envisioned by composers Leonard Bernstein and Stephen Sondheim, had been to depict the rivalry between a Jewish gang and an Irish gang; this was jettisoned in the service of a more general "American" profile. But why was a Puerto Rican gang more American than a Jewish gang? Just the question speaks volumes about Jewish caution and discomfort (although, as the joke goes, nobody would cross the street in fear if they saw a gang of Jewish accountants coming toward them).

One sign of Jewish caution during the fifties was their apparent lack of visibility in the music business. The radio, by and large, continued to play songs of impossible happiness, musical confections like Perry Como's "Hot Diggity Dog Ziggity Boom," and when one looked under the surface one still found Jewish composers—that particular song, for example, was written by Dick Manning; a bit more digging and one discovers that Manning was actually Samuel Medoff, the former leader of Sam Medoff and His Yiddish Swing Orchestra. In the fifties, Sam Medoff would not have been admitted to most private clubs across America, nor would his name secure the best table in many restaurants; but Dick Manning's might. One notices fewer and fewer Jewish pop singers (Steve Lawrence, Eddie Fisher, Tony Martin), fewer flamboyant Jewish composers in the Berlin/Gershwin mold, fewer confrontational themes in Jewish pop music, certainly nothing as bold as "Strange Fruit" or "Brother, Can You Spare a Dime?"

While the HUAC hearings had damped down the spirit of confrontation, the rising affluence had propped up a kind of country club sensibility: while most of the old Jewish lefties had been driven underground, the "all-rightniks," the majority of Jews just looking for a nice night out, quite literally took up the mambo. Arthur Murray (born Moses Teichman) set up a chain of social dance schools, which at its peak had more than 3,600 locations, teaching folks how to push their tush across dance floors from Miami Beach to the Catskills. The "Latin Craze" of the fifties was centered on kosher hotels and Caribbean cruises, and several successful Latin music record labels (Gee and Rama) were owned by a Jewish "mambonik" from the Bronx, George Goldner. Goldner married a Latina and produced salsa greats like Tito Puente and Eddie Palmieri. For him and other serious connoisseurs of Latin music, there was the Palladium, a large dance hall in midtown Manhattan where hundreds of mambo dancers gathered nightly and got physical to some of the best musicians in the world. The scene at the Palladium became definitive for many of its habitués; one of them, a Jewish refugee from Berlin named Wolfgang Grajonca (aka Bill Graham) would attempt to recreate its ambience, down to the rotating crystal ball, years later in San Francisco. But for those not subsumed into the Latin culture, a nice turn around the dance floor at the club would do.

Dancing, dining, golfing at private Jewish country clubs, one rarely heard the sounds of this new music called rock and roll beating against the windows, and if one did, it was dismissed as a fad that would soon pass. All the old Jewish Tin Pan Alley composers said it was temporary, and younger Broadway composers agreed with Stephen Sondheim's opinion that this new music would never last because it couldn't grow up. Rock and roll could never transition to "legitimate" venues, he said: "They can't go into Broadway theaters because they need amplification. Everything is loud. And if everything is loud and at the same level, well, then a love song is the same as an action song and so there's no nuance in rock and roll." And while this was more or less true, he and the others hadn't counted on this being the essential point of rock and roll—not growing up. Furthermore, it missed another essential point about rock and roll: unlike the music of Broadway, unlike the music of the great Jewish composers and the Great American Songbook, rock and roll was not so much about words or music as it was, and still is, about *sound*. Perhaps because on occasion it got "loud," it was hard for the older folks to hear it at all.

But loud was only part of what this music was. It was also a budding new form of musical theater, taken off the stage and staged on the streets. In some aspects, it was just as contrived as vaudeville, but it posed as being more real than real life. Rock and roll was the heartbeat of the "teen era" that accepted James Dean in *Rebel Without a Cause* as an existential hero and Elvis Presley in *Jailhouse Rock* as a musical tough guy. As such, rock and roll was symptomatic of a new bifurcation of the American experience: if American society was no longer split among various cultural hyphenates—Jewish-Americans, Italian-Americans, African-Americans, and the rest—rock and roll was clearly splitting society along age lines, the young versus the old, the modern versus the nostalgic, the future versus the past. Youth trumped all. The American teenager became positioned as a kind of cultural outsider, and advertising men rushed to sell this newly identified cohort the artifacts they needed to sustain that self-image. The teen era proclaimed truth in expression; it mocked the *Father Knows Best* lifestyle promoted on television (an echo of the previous revolution against Victorianism at the turn of the century). With rising teen alienation and growing materialism, to point out that older folks didn't like their music was like fighting fire with gasoline: soon the teen era was a runaway cultural phenomenon.

The constituent parts of early rock and roll are well known. It combined elements of jazz (the walking bass line), rhythm and blues (the stripped-down incessant backbeat), country (the relentless major-chord guitar patterns), and blues (vocals that didn't need to make sense in order to make sense). Whereas the separate idioms from which it was taken were all more or less authentic (that is, originating in some living cultural subgroup), rock and roll represented a kind of hybrid American life that was manufactured in studios and shipped out to the kids on the streets. Idiomatically, it was a pose. Elvis was not a sneering tough guy; he was a sweet, sad mama's boy. Chuck Berry was not a wild and crazy teenager; he was a dirty old man with a jump blues background. And over in England, where Chess had struck a new distribution deal, young kids were getting their first shot at this new American rebellion, grasping the aspect of pose as much as the sound of the blues. A teenage Mick Jagger and his pals, for example, sat listening to the music of Muddy Waters and decided to pick up instruments and reshape themselves into the ultimate "street fighting band"; they were not, nor would they ever be, street fighters: Mick himself was essentially an effete art student. Some years later, a piano player engaged to record with the Rolling Stones at London's Olympic Studio arrived to find Jagger sitting at the piano playing a lovely, sophisticated ballad. When asked if this was the song they would be recording, Jagger's response was rather sad: "No, mate," he said, "this is just something I'm fooling around with for myself." Shortly thereafter, he was leading the group through six hours of a hammering, monotonous cycle of major chords.

No, from the beginning, rock and roll was a pose: it claimed to be dangerous, unpredictable, alienated, passionate, decadent, excessive; its followers were slaves to the groove, driven by a sound that came up from the bottom of their shoes, from the "good foot," with the promise of menace and an undercurrent of violence. This pose became fact in the marketplace, if not on the ground; that is, while kids acted out fantasies of alienation, they inherently understood that America was the only place where they could get away with it. It was a game. Too, even as the music was being sold as something wild and free, the fact remained that at bottom every hit song said that love ruled and relationships mattered most of all. From the most treacly ballad to the most antisocial groove, at heart all pop music supported core "family values." So, for all its airs of disaffection, early rock and roll was really quite patriotic. It was alienation as fashion, perhaps, but in time it would lay the groundwork for something deeper and more profound in the youth culture.

Rock and roll sold what the kids wanted (and parents hated) at a time when kids had disposable income (mostly given to them by their parents); it was easily packaged and distributed through the new technologies (45 rpm records, radios, disc jockeys, jukeboxes); and it was the answer to the question that never arose: How are kids going to find and identify each other, given their desire for change and lack of real-world experience? Rock and roll kept the operating system in place—in fact, it made the marketing machinery billions of new dollars, selling ice cream to the Inuit—delivering outsider status to insiders; it disguised rebellion as true love and love as rebellion ("they say that we're too young"), all for 99 cents; and finally, it proved that one should never underestimate the ability of the American system to absorb dissent by turning it into a commodity and selling it back to its instigators as a must-have affect.

At first, this new music came mostly from jukeboxes in malt shops and from AM car radios at traffic lights. One can't imagine today how wild and weird it was to hear Bill Haley shout "One two three o'clock, four o'clock rock!" right after hearing Kitty Kallen's "Little Things Mean a Lot" (1955's biggest hit) or Eddie Fisher's "Oh! My Papa." Just as car culture was growing more important in one's life—where else could one go to be alone with that special boy or girl and hear the words "They say that we're too young"?—this new sound came along. You got your driver's license at age sixteen, and the first thing you did was reset the buttons on your dad's car radio to the stations that might be playing your music; resetting the buttons on the car radio became the first overt act of rebellion for many kids in fifties America. By 1955, the first "muscle cars" emerged, souped-up Chevys and Fords that boys drag-raced up and down city streets to impress girls; that same year, President Eisenhower signed the interstate highway system into law, promising that soon the entire country would be one long drag strip and getaway. Suddenly, cars were the center of the teen world, and the soundtrack for this adventure was emerging from a single four-inch speaker in the dashboard.

By 1955, in response to the growing white teenage market, the sound of popular music was shifting: ethnic voices were "in"—black voices, Southern voices, country voices (for example, the Everly Brothers' hillbilly harmony); no longer did middle-American diction characterize popular song; something raw, something a little more dangerous was brewing. Disc jockeys were showing up at local dances with Eddie Fisher and Jo Stafford records while the kids were clamoring to hear the latest by Lloyd Price ("Lawdy Miss Claudie") or the Clovers ("Good Lovin'," "Lovey Dovey"). Once again technology was leading the way, because when kids got their hands on portable radios, the business of rock and roll really took off. And when kids started driving endlessly around the cities in the north (often in circles, called "scooping" or "looping the loop") listening to the radio and flashing their friends, this music was out of the box. Airplay became the great leveling force; even major retail outlets, like the RCA Victor stores, started selling independent recordings. Once this music was played on the radio and was available free in the air to anyone, everyone wanted a piece of it.

The rise of radio play dramatically and immediately began to drive down the barriers between black and white kids in America. Everybody loved Ray Charles; his first hit on Atlantic, "I Got a Woman" (1955), was basically a series of sanctified chords straight out of the gospel church, but the kids couldn't care less whether it was black or white, sacred or profane. It was pure pleasure. Jerry Wexler, who produced all the early Ray Charles hits, confirms that it was nothing but a party: "The idea of producing [Ray Charles] is a misnomer," he said. "What we were doing was presiding at a happening starring Ray Charles." That simple veracity in the music came through loud and clear, and distributors began to report that white high school kids were picking up on rhythm and blues and, in the South, calling it "cat music."

In order to break through those small speakers in the car or the transistor radio, this music needed to have an immediately identifiable sound. The sound was everything; you didn't need to be told about rebellion or the new reality, you heard it and you felt it and you acted upon it. Interestingly, rock and roll sounded bigger (louder) to the old folks specifically because it was smaller. That is, in the days of the big bands, if one wanted to emphasize a musical passage, one would add additional horns to emphasize the part—make it bigger to make it louder. In recording, especially rock and roll, one would simply turn the single part up in the audio mix, whether it was the guitar or the drum. In the world of recording, less is dramatically more, as the architect Mies van der Rohe so succinctly put it. This is the profound modernism at the heart of today's recorded music: it is essentially a *deconstructed* experience; its constituent elements exist in isolation and are rebalanced to approximate a communal experience. And like all good art, it can be highly effective, but it is artifice.

Ironically, the production of rock and roll was infinitely more sophisticated in its use of technology than that of the Tin Pan Alley adult music of the era. For one thing, it was scientifically designed to deliver a specific emotion by way of a rhythm premise. Not only was the snare drum (backbeat) exaggerated, but, in 1949, an engineer named Al Schmitt happened to place an extra microphone in front of the bass drum (or "kick drum" as it was called), and the bottom-end (low frequencies) became equally exaggerated. This new approach helped institute the big beat and furthered the process of "collective entrainment" (the phenomenon of people's physical and emotional beings becoming coordinated by an external pulse), a hallmark of rock and roll ever since. Starting in the fifties, rock and roll literally bound teenagers together on a level never before experienced. This music was built from the beat on up to the voice, where the narrative was told, either through lyrics or simply through the anguish in the singer's voice (love, loss, and what I wore); everything else (the guitar or strings or piano) became part of the stage set for the communal groove. By discovering that fewer elements created a more dramatic acoustic image, the sound of the record became the most important thing.

This distinction between making records and making music will become more clear as the record industry gradually gathered the entire music business unto itself and recording technology took center stage in the process of communal storytelling. But all the signs were there in the original rock and roll hit, "Rock Around the Clock." For example, the guitar on that record has a certain kind of reverb on it that describes a particular-sized room, but it's not real; that is, it has nothing to do with how big the room actually was. There are several ways to create this illusion of space. The most common way, before digital technology, was to use "tape delay" (also called "slap back," which meant using the space between the recording and playback heads of a machine to create a delay in the signal) or, alternatively, a metal "plate" to extend the electrical path of the signal; and finally, there was an actual concrete echo chamber beneath some recording studios where the signal of the guitar (or the voice or whatever needed reverb) was sent, creating an echo indicating a space of approximately the physical size of the enclosure, and that signal was then fed back and mixed in with the original guitar sound. All these ways to create a synthetic space, along with various other effects, were used, starting in the fifties, by producers to create a false ambiance, a sense of grandeur, or intimacy, that the raw music did not necessarily possess. The grandeur was created. Today, there are programs on the computer that allow one to design an acoustic environment that's as intimate as a closet or as vast as the Taj Mahal.

Starting in the fifties, the space that popular music pretended to occupy was not actually there. From that point on, one was manufacturing something that distinctly did not exist in the mundane world. It did not exist, and yet it was very clear and present when the record was playing and in the effect it had on people's lives. Hence, pop music is a kind of parallel universe created through the technology, and technology, beginning in the 1950s, became a central part of the grammar of musical storytelling. The sound, as much as, if not more than, the words and music, cued the listener's emotions and drove the narrative home.

What made rock and roll so powerful, even dangerous, wasn't the words or music—which were rightly recognized as puerile in the beginning—so much as the sound and feeling. The sound described a world where the pose was real; it was emotional adrenaline, truth serum for a lying world. Nobody asked what Little Richard was singing about in "Tutti Frutti" (in fact, it was anal sex); it was just the sound of his voice—you couldn't turn away. And when Ray Charles would ask, "How do you feel when your baby's loving your best friend?" you were right there with the Raylettes demanding "I want to know," and there was more information in the sound of their voices than in all the dictionaries in the classroom. Musical theater on the streets; authentically dangerous in a fictitious world: kids were being sold an acoustic movie in which they could be actors too and fill in the details with their own lives.

Beginning in the mid-1950s, through the use of new recording technology, the record business was musical theater of the mind, and the next generation of songwriters, producers, and record executives would understand this implicitly. "Rock Around the Clock" was idiomatically a kind of dividing line: there was music before "Rock Around the Clock," and there's the music after "Rock Around the Clock"; after came the explosion of technologies used to illuminate the story of rock songs—compressors, gates, flangers, phasers, aural exciters—until finally the process of recording collapses back in on itself, calling forth the darkness and simplicity of its origins, only to flare up again in a new extravagance of technology as money increases and youth searches for a way to spend it. Like a constantly pulsing dark star, generating and then losing its own source of heat in an ever diminished universe, American popular music from this point forward continues to ebb and flow on the currents of technology.

Before this dividing line, fans were connected to the people singing the songs: stars were stars, Frank Sinatra had Frank Sinatra fans, and great songs were the vehicles in which they arrived. After this point, fans were connected to *records*. Songs were the premise for *productions*, and the singer was part of the script. Before, songwriters wrote songs. After, songwriters wrote records. Once it became a record business, the artifact (the recording) became the heart of the popular music experience and the "artist" began to fade into disposability. Today there are still several aggregations touring the country calling themselves the "original" Coasters; these groups don't necessarily have anything to do with the actual musicians who cut the recordings; they don't even own their own name—the music is reduced to a sound, a look (a spit curl), a move, a step; a narrative that you can insert yourself into; music as theater.

In this new world, the producer of the record became the artist and the performance became what was being sold, the product. The underlying asset was still the song (because it could be performed and recorded many times, many ways, each one a new dramatic narrative paying a new royalty to the publisher) and the songwriter was the engine that drove the machine. In fact, if one checks the top pop songs of 1955, it's interesting to see alternative versions of the same song appear, usually one raunchier black version and one cleaned up "white" version: "Ain't That a Shame" by both Fats Domino and Pat Boone; "Work with Me Annie" by Hank Ballard and "Dance with Me Henry" by Georgia Gibbs; "I Hear You Knocking" by both Smiley Lewis and Gail Storm. What you don't see is a lot of nice Jewish boys and girls performing any of them.

On the surface, there was, stunningly, almost no visible Jewish aspect to rock and roll at all. Bill Haley, with his little spit curl, was pure hillbilly. So were Elvis, a Memphis boy, and Jerry Lee Lewis. Little Richard, Chuck Berry, black but, it was assumed, sanctified Southerners all. Rock and roll was dramatically rural and Christian; "cat music" presented itself as totally disconnected from the Jewish show business types of the era, the popular television icons like Milton Berle (Uncle Miltie, who liked to appear in drag), or Sid Caesar (with his staff of brilliant Jewish writers—Woody Allen, Mel Brooks, Carl Reiner—dressed up as a series of characters), or Phil Silvers as the scheming Sergeant Bilko, or, heaven forfend, Jack Benny and his black chauffeur Rochester (now there was a stereotype: Benny who squeezed his nickels until the buffalo cried and Rochester who remained vaguely chagrined by the whole affair). No, there was initially nothing identifiably Jewish about this music—and yet "Rock Around the Clock" itself was written by two Jewish composers, James E. Myers, aka Jimmy DeKnight, and Max Freedman. The world of rock and roll, with its string of apparently "dangerous" bad boys and girls, outlaws, alienated, misunderstood teens, would be almost entirely written and underwritten by members of the Jewish community.

This is not to say that the songs of Little Richard didn't reflect the true wildness that was part of the man or the rawness of the sanctified church—that was undeniable—or that there weren't true hillbilly roots in the music of the early fifties; white hillbilly roots aerated the ground of early rock and roll. Take Carl Perkins, born near Tiptonville, Tennessee, in 1932; at age seven he started listening to country music and playing a guitar that his father had made from a cigar box, broomstick, and baling wire; at thirteen, he formed his first group, which began to perform at local honkytonks; after hearing a boy telling his prom date not to step on his blue suede shoes, he went home to the housing project where he lived and wrote down his song "Blue Suede Shoes" on a brown potato sack. He then recorded the song at Sun Records in Memphis in December 1955, and it reached number two on the pop and country charts in 1956. Straight-up hillbilly. This record, like so many of the era—Buddy Holly's "Peggy Sue" or Gene Vincent's "Be Bop a Lula"—wasn't really about anything. It was pure sound, not even a song (melody, lyrics) so much as an anarchic feeling: a voice, an electronic effect, a backbeat; elemental information, raw material as vital as the crude oil bubbling under the American ground or the trees growing in the American forest. Fashioning it into a product and bringing it to market—and then telling people what to think about it—that was the work of another kind of expertise.

One of the reasons rock and roll became so popular at this particular moment in time—aside from the availability of new technologies (e.g. the transistor radio and the 50,000-watt clear-channel signal)—was that it allowed all the various ethnic groups—Jewish-Americans, African-Americans, Italian-Americans, etc.—to hide behind the all-American country roots of the music. It smoothed the transition already under way. If the fifties was a time of opportunity and indecision for Jews, unsure about whether to step up and claim the future as Jews or step back and become part of the future as Americans, the young Jewish songwriters managed to do both: they stepped up by stepping back (a very Talmudic solution, the uniting of apparent opposites). By adopting this pose, Jewish writers were able to continue to develop music that had historic values, a native optimism and a belief in the inevitability of change and social progress, a narrative that, perhaps ironically, also recognized the importance of alienation and exile in the modern world.

The Jews didn't put the danger into the music; they gave that danger a context and a story. They made it *about* something. And if, in the new age of rock and roll, the *performance* was what was being sold (as opposed to, in the past, the melody or the harmonic invention or the dream-inspired lyric), the vehicle for that performance, the premise, would be critical. Bob Dylan, who grew up listening to music from a 50,000-watt clear-channel signal on his transistor radio at night, once said that it was Elvis Presley singing "Hound Dog" in 1956 that made him want to be a performer. He said it was the *performance* that was just overwhelming. It didn't matter who wrote the song, it was just there. But of course the song wasn't just there. It was written by Jerry Leiber and Mike Stoller, a couple of Jewish kids carrying on a tradition that went back to George Gershwin and Irving Berlin, constructing songs out of the raw cultural materials at hand.

Leiber and Stoller met as teenagers at Fairfax High School in Los Angeles, arriving there by very different routes. Jerry grew up in Baltimore at the edge of two worlds, where the Jewish and the black ghettos met. His father died when he was four, and his mother ran a small grocery store to support the family. She was one of the few shopkeepers who would give credit to black families, so Jerry was always welcome in their homes when he made deliveries of kerosene and coal. That's where he heard R&B. "Inside those households, radios were always playing," he said. "Music was everywhere. Music was running through my head and coursing through my veins. My heart was flooded with boogie woogie." The boys in the hood never gave him any trouble: "I was trusted and therefore untouchable," he remembers. "I think they saw me as a bringer of light, the white boy who was serving black people."

In 1945, when Jerry was twelve, the family moved to Los Angeles. He was encouraged to write songs while still in high school by his older sister, who was dating a songwriter. Now, in America during the forties, becoming a songwriter was not a serious career option for a WASP. But in Jewish America, songwriting was something your sister's date might do, especially in L.A. As a thirteen-year-old, Jerry heard the great blues shouter Jimmy Witherspoon singing "Ain't Nobody's Business."

"At that very moment," he remembered, "I was transported into a realm of mystical understanding. The light came on. Witherspoon turned on the light. Maybe it was the power and absolute confidence of his voice. Maybe it was the lyrics, I don't know. Whatever it was, I was never the same again. Whatever Witherspoon was doing, I could do. Whatever Witherspoon was saying, I could say. The doors had opened. I had entered his world."

Mike Stoller was a gifted musician whose mother had been an actress, loved show business, and encouraged him to play piano; she hung a signed photo of George Gershwin over the piano in their apartment on the Upper West Side of New York City to inspire him. Like Leiber, he too fell in love with boogie-woogie and, as a young boy—along with his pal Al Levitt (another Jewish prodigy who would eventually become a noted jazz drummer)—he ran in the streets of Manhattan, collecting records and peeking into clubs. By chance, someone in the neighborhood heard him play piano and introduced him to the great Harlem stride pianist James P. Johnson. Johnson gave him some lessons, introduced him to the classic twelve-bar-blues structure, and told him, "Keep at it and someday you'll make a living banging those keys."

On Saturday afternoons, he and Al would go to Harlem, shoot pool, and feed the jukebox at a black social club. "It was the late forties," he remembered, "and Harlem was the right place at the right time." He dated black girls, dressed in the hip style of Harlem, and fell in love with the mix of bebop and blues. When his family too moved to Los Angeles, he went to Fairfax High, in the heart of the Jewish neighborhood. It was there that the two met.

Although very different in many ways—Mike was a skilled musician, interested in all the technical aspects of jazz, and Jerry was strictly a rhythm-and-blues man—they shared an overriding passion for the blues. "The blues broke him down," said Jerry, "and the blues freed him up. For all of his love of that high-minded technically complex jazz, Mike's heart was in the blues. He was as passionate about blues as I was. Blues was the bottom line." Mike put it more simply: "We wanted to have fun," he said, "and our notion of fun was rooted in authenticity . . . black music and black music only." They felt that the middle-class Jewish environment around them was terminally square and started hanging out in the black neighborhoods and the Latino barrios.

They began writing songs together and immediately knew their songs were good. "We knew they felt authentically black. Black was our criterion for quality," Mike recalls. A family friend just happened to be a well-known music publisher named Lester Sill (perhaps only in the Jewish community of L.A. could a couple of high school kids come face-to-face with such a major industry connection in such a casual way) and Lester got their songs to a black group called the Robins. From this connection, they began writing for Lavern Baker, Jimmy Witherspoon (the same singer who had ignited Leiber's imagination), Amos Milburn, and Joe Turner, all recognized as being among the precursors of rock and roll.

From the beginning, Leiber and Stoller had their own style. Perhaps it was inevitable, for they had to write from what they knew, and there was no way for them to actually know what it actually felt like to be black. Their music departed dramatically from the original black idioms of the forties, the ones that they loved, and yet their songs were recorded as often, if not more, by original black artists than white artists, proving it too had its own "authenticity." One difference was in the narrative range of their compositions: their music was not just about having a good time (although it certainly was that) and it was not merely a "sound," although it definitely was that too. Rather, their songs also had a backstory and an overarching narrative that went beyond the traditional moon-June kind of teenage song. This was the Jewish move, of course. And by the time they came of age, the old R&B approach was also growing a little thin; the good-time party pose of songs like "Drinkin' Wine Spo-Dee-O-Dee" (Stick McGhee) was like the black equivalent of the some old Jewish comic (think Milton Berle in a dress), a one-trick pony, a sight gag that was becoming frayed around the edges. Even Little Richard, after a year in the limelight, quit show business and joined the ministry. There was a crying need for some kind of narrative progress.

All Leiber and Stoller songs, even the early ones, had a special little narrative or harmonic twist. Like the one that they wrote for a singer named Wilbur Harrison, called "Kansas City": it followed the standard blues form, three simple chords, twelve bars, yet there was something slightly more sophisticated about this particular blues; the melody was a little hipper than the average blues shouter would reach for (it was composed, not thrown away), and the words too were just a little bit more well organized ("I might take a bus, I might take a train, but if I have to walk, I'm gonna get there just the same"). It was simply more *modern* than the "authentic" blues they had heard as kids; and yet it became a huge hit and was recorded by a lot of other black groups.

There was something seductive about the way they approached and updated the classic blues form even while trying to be traditional. Again, consider the song "Hound Dog," the one that helped turn Bob Dylan around; it too is a simple three-chord blues, but it employs one simple little trick (the same one Berlin employed with "Alexander's Ragtime Band"): it opens with a pick-up phrase ("You ain't nothin' but a . . . ") which becomes the clarion call (Berlin called it the "happy ruction") that launches the groove every time the hook comes around. Written for Big Mama Thornton, a 300-pound lesbian blues shouter, its original subject was a freeloading gigolo. The intrinsic metaphor of a man as a no-good dog was handled with some finesse:

> You ain't nothing but a hound dog
> Quit snooping round my door
> You can wag your tail
> But I ain't gonna feed you no more

But when Elvis recorded it, he changed the lyrics to

> You ain't nothing but a hound dog
> Crying all the time
> You ain't never caught a rabbit
> And you ain't no friend of mine

The Presley version didn't sound anything at all like Big Mama Thornton's—her version was so bawdy and outrageous it sounded like it was from outer space compared to what Elvis did; aside from her ribald vocal performance, the rhythm section, driven by hand clapping on beats 2 and 4 and a bass line that played against it with a clave feel, created a rhythm that can only be described as "ass shaking." In 1952, it was on the R&B charts for seventeen weeks. "Of course, by the time Elvis Presley got a hold of it [in 1956]," said Leiber, "he de-sexed it but it was enough that it freaked out the white folks." And it sold more than seven million copies.

By virtue of that Presley cover version, Leiber and Stoller were thrown into "the biggest commercial revolution in American music: teenage rock and roll. In the postwar prosperity of the fifties, teenagers had money and they were restless. Elvis' success was the prime example," said Leiber. "When the music was sung by one of their own, teenagers liked it even more."

"One of their own," said Leiber, meaning not black nor white (nor Jewish,) but *young*. It was this pose that Presley represented—something wild, something new—that had captured the heart of Bob Dylan. (As an aside, however, it can be noted that Elvis's mother's mother was Jewish, thus, according to the matrilineal tradition, making Elvis himself Jewish; it is also a fact that when Elvis died he was wearing a Jewish Chai—the symbol for life—around his neck.) Leiber and Stoller went on to write twenty more songs for Presley, and while none had the raw power of a Little Richard lyric (what could equal his righteous scream, "awopbopaloobop alopbamboom"?), it had something else.

"They created characters and stories," writes biographer David Ritz, "using black voices and black slang, yet at the same time, they depicted universal themes of love, life and above all, teenage insecurity. It was an important step: in a world dominated by white

Anglo-Saxon images, black life was being presented as a mirror in which all teenagers could recognize themselves."

By the time Leiber and Stoller began writing hits for the Coasters, between 1957 and 1959, they were creating full-on mini-operas that had humor, pathos, and a moral point of view. Songs like "Yakety Yak, Don't Talk Back," "Along Came Jones," "Young Blood," and "Charlie Brown" presented characters, told tall tales, and cracked jokes all within a couple of minutes. It was compressed short-story writing, using musicians who had started out as gospel or doo-wop singers as actors in their little plays. They actually cast certain songs based on the voices at hand. And it was obvious that they were having a great time making this music. It was not only fun but funny; they not only altered the pose of rock and roll but threw open the doors of the music much wider. As Ahmet Ertegun, the founder of Atlantic Records, once said, "The best way to cross boundaries is the promise of a good time." Leiber and Stoller not only promised but delivered.

The explosion of "Rock Around the Clock" had been a sensation in part because it marketed teenage disaffection and legitimized the juvenile delinquent aesthetic, much as hip-hop would do several decades later; teens were presented as alienated and dangerous (fear sells). But what Lieber and Stoller were doing wasn't about danger at all. It was about love and life and the themes that all young people understood: the conflict between the generations ("Yakety Yak"), the desolation of school ("Charlie Brown"). These songs were important because in 1950s WASP America, they were letting kids across the country know, "Hey, we *all* feel this way, black kids, white kids, all kids; we all feel the same way." Finally rock and roll was *about* something; it was communal music used to express universal themes; a party with a purpose.

Jewish songwriters of an earlier generation may have picked up the craft because it was a quick way to make money, but Leiber and Stoller did not write simply because they had found an opportunity that WASP America wasn't already covering. Nor were they "identifying down" to the black culture through their music. Like Milt Gabler or Jerry Wexler before them, they were identifying *up*: working in black music was the high ground. Their writing was part of a larger moral universe, growing out of the fertile detritus of early-fifties America: on the one hand, it was the era of Eisenhower and conservative politics, ponytails and poodle skirts; on the other, the breaking news story of December 1955 was that Rosa Parks, a black woman, refused to give a white man her seat on the bus, thus launching the historic Montgomery, Alabama, bus boycott, the putative origin of the Freedom Rides. This tension between the old world and the new was the underbelly of "cat music," and young Jewish composers felt intuitively that here was an opportunity to do well by doing good.

In 1957, the year that tail fins appeared on American automobiles, Ahmet Ertegun and his partner Jerry Wexler brought Leiber and Stoller out to New York and set them up in business in the Brill Building at 1619 Broadway. (It was called the Brill Building because there was a men's clothing store on the first floor owned by Maurice Brill, "the one guy who didn't go into songwriting and was still selling pants.") The place was a hotbed of young songwriters. Think of it as the old Tin Pan Alley neighborhood compressed into one large vertical space (although there was also another building across the street at 1650 Broadway that served as a kind of annex). Back in the late forties, when Jerry Wexler was working for *Billboard* magazine, he would start on the eleventh floor of 1619 Broadway and work his way down to the first floor looking for stories. The building was a warren of songwriters, publishers, record company touts, and promotion men, all hustling each other. The music business was all about "the song," and everybody had one to pitch.

Leiber and Stoller did everything, from writing the songs to casting the voices to producing the records. They spent days in the studio developing this new narrative technique, leading the city's finest session musicians (mostly jazz players who could read anything and turn around on a dime) through the rigors of inventing a new sound. By the time they wrote "There Goes My Baby" for Ben E. King and the Drifters (1959), they were creating small pop operas, combining an R&B backbeat, a Latin clave beat, and dramatic narratives employing orchestral strings that recalled classical motifs ("a Rimsky-Korsakov-Borodin pseudo line," Leiber called it). By the following year, 1960, when they produced "Spanish Harlem" for King, which also combined the singer's gospel tenor with Latin rhythms, electric guitar, and orchestral strings, they had perfected a kind of Technicolor musical adventure that synthesized European, African-American, and Latin music into something completely original.

They didn't write songs, they said, they wrote records, and they invented the grammar as they went along. As in the evolution of the film business, in which techniques like slow motion and multiple imaging were invented as needed, they too had to discover ways to express their aural visions. This grammar was nothing that could be formally learned or written down; it had to be created in the moment and for the moment. This was *performance* music, down to the level of production. The birth of the modern record producer lives here. For example, consider the song "Yakety Yak, Don't Talk Back." One could buy the sheet music, but what would that tell you? The words and chords, perhaps. But you wouldn't get any idea what the song sounded like, or why it was so captivating. This music, like the straight-up black blues before it, was dependent on new technology specifically because it could not be written down. It depended on a new kind of technology to exist, for it to be passed on, for it to have any impact or existence at all. It was an ongoing experiment, and Leiber and Stoller were there at the beginning; but they were not alone.

If the Brill Building in the forties was initially full of old-timers from the sheet music era, middle-aged men writing for Broadway and *Your Hit Parade*, by the 1950s it was home to dozens of young songwriters, some barely out of high school, all working in small cubicles and getting paid $100 per week to crank out songs. They received royalties if the songs became a hit, but until then, they survived on this small advance, doing a kind of musical piecework; the faster they worked, the better their chances. These conditions made songwriting in the Brill Building highly competitive—if you didn't turn out a good song every day, the couple in the next cubicle might beat you to it—and this intensity in turn generated a wealth of popular music. It was a hothouse, a new phenomenon: American teenagers writing songs for their peers.

Most of the record labels were also located in Midtown Manhattan and were always looking for new songs for their artists (who, as a rule, didn't write their own material); the Brill Building was a veritable factory of teenage angst. Indeed, it became the pumping chamber at the heart of the music business: the songs that dominated radio in America for most of a decade came out of this eleven-story building, day after day, week after week, written by a small collection of kids, most of whom came from Brooklyn. It was really a golden moment in American songwriting. The songs, by and large, were highly experimental, universal in appeal and inclusive in nature. They were for blacks as well as whites. They were optimistic. They gave one the feeling that "we were all in this together and there is going to be a better future in America because of it." But who were these kids who started writing songs when they were fifteen years old, serious songs that exhibited craft and insight, and started this musical gold rush?

They included Carole King and Gerry Goffin ("Will You Love Me Tomorrow?" and "Up on the Roof"), Barry Mann and Cynthia Weil ("On Broadway" and "You've Lost That Lovin' Feelin'"), Jeff Barry and Ellie Greenwich ("Be My Baby" and "Chapel of Love"), Neil Sedaka and Howard Greenfield ("Calendar Girl" and "Breaking Up Is Hard to Do"), Mort Shuman and Doc Pomus ("This Magic Moment" and "A Teenager in Love"), and Burt Bacharach and Hal David ("Walk On By" and "Anyone Who Had a Heart"). Jews one and all, and each with a story that had a subtext of hope for a better world, usually by way of a teen romance.

A brief glance at some lyrics gives a sense of their narrative breadth, and their identification with the underdog, even if it can't convey the impassioned angst of their melodies and arrangements. Take, for instance, this verse from Mann and Weil's composition "On Broadway":

> They say the neon lights are bright on Broadway
> They say there's always magic in the air
> But when you're walkin' down the street
> And you ain't had enough to eat
> The glitter rubs right off and you're nowhere.

Or consider, for example, the personal story of Doc Pomus (born Jerome Felder). A large, gnarly-looking man with a goatee, he was rendered paraplegic as a child after a bout with polio. He said that even as a young boy, he felt connected to the poorest blacks because of his disability, and as a teenager, he was transformed by hearing the blues singer Big Joe Turner. He decided to become a blues shouter himself, and often performed in funky

Harlem clubs while propped up on his crutches. His family was ashamed of him; his brother Raoul Felder (the infamous divorce attorney) said, "Most people spend their lives trying to get out of the slums. Instead of getting out of our slum, he was going to a worse slum."

He came to a crossroads in his career when he wanted to get married but wasn't making enough money to support a wife; it was then that he and his friend Mort Shuman went into the business of songwriting. Their songs always took the side of the weak against the strong. His masterpiece was "Save the Last Dance for Me," which turned a profound personal hurt into an emotion that every teenager could understand. The song is about a man watching his girl dance with another man, and it is autobiographical: Pomus would take his wife, a gorgeous woman, to dances, where she would dance with other men while he sat watching. And so the song was written to his wife, saying, "Darling, save the last dance for me."

This was not trivial music. This was very personal: but in taking this deep personal moment and making it an anthem with which any teenager could identify, he was really raising the bar on what popular music was about. It was the beginning of the intellectualization of teenage music, which would blossom further a few short years later. In fact, there is a famous story of B. B. King bursting into tears after he recorded Pomus's "There Must Be a Better World"; it was not, he said, because he felt that Pomus had so finely understood black sensibilities, but rather that he himself finally understood what Pomus was saying. Pomus, like the other young Jewish songwriters, came from a background in which prejudice and poverty were ongoing themes and where escape from pogroms would have been part of the family history. Hence their own songs all expressed this possibility of escape, through love, ambition, or even just a night up on the roof.

That, of course, was the theme of Carole King and Gerry Goffin's hit song of the same name. The story of this songwriting team is particularly interesting in that it demonstrates both the informality and the remarkably close-knit aspect of the Brill Building family. It started when a young Jewish hustler named Don Kirshner met a singer named Bobby Darin in a candy store; they decided to write a song together and came up with something called "Splish Splash," which became one of the biggest hits of 1958. On the strength of its success, Kirshner, only twenty years old, talked his way into a music publishing partnership with a man named Al Nevins, a guy twenty years his senior. Kirshner's dream was to manage songwriters, not become one, to help shape the career of "the next George Gershwin." Nevins and Kirshner called their company Aldon (for Al and Don) Music. One of the first guys to walk through their door in the Brill Building was a young Jewish kid named Neil Sedaka, with a song called "Stupid Cupid." It became the first song Aldon published and a Top Ten hit for singer Connie Francis. In 1959, Sedaka himself recorded another song he wrote called "Oh! Carol," dedicated to a girl at his high school named Carole Klein (Carole King), and this too became a hit. Meanwhile, Carole, who was then a seventeen-year-old freshman at Queens College, met a chemistry major named Gerry

Goffin; she was interested in writing rock-and-roll songs, he was interested in writing a Broadway musical about beatniks. They joined forces, and the first song they wrote was an answer to "Oh! Carol" called "Oh! Neil"; Kirshner heard their song and hired them too.

And so Goffin and King left school, got married, and joined the party at the Brill Building. They became friends with Barry Mann and Cynthia Weil, also married and writing songs for Kirshner. The couples were unbelievably competitive. Cynthia Weil remembers, "We rented a ski house together and we would all go up there. We didn't want to leave them for a weekend—partially because they were our pals and partially because we knew they'd be writing their asses off if they weren't skiing with us."

From 1961 to 1963, Goffin and King had a string of hits that included "Will You Love Me Tomorrow," "The Loco-Motion," "Chains," "One Fine Day," and their masterpiece, "Up on the Roof." Recorded by the Drifters and produced by Leiber and Stoller in 1962, "Up on the Roof" had all the elements of their by now famous storytelling technique, a small movie of hope and optimism in the heart of the city:

> Right smack dab in the middle of town
> I've found a paradise that's trouble proof (up on the roof)
> And if this world starts getting you down
> There's room enough for two
> Up on the roof (up on the roof)

This recording, however, like so many of the new productions, was no longer, in the literal sense, a "record" of a live event: it did not represent a document of what the artist sounded like so much as what the writers and producers had envisioned for the song. Along with the chimes, strings, a choral background, and a catchy little piano part that sounded cool on the recording but would have sounded trivial in life, the voices of the Drifters were just so much additional texture. The record became the thing in itself, and the producer had become the star. Indeed, a few years later, Goffin and King would be singled out by the Beatles as songwriting influences; the Beatles, along with their producer, George Martin, had grasped early on that pop songwriting was linked to production as much as (if not more than) the words and music, and that the artist existed to serve the recording.

Enter Phil Spector. He arrived in New York from Los Angeles by way of a phone call to Leiber and Stoller from their old mentor Lester Sill. Sill called to say, "I got this kid. He's talented. He wants to move away and hang with you guys." So they sent the kid a ticket. Spector, from the beginning, was a kind of odd duck, a self-involved young man with a gift for intrigue and a laserlike focus on his own career. His personal story is as strange as any in rock and roll: in 1949, when Phil was just a boy, his father committed suicide and, weighed down by increasing debt, his mother took them west to Los Angeles (just as Jerry Leiber's mother had done), where the young Phil also attended Fairfax High. As a kid, he dreamed of being a star, and because of his odd looks and average voice, he knew that the way to do it was to write and produce records. He used his own father's death as the hook: when he was eighteen, the title of his first professional song came from the inscription on his father's gravestone back in Long Island: "To Know Him Was to Love Him." Spector crafted a teen ballad around the phrase, recruited a couple of friends from high school to sing it, played all the instruments himself, and cut the demo. When a producer named Lou Adler heard it, liked it, and arranged a full-blown recording session, they called the group the Teddy Bears, and by the end of 1958, "To Know Him Is to Love Him" was number one on the *Billboard* chart. The inscription in the cemetery had been transmuted into the breathy words of teenage love for the whole of America. No hint of the personal tragedy was audible. What this story doesn't tell us about Spector's emotional compass we would eventually discover several decades later.

Spector started working with Leiber and Stoller in 1959. He was musically talented, and he generally made himself both useful and a nuisance in the studio. The problem was that he wanted to be in total control. He was not interested in working with anybody else; in fact, as he saw it, everybody else was a pawn in his own ongoing production. Therefore he preferred to work with unknowns, especially black unknowns who would give him little resistance.

"He actually preferred to use session singers on the records," recalled one former singer, "and then sent the groups [including the Ronettes and the Crystals] out on the road. (Apparently the Crystals were surprised when touring in Ohio to discover they had a number one song called 'He's a Rebel.' They knew nothing about the record; they hadn't even sung on it)."

He was developing what he called his "wall of sound," a production technique that remains unrivaled in its scale of pretension and grandiosity. Writing what he said were "little symphonies for the kids," using multiples of everything possible—instead of one guitar or mandolin playing a part, he would use four; instead of six violins, he would use two dozen or more—he created great waves of sound that would flood the studio; his productions soon became Wagnerian in scale.

As a production style, Spector's "wall of sound" seemed to refute the communal nature of popular music; like the huge fins on the 1959 Cadillac, it was no longer just good dirty fun; it was obscene. By the time of Spector's epic production, "You've Lost That Lovin' Feelin'" by the Righteous Brothers, the title was both prescient and absolutely correct: he had, with the size and cynicism of the production, lost the human scale, the intimate, hand-holding function of popular music; the "wall of sound" was Spector's ego propped up by the bottom line. Four mandolins playing the same part doesn't equal a part four times better; in fact, it works the other way around; the result is perhaps one-fourth as easy to hear; sound gets buried in sound. It would have been more accurate to call it "a cloud of sound," and the lack of sonic focus was due to the fact that the music was all about the producer, who in this case was insular and hidden. And so, quite naturally, were his productions. As long as the records he made were hits, however, Spector was considered a genius. But they were no longer about the feeling of love; it was all theater: a three-minute symphony that starts with a man alone and ends on a mountaintop of music, a cheap thrill, an E ticket ride for the kids.

This focus on size was a growing American obsession. In 1959, even President Eisenhower, on his way out of office, made a point of warning Americans about the dangers of excessive growth in the "military-industrial complex," as if to confess that bigness itself might be a looming danger in the future. At the same time, there was a growing backlash in teenage America against the phoniness of pop artifice. Many young Americans had learned to question authority as kids through the pages of *Mad* magazine, Harvey Kurtzman's groundbreaking parody of popular culture. *Mad* was hip, ironic, madcap, and visceral, the iconic precursor of *Saturday Night Live,* and, in its own way, a beacon of Jewish righteousness: totally unafraid to mock the excesses of the status quo, "Kurtzman drew a bead on the phony aspects and idiosyncrasies of modern commercial culture. . . . He took on Senator Joseph McCarthy as surely and seriously in the pages of *Mad* as Edward R. Murrow did on television." *Mad* had the irreverent spirit of an old-school Jewish tummler combined with the outrageous timing of contemporary comics like Lenny Bruce. There was a new aesthetic bubbling up here, a more freewheeling, down-at-the-heels idea of what American pop culture could be; this aesthetic became romanticized in the 1957 publication of Jack Kerouac's *On the Road,* which glorified the "beat" aesthetic.

Simultaneously, a new congressional investigation was shaking the trees of the music business, and the fruits of corruption were falling to the ground for all to see. "Payola," a word combining the words "pay" and "Victrola," entered the English language in 1960. On May 9 of that year, a disc jockey named Alan Freed was indicted for accepting $2,500 in "pay for play" money (aka bribes), which he claimed was merely a token of appreciation from grateful record companies and did not affect what he played on the air. He paid a small fine and was released, and immediately faded into oblivion. Who was Freed, and how did this case not only end his career but help usher in the age of the singer-songwriter? To understand this, one has to go back to the turn of the decade and the historic coming together of teen songwriters and old-school hustlers at a time of rising prosperity and expanding technology. It was a kind of perfect storm in the record business, a climate that set loose forces still very much in play today.

Until 1940, the American Society of Composers, Authors and Publishers (ASCAP) had a virtual monopoly on collecting money from radio stations for airplay. They were lily white and controlled the music of the masters—Kern, Gershwin, Rodgers, Berlin. In 1940, ASCAP decided to raise its rates to the radio stations. In response, the big broadcasters started their own performing rights organization called Broadcast Music Inc. (BMI). BMI quickly became the sole representative for all the smaller, independent writers and publishers. Subsequently, music previously ignored—rhythm and blues and hillbilly music, for example—began getting a lot of play at radio stations. By 1950 it was not unusual for every song on the *Billboar*d R&B jukebox and sales charts to be registered with BMI. Since BMI was started by the broadcasters, it was a bit like leaving the fox in charge of the henhouse, but initially, the size of the indie business and the nature of the music was not of a scale to bring down the wrath of ASCAP: a promo man would show up at the radio station and slip the disc jockey $50, get his song played, and leave. No harm, no foul.

But as the rock-and-roll business grew, the value of a hit song increased dramatically. A disc jockey on a top station could make a considerable amount of money on the side, and often times, a fifty-dollar handshake was not enough to get the ball rolling. It was clear by the early fifties that radio play was what created hit records. So the radio stations simply stepped up: for example, WKMH in Detroit openly offered an album-of-the-week deal for $350. They would play a record 114 times with a commercial before and after each play for six weeks. At the same time, the indie record labels had all started their own publishing companies to maximize profits. Hence, if Willie Dixon, part of the Chess Records organization, wrote a song like "Hoochie Coochie Man" for Muddy Waters (a Chess artist) and another group, say the Crewcuts, did a cover version of it, it meant more money for everybody—except Muddy Waters, whose sales of the song would certainly be diluted.

As airplay became a more cherished commodity, the indies began offering disc jockeys something much more valuable than a few dollars, or a night out on the town: they offered a piece of the song itself, a percentage of the publishing rights. Who wouldn't play a song if every spin meant money in one's own pocket—forever? And while this may have meant a nice little taste for a disc jockey initially, it soon took on greater import when, in 1955, Atlantic records made a deal with a company in England to export their music and then, in 1958, Chess followed suit. By 1958, England was rhythm-and-blues obsessed; when Chuck Berry went straight to the top of British charts in 1958, it was clear this music was international and the revenue stream was potentially enormous.

Meanwhile, back in Cleveland, a record store owner named Leo Mintz persuaded a young man named Alan Freed to emcee a program of rhythm-and-blues records over a local radio station. On July 11, 1951, calling himself "Moondog," Alan Freed hit the air. Within a year he had become a sensation with the local kids, and at his "Moondog Coronation Ball" in March 1952—credited with being the first rock and roll concert in the United States—twenty thousand fans crashed the gates at the Cleveland Arena. His audience, which was initially mostly black, began to include an increasing number of whites, and Freed began to refer to the music he was playing as "rock and roll" instead of "rhythm and blues" or "cat music." Indeed, Freed is credited with inventing the term "rock and roll," but it was not something he made up out of whole cloth. The terms "rock" and "roll" had been associated with rhythm and blues for a long time and were usually used as verbs (e.g. to rock with your baby), and, like the term "jazz" before them, connoted sex. For example, back in 1951, there was a song by the Dominos called "60 Minute Man" that included the line "They call me lovin' Dan, I rock 'em and roll 'em all night long, I'm a 60 minute man." So "rock and roll" was just something that came out of Alan Freed's mouth, and it caught on. His friend Hy Weiss said, "He knew it meant 'fucking' in the black community but he went with it anyway, saying 'the whites will never know.'"

By 1954, Freed had become increasingly important in the world of R&B, a one-man promotion phenomenon. If he played your song, it was well on its way to becoming a hit. In the process, he had become good friends with many small label owners, including Leonard and Phil Chess, and was responsible for breaking many of their records. In return, label owners gave him expensive gifts—cash, crystal, furs for his wife—and then they began to offer him a piece of the song publishing in return for playing it on the air. Freed claimed he never asked for anything and insisted the gifts and favors and cash were "for consulting services." But when he hired the mobster Morris Levy to be his personal manager and moved to WINS in New York, it was pretty clear to everybody in the business that his playlist was for sale. Soon Freed was making money from management fees, record sales, distribution deals, and songwriting royalties as well as from his radio program. In addition, he would occasionally discover songs or acts and pass them along to labels, in return for a "consideration"; for example, he discovered a group called the Moonglows and had them signed to the Chess label. Their first release was a song called "Sincerely," published by Chess, which became a big hit on the R&B charts after Freed played it. Then the Chess boys in turn got the song to the McGuire Sisters, who also cut it and had an even bigger hit on the pop charts. Not surprisingly, Freed was listed as one of the writers of the song.

Ultimately, Alan Freed was credited with cowriting fifteen major rock-and-roll hits, including Chuck Berry's "Maybelline," even though he did little more than play them on the air and hire the artists at his concerts. And while many in the business were righteously indignant at his boldness, to many black artists, Freed was the one man who saved them from obscurity, and they were vocal in their gratitude to him. Recalling how Freed helped popularize his music, Little Richard once said it was "a little Jewish boy" who played his songs when so many mainstream radio stations had refused. It is interesting to note that to Little Richard, Freed's being Jewish was the salient factor, not his white skin. "Had Freed been a Methodist, it is hard to imagine Richard praising 'the little Methodist boy' who played 'Tutti Frutti.'"

In 1954, Freed's first year at WINS in New York, the station posted a 42 percent rise in advertising sales. Meanwhile, while his early stage shows in Cleveland had attracted large but mostly black audiences, his new rock and roll shows in New York were filling New York's Paramount Theater and were equally divided between black and white teenagers. This meant a potentially huge market for the labels. Their challenge was to understand this cultural explosion and meet the growing demand.

Freed's close friend Leonard Chess was one of the main beneficiaries of this new teenage environment. And if he occasionally gave away pieces of hit songs, he also earned them. For example, in early 1955, an odd guitarist who built his own instruments named Ellas McDaniel and a harmonica player named Billy Boy Arnold cut a demo of an odd song called "Uncle John" and brought it to Chess. Leonard liked it and signed them, but he wanted both a new name for the act and different lyrics for the song. The original lyrics began "Uncle John got corn ain't never been shucked, Uncle John got daughters ain't never been . . . to school," and Leonard knew disc jockeys would never play it on the air. One of the musicians at the session claims the name "Bo Diddley" popped into his head when he recalled a circus clown on the street who used that name, and he suggested it. "Bo Diddley" fit the cadence of "Uncle John," and the band changed the first verse to begin, "Bo Diddley bought his baby a diamond ring. . . ." In March 1955 the group went into Universal Studios in Chicago and cut the song with Leonard very much in charge: he told McDaniel where to play his solo and how to turn up the tremolo on his amplifier. Within weeks, the single was on the charts, with Alan Freed at WINS leading the charge. To the end, Arnold insisted the success of the song was owed to Leonard Chess. "If we had recorded for any of the other record companies, the word 'Bo Diddley' would have never come about because they would have recorded exactly what we had. They wouldn't have sat down like Leonard did and sort of like made the record what it was."

A couple of months later, in May 1955, a guitar player named Chuck Berry showed up at Leonard's office. He had a song called "Ida Red," but because there already was a song by that name, and seeing a mascara box in the office, Leonard suggested he change the title to "Maybelline." The record was released in late July, and Leonard personally flew to New York to hand it to Alan Freed, who played it to death. By August 15, it was on the bestseller chart. By September it was number one. Not just on the R&B charts but on the pop charts. A black artist had finally crossed all the way over. Suddenly, rock and roll had become, in the words of *Cashbox*, "the great unifying force." At *Billboard* they were talking about "the integration of chart categories."

It wasn't just the chart categories that were being integrated. At the bar mitzvah of Leonard's son Marshall, "Hebrew chants mixed with blues guitar." The guests included, along with family and friends, dozens of industry insiders: from New York, Jerry Wexler and Alan Freed; from Nashville, Randy Wood of Randy's Record Shop and WLAC's Gene Nobles; from Memphis, record pressers; distributors from Atlanta; and of course dozens of black Chicago radio personalities and musicians. Marshall himself said that when he stepped to the altar to begin the service, he nearly broke out laughing: halfway back in the sanctuary was a row of black guests, yarmulkes perched precariously on their pompadours. It may have been the only bar mitzvah ever written up in both *Billboard* and *Cashbox*. Obviously, everybody was getting along nicely—except those not invited to the table.

This included the very powerful American Society of Authors, Composers and Publishers. ASCAP believed that the only reason that BMI songs, like the ones in the Chess catalog, became such big hits was because of payola; rock and roll was just a fad, they felt, sustained by greed and payoffs. If DJs (who got bribes to play BMI songs) were exposed, and if the playing field was leveled, so the thinking went, rock and roll would fade away. At the same time, the country was reeling from a major congressional investigation into a scandal involving television quiz shows, when a committee had established that the most popular ones, like *21,* were rigged. Following this lead, ASCAP urged the House Oversight Subcommittee to look into the recording industry's practice of payola. The committee agreed and began to investigate DJs who took gifts from record companies; next, the IRS announced that it too was going to look more closely at business expense deductions for gifts and promotion. When the FCC got involved as well, and ruled that payola was an unfair and deceptive trade practice because the public didn't know that money had changed hands, the game was up. In the end, twenty-five DJs and program directors were caught in the scandal, including New York's Murray "the K" Kaufman, Dick Clark, and Alan Freed. Kaufman and Clark pled guilty and got a slap on the wrist. Freed refused to plead, claiming he programmed records "solely and completely on the basis of my evaluation of the records and their appeal to my listening audience." Two days later, he was fired.

One record executive found the whole episode bizarre and unfair, "that one American business is singled out for industrial gift giving. At the same time record people were being thrown in jail, professionals in Washington were doing the very same thing. They're called lobbyists." In the end, although the investigation destroyed Freed's career, the scandal did little more than shine a light on a practice that would become even more prevalent in the passing years—pay for play, they called it—and in its own way, accelerated the vogue for singer-songwriters.

Singer-songwriters (generally young white middle-class kids who performed original material and generally controlled their own work) had been coming to the Brill Building along with the other "assembly line" songwriters for some time. One such collaboration called itself Tom and Jerry, two fifteen-year-old Jewish kids from Queens. The one who called himself Jerry Landis had a father who had been a professional musician and along the way gave his young son his old guitar and encouraged him in music. By the time the boy was thirteen, he was already writing songs. He would go into the bathroom at home, pull down the shades, turn on the water tap, and practice; he said he liked what he called "the sounds of silence." From the beginning, he said his songs arrived "nearly intact," and he reported, "I realized what I was fascinated with, couldn't explain, was *sound*—that you can't really say why a combination of sounds is moving or feels really good and right—and the whole game was: Can I get the sounds in my head on tape?"

He met his partner, "Tom Graph," in grade school and by the time they were thirteen, they were singing together. When they were fourteen they began looking up record companies in the Yellow Pages, and with a little help from a father in the business, they were able to arrange a few auditions in the Brill Building. One day, in 1956, when they were fifteen, they were recording a demo and a man named Sid Prosen, who had a small label, happened to be standing in the hallway. Liking what he heard, he signed "Tom and Jerry" and they recorded their original song "Hey, Schoolgirl!" for his label. Prosen paid Alan Freed to play it, *Cashbox* picked the song as its Sleeper of the Week, and within months, the record had sold one hundred thousand copies. The duo of Tom and Jerry appeared on American Bandstand on the same day that Jerry Lee Lewis sang his new hit "Great Balls of Fire."

After several failed attempts to repeat the success of that first hit, Tom and Jerry broke up. For a while, Jerry recorded demos of songs (not his own) for presentation to stars like Dion, Fabian, and Bobby Vee, but at $25 apiece, that didn't last long. Next, he enrolled in Queens College, where he majored in English, graduating in 1962. Not knowing what to do next, he went to England and began busking on street corners. That could have been the end of his career but for a lucky twist of fate; as it happened, he returned to the States shortly thereafter and reunited with his old pal Tom, and this time they used their real names: Paul Simon and Art Garfunkel.

The singer-songwriter archetype was part of an American tradition, and like rock and roll itself, its roots were rural and Southern; but unlike rock and roll, this tradition was also connected to the politics of change—fallout from the Great Depression—specifically the worker's parties and labor union rallies. For years, songs like "Solidarity Forever" and "Joe Hill" were known to workers' groups everywhere, and were often mixed with tent-show sing-alongs like "Michael Row the Boat Ashore." This singer-songwriter tradition remained within the labor movement until 1950, when the song "Goodnight Irene"—written by Huddy Ledbetter (aka Leadbelly) back in 1932 and often included in union sing-alongs—became a number one hit for a group called the Weavers. That's when "folk music" appeared on the national radar.

American folk music was essentially utilitarian; like the blues, anybody could sing it (you didn't need a great voice), but unlike the blues, it was about group dynamics rather than individual heartbreak, about perseverance rather than passion: the subject was more often *we* ("this is how *we* feel"), not *I* (this is how *I* feel). For example, "John Henry" (a folk ballad) is about the plight of the exploited worker fighting the encroaching machine age, while "Frankie and Johnny" (a blues) is about a fight between two lovers. Jews had been active in the workers' parties and labor struggles since the turn of the century and knew this folk tradition well, but they were not known for their contribution to the singer-songwriter tradition; that is, not until a cowboy from Brooklyn named Elliot Adnopoz picked up the guitar and began to follow the lead of Woody Guthrie. He changed his name to "Ramblin' Jack" Elliott and became the role model for a generation of young singer-songwriters. In an era of lefty East Coast Jewish summer camps, where kids learned their politics while they shared their first kiss, "Ramblin' Jack" helped set the stage for Bob Dylan and the "music of conscience" in the sixties.

Woody Guthrie was an American legend by the time he died in 1967, but he lived most of his life as an ordinary man, bumming around the country with a guitar on which was written "This machine kills fascists." Guthrie had traveled with migrant workers from Oklahoma to California to learn the traditional folk and blues songs, and many of his original compositions were about his experiences during the Dust Bowl era of the Great Depression, earning him the nickname "the Dust Bowl Troubadour." He wrote hundreds of political, traditional, and children's songs, but his best-known song is "This Land Is Your Land," written in 1940 as a response, he said, to Irving Berlin's "God Bless America," which he considered "unrealistic and complacent." The song was not published until 1951, when it was included in a small mimeographed booklet with typed lyrics and hand drawings and sold for 25 cents at rallies. Eventually it became one of the most famous songs of the twentieth century. What is not so well known, however, is Guthrie's connection to Jewish tradition.

Guthrie moved to New York in 1940. There he met and married a Jewish dancer named Marjorie Mazia and settled in a primarily Jewish neighborhood in Coney Island, Brooklyn. According to his daughter Nora, keeper of the Woody Guthrie Foundation and Archives, Woody found "common ground" with his Jewish neighbors and, in particular, a kindred spirit in his mother-in-law, Aliza Greenblatt, a Yiddish poet with a strong social consciousness. He became immersed in Judaism and churned out lyrics reflecting this passion. "He put himself in the camp," Nora said. "This is really fascinating to me—that he suddenly became a Jew, in his own way." He eventually wrote hundreds of pages of unpublished lyrics about Jewish holidays, Jewish history, and Jewish spirituality.

Elliot Adnopoz, on the other hand, was *born* in Brooklyn in 1931, a Jewish boy whose father was a respected surgeon. Elliot was expected to follow the same career path, but, inspired by the rodeos he attended at Madison Square Garden, decided he would rather be a cowboy. Unlike 99.9 percent of young boys who shared this dream, Elliot actually did it. When he was fifteen, Elliot ran away from home to join Col. Jim Eskew's rodeo, the only rodeo east of the Mississippi. He was with them for three months when his parents tracked him down and had him sent home, but while on the road, Elliot had heard his first singing cowboy, a rodeo clown named Brahmer Rogers, and decided that's what he wanted to do too. Long before every kid in America wanted to play guitar—before Elvis, Dylan, Bloomfield, or Slash—Ramblin' Jack had picked it up and was passing it along. When he met Woody Guthrie in 1950, he traveled America with him, from California to Florida, from the redwood forests to the Gulf Stream waters. Elliott (when he changed this from first name to his last, he added another T.) became so enthralled with Guthrie that he completely absorbed his inflections and mannerisms, leading Guthrie to remark, "Jack sounds more like me than I do."

Elliott was a born storyteller. Even his nickname, "Ramblin' Jack," came not from his love of travel but from his love of talking. The folk singer Odetta claimed that it was her mother who gave him the handle, remarking, "Oh, Jack Elliott, yeah, he can sure ramble on!" This tradition of storytelling, and of integrating songs with stories or political messages, was being passed down by many performers, including Guthrie as well as others like Leadbelly, Mississippi John Hurt, Jesse Fuller, and the Reverend Gary Davis. But the way it came through Elliott—with his laconic, humorous style of talking, his traditional flat-picking style of playing guitar, his habit of accompanying himself on harmonica, the strained, nasal quality of his voice—is almost verbatim the way a young Bob Dylan would sound at the start of his own career. Thus the person of Elliot Adnopoz is an important piece in the developing American singer-songwriter continuum.

Similarly, the existence in the fifties of several Jewish-owned record labels devoted to folk music assured its survival: Vanguard Records, started by Maynard Solomon, recorded both Joan Baez and Buffy Sainte-Marie; Folkways Records, started by Moe Asch, released more than two thousand albums, including spoken word, poetry, and the works of Woody Guthrie, Pete Seeger, and Leadbelly; and Elektra Records, started by Jac Holzman, recorded Judy Collins and singers Phil Ochs and Tom Paxton, who helped shape the protest-slash-art music that became a commercial phenomenon in the sixties.

By the late 1950s, American folk music had become a good deal more complex than the simple traditional style of singing and playing that came out of the Dust Bowl and work camps; if that was all it was, it would have disappeared in the rush toward modernism, long before the sixties. It survived and became an influential aspect of the antiwar counterculture because, during the fifties, it addressed a key issue for an influential group of young people in major urban areas; the ongoing question of "authenticity." Just as Leiber and Stoller had discovered their own version of authenticity in the music of black R&B, so too a thriving coffeehouse scene had developed around the issue in major cities such as Boston, Chicago, and New York. There, a distinctly Jewish-beatnik milieu, a loose-knit community where jazz music, pot smoking, a love of literature, and an open, interracial dating scene (prompting Normal Mailer's famous "white Negro" essay in *Esquire* magazine) offered a radical alternative to the *Leave It to Beaver* image of America being sold on television. Given a choice between lying around some "pad" in the Village listening to Miles Davis or being propped up on a suburban sofa digging Patti Page singing "How Much Is That Doggie in the Window?" many young people made the same decision Mezz Mezzrow had made two decades earlier. The folk movement was part of this larger experiment, and it hinged on the concept of "being real," of defining the space you occupy and owning it.

There is an obvious irony in sophisticated urban kids working to be "authentically" rural and primitive. But for Jews who grew up on the outside of mainstream society, always sensing their difference, to be fully American was a powerful draw, and in seeking authentic traditions that were congruent with Jewish epistemology, the left-wing people's movement (that also included a rich base of hedonism and intellectual activity) was an obvious draw. Besides, part of being an "authentic" American is being able to invent and reinvent yourself, and so, in the broadest sense, perhaps there is no more authentic American than an inauthentic one, or at least one who is trying on different personas.

The New York folkies had a kind of clubhouse in Izzy Young's Folklore Center on MacDougal Street between Bleecker and Third streets. There, Young was constantly organizing events and putting people in touch with each other. By the mid-sixties, there were folklore centers all over America, many inspired by this one dedicated Jewish entrepreneur. If the Folklore Center was the clubhouse, Washington Square Park was the playground. Singer Dave Van Ronk, an important figure on the New York folk scene during the fifties and sixties, described an average afternoon in the park in 1956:

> There would be six or seven different groups of musicians, most of them over near the arch and the fountain. The Zionists were the most visible, because they had to stake out a large enough area for the dancers, and they would be over by the Sullivan Street side of the square, singing "Hava Nagila." Then there would be Stalinists: someone like Jerry Silverman would be playing guitar, surrounded by all these summer camp kids of the People's Songs persuasion, singing old union songs and things they had picked up from *Sing Out* [the magazine edited by Irwin Silber], the Bluegrassers would be off in another area, led by Roger Sprung, the original citybilly. As far as I know, Roger single-handedly brought Scruggs picking to the city—not just to New York but to any city. Lionel Kilberg would be playing bass, and there would be a little group around them that gradually grew to include a lot of people who would go on to spearhead the bluegrass and old-time string band revivals.

"A lot of both the middle-class left wingers and the workers back in the 1930s were first or second generation immigrants," Van Ronk notes, "and the folk revival served as a way for them to establish American roots. This was especially true for the Jews. *The folk revivalists were at least 50 percent Jewish* [italics mine], and they adopted the music as part of a process of assimilation to the Anglo-American tradition. . . . Of course that rush to assimilate was not limited to Jews, but I think they were more conscious of what they were doing than a lot of other people were."

And, as if to cement the deal, he recalls, "When Roger Sprung, one of the original Washington Square bluegrassers, showed up with a couple of his buddies at the Asheville Folk Festival in the early 1950s, Bascom Lamar Lunsford, the festival organizer [a racist, anti-Semitic white supremacist] got up and announced, 'Now, Ladies and Gentlemen, I would like to present the three Jews from New York.'"

This urban folk music was essentially a new music, consciously and often carefully crafted, politically motivated, and in many ways quite different from the rural folk music that had come before it. It was in part a reaction to the Red Scare of the forties and fifties, a witch hunt in which thousands of people lost their jobs and were harassed by the FBI, and it was also a new form of show business: the "authenticity hustle." Bob Dylan became a master at this game, but he was not alone in inventing characters for himself to play. Trying on different realities ("authenticities") was becoming a popular game. And it spawned a new style of songwriting that was quite different from any that had come before.

"Any music is the music of its time," writes Van Ronk, but a great deal of the music written in the 1960s was also *about* its time. It dealt directly, almost on a one-to-one basis, with the experiences that people were going through at that moment. This self-referential, "history made while you wait" attitude would become a watchword for the sixties.

In the end, the folk revival was historically important if only because it welcomed thinkers and populists into the contemporary American songwriting business. But perhaps equally important was its contribution to the new *sound* of popular music. First, folk songs were often sung by people who did not have pretty voices, and as delivered by Bob Dylan, this rough and raw approach would propel waves of singer-songwriters and punk rockers for generations to come. One didn't have to sound like a professional in order to be a professional. And second, the introduction of the long play recording was hastened in part by this urban folk music; songs like "How Much Is That Doggie in the Window?" were sold as 45 rpm singles for 99 cents each, but folk music was sold on albums. And while it was true that long-play albums allowed the industry to repackage groups of singles and resell them in the new format (much as the CD technology would do several decades later), phonograph equipment was quickly improving and LPs delivered the superior sound that jazz and folk music customers, urbanites by and large, demanded.

Popular movements invariably lose momentum when they become institutionalized (nothing can kill a social movement like corporate success), and by 1963, it was evident that the Brill Building style had peaked. That year, Don Kirshner sold Aldon Music to Columbia Pictures / Screen Gems and all the young writers, who had been so fresh and experimental only a few years earlier, were now assigned to come up with theme songs for mainstream TV shows or to provide pop confections for Columbia's contract actors who wanted to dabble in singing. When Phil Spector brought Barry Mann and Cynthia Weil to the West Coast to write "You've Lost That Lovin' Feelin'" for the Righteous Brothers, that particular mountain had clearly been scaled, even though the Brill Building writers would continue cranking out hits throughout the sixties. And the view from the top was not immediately clear. Because by then, folk music too was diluted with Kingston Trio–type happy talk; at college campuses everywhere, "folk" music was referring less to the sociology of its source and more to the fact that most of the kids buying it were supported by their folks.

It was all fun and games—until that morning in 1963 when President Kennedy was assassinated, and then everything changed. There was a tremendous sense of vulnerability: it was like an attack on youth itself; if they could get Kennedy, then no one was safe anymore, all bets were off, and reality was what you made of it. That day, we all sailed off into uncharted waters.

HIDING IN PLAIN SIGHT

HIDING IN PLAIN SIGHT

November 22, 1963, arrived as a cold gray morning in Madison, Wisconsin. At 9 a.m. I was in the basement of Discount Records, opening boxes and checking in stock. As in most small college towns, phonograph records in Madison were sold primarily in variety stores (Woolworth's) or appliance stores; there were very few stand-alone record stores. So when Discount Records opened on campus the year before, it became a meeting house for a group that included record collectors, film buffs, musicians, lefties, historians, artists, philosophers, hipsters, and musical adventurers of every stripe—not unlike the scene described by Milt Gabler at the Commodore Record Store in New York decades earlier. In the sixties, music was a kind of code word for so much more than just music, and unraveling what that "more" involved required meetings, hangs, listening parties, and jam sessions well into the night, some in the store itself after hours and behind locked doors. Down in the basement, we were taking in boxes and boxes of albums by Peter, Paul and Mary (containing their hit single "Blowin' in the Wind"), and we were starting to see a lot of Bob Dylan as well. There was a trend here. Previously, the big sellers at this store had been classical records (Herbert Von Karajan's Beethoven's Nine box set on DGG), Broadway soundtracks (*My Fair Lady*, always popular), and jazz. In fact, after the symphonies and operas, the biggest seller at the time had been the new "bossa nova" sound of Stan Getz.

Getz (born Stanley Gayetsky in Philadelphia to Ukrainian Jewish immigrants) was a tenor saxophone player with a wonderfully lyrical sound, a star in the swing era and now, having returned from a U.S. State Department tour of Brazil, a pioneer with *Jazz Samba*. His adaptation of Antonio Carlos Jobim's "One Note Samba," and his solo on the song "Desafinado," won a Grammy award in 1963, and then, when he recorded the album *Getz/Gilberto* with João Gilberto and his wife, Astrud, "The Girl from Ipanema" won him another Grammy and made Getz one of the best-selling jazz musicians ever.

But that summer, Peter, Paul and Mary's single "Blowin' in the Wind" had been a huge hit (released in June, by July it had sold more than a million copies nationwide), and the album continued selling hundreds of copies to college students at our small campus store; this was unexpected: at the time, all album sales were relatively modest, and our biggest sellers—like the *West Side Story* soundtrack or *The Second Barbra Streisand Album*—were generally pitched to wealthy customers with high-end audio gear. The former was a kind of populist musical with romantic social-justice overtones, whose revolutionary dance grammar, invented by Jerome Robbins (Jerry Rabinowitz)—with groups of jazzy kids in street clothes swinging in unison—was the forerunner for so many Michael Jackson videos. The Streisand story was something else.

Barbara was a phenomenon in the Judy Garland mode, a kind of waif with a tragic back-story and an extraordinary voice (some have called it "the voice of the century"). It was not only her sound but her persona that was remarkable: first, she was a rising Jewish star who did not change her name, and it was obviously a Jewish name; and second, she was a good-looking girl who did not change her nose, and it was obviously a Jewish nose. These were not small things (no irony intended) because, as we have seen, in the 1950s, not only did one routinely change one's name in show business, but prospective divas regularly altered their profiles. But significantly, Streisand did not consider either of these options.

As a teenager, Streisand had been a gawky kid from Brooklyn, very bright, very willful, who was tormented with names like "big beak" and "*mieskeit*" (the Yiddish word for a person who was an ugly mess). She went to a large school—Erasmus Hall High School in Flatbush—but her life was played out in a small social Siberia. "I wouldn't know who to talk to," Barbra said. "I was smart, but the smart kids wearing oxfords and glasses wouldn't look at me, and the dumb kids I wouldn't want to associate with. So I was a real outsider." Her response was to develop the demeanor of a star, a kind of "haughty, defensive air" that only spurred her tormentors on.

She always felt there was something missing in her life. "When I was young," she said, "I felt like I came from another planet. And at the same time, I felt like I was chosen, that I was somehow special." Feeling chosen is of course the classic Jewish reaction to the experience of living on the outside, which was only heightened for Barbra when, on her fourteenth birthday, her mother took her to see the Broadway production of *The Diary of Anne Frank*. (She had wanted to see *My Fair Lady*, but her mother wouldn't pay the extra dollar for the ticket.) The choice was fortuitous, however, because after the lights went down, Barbra came face to face with a story she recognized as very close to her own: here was a girl of thirteen, dreaming about living a glamorous life, being asked, "Why do you show off all the time? Why can't you be more like other domestic girls? Sewing is important. Cooking is important." Anne Frank says, "I'd open my veins first. I'm going to be remarkable. I'm going to be a famous dancer or singer, something wonderful." To the young Barbra, it was like watching her own story play out on stage; leaving the theater, she told her mother she could have played Anne Frank at least as well as the actress on stage (Susan Strasberg). She said, "I knew what she was feeling."

Streisand had a tremendous sense of self and a desire to "make it" on her own terms, to be accepted for who she was, Jewishness and all. The gawky Jewish girl would step up and reveal something remarkable. Her earliest performances at Max Gordon's Village Vanguard, when she was still a teenager, were transforming. The acceptance she received there was the opposite of the experience she had known in high school. Here, in front of New York's hip elite, she became the diva, the butterfly that emerged from the chrysalis of rejection. Her large Semitic nose became a dramatic profile, a thing of beauty, and ultimately her story became a new kind of morality tale for Jews across the country: here was a Jew who was fearless in letting her Jewish flag fly. Her greatest hits rode on the waves of these emotions, and her fans—many of them gay and in the closet as well as Jewish and passing—took her success to be something larger than life, something personal as well as professional: a statement of authenticity. Much as Bessie Smith and other black female blues shouters had delivered the similar message forty years earlier, her story—one of justice in a world of injustice—made her a diva in a much larger production than the world of popular music. This conflation of pop music and social justice was just starting to be felt on college campuses.

A brief glance at the hit songs being played on the radio at the time would give little indication that popular culture in America was about to undergo a dramatic transformation: songs like "Deep Purple" by Nino Tempo and April Stevens, "Washington Square" by the Village Stompers, "Be My Baby" by the Ronettes, "Busted" by Ray Charles, "Bossa Nova Baby" by Elvis, "Walking the Dog" by Rufus Thomas, "Dominique" by the Singing Nun, "Heat Wave" by Martha and the Vandellas, "Surfer Girl" by the Beach Boys, and last, but surely not least, "Louie Louie" by the Kingsmen. Still, the phenomenal success of "Blowin' in the Wind" was right there for all to see: at Discount Records we were selling hundreds of copies of Peter, Paul and Mary and Bob Dylan albums weekly (sometimes daily).

If Streisand was the ugly duckling who became the swan by embracing, indeed glorying in her past—like a modern-day Cinderella, she was revealed through her suffering—Bob Dylan, by rewriting his past and transforming himself into something completely other (a narrative), receded into the poem he sang and erased his personal story. And yet, more than Streisand, he signaled the shift at the base of American popular culture: he was a gifted "everyman," a self-professed anti-star. In the process, his story became the stuff of legend: henceforth, American popular music would by necessity reference the glory of the average man. Music, as the saying of the day went, "belonged to the people." At the time, no one could know that Streisand represented the end of the beginning—the last of the great Broadway divas—while Dylan represented the beginning of the end, the demise of the professional Tin Pan Alley songwriter. Yet looking at him, he appeared to be just another scruffy kid, like so many others walking down State Street in Madison.

Indeed, just one year before his great success in New York City, Dylan *was* just a scruffy kid walking down State Street. He had arrived in Madison in December 1960 to visit an acquaintance named Fred Underhill, a member of Madison's folk music / political activist scene. At the time, the main topic of discussion on campus was the Freedom Rides taking place in Mississippi, but Bob was not particularly interested in that or any of the politics of the day. He was completely captured by the transformative nature of the music, particularly as it played out in the social activist's environment: the revelation was that music could be serious as well as popular. Bob appeared to be transfixed by this aspect of folk music—its credibility. By the time he showed up in Wisconsin, his transformation from Robert Zimmerman to Bob Dylan was well under way but not yet complete; he had adopted the new last name, had abandoned ties to his home in Hibbing, Minnesota, but had not yet started telling the wild, phantasmagoric stories about his past nor developed the compelling, "howling" stage persona that would eventually drive his future.

There Was a Fire: Jews, Music and the American Dream

Dylan is arguably the most widely researched American artist of the twentieth century. Fans have done everything from paw through his trash to write dissertations on his work, searching for clues to the Dylan conundrum: Who is he *really*? Fifty years on, the question is still relevant, and still impossible to answer. This in itself is remarkable and virtually unprecedented in modern media culture; few other artists (one thinks perhaps of Thomas Pynchon and J. D. Salinger in the world of literature, or Thelonious Monk in the world of jazz) have guarded their privacy as closely as Dylan has guarded his. Virtually everyone, from fans to critics, presumes he has played some kind of game with his public; it rarely occurs to anyone to take him at face value. Yet in the end one is left with the feeling that Bob Dylan meant exactly what he said and said precisely what he meant. His gift with words is what got him into trouble. His indirect answers to direct questions were often ludicrous. Take for example his response to the question "How did you choose your career?" "Carelessness" he said.

> "I lost my one true love. I started drinking. The first thing I know, I'm in a card game. Then I'm in a crap game. I wake up in a pool hall. Then this big Mexican lady drags me off the table, takes me to Philadelphia. She leaves me alone in her house, and it burns down. I wind up in Phoenix. I get a job as a Chinaman. I start working in a dime store, and move in with a thirteen-year-old girl. Then this big Mexican lady from Philadelphia comes in and burns the house down. I go down to Dallas. I get a job as a 'before' in a Charles Atlas 'before and after' ad. I move in with a delivery boy who can cook fantastic chili and hot dogs. Then this thirteen-year-old girl from Phoenix comes and burns the house down. The delivery boy—he ain't so mild: He gives her the knife, and the next thing I know I'm in Omaha. It's so cold there, by this time I'm robbing my own bicycles and frying my own fish. I stumble onto some luck and get a job as a carburetor out at the hot-rod races every Thursday night. I move in with a high school teacher who also does a little plumbing on the side, who ain't much to look at, but who's built a special kind of refrigerator that can turn newspaper into lettuce. Everything's going good until that delivery boy shows up and tries to knife me. Needless to say, he burned the house down, and I hit the road. The first guy that picked me up asked me if I wanted to be a star. What could I say?"

Lies, of course, but the feeling of adventure, escape, frustration, entrapment, of being on the run, of facing imminent danger, free floating lust, of being in the wrong place at the right time, of needing to constantly reinvent oneself, this was all true. At the time, young people were all caught up in a dream of self-transformation, in the adventure of changing themselves and changing the world. This too was the American dream, perhaps more so than the dream of a house with a white picket fence, or forty acres and a mule. "I'll let you be in my dream," Dylan sang in 1962, "if I can be in yours," and a generation took him up on it. So while Dylan's stories were often composed of lies, they were lies that told a much greater truth. And the *way* he told these stories was equally important: he used vernacular language that, like the language of Irving Berlin decades before, was not his own natural language but reflected something larger, something deeply poetic in the American soul: it swung.

There was no way to plumb the deeper subconscious yearnings of the time with simple political rhetoric, although many tried. Indeed, as Dave Van Ronk noted, the core problem with the New Left (the sixties term for the "politics of change") was that "it wasn't an ideology, it was a mood." Dylan's narratives, on the other hand, were exactly that: they conjured this mood, seemed to ride a profound wave of emotion that somehow rang true—whether or not the message was always clear. Dylan himself maintained that he didn't know what many of his songs meant, that he was the last one to ask. If we take Dylan at face value, his story is the story of a grand interior journey; he says he was in the circus? Well let's assume he *was* in a circus, both in terms of his interior journey and the circumstances of his external life: Bobby Zimmerman, through his artistic will, created that circus, and Bob Dylan was its ringmaster; today Zimmerman is gone, a myth, while his creation remains in full flower.

Bob's grandparents fled Odessa, Russia, in 1905 when fifty thousand czarists marched through the streets screaming "Down with the Jews," shooting, stabbing, raping, and strangling thousands. His grandfather made it to Duluth, Minnesota, which had the advantage of a climate similar to Odessa's. Bob's father, Abe, was a musician who played "the Jewish guitar" (violin); his mother, Beatty, came from a prominent Jewish family in the mining town of Hibbing. When his father contracted polio in 1946 and lost his job, the family moved from Duluth to this small town. Hibbing had a thriving Jewish community, more than twenty-five hundred members, almost half born in Russia or Lithuania. The Zimmermans lived on the second floor of a frame house a couple of blocks from the synagogue. His family kept kosher, observed the Sabbath, and in 1954, when it came time for Bob's bar mitzvah, brought in a special rabbi from New York to prepare him to be a man. The rabbi, a very old Jew with black robes and a white beard, must have done a good job, because, as his later work testifies, Bob was clearly well grounded in the tales of the Old Testament.

In Hibbing, there were "bears in the pine forests; the northern lights could be seen flashing across the bleak horizon." "In the winter," Bob said, "everything was still, nothing moved. Eight months of that . . . you can have some amazing hallucinogenic experiences doing nothing but looking out your window." Many years later, when an interviewer asked Bob if he was "a mystical person," his answer was telling in the connection it made between his origins and his outlook: "Absolutely. I think it's the land. The streams, the forests, the vast emptiness. The land created me." At night, Bob's portable radio (a bar mitzvah gift) picked up stations from as far away as Nashville, Tennessee, and Shreveport, Louisiana. He heard Johnny Ray ("he was dynamic and different and really had heart and soul") and Hank Williams ("the ol' Lovesick Blues Boy"). He heard Muddy Waters, John Lee Hooker,

Jimmy Reed, and Howlin' Wolf. "I used to stay up till two, three o'clock in the morning," he remembered. "Listened to all those songs, then tried to figure them out." The experience of hearing this magical music coming to him in the dark was the core experience of his life. He later said, "The reason I can stay so single-minded about my music is because it affected me at an early age in a very, very powerful way and it's all that affected me. It's all that ever remained true for me, and I'm very glad this particular music reached me when it did. Because frankly, if it hadn't, I don't know what would have become of me."

In the summer, like other Jewish kids, Bob went to Camp Herzl, a Jewish enclave in the northern Wisconsin woods. There he spent most of his time playing piano in the lodge, maintaining an aura of introspection, of mystery; even at age fourteen, according to a childhood friend, he was already "cool," not disenfranchised but focused, smart, funny, "kind of a star" who had "a lot of girls around him." It is important to note that whatever possessed the young Bob Zimmerman to transition into the magnificent narrative that would become Bob Dylan, it was not peer-group alienation or the kind of humiliation that had driven previous generations of Jewish artists (one thinks of Artie Shaw). Bob was not on the outside looking in; if anything, he was on the inside looking out.

Back in Hibbing with his friends, Bob was a fan of modern films as well as popular music, and his favorite was *Blackboard Jungle*. He also loved James Dean, seeing himself as the young "rebel without a cause," and he and his friends memorized lines from that film ("I don't want an answer in ten years, I want an answer now!"). His first instrument was piano, and he began forming bands early on. He had been, like so many others, transformed by seeing Elvis Presley on *The Ed Sullivan Show*, the way Presley moved, his whole bad-boy image, and Bob also loved the outrageous pompadour and standup pyrotechnics of pianist Little Richard. Then, in 1958, a tragedy struck close to home: one of Bob's bandmates, a good friend from camp named Larry Keegan, jumped into a swimming pool and broke his neck, paralyzing him for the rest of his life. From all accounts, this event affected Bob dramatically, became a glowing coal at the heart of his self-transformation. Life was fragile, subject to change at any time, and, as he would write later, "those who are not busy being born are busy dying." His frantic years of self-transformation speak of a kind of near panic to do the work before it was done to him by some unknowable, unanticipated force. Years later, he wrote to Keegan that when he thinks about what had happened, "I become speechless unto myself." "It set him off in a way," remembers his friend Bob Cohen. "He became inward, keeping most things to himself."

Oddly, it forced him into a reality that was more imagined than actual: he described his own roots as "eccentric," continuing,

> Mass media had no overwhelming reach so I was drawn to the traveling performers passing through. The side show performers—bluegrass singers, the black cowboy with chaps and a lariat doing rope tricks. Miss Europe,

> Quasimodo, the Bearded Lady, the half-man half-woman, the deformed and the bent, Atlas the Dwarf, the fire-eaters, the teachers and preachers, the blues singers. I remember it like it was yesterday. I got close to some of these people. I learned about dignity from them. Freedom too. Civil rights, human rights. How to stay within yourself. Most others were into the rides like the tilt-a-whirl and the rollercoaster. To me that was the nightmare. All the giddiness. The artificiality of it. The sledge hammer of life. It didn't make sense or seem real. The stuff *off the main road* was where the force of reality was. At least it struck me that way. When I left home those feelings didn't change.

This passage holds a key to Dylan's path — a life on the road driven by identification with the outsider. Although from all accounts his daily life was small-town normal, still, as a skinny Jewish kid growing up on the Minnesota iron range, Bob had grasped that the reinvention of self was not only a possibility but that, in America, identifying "down" was also, potentially, a way of moving up and out.

Upon graduation from high school, Bob took a bus to Fargo, got a job busing tables, and began using the alias Elston Gunn. He managed to insinuate himself into a local band led by a singer named Bobby Vee (who three years later would have a number one hit with the song "Take Good Care of My Baby"); Vee later remembered Elston Gunn as a "spacey little guy, you know, just sort of worming his way around." On returning to Hibbing, Dylan told his friends he had played on a new record (not true) and implied that he himself was the one with the recording contract. Bob was nothing if not resolute in his desire to differentiate himself from his ordinary roots, using all his narrative powers to accomplish the task.

Exaggerating one's past is not uncommon among kids or in show business (even today, every rapper claims to be a felon), but having the wherewithal to surpass the normal white lies with enormous fantasy was unique to a gifted storyteller—or a sociopath. Bob made up one story more outrageous than another and then told them all as if they were the gospel truth. For example, he once told his high school girlfriend Echo Helstrom that he had come upon a snake wrapped around a tree and "made both the snake and the tree so vivid" that she believed him. Bob was a fantasist, but not in a malicious way, and this was part of his charm. In the spring of 1958, he announced to Echo, "I've got my name. I know what my name's gonna be now." He showed her a book of poetry; it was by Dylan Thomas.

It was Bob Zimmerman, not Dylan, however, who enrolled at the University of Minnesota in the fall of 1959. Just two years after Kerouac's *On the Road*, every serious seeker, including Bob, was reading "beat" literature and listening to folk music. Dylan, who was clearly more comfortable on the social fringes, nonetheless joined the Jewish fraternity Sigma Alpha Mu so he could live off-campus; there was method to his madness: the Sammy who got him in remembers, "I would run into him at seven in the morning when I was going out and he was coming in." Bob was living an alternative life in a neighborhood known as "Dinkytown." There he met musicians Dave "Snaker" Ray and "Spider" John Koerner, older heroes on this street of bookstores and coffeehouses. Compared to Hibbing, Dinkytown was a magical place. In the fall of 1958, the Kingston Trio had the number one hit with "Tom Dooley," and while their style was rather prissy for serious seekers like Bob, other folk singers, like Leadbelly, Pete Seeger, and Woody Guthrie, had real currency there. Dylan was especially influenced by Odetta, a singer of traditional songs like "Jack o' Diamonds" and "Mule Skinner Blues." "I heard a record of hers in a record store," he recalled, and "right then and there, I went out and traded my electric guitar and amplifier for an acoustical guitar." The young Elvis imitator was heading underground.

On college campuses in the sixties, musicians regularly hung out with political activists, film buffs, social historians, and other offbeat characters, sharing food, partners, pot, and politics in an extended bohemian family that had a decidedly Jewish cast to it. Bob fit right in, and even took up with a young Jewish woman named Tova Hammerman. She remembers him hanging out at her house where political discussions were de rigueur, but rarely joining in; instead, "he was like a sponge," Hammerman said; he was taking everything in. Another acquaintance at the time likened him to "a vessel waiting and wanting to be filled." Tova got the impression that Bob was not entirely comfortable in her company, perhaps "because I was too Jewish for him." It was not that he was ashamed of being Jewish, she thought; rather, he did not want to be defined as Jewish. Or, to maintain the metaphor, he did not want to limit that which was pouring into him. It is clear, however, that, had he been raised a Christian, the issue of religion would probably not have been a factor for him at all; indeed, if he hadn't been born Jewish, he might not have found his way to folk music in the first place. Throughout his career, he remained keenly connected to the Jewish roots of his personal narrative. Even during his "born again" period, there seemed to be something profoundly Jewish about his conversion.

"Bob was painfully shy and very nervous," said an early friend. "He used to twitch all the time; but he always had a guitar in his hand and a great sense of humor. He had a sense that fortune had put her hand on his shoulder, but he didn't really know how, or what, or why." In the beginning, when he wasn't much of a guitar player or a singer, he was still impressive as a performer, according to Koerner: "It may not have been confidence, but it's acting like confidence. You know, I'm doing this. Here's my thing. Take it or leave it. He was definitely one of the most noticeable people around." At the same time, he made a first attempt at writing songs, which, although not fully formed, were "Really nice and clear and had bite to them . . . none of the others of us were doing that." Writing your own songs back then was highly unusual; college kids rarely tried to do it because of their great respect for, or their intimidation by, the popular canon. Young white college kids in particular did not have the "authenticity" (the street credibility) to try. It was the rare individual who even attempted the move. For Bob, it wasn't so much about charisma but about commitment; the innate confidence recognized by Koerner enabled him to make his audience suspend disbelief.

In Dinkytown, Bob had become obsessed with a collection of obscure American folk songs that he discovered on a friend's rare six-record set called *The Anthology of American Folk Music*. The songs sounded as if they had come out of "a lost world, sometime around the Civil War," and they contained archaic words and strange images that seemed haunted, out of time and place. The mountain singer Dock Boggs sounded like a man "going down to Hell" as he grumbled about what to do with his child now that his "sugar baby" had gone. Other songs were about calamitous events—train wrecks, mining disasters. There were songs that documented changes in the social fabric of America, how machines had destroyed the workers' world. The language was quirky and surprising, with words and images taken from the Bible or the folklore of seemingly foreign lands. Bob borrowed the set from his friend and never returned it. For years, fragments turned up in his performances.

In the summer of 1960, Bob hitchhiked to Denver. After a month, he returned to Dinkytown with a flat Oklahoma twang and a penchant for using double negatives, an uneducated air that he had discovered in Woody Guthrie's book *Bound for Glory*. Guthrie was the real deal, and his romanticized account of a musician's life, which opens with hoboes riding in a boxcar across Minnesota—trains that Bob had seen in his youth, hearing their whistles in the night—was delivered in spare, down-to-the-bone, yet colorful language. Bob also began using Guthrie's "talking blues" style, a format that allowed one to slip in and out of conversation, to stretch the song form to accommodate insights, asides, and odd bits of humor. By channeling Guthrie, Dylan was discovering himself, and he would use the "talking blues" technique throughout the sixties to express his wildest visions. Bob even started speaking like the characters in Guthrie's book when he was offstage. When he was drunk or stoned, he would put on an old hat and pretend to *be* Guthrie. "If you didn't call him Woody," says an old girlfriend, "he wouldn't answer."

Guthrie himself was still an important icon on the folk music scene. He had actually traveled the back roads, ridden the rails, sung in lumber camps for labor causes and integration: he was a hero to outsiders, both real and aspiring, the friend of the underclass and a source of authenticity to young folk acolytes. His music lived where politics met poetry and existed to serve a community. Just as important to Dylan was the *sound* of Guthrie's voice and music. When he heard Guthrie for the first time, he explains in his autobiography, "a voice in my head said, 'So this is the game.'" It was a magical, lonesome sound, and he knew he could get it. Perhaps because of the seriousness of his purpose, Guthrie, who wasn't an educated musician but a self-made WASP folk musician, became Dylan's role model.

In December 1960, nineteen-year-old Bob Dylan decided to make a pilgrimage to New York to meet his hero, and he stopped in Madison on the way. He stayed with Fred Underhill and Fred's girlfriend, a young woman named Ann Lauterbach, who not only knew her way around an acoustic guitar (she was a former student of Pete Seeger) but was active in politics. "I remember very clearly," she says, "his being in a kind of spare room with a mattress on the floor, and I have a very strong memory of his sitting on that mattress and hiding out because somehow his very presence seemed to have elicited phone calls from women." In the alternative folk music scene, he was still not an outsider by any stretch of the imagination, but he used his image as an outsider to maneuver the rocky shoals of personal relationships. "He was already quite averse to a certain kind of attention. There is no doubt that he—it's something that happens with a certain form of ambition or charisma where it's dependent on withdrawal, in the sense that he was creating mystery—and I think he had already done that; he was extremely attractive in his mysteriousness."

At barely nineteen, slight and scruffy, Dylan was indifferent to his appearance in a somewhat studied way. "While the rest of us were really busy trying to figure out what our image was," says Lauterbach, "he was in another kind of space. . . . He seemed to be very shy until he was sitting and playing his guitar." And what about his interest in the great issues of the day? "He was absolutely not political at all, except that he understood that Guthrie, and by association, Seeger, had their roots in this kind of populist progressivism. And I think that attracted him. But I don't think that he was terribly interested in transforming that into New Left agendas. He felt that everything was *in* the music; that whatever would happen would come right out of the music and not because the music represented something beyond itself. He didn't come there for that and he wasn't going to get engaged in it." In other words, Dylan had no taste for being a spokesman for the cause. Any cause.

His fierce artistic resolve was an important part of his charisma because at the time, many students were conflicted about their relationship with authority (reflected in their somewhat hesitant commitment to a university education), while Bob had already burned that bridge behind him. "All of us were straddling this fence and the fact that he seemed indifferent to the academic setting, he really was not interested, that was kind of exciting. He was an avatar of this kind of troubadour energy," said Ann. While others were trying to understand the information, Bob was in the process of *becoming* the information. His rawness (indeed, his indifference to the niceties of an academic environment) was something that set Dylan apart from other folk troubadours. One thinks of Joan Baez, for example, who had a rather studied and glossy air about her—she with the bare feet and the ethereal soprano voice—while Dylan seemed to be much more rooted, not in the past, or in a particular tradition, but something more interesting and more immediate: he was clearly in the process of *doing* something as opposed to trying to remember something into existence. "I think that's partly why so many people made this astonishing identification with him," said Ann. "He had this notion of being inside of a time—being a part of a time." Others might have been trying to do the same thing, politically and socially, but they lacked the innate tools or commitment to illuminate the path that many were trying to walk.

And then there was his sound. For it was the *sound* of Dylan, something primary, beneath the surface of the lyrics or the song forms, that was a call to action. His work was not about idealism; it was about the conflicted, difficult journey he was on: it was messy (not something that could be captured in a course syllabus), and the mere sound of his voice confirmed the fact that this was a struggle and we were in it together. It wasn't some "gaga, hippie, vulgar, self-indulgent space we were occupying," said Lauterbach. "That's the thing about his work. It had a kind of ground of difficulty, of negativity even, that, for some of us, was crucial to the experience of the sixties." This was something new for the youth culture: ugly beauty.

This resolution of apparent opposites, of course, is directly connected to the classic Jewish experience; even the fact that his voice wasn't beautiful was a very important part of his Jewishness. You couldn't talk about Dylan's work in terms of pure aesthetics. It couldn't be turned into a kind of beautiful truth. It was more difficult than that: it suggested that change doesn't happen without suffering. Dylan's music implied a kind of actual reckoning with experience. In the process, he was mastering the dramatic persona of the "flawed hero" and thus making himself much more useful to his generation than those who pursued the path of pure idealism or rigid optimism. Pete Seeger, for example, represented this kind of idealism and set an example of such absolute goodness or social commitment that it was impossible for the average person to maintain, especially in the face of the beatings they were witnessing in Selma and Birmingham. Dylan, on the other hand, made people know that whatever it was that they were after, it probably wasn't going to end happily, or come purely as a kind of fulfillment of their hopes or the rightness of their dreams. There is in his work a kind of tragic space, which was invaluable in the sixties as it spoke to the young men and women whose lives were being wrenched by the war in Vietnam and whipsawed by the mind-altering substances they were taking.

Late in December, 1960, Bob jumped in a car with Fred Underhill and drove east to New York City. Within twenty-four hours of their arrival, he had gone to Woody Guthrie's home. Guthrie, who was suffering from a degenerative disease called Huntington's chorea, was not there (he was hospitalized), and perhaps Dylan knew this, but he knocked on the door anyway; when it opened, he announced, "I'm here to pay tribute to Woody Guthrie. I must tell him how important he is." Eventually, Woody's wife invited him in, in part, says Guthrie's son, Arlo (who was home at the time), only because she was Jewish and clearly responded to this skinny, ragged, obviously Jewish young man at her door. So here is Dylan trying not to be Jewish, trying to be a Christian redneck like Woody Guthrie, and it is the charismatic Jewish part of him that gains him access. In a way, it is a metaphor for his entire career.

By the following fall, Bob had become a regular on the "basket house" circuit in Greenwich Village (so named because the singers would pass a basket after their performance for audience donations). He met singers Carolyn Hester, Eric Von Schmidt, and Liam Clancy; musicians Tom Paxton and Dave Van Ronk also facilitated Dylan's entrance into the New York folk scene and noticed his unusual approach to learning. "Bob was unteachable," says Van Ronk. "He had to reinvent the wheel all the time. Any number of people tried to show him finger picking of the guitar, but he just seemed to be impervious. He had to work it out for himself . . . you could almost say he could not acquire anything except by stealing it. That is to say that he would watch, and if you tried to explain to him, he would affect a lack of interest."

Bob apparently needed to reinvent every aspect of his life. He told guitarist Happy Traum stories about his past, but it was not about Minnesota. Instead he made up adventures about coming from Gallup, New Mexico, where he claimed to have been a carnival hand and an itinerant blues singer. "We bought into the whole myth," laughs Traum. "That he was just this street urchin who rode freight trains and hitchhiked his way around the country. He fed right into that romantic myth we all had of the nouveau Woody Guthrie." One of Bob's most outrageous tales was that he was descended not from Eastern European Jews but from Native Americans. His claim that he was in fact part Sioux Indian was a devious yet interesting way to explain his large nose; like Streisand, he was acknowledging the obvious; unlike Streisand, he was also lying about it. "Nobody held it against him," chuckles Van Ronk. "Reinventing yourself has always been part of show business. But he sort of got backed into a corner with his own story. I remember he solemnly gave us a demonstration of Indian sign language, which he was obviously making up as he went along." Why was being an American Indian more authentic than being a descendant of a Jew from the Pale? Again, it was a lie that told a deeper truth.

Yet Bob always had what Jews call *kavanah*, spiritual dedication, being ruthlessly focused on one's life purpose. When he performed, you couldn't take your eyes off him—and when he opened his mouth, it didn't matter that he did not try to use a beautiful voice. In fact, perhaps *because* he did not use a beautiful voice, he was forced to invent a vocal delivery that was even more compelling, immediate, profound. As a singer, he was as influenced by the black R&B tradition as by the folk tradition, and this combination of a casual, "aw shucks" Guthriesque stage presence and a "howling" vocal style really set him apart. "Bob loved to perform," said Happy Traum, "and he had a magnetism and a strength up there that would sometimes just make me laugh. . . . People saw it as a happening thing and this was an exciting place to be. So the girls started coming and the guys started following the girls. He was very animated, very funny. We just loved him. The audience wasn't so sure because he was pretty rough." The writer and broadcaster Oscar Brand noticed it also. "He wasn't just singing for a little while until he could become a doctor or a lawyer," says Brand. "This is what he did and this is what he was gonna do and nothing was gonna stop him."

The New York folk scene took Bob to its heart, and Izzy Young of the Folklore Center took it upon himself to promote the young singer. He took Bob to Folkways Records, where Moe Asch was not interested in signing him. Bob then went to Elektra Records, where Jac Holzman also turned him down. Next he went to Vanguard Records, where Manny Solomon showed little interest. Rejected by the Jewish folk labels—much as a young George Gershwin had been turned away from the Yiddish theater for his lack of orthodoxy—Dylan eventually scored through the same musical aristocrat that "discovered" Billie Holiday and Benny Goodman: John Hammond of Columbia Records.

Bob had met folk singer Carolyn Hester in Cambridge; she was signed to Columbia Records, and Hammond was her producer. In 1961, Bob wound up playing harmonica on her record, and in the studio, Hammond couldn't take his eyes off the young Dylan. He wasn't sure what to make of the scruffy kid, but he recognized that something significant was happening. Later that week, Hammond attended Dylan's gig at Gerde's Folk City, and within days, he offered him a contract at Columbia. It was a huge break. At the time, folk musicians had no expectation of recording on a major label. Some say Hammond's interest was driven by the fact that he had failed to sign Joan Baez a few years earlier when he had had the chance and he wasn't going to make the same mistake again. Whatever the cause, it was still a long shot in 1961. Dylan's sound was nothing at all like the standard folk music of the time—the earnest, reverent, and completely sexless appeal of Pete Seeger and Joan Baez was everything that Dylan was not. Dylan had a kind of danger about him; he was wrapped in mystery. At Columbia, Dylan was known as "Hammond's folly."

And yet onstage, Dylan was natural and loose, friendly even. He had invented a kind of bumbling, Chaplinesque persona; he channeled dozens of personalities that he couldn't possibly have experienced—religious, historical, philosophical; he was assiduously trolling the waters for stories, narratives that would suggest some kind of authentic truth about himself and his songs. Most performers on the folk scene were playing the old songs exactly the way they had always been played; this was their definition of authenticity. Bob played it differently; he put himself in the middle of his songs; he became a character in the narrative, using folk forms to tell *his* story. In so doing, he personalized the moral and philosophical storm that was raging all around him.

And then there were the songs themselves. Dylan's gift for language arrived in a torrent, and when the dam broke, the result was a gusher of narrative—often hallucinogenic, humorous, scathing, topical, tender, absurd, or just plain simple—storytelling of every stripe, with Dylan playing a kind of prophet who emerged from some timeless desert of popular culture to bring the news of a dire future: "A hard rain is gonna fall." Dylan's voice became, in the words of Joan Baez, the "missing piece" in the arsenal of the social justice movement, ultimately its "greatest weapon." But weapons also transform those who use them. Sixties music was not just a soundtrack to the revolution; it was also a cause. This was Dylan's genius; he was among the first to be transformed, and to let others know it was possible.

It was only natural that his audience should take him for their leader. But Dylan wasn't having it. Over and over he told the press he wasn't the leader of anything. He was not interested in polemics; he was interested in performance. It was the process of music that was transformative for him, not the politics; the words were simply the vehicle for his transformation. "I am my words," he famously said. As the kabbalistic Jews of the past had noted, "mere words" had vast power, and one needed to enter them as if they were whole universes. Dylan plunged headfirst.

If Dylan's transformation into a songwriter seemed to come out of nowhere, it was not without precedent. At the time, he was taken with several works of art and performance that informed both his sense of style and his sense of direction. First was François Truffaut's film *Shoot the Piano Player*, in which Charles Aznavour played a barroom pianist with a mysterious past. The character was like Bob in many ways—a shy, unassuming, and diminutive man with enormous talent who lived for music and for the love of women. Bob saw the movie again and again. "Everything about that movie I identified with," he said. It was a style he would take to heart. More important was the music of the German-Jewish composer Kurt Weill . Dylan emerged from seeing *The Threepenny Opera* obsessed with Brecht's "songs with tough language." This would be his direction in the future: the "elevation of dialectic to a theatrical style, the mythologizing of the craven, the revolutionary aesthetic strategy to deny the bourgeois audience the treat of escape and to promote thought by keeping the audience emotionally detached," so that, as Brecht wrote, "the spectator adopts an attitude of smoking-and-watching."

In his memoir *Chronicles: Volume One*, Dylan writes of Brecht's songs, "They were erratic, unrhythmical, and herky-jerky—weird visions. . . . Every song seemed to come from some obscure tradition, seemed to have a pistol in its hip pocket, a club or a brickbat, and they came at you in crutches, braces and wheelchairs. They were like folk songs in nature but unlike folk songs, too, because they were sophisticated." The song "Pirate Jenny" became a template for Dylan: "I took the song apart and unzipped it. It was the form, the free verse association, the structure and disregard for the known certainty of melodic patterns to make it seriously matter, to give it a cutting edge."

Released in 1962, Dylan's first album (*Bob Dylan*) featured mostly traditional songs like "Baby Let Me Follow You Down" and Dave Van Ronk's unique arrangement of "House of the Rising Sun," but it did have one original composition, "Song for Woody," an homage to his hero and the others (like Cisco Houston and Leadbelly) along whose path he now trod. The record sold poorly, but as it was distributed by Columbia, it brought Dylan to the attention of many important people, including a man named Albert Grossman. Grossman had a small but growing management agency, located in Woodstock, New York, with a roster that included Odetta (one of Dylan's first influences) and a group, which Grossman himself had created, called Peter, Paul and Mary. In fact, he had had his eye on Dylan for several years before making his move.

Albert Grossman was born in Chicago in 1926 to Russian-Jewish immigrant parents and received a degree in economics from Roosevelt University. The way Grossman entered the music business says a lot about both the man and the business: he had secured a hot dog concession and came up with the idea to start a folk club in Chicago as a way to sell his hot dogs. It was called the Gate of Horn. Along the way, Grossman made a string of enemies, many of them musicians. "Asses on seats. People buying drinks. Money in the cash register. That's what Albert knew," says Nick Gravenites, a Chicago musician Grossman once managed. "He didn't know music from dog shit. But he knew the cash register. He knew it real well." The saintly Pete Seeger, who rarely disparaged anyone, said, "I pitied the people who had to work with him." A man of mystery, duplicity, and ambition, Grossman was initially interested in Dylan not as a performer but as a songwriter. (He eventually wound up owning 25 percent of Dylan's song royalties, a small ongoing fortune.) However, he was a perfect wingman for Dylan just as he was entering the world of show business.

In 1962, Grossman made a deal with his old friend Artie Mogull, a music publisher at M. Witmark and Sons (a division of Warner's music publishing), whereby Grossman would receive a 50 percent kickback for every artist he brought to Witmark; the money came out of the publisher's share, which meant in effect that it was in Grossman's interest to cut the worst deal he could for the artist. That summer, Dylan, who had already signed a provisional deal with another publisher, Duchess Music, became Grossman's client. As he hadn't yet recorded a demo of the song that would make him famous—"Blowin' in the Wind"—Duchess had no idea he was going to be a hot property. But Grossman knew of the song from the buzz on the streets (it was being performed all over the Village) and, recognizing its worth, he gave Dylan a thousand dollars and told him to go over to Duchess and buy back his contract, which Dylan did. On July 12, Dylan went into a demo studio and recorded the song, which was then registered to Witmark.

During the summer of 1962, Dylan was on fire, writing original songs and expanding his biography nonstop; now he admitted he was born in Duluth, but then claimed he raced motorcycles, worked as a farmhand, and had sung in carnivals from the age of thirteen. The songs included "Talkin' John Birch Society Blues," "Blowin' in the Wind," "Masters of War," and "Let Me Die in My Footsteps," all of which were taken up by Pete Seeger and the folkies as modern masterpieces of the protest genre. The tunes were almost always borrowed or adapted from older things Dylan had heard, traditional pieces. The melodies were simply not that important to him—just something he knew, vehicles for his words—and most of his listeners had no idea that the songs came from a long tradition; but they certainly *felt* the tradition in the songs. There was a subtext of authenticity—a past presence—to Dylan's earliest compositions because of his use of classic folk melodies. Perhaps because of this, and because of the enigmatic nature of his lyrics, many in the audience turned to him for direction. He was often hailed as the leader of his generation, a generation that he often and actively seemed to dislike. And while he had great sympathy for the social issues of the day, his mind was similarly preoccupied with music, French symbolist prose poems, biblical stories, and more. "To be on the side of people who are struggling for something doesn't mean you're necessarily political," he said; but to no avail.

One of the few overtly political appearances Bob made was at the March on Washington in August 1963, a key event in the history of the civil rights movement. There, just a few short months after the release of his second album, *The Freewheelin' Bob Dylan* (which contained "Blowin' in the Wind" along with "A Hard Rain" and "Don't Think Twice"), Bob sang "Only a Pawn in Their Game," about the racial hatred in the South that led to the assassination of Medgar Evers. Dylan stood only a few feet away from Martin Luther King when he sang it, and was there when King made his famous "I have a dream" speech. He was not a political junkie like Joan Baez and all the others in attendance that day, yet his music had a greater impact on the crowd than many of the incendiary speeches. As Baez recalled, "everybody wanted him on the team," but he didn't want to join and didn't need to—he wrote the songs, "and the songs were the most powerful thing in our arsenal." It was wartime, and for the younger generation, anything was possible and nothing was inevitable. Perhaps Dylan's lack of a specific agenda—his indifference to party politics—was what made it easier for the average student to accept his music; it contained the essential questions of social justice without all the political rhetoric.

A major part of Dylan's success, however, was a result of Grossman's strategies. When *The Freewheelin' Bob Dylan* was completed in spring of 1963, Grossman immediately had Peter, Paul and Mary record the song "Blowin' in the Wind" (setting himself up to collect royalties three times over: from the song publishing, and from the royalties of both the group and Dylan), but he did more than that. By having a vocal group in the tradition of the Kingston Trio (already popular on the radio) record the song, he gave Dylan a chance to be heard by the millions of Americans already troubled by the Cold War or the racial struggle in the South; had he tried to promote Dylan's own version first, the song would never have been a hit because no one would have played that voice on the radio back in 1963. When Peter, Paul and Mary's single was released, it quickly became one of the year's biggest hits, and Dylan too became famous along with the song. After that, radio couldn't *not* play Dylan. By that fall, because of that one song, not only the careers of both of Grossman's clients had changed, but the political and musical landscapes had changed as well. Plain and simple, Grossman's handling of "Blowin' in the Wind" not only made popular music socially relevant to average Americans but helped make disparate Americans relevant to each other.

In Martin Scorsese's documentary on Dylan, *No Direction Home*, the gospel singer Mavis Staples expresses her astonishment on first hearing "Blowin' in the Wind," saying she could not understand how a young white man could write something that captured the frustration and aspirations of black people so powerfully. The soul singer Sam Cooke was similarly so deeply moved by the song that he later wrote his own song "A Change Is Gonna Come," considered to be a soul masterpiece, as a response to Dylan's song. "Blowin' in the Wind" moved an enormous amount of social history. And yet Dylan said he wrote the song in just a few minutes while sitting backstage at a club in Greenwich Village, Gerde's Folk

City. The melody itself was taken from an old abolitionist folk song called "Many Thousands Gone," which was compiled as early as the 1860s. Dylan's lyrics too were deceptively simple. The language was plain-spoken, seemingly part of a long-running dialogue that stretched back to biblical times, containing classic imagery—white doves, cannonballs (not modern bombs), seas and oceans (in this way, it referenced Irving Berlin's "God Bless America" as well). It also employed devices that worked to plant the language deep into the memory; the repetition of the word "yes," for example, was a kind of call-and-response technique, posing a question and answering it at the same time, signifying an invisible choir that the listener was part of, a kind of ongoing internal dialogue that we were all having.

That summer, Dylan's girlfriend, Suze Rotolo, took off to study art in Italy, and Bob borrowed another old melody, this time from a song called "Who's Gonna Buy Your Chickens," to write a bitter going-away song for her. It was called "Don't Think Twice," and it too appeared on the *Freewheelin'* album. Like "Blowin' in the Wind" it made clear that its author had moved well beyond the reach of his hero, Woody Guthrie, and was in no sense limited to writing songs of protest. If the storytelling of the Brill Building writers had been clever, sensitive, upbeat, and often warmly humanized—a prelude to the music of Bob Dylan in that it made a place for the intellectual in pop history—Dylan's work was profound, often troubling, and suggested layers of meaning buried beneath a rolling surface. In a stroke, Dylan had raised the bar for all popular songwriters; if it was possible to achieve such an intellectual and musical synthesis, then in a sense it was necessary. Songwriters everywhere took up the call; upon hearing Dylan, the Beatles changed direction and started playing with disconnected images in their songs (their album *Rubber Soul* was heavily Dylan-influenced). But nobody was able to channel the collective unconscious the way Dylan could.

And yet even as he kept pushing the boundaries of the popular song, constructing "flashing chains of images" that opened up the social dialogue all around him, he became more reclusive, more introspective. Some say this personality shift was in part a result of Grossman's own paranoid worldview; in any case, Dylan became fixated on songwriting above anything else. "He began writing anywhere and everywhere. He'd be in a booth somewhere and everybody else is jabbering and drinking and he's sitting there writing a song on the napkins. And you couldn't interrupt it. He was driven, and obviously enlightened." One night, sitting in the apartment of Hugh Romney (aka Wavy Gravy), Bob started typing on an old battered Remington, channeling "a song of desperation, a song of terror." It was called "A Hard Rain's A-Gonna Fall," and it "kind of roared right out of the typewriter," said Romney. "It roared through him the way paint roared through Van Gogh." "A Hard Rain," which took its melody and structure from the old English ballad, similarly stunned everybody.

He later said the hard rain wasn't nuclear fallout but something more encompassing, like a biblical apocalypse. "It was a song of desperation," said Dylan. "We were sitting around wondering if we were gonna survive; what could we do? Could we control men on the verge of wiping us out? The words came fast, very fast. It was a song of terror. Line after line after line trying to capture the feeling of nothingness." Dylan wasn't writing politics; he was already way beyond politics. At twenty-one years old, he was already operating as a full-blown artist, and, as he wrote in the song "She Belongs to Me," he didn't look back.

Now even the skeptics at Columbia Records started to come around. A hit song will do that. The label's publicist, Billy James, spoke for many when he said, "I had never heard a skinny little white young kid sounding like an eighty-year-old black man before and doing it with that sureness and intensity, and that unswerving understanding of who he was, and what he wanted to do." And Tom Wilson, the young black producer who had replaced John Hammond after the failure of the first album—a man who actually claimed to dislike folk music (he was a jazzman who had worked with John Coltrane)—was similarly taken by surprise. Going into the studio, his expectations were low; he too played like "those dumb guys . . . but then these words came out and I was flabbergasted." Dylan had played the authenticity game in a brand-new way—and won.

However, his victory was not without a fight. The first sign of trouble came early from the CBS general counsel, a Harvard-educated lawyer named Clive Davis. Davis, who eventually dragged CBS into the rock-and-roll business by its heels, had taken over from Goddard Lieberson, an aristocratic music maven who had built the label up by fostering knowledgeable A&R men like John Hammond. Davis, however, was a rough-and-tumble Jewish kid from Brooklyn, but he too aspired to be a stylish patron of the arts (in time, he even assumed an odd, untraceable upper-class accent), but unlike Lieberson, he was not necessarily driven by higher aesthetics. His very first assignment at CBS had been to try to find a way to stop Dylan from breaking his contract. Back in 1962, when Dylan's initial record for CBS had been a flop, the singer wanted to leave the label (possibly to sign with Warner Bros., where Albert Grossman was connected). Because he was under twenty-one when he had signed his contract with CBS, Dylan had grounds to leave, but Davis found a loophole. He claimed that Dylan had used the CBS recording studio, and this, he argued, implied Dylan had consented to being a CBS artist. Davis prevailed, and Dylan was stuck.

The conflict between Dylan and Davis didn't end there. The following year, when Dylan wanted to include the song "Talkin' John Birch Society Blues" on the *Freewheelin'* album, Davis, on behalf of the legal affairs department at Columbia, informed him that the label considered the song potentially libelous (to the KKK), and too risky to be included on the album. Dylan went ballistic, demanding, "What *is* this? What do you *mean* I can't come out with this song?" Davis said Columbia would not back down, and Dylan proceeded to replace it with something equally incendiary, an improvised talking blues, this time taking aim at the Cold War in general rather than the politics of the South. It seemed that for Dylan, the subject matter was not as important as the intent; if he "was his words," as he had said, he could sing himself into existence in any number of ways.

This drive for a new transparency in the lyrics of American popular music—due in great part to Dylan's influence—was turning up in many other places. Take for example the case of Tom and Jerry (Paul Simon and Art Garfunkel). They reunited in 1966 after the song "The Sound of Silence" became a million-seller. The evolution of this song goes back to 1963; with the record industry being fueled by Dylan's "finger pointing songs," Simon had recorded a demo of an original composition, "He Was My Brother," which protested racial injustice in the South. There was a story going around that the song was written by Paul for an old school friend of his named Andrew Goodman, who, along with another Jewish activist from New York, Michael Schwerner, and a black young man named James Chaney, had gone to Mississippi to register voters and all three had been murdered there. (A disproportionate number of students who went to Mississippi that summer—in fact, more than one-third by some estimates—were Jews.) On the basis of the demo of this song, Tom Wilson at Columbia signed the duo.

In 1964, Paul and Artie recorded an album that included "The Sound of Silence," a song Simon had written as a response to the assassination of President Kennedy. Upon completing the album, Simon and Garfunkel called a meeting with Wilson to choose a new name under which they could release the album, something more serious-sounding than Tom and Jerry. Wilson insisted they use their own names, especially while singing about racial injustice; eventually, the album, called *Wednesday Morning, 3 AM*, was released under the boys' real names, Simon and Garfunkel, but went nowhere. In 1965, the duo broke up yet again and Simon moved to England, where he began performing as a solo act. A few months later, however, Wilson went back into the studio and added electric guitar, bass, drums, and organ to the original acoustic track of "The Sound of Silence." Rereleased in September 1965, the song was the number one single in the country by New Year's Day 1966. Simon returned to the States and reunited with his old pal again, and the duo became hugely successful.

In the sixties, with the commercial focus on acts like the Beatles, the Stones, and other "British invasion" bands, everything English was of interest to Americans. It was ironic, of course, in that the Stones and the Beatles were basically playing stripped-down, simplified, and rearchitected American music. The Rolling Stones favored Muddy Waters and Howlin' Wolf; when the Beatles started out, their hero was Little Richard. So one thing the British pop bands ultimately accomplished was introducing American kids to their own culture. If these guys were coming over here and making a big deal out of Muddy Waters, maybe Muddy Waters *was* a big deal. On the other hand, the Brits had qualities America lacked: aside from a wildly theatrical approach to pop music, they also had a long tradition of compiled folk music. Both Paul Simon's and Bob Dylan's use of traditional English folk melodies and images (e.g. "milk-white steed") was simply part of this larger exchange; authenticity for authenticity. The Brits gave the Americans a vast repertoire of ballads and folk melodies; the Americans gave the Brits a whole new reason to get out of bed in the morning: the blues.

Simon, like Dylan, often mined the archives of traditional British folk songs. His "Parsley, Sage, Rosemary and Thyme," for example, was a reworking of the English folk song "Scarborough Fair." Simon's interest in traditional musics would continue throughout his career, and ultimately he employed themes and structures from around the world, from Peru and South Africa, Brazil and Puerto Rico. However, throughout his long and celebrated discography, there remained a missing piece: he never incorporated nor artistically acknowledged Jewish culture or his connection to it. Unlike Dylan, whose biblical, even Talmudic, references seemed to cross ecumenical boundaries, Simon, who often borrowed from Christian church forms (as in "Bridge over Troubled Waters"), was not particularly inclined to consider his Jewish roots through his work. And while he was proud that his grandfather had been a cantor, and at one time hired a genealogist to trace his ancestors in Rumania, none of this surfaced in his songwriting. The Jewish experience seemed to remain an open question for him: "I had no idea what I was," he said, "or even what my family's original name was."

When asked about his ethnicity in an interview, like Irving Berlin before him, he said "I don't think there's a connection" between his Jewish roots and his musical gift. When the interviewer pressed him, saying that so many great songwriters were Jewish, Simon did not take the bait. On the other hand, part of Dylan's genius was that his imagery—the language he used—integrated the deepest aspects of Jewish tradition with contemporary American life, without appearing to be specifically Jewish or narrowly religious. To some, next to Dylan, Simon and Garfunkel seemed "polite, studious and eager to please—college boys." It wasn't that Dylan had graduated from anywhere; he had simply *become* the information, created his own institution.

For many middle-class kids in the 1960s, this possibility of self-transformation (to become the information) was in the air. In the face of their growing alienation from their parents' generation and the looming personal danger of the Vietnam War, it often appeared to be their only alternative. Indeed, self-invention was a very real and immediate issue for the thousands of young men of draft age who would not go to fight in Vietnam but needed to decide how to avoid it in a way they could live with. Any decision they made would be with them for the rest of their lives. The growing presence of psychoactive drugs poured fuel on the fire: pot, LSD, and other chemicals drove the user inward, deeper into the self where the question "Who are you *really*?" demanded an answer. If one was going to respond to this great personal and historical challenge in a responsible way, it meant one needed to define a new "authentic" American identity, with little or no help from the previous generation. For the first time, and possibly the last, a whole cohort of young people was wandering through both their inner and outer landscapes, often stoned on drugs and fearful of dying, firmly believing the previous generation was lying to them (telling each other "Don't trust anyone over thirty"). With no one or nothing to turn to for direction, the music became the one thing they could trust, that felt real, "authentic." It was only natural that popular musicians, even those more stoned and confused than themselves, often took on a kind of high moral sheen.

For the generation of this sixties "counterculture," then, popular music became a literal and spiritual path, a transformative medium. Whereas the music of the fifties had relied on the exploration of the mundane world, a parsing of the teen narrative of escape, longing, and displacement, starting in the sixties, the characters in the story broke out and were considered living examples. No one, for example, wondered or even cared if Paul Anka was personally involved with the girl "Diana" that he sang about in the fifties, but everybody needed to believe that the life of Bob Dylan was somehow congruent with his songs. As they say, action is character, and how one lived now determined who one was. With Dylan, there was a closing of the gap between author and narrator, perhaps to a degree not before seen in American music.

SORRY, SON,
YOU CAN'T
DO BOTH

In the past, one sang about the life one lived; now, one needed to live the life one sang about. This in itself was a radical departure from both the old folk tradition (which celebrated the historical struggles of the people) and the rhythm-and-blues tradition, which was being polished into a kind of final form during the sixties by Jerry Wexler. In 1960, Wexler had taken the power of Atlantic Records deep into the American South, recording, among others, Wilson Pickett and Otis Redding in Memphis and Aretha Franklin in Muscle Shoals. This music had a bedrock verisimilitude about it; it was about what it was about: having a good time, the tragedy of losing a good woman, the heartbreak of loving a bad man. In addition, Wexler's productions all had a crisp sparkle to them without sacrificing the gut-bucket heart and soul of the music's origins. He called it "immaculate funk," and it too set a standard for future dance music, a deep rhythmic groove, tight flashy horns, focused guitar patterns, and a sound so clear you could hear all the way to the bottom of the acoustic spectrum, to the lowest notes of the bass.

Wexler's soul sessions were extraordinary in that they exemplified a thoroughly integrated musical environment, black and white players all creating the music equally. In Memphis, Wexler used Al Jackson on drums and Booker T. Jones on organ (both black), Steve Cropper on guitar and Donald "Duck" Dunn on bass (both white); it was the beginning of what came to be known as the "soul era," and in Wexler's hands, this recording studio was more open and more integrated than virtually any other social institution at the time. For this and many more reasons, many musicians considered Jerry Wexler to be part of the civil rights movement.

What was unique about Wexler's approach was that it represented integration on black terms. Whereas Berry Gordy at Motown Records was having great success at the time running a black company, he was doing it by making music for an essentially white audience. Wexler's sessions might have been integrated, but the music was as down and funky as it could be. (The difference between the audience for Motown's biggest act, the Supremes, and that of Wilson Pickett was akin to the difference between caviar and grits.) Wexler was a white man making black music, yet his technique was in keeping with the philosophy of Martin Luther King; his whole approach was based on assimilation. "In the studio," one musician said, "he [Wexler] doesn't draw the line, he erases it." This is how the classic soul hits of the period were cut—Pickett's "Mustang Sally," "Funky Broadway," and "Land of a Thousand Dances," for example—with a broad communal spirit. American society is premised on the proposition that we all fit in together, and Wexler's music was the sound of integration. These are white people. These are black people. This is their music (our music), popular music being bought by white people and black people alike. It's not apologizing for itself. It's not trying to be polite. It's exactly what it is. "A lot of contemporary production tried to homogenize the music," said pianist Jim Dickinson, who worked with Wexler in the South. "They take away the element that's alien. Jerry Wexler always turned that element up."

The key to Wexler's success was his belief in both the commercial possibilities of rhythm and blues and in its potential to be art, a notion he brought with him from the world of jazz. At the time, there was also a movement called "soul jazz," inspired in part by Ray Charles's success, in which jazz musicians went back to their ethnic roots (e.g. Johnny Griffin's "Wade in the Water," Art Blakey and the Jazz Messengers' "Moanin'," Horace Silver's "Filthy McNasty," Cannonball Adderley's "Dis Here," and Jimmy Smith's "Back at the Chicken Shack"). It was good-time music but at the same time it was "serious as a heart attack," with a level of harmonic sophistication in the solos that came directly from the further explorations of Charlie Parker. Wexler "brought the depth of literature to a music that was basically treated as if it was primitive." When one thinks of the two Jewish boys, Andrew Goldman and Michael Schwerner, and their black coworker, James Chaney, cold and alone in the back seat of a beat-up car roaring through a dark Mississippi night, one thinks of soul music.

It's hard to imagine what these records meant to young listeners at the time. It's easy to hear Aretha Franklin singing "I Never Loved a Man (the Way That I Loved You)" today and say, well yes, it's a brilliant vocal. But at the time, just the *sound* of this soulful voice, the lonely piano chords that opened the recording, the rising, searing horns, her cry at the top of the chorus, these things arrived in college apartments across the country as if coming from a "Land of a Thousand Dances" itself, a place where there was no confusion about mundane things like love and death. Soul music said what it said and it meant what it meant; there was no question.

"That singer was talking about you," remembers one young white musician. "He's talking about your underwear, he's talking about what he's talking about but that's what he's talking about. And that kind of reality, that sense of understanding who you are and where you are was what young people wanted in the sixties. That kind of gritty earth-driven music is what soul music was about." For integration to be real, it had to work both ways.

In the world of popular music, there is no more poignant example of musical integration than that of a young Chicago guitarist named Mike Bloomfield. He was born and raised until grade six in a hillbilly-Jewish neighborhood, situated between the wealthy Gold Coast and a funky Puerto Rican neighborhood. As a child driving with his parents through the city, he'd hear all kinds of music coming out of record stores and jukeboxes and remembered loving it all. Just as he was entering his most formative years, at age twelve, the family moved to Glencoe, a rich Chicago suburb. There, this streetwise, hip little kid was clearly an outsider; everybody else was either a jock or a social maven and he was, as he said, "just a fat kid. Bad at school, bad at sports, bad at everything." All of a sudden, he was another stranger in a strange land. People laughed at him; in response, he became a troublemaker, a lawbreaker.

His father was rich, owned a large company called Bloomfield Industries that made stainless steel—during World War II the company had manufactured bomb hoists, oxygen masks, K-ration can openers—and he belonged to a club downtown where old Jews sat around in the steam room kibitzing and kvetching. Michael and his friends would go to the club sometimes, where their presence embarrassed his father. But the black waiters at the club were nice to Michael; his father would say "Sit over there and don't tell anybody you're my son," but the waiters would bring him things to eat and talk music with him. His father was only interested in business; it was the language he spoke. In the Bloomfield family, "If you didn't have the ability to add and calculate quickly and find the leverage point, that was regrettable."

One of his friends recalled, "When I told Michael's father that I wanted to be a writer or a college professor, he got mad at me. He said, 'Your parents spend good money. They raised you in Glencoe and got you a good education. You want to be a goddamn college professor? Do you know how much money they make? They don't make shit. Get a real job. Go into business and make something of yourself. Be a businessman. Make some money. Make your parents proud." This was the environment in which Michael Bloomfield grew up. The generational chasm was enormous.

For his bar mitzvah, Michael got a small transistor radio, which he took to bed with him to listen to WVON (the "Voice of the Negro"), the Chicago radio station owned by the Chess brothers that played raw, serious music. He also loved Scotty Moore, Elvis Presley's guitar player, and he became transfixed by Elvis himself: "Man, I had every Elvis Presley magazine," he said. "This little fat Jew with his hair combed like Elvis Presley, waddling around. It was very serious to me . . . I saw myself, in my mind, as this lanky hillbilly and the radio was a reinforcement of that whole lifestyle." This was the transformative power of music in the fifties and sixties: one could look in the mirror and see a complete lie and believe it was the living truth. The parallels between Bloomfield's inner world and that of Dylan—who also had his portable radio at night and was obsessed with Presley's bad-boy image—are striking, and they were no doubt repeated all around the country.

The black maids in Michael's house and the houses of his friends also listened to WVON while they worked, to Muddy Waters, B. B. King, and Jimmy Reed. "All of us had bad parenting but we loved our maids," a friend of Michael's said. "The parents were mean, unpleasant middle-class people who didn't understand us. The maids were cool, hip, sophisticated people who didn't understand us, but liked us." The music they had in common came to represent an alternative world, a world where someone trusted you with serious emotional content at a time when it didn't seem parents trusted you with anything at all.

A defining event for Michael—like the butterfly in China that starts the storm in Australia: small on the surface, large in its implication—occurred when the kids at New Trier High School (considered one of the nation's best) put on a program. Michael entered his rock-and-roll band and the show's director told him, "You can play whatever the tune is, but you can't do any type of encore." Michael and his band tore it up and kept going. The kids went wild and he was kicked out of school for failing to obey the director. In response, his parents sent him to a private school in Massachusetts to try to "straighten him out." There he was introduced to drugs; he returned home for vacation at age fourteen smoking pot. Out east, he had also become a voracious reader, following politics and literature, Salinger and Bellow, Mailer and Kerouac. That, combined with the street radicalism of Chicago's South Side, where the blues was being played, made him aware of a much larger world than the world of his parents. "We didn't realize that the black people we were hanging out with were something that serious intellectuals would think about or care about or put in the Library of Congress," he said. "But then we found out that people like John Hammond and Alan Lomax had recorded people like that and considered them great poets and artists. So that proved to us even more that these white people we knew were really stupid. They didn't know anything about what was going on."

If Michael's music was a source of enlightenment for him, it was also a source of tremendous pain. His father actually broke his guitar on more than one occasion. "He called them 'fruit boxes,' and he'd just take them and break them up. He wanted me to be everything that I wasn't. He wanted me to be a jock and he wanted me to be a good student . . . he just didn't understand." Michael desperately wanted his father's love, and in a last-ditch attempt to secure it, he tried playing show tunes for his father, who loved them. "Michael would bring his guitar and amp into his father's bedroom and play every one of them for him. I don't think he did that for anybody else in his life. But for that type of appreciation, for a sense that he could get his father's love, he was banging out those show tunes."

Ultimately, it was the blues that delivered the father figure that Michael so ardently sought. But first, he had to learn the difference between playing the notes and playing the music. "The first blues I remember was a T-Bone Walker song called 'Glamour Girl.' That was just a whole other thing. I was playing the same notes that they were playing, but when I would take my solos they weren't the same. What I was playing was like fast bullshit. I couldn't play it. All I could do was play rock and roll. I just couldn't figure out the difference." While there was a growing core of people at the time who understood rock and roll to be a radical, revolutionary music (which in a way it was), Bloomfield, among others, had already sensed that as a form, it was primarily an act, a pose, and that there was a deeper level to the music.

This gap between authentic and inauthentic music—between captured and manufactured music—music made from the heart and music made from the wallet—was exacerbated by the enormous expansion of the recording industry and its increased reliance on technology. In the sixties, with the explosion of album sales (due to the new "serious" music coming from popular artists), the recording industry had virtually wrested control of the business from the old-time publishers and promoters. And while they made a real business out of music, in the process, with multitrack technology and the producer as the ultimate creator, came the ability to literally invent artists, to manufacture them rather than capture them. A lot of the music that was being sold as "authentic," a voice from the underground, was clearly being invented in the studio. But for music to have an authentic feel, it has to have captured something living, in the moment: something real. For Michael, what he heard and felt on the radio late at night could only be found in the black nightclubs of Chicago; this too was a revelation.

Bloomfield's maid, Mary Williams, was a friend of the singer Josh White, and that's how he and his friends first got entrance into a real nightclub. White got them special seats in the balcony. Mary also took them to the Regal Theater to see the jazz musicians Art Blakey and Miles Davis.

"There was this black world that doesn't exist anymore," said one of Michael's boyhood companions. "It was part of the old jazz world, 'black and tan' clubs. They were clubs where whites could go in black neighborhoods and it was okay because they were there to hear the music. In the late fifties, there were blues clubs that were like black and tan clubs, where white people could go to hear the blues. But hardly anybody went. And so, when we got to be about fifteen years old, these maids, Michael's maid, primarily, would take us . . . they would invite us down to their apartments on the South Side on a Sunday afternoon and make dinner for us. And they'd have relatives over. A big Sunday dinner with fried chicken and okra and squash and sweet potatoes. And they'd play the records of Wolf and Muddy and Chuck Berry. We would take the El downtown on Sunday afternoon and they would take us out to these clubs, to Pepper's Show Lounge on Forty-third Street, or Theresa's, these famous blues clubs. Here was this other world that was totally unimaginable to us. And we were just overwhelmed by this music."

It sounds like nothing so much as the story of Louis Armstrong fifty years earlier, but in reverse: a black household taking in a young Jewish child who came from an emotionally impoverished home. Like a lot of other kids from rich Jewish families, Michael didn't see a lot of happiness around the house; mostly it was frustration and anger, the focus on affluence being the sad underside of the Jewish experience. Perhaps it came from years of poverty, but he wanted no part of it.

Michael's brother Alan recalled, "Michael and me looked at it as if it was pretty onerous to have a lot of money. Nobody looked real happy owning a lot of money. In fact, we saw a lot of misery. We saw a lot of anger. We saw a lot of tough stuff. . . . It was like something that could be ripped away in a second . . . I don't think Michael wanted to distance himself from the money as much as what he looked at as the price you have to pay to make the money." It was all part of the great cultural reevaluation of the sixties.

Michael's girlfriend at the time said, "You know how people were in those days—the repressed fifties—and both of us needed to get away from that. I know my father thought

Michael was stupid and pretentious because he wanted to know about eating beans, or he wanted to know about being poor. My father used to yell at me for singing Pete Seeger union songs. My father was a steelworker and he was in the union and he used to think that our point of view was really stupid. But we were children. Our hearts were in the right place, and Michael was not a phony. He really did want to know about the funkier side of life. And he was a funky guy. It's hard to know what he was fighting against. Everything was so awful back then for everybody, and we were all trying to get out of it."

The black people understood this funky side all too well and were amazed to see these little Jewish kids down in their clubs. When they discovered that the kids knew about Muddy Waters and Howlin' Wolf, they would sit at the table and talk to them and buy them beer. And they'd take them out in the alley to smoke joints with them. All the lines—age, race, class—were being erased. Michael remembered these nights with great delight.

"It'd be crowded," Michael described.

> If it was Saturday night, everybody was determined to get it on. They'd be jukin' . . . they'd be partying. The women dressed up as fine as they could, with red hats and wig hats on their heads, and the cats'd be pressed out slick . . . they wanted to dig that music . . . cats'd be up in front of the bandstand screaming at you, man, telling you to "Play that music!" Lord, they would want to hear that music. And when you played that music, oh man, you'd be talking right to these people and they'd be screaming back at you and dancing and everything. Lots of times there were incredible good feelings, just the best feelings of all. Because there was so much correspondence between the musicians and the people. Sometimes a cat would be up there, and the groove'd be so strong, the joint would be jumping, people'd just be rocking and screaming and shouting.

"Muddy Waters, he was like a god to me," said Michael. "B. B. King was a deity where I couldn't even imagine ever knowing someone of his magnitude and greatness. But Muddy was in Chicago. I would go down the street and from two blocks away I'd hear that harmonica . . . and I'd hear Muddy's slide. I'd be tremblin'. I'd be like a dog in heat." Muddy would get up on the stage and tell everybody to let the white kids alone, that they were his friends from the North Side come down to hear the music. When Michael was fifteen, Muddy finally let him sit in. Muddy would introduce him and tell the crowd to pay attention and give the kid a nice big round of applause. "He's a great musician and a good friend of ours," Muddy would say, and everybody would laugh, or say, "Come on man, get that fucking kid off." But then Michael would play, and the audience would be stunned. "He was real good. . . . Later on we got to be friendly with Muddy and his wife and Otis Spann. They all lived in the same building. We would spend a day there. We'd start out at Muddy's house for dinner, and his wife would make, like gumbo or some real hot New Orleans kind of dinner. And then we'd go downstairs to where Spann lived, in the basement, and jam. Michael would play and Muddy would play and Spann would play."

"A lot of these cats was old enough to be my father," said Michael. "And I had that sort of feeling—they were like dads, you know? Like a father relationship. And I had to be polite. They were the older masters of this thing. It was like being with classical musicians. . . . You couldn't shuck. Just to be in that environment, and to be accepted in that environment as a man when in my own mind I felt like a little kid, was a very flattering thing. . . . And there was an amazing amount of fantastic passion and getting it on, too, man, an incredible love for the music. It was just an amazing thing for my eyes to behold. To see that lifestyle, and to be swept into it. . . . Several guys took me to be almost like I was their son—Big Joe Turner, Sunnyland Slim, and Otis Spann. They took me to be like their kid. They just showed me from the heart. They took me aside and said, 'You can play, man. Don't be shy. Get up there and play.' What I learned from them was invaluable. A way of life, a way of thinking, a whole kind of thing—invaluable things to learn." Bloomfield, like so many of his generation, found on the streets and in the clubs what he couldn't find at home: love, acceptance, and trust.

The role of traditional values was being reexamined by Jews and non-Jews alike; for older Jews, it found an apogee of its expression in the Broadway play *Fiddler on the Roof*. As conceived by the play's creators, Jerome Robbins, Sheldon Harnick, Joe Stein, and Jerry Bach, the power of tradition in the Jewish culture was that it added stability in a world that was as precarious as a "fiddler on the roof." During the sixties, the second- and third-generation American Jews were looking back at their own family history, taking the experience of the Pale of Settlement out of the closet and examining it for the first time. But making show business out of the pogroms meant that much needed to be glossed over.

In the 1960s, many Jews had Christmas trees. Perhaps they thought of them as "holiday trees," or "Chanukah bushes," but this too was part of an American tradition, and they wanted in. Like Irving Berlin before them, perhaps they felt they were Americans first and being Jewish had little or nothing to do with it. Yet they *were* Jews, and so within the structure of *Fiddler on the Roof* is the notion that for Jews, the only constant is change, that tradition is malleable, and this was something that all Americans could accept. The play became iconic and was produced around the country. In fact, it was the way many people in rural areas saw their first "Jew": in schools and community groups, with people dressed up "as Jews" and doing what they thought Jews did. All Americans were trying to understand the issues of tradition and what happens when the young people don't follow their parents' wishes. It was a very powerful metaphor for the sixties, and in some instances it was a way for Jews to learn about themselves, as well as the way America learned about them.

For the young Bloomfield and for many young Jews, however, tradition was taking on new forms. Instead of the currency of change, life on the streets became about the change of the currency; it was not so important *how* one engaged in the old traditions but *whether* one engaged in them. For example, in Chicago, the blues scene overlapped with the Hyde Park neighborhood, home to the University of Chicago. It was "an extraordinary place," recalls Bloomfield's friend Norm Dayron. "We had people on the faculty like Saul Bellow, Hannah Arendt, Harold Rosenberg—surrounded by this rich culture of black people who found a mode of self-expression that had migrated up from the South. . . . These were times when the culture was saying that anything was possible. You could be anything. You could do anything."

What Michael wanted to be was an authentic bluesman, and he discovered a partner in crime in the person of a young singer / harmonica player from Hyde Park named Paul Butterfield. "Paul Butterfield was the real thing . . . this cat went down there, went in the baddest black ghettos and was as bad as the baddest cats down there. He wouldn't take no jive from anybody. And he held his own. God, did he hold his own. I learned that was the secret. If you wanted to play with some authority, you had to go down and prove yourself. You had to burn. You had to be up on the stage with Buddy Guy or Freddie King . . . and hold your own. You had to be a man up there, or you'd blow your whole scene. You'd be lost."

Things progressed quickly. In 1963, Paul formed a band with two young black veterans from Howlin' Wolf's band, bassist Jerome Arnold and drummer Sam Lay, and a white guitarist from Oklahoma named Elvin Bishop. They became the house band at Big Johns, a fashionably hip club in the Old Town section of the city that attracted a lot of college kids but was still funky enough to welcome authentic bluesmen. When Bloomfield joined the band in early 1965, Jac Holzman signed the band to Elektra Records and put them on a sampler for $1.98 called *Folk Song '65*. Butterfield's signature song "Born in Chicago" was included; the sampler itself sold 200,000 copies, and suddenly everybody was talking about the Paul Butterfield Blues Band. The Chicago music scene became a kind of beacon to young musicians around the country, and the Paul Butterfield band lit the signal fire. The subsequent release of their first album had a huge effect on the college crowd. Here was a racially mixed hard-driving blues band that was completely authentic, not a pale imitation or tribute to the blues (like those coming out of England); it was comprised of young people who played with total conviction. Chicago-style blues, with all its energy and rough edges, was no longer just the province of old black men.

At the time, the raw blues was not as popular in the black community (where soul music and R&B held sway) as it was on college campuses. There it really took off, and the song "Born in Chicago" opened a lot of doors. First of all, it was obviously a white person singing it, which just leaped out at you; and, second, the song opened with the line, "I was born in Chicago in 1941; my father told me 'son you better get a gun.'" This was different from every other blues that young people were hearing, which was invariably sung by an older man who had been born in the Mississippi Delta. This was obviously a hard, cold truth being told to you by someone who could just as easily have been a student like yourself; in fact, Butterfield had gone to the University of Illinois but dropped out after a year to be a full-time musician. The subtext was that being an authentic bluesman was now an option for educated young white kids; this one band launched a lot of young white musicians.

In 1963, by coincidence, Mike Bloomfield also met Bob Dylan in Chicago, when Dylan came to play at the Gate of Horn. "I had heard the first Dylan album when it came out," he said.

> I thought it was just terrible music. I couldn't believe this guy was so well touted. I went down to see him when he played in Chicago. I wanted to meet him, cut him, get up there and blow him off the stage. He couldn't really sing, y'know. But to my surprise he was enchanting. I don't know what he had, but he got over. He could get over better than anybody I ever saw. I thought Jack Elliott was the best single guy, for just a man with a guitar, for getting over, I mean, winning you. But Bob got over better than anyone I'd ever seen in my whole life. Anyway, we jammed that day, and way later he phoned me up and asked me to come play on his record.

The record he's referring to was recorded at the famous 1965 session in New York that produced Dylan's six-minute landmark song, "Like a Rolling Stone." "You wouldn't believe what those sessions were like," said Bloomfield. "There was no concept. No one knew what they wanted to play, no one knew what the music was supposed to sound like, other than Bob, who had the chords and the words and the melody." Another young Jewish musician named Al Kooper was also at the session. He had hustled producer Tom Wilson to invite him down to watch Dylan record and had hatched a plan whereby he would get to play. The session was called for 2 p.m. the next day but Kooper arrived an hour early, walked into the studio with his guitar, and set up as if he had been hired to play. He knew some of the other musicians, so when they saw him setting up they just assumed he was on the date. Everything seemed cool, and Kooper was planning to tell Wilson, when he arrived, that there was a miscommunication and that he thought he had been asked to play with Dylan. Hopefully, the scam would work.

"Suddenly," recalls Kooper, "Dylan exploded through the doorway with this bizarre-looking guy carrying a Fender Telecaster guitar without a case. It was weird, because it was storming outside and the guitar was all wet from the rain. But the guy just shuffled over into the corner, wiped it off with a rag, plugged in, and commenced to play some of the most incredible guitar I'd ever heard. And he was just warming up. I was in over my head. I embarrassedly unplugged, packed up, went into the control room and sat there pretending to be a reporter from *Sing Out* magazine." The guitar player with Dylan was Mike Bloomfield.

When Wilson finally showed up and the recording got under way, the organ player was asked to play piano, and, seeing an opening, Kooper told Wilson he had a great organ part for the song. Wilson said, "Hey, you don't even play the organ." He shot back, "Yeah, I do and I got a great part for the song." He was still angling to get onto the session somehow: in truth, he had never played organ and didn't even know how to turn the instrument on. But when Wilson was distracted, Kooper ran into the studio and sat down at the organ. Luckily, it was still up and running.

"There is no music to read. The song is over five minutes long, the band is so loud that I can't even hear the organ, and I'm not familiar with the instrument to begin with. But the tape is rolling and that is Bob fucking Dylan over there singing, so this had better be me sitting here playing something. The best I could manage was to play hesitantly by sight, feeling my way through the changes like a little kid fumbling in the dark for the light switch." After six minutes, they'd gotten the first complete take of the day and everyone adjourned to the control room to hear it played back. Thirty seconds into the second verse, Dylan motioned toward Tom Wilson. "Turn up the organ," he ordered. "Hey, man," Tom said, "that cat's not an organ player." But Dylan just said, "Hey, now, don't tell me who's an organ player and who's not. Just turn the organ up." At the end of the session, Dylan asked for Kooper's phone number and told him to come back the next day. And that's how Al Kooper became one of the most influential rock-and-roll organ players of the sixties. Soon he was getting calls to play organ on a lot of records because "Like a Rolling Stone" went to number one and then everybody wanted the "Dylan sound."

Dylan was really word-gaming at this point—composing long screeds that he then tied together with a strong vocal hook ("How does it feeeel? To be on your own. A complete unknown. Like a rolling stone"). When he heard the final mix, he called it "religious carnival music." He was now using drugs regularly to prime the poetic pump (pot mostly, but also stronger chemicals) and using religious imagery to talk about his music. When asked what his songs were about, he said "The second coming." When asked what he had to look forward to, he said "Salvation." One of Dylan's favorite poets, Arthur Rimbaud, once said, "When the poet makes himself the seer . . . he reaches into the unknown and even if, crazed, he ends up by losing the understanding of his visions, at least he has seen them." The crazier Dylan became, the more durable the visions that remained.

Dylan had pushed his transformation so far that now the meaning of his epiphanies and clever turns of phrase often eluded him as well. Perhaps he remembered the initial feeling that launched the rant (anger, need, sorrow, lust), but as for "meaning" (definition), that was now pretty much in the past. It was pure process and conjuring with no end in sight and no beginning to hold on to. It was liquid, moving poetry coming from a contemporary consciousness being driven deep by personal need and with no brakes. Songwriting had become a magical gesture and Dylan became inscrutable; he let his mind run free and fueled the process with chemicals. There was no map to this territory.

Many years later, Dylan tried to describe the sound he had been hearing in his head at the time:

> It's that thin, that wild mercury sound. It's metallic and bright gold, with whatever that conjures up. That's my particular sound. That's the sound I've always heard. . . . It was the sound of the streets. It still is. I symbolically hear that sound wherever I am. That ethereal twilight light, you know. It's the sound of the street with the sunrays, the sun shining down at a particular time, on a particular type of building. A particular type of people walking on a particular type of street. It's an outdoor sound that drifts even into open windows that you can hear. The sound of bells and distant railroad trains and arguments in apartment buildings and the clinking of silverware and knives and forks and beating with leather straps. It's all—it's all there . . . no jackhammer sounds, no airplane sounds. All pretty natural sounds. It's water, you know water trickling down a brook. It's light flowing through the . . . crack of dawn.

With the addition of electric instruments to music that had variously been described as "protest" music or music of conscience, Bob was now, in albums such as *Blonde on Blonde* and *Bringing It All Back Home*—the title was a reference to the fact that Dylan was repatriating the American music that British groups had borrowed—changing the set point for rock and roll; it was now possible to introduce meaningful political and social ideas into Top 40 songs. This simple but revolutionary idea (pioneered decades earlier by Yip Harburg but unknown to America's young) drove hundreds of musicians to write thousands of pop songs that aspired to the intellectual level of art. "I knew I was listening to the toughest voice I ever heard," recalled Bruce Springsteen; "Bob showed all of us that it was possible to go a little further," said Paul McCartney.

Young white pop musicians were now voicing their opinions on everything from philosophy to politics, literature to fashion. Of course a lot of it was pretentious—even Dylan's gift with words did not make him immune—but it had a scene-changing effect nonetheless. He remained aloof from the pandemonium he had set in motion. In his autobiography, he wrote, "I had very little in common with and knew even less about a generation that I was supposed to be the voice of." The person who started out in Hibbing as Bob Zimmerman was disappearing and the creation of Bob Dylan was dissolving into a whirlpool of words and sounds.

"Like a Rolling Stone" went to the top of the pop charts in the summer of 1965, just a few weeks after its release. That summer, Dylan appeared at the Newport Folk Festival with members of the Paul Butterfield Blues Band. Their set caused anger both in the back-stage area, where promoter Alan Lomax and musician Pete Seeger resented the amplified music (considering it counter to the principles of the folk tradition) and got into a skirmish with Albert Grossman, and out front, where the sound system was not up to the task of delivering the new electric sounds to the audience; people starting catcalling and booing the band. It was the moment that the down and dirty Midwest blues ran head-on into the intellectual pretensions of the East Coast folk establishment—by that time, Chicago bands like Muddy Waters, James Cotton, and Howlin' Wolf had a lot of young white kids playing electric guitar—and there was a wreck on the highway of American pop music. When the dust cleared, it was Dylan who walked away, bruised but not broken. Keyboard player Barry Goldberg said, "I remember Michael [Bloomfield] counting it off and saying 'Let's go!' and it was like POW!—we went into this whirlwind. Bob was like a warrior, and we were all on this mission."

The saga of "Like a Rolling Stone" was a kind of Jewish morality play; many of the lead characters in the drama—manager Albert Grossman, musicians Mike Bloomfield, Harvey Brooks, Al Kooper, and Barry Goldberg, to name a few—and, of course, Dylan—were Jews. Too, the most Jewish aspect of the songs Dylan was writing during this period, including "Like a Rolling Stone," was not his use of biblical language so much as the scope of the narrative, the inconclusiveness of the morality, and the implication that there is something important and profound behind popular music—the *sound* of the music—and that you have to figure it out for yourself; he's not going to tell you. "How does it feel?" he kept asking in "Like a Rolling Stone." You were on your own. We will not tell you the answers, only the questions. Even in the midst of the sixties chaos, the part of Dylan that came across, just as it came across to Woody Guthrie's wife that day, was deeply Jewish.

With the success of this song and his new electric sound, Bob was catapulted into a much higher level of commercial success, and all the musicians who took part in the recordings were eager to tour with him—all except Michael Bloomfield, who chose instead to go back with Paul Butterfield. "Michael was going to stay with Butterfield, because he felt that was his obligation and that's what he should do," said Harvey Brooks. "That's what he felt was best for him. He said we'd go on and be stars and everything, but he was going to play the blues." Unwittingly, by choosing to leave the starmaking machinery behind, Bloomfield was ultimately able to contribute as much as, if not more than, he ever could have as part of Dylan's circus. Because by 1966, he, Butterfield, and many of the other hardworking Midwest musicians had migrated to San Francisco.

They left Chicago in part because their impulse to expand the music—to combine the electric blues with elements of Dylan's long-form lyrics, James Brown's extended dance grooves, and John Coltrane's inspired improvisations—was essentially underappreciated on the Midwest scene, where audiences were more conservative. Particularly in parts of Chicago where there was a strong presence of street violence in the clubs. Nick Gravenites recalls, "Most of my memories of Chicago were hard memories, but in San Francisco there weren't that many hoodlums around. People were more open and more relaxed and didn't have that gangster mentality. Chicago was great for the blues, but stretching out from it, nope. That's why everybody went west. Everybody wound up going to San Francisco, because it wasn't so restricted."

Also in San Francisco was an aspiring music promoter named Bill Graham—the same Wolfgang Grajonca who had so loved the world of mambo back in New York during the 1950s. After surviving ten years of straight jobs, working for major companies like Allis-Chalmers and the 3M Corporation, he was on the West Coast and looking to do something else, something with soul. For a time, he helped raise money for the defense fund of the San Francisco Mime Troupe, a radical performance art group. When the troupe was busted for obscenity (they occasionally performed nude), Graham organized a fundraiser for them at the Fillmore Auditorium; it was his first large-scale promotion and its success led him to develop more large-scale concerts and "happenings." Another one of Graham's earliest promotions was author Ken Kesey's Electric Kool-aid Acid Test, also staged at the Fillmore, using strobe lights and swirling projected patterns on the walls to entertain the stoned-out audience. These would become standard features at the rock-and-roll shows he would eventually organize.

Graham's first booking of the Paul Butterfield Blues Band was an overwhelming success. Subsequently, he called their manager, Albert Grossman, and secured exclusive rights to promote the band on the West Coast. This was how he met Mike Bloomfield, and it was through Bloomfield that he learned about the music he would promote for the rest of his life. Michael saw his friendship with Graham as an opportunity to reward some of the musicians who had affected him, indeed, had saved his life, back in Chicago.

"It was like payback," said a band member. "We weren't out there saying, "Oh yeah, we're great.' We were saying, 'Sure, we can play, but the guys who really are good, who taught us, they're the *real* players.' And we tried to see if we could help the people that helped us. We were really happy to do that. Michael, I think, was the guy, *the* guy, that got a lot of the black blues bands playing in the major venues."

Michael and Bill became close friends. "Bill Graham was totally freaked out by Bloomfield," said one musician. "Here was a *landsman* who was a brilliant guitarist, a crazy son of a bitch with a crazy sense of humor. They hit it off really well . . . Bloomfield and Graham, they're both like funky Jews. They appreciate the funk side of existence." "Michael was my teacher," said Graham. "He always had somebody he was pushing. If it wasn't the Staples Singers, it was Albert King or B. B. King or Otis Redding or Howlin' Wolf. He more than any single musician, kept bringing me records. . . . Prior to 1965, I knew nothing. I think the music industry owes Michael far more than they realize. Besides being a very special musician in what he brought out of the guitar and how he made people feel . . . as great a guitar player as Michael was, he was really a teacher."

More than once, after Mike got Bill Graham to promote one of his favorite musicians, a record company, seeing that a young white audience was interested in a black artist, signed them to a recording contract. A lot of these musicians—whether it was Howlin' Wolf or John Lee Hooker or Albert King—who might well have disappeared without being "discovered" by Graham and the San Francisco scene in the sixties, owe their longevity, if not their very survival, to a formerly overweight Jewish kid from the Chicago suburbs who found a home and a family in their music. This is part of Michael Bloomfield's legacy.

His dénouement was less elegant. Michael became addicted to heroin, and although he had access to a trust fund his whole life, he often suffered money problems. By the early seventies, primarily to support his drug habit, he and Al Kooper formed a so-called "super group." The idea of the "super group" was Kooper's; he had been working on and off as a record producer and understood the mentality of the business: bigger is better and nothing less than "super" will do. The concept of the "super session" was basically to put famous musicians together, have them jam for a couple of hours, call it "super," and then parade the show around the country. The process often had little to recommend it in terms of authenticity; the musicians need not be particularly sympathetic to each other nor stylistically matched. Indeed, they need not even like each other personally; it was purely a play to generate cash and hustle the rubes.

Michael described the whole process as a kind of sellout: "The first thing we had to do is get a record company so we went to Hollywood to showcase. It was like *Roots*. We were up on the auction block. All those execs who came to see us looked the same. Pinky ring, leisure suit, shirt open to the tits, fabulous complexion, blow-dried hair. One word I heard over and over again was 'bankable.' We were a product. We were hula hoops. We were skateboards. We were beef. We were plastic. We got a deal, though." The irony, of course, was that in the end, Michael couldn't avoid becoming fodder for the same kind of businessmen that he had met in his father's steam room and spent his entire life trying to avoid. This too could have been a metaphor for his whole generation. Michael eventually died of a heroin overdose.

Like Bloomfield, many young musicians in the late sixties were being blown off center by drugs. Dylan too had begun experimenting with harder chemical substances, and his music was in a kind of free-fall as heroin joined speed and coke in the regime. Drug use leads to self-absorption, and, as the interior life was where Dylan spent most of his time anyway, he became even more reclusive, smacked out and jacked up at the same time. "The magic swirling ship" provoked wild mood swings; he no longer seemed to care whether he was communicating or not. Unlike Irving Berlin, who believed the people were always right, Dylan arrived at a place where the people could never understand. He was letting the words and images sing themselves into existence and he along with them. "Dylan was physically vibrating . . . there was a yawning chasm between him and any kind of human activity."

He had just turned twenty-five. In five years he had totally transformed popular music. Perhaps he felt he had done it all. Where could he go from there? Out: on July

29, 1966, the question was answered when he had a serious motorcycle accident; it was rumored that he almost broke his neck. Others claimed that it was not so serious but that he used it to get off the treadmill he was on. In any case, it becomes a convenient point of demarcation in his career. Overnight he seemed to disappear from the public eye. In a way, it reconnected him to his past—he stopped wandering, set up a house and family in Woodstock, fathered three children; he was interested in religion and became fascinated with both the King James Bible and the Jewish iconography of Marc Chagall (the "things flying, things walking, clocks flying, rabbits with green faces"). He was also reading the stories of Isaac Bashevis Singer, like "Gimpel the Fool," about the existence of God, moral choices and inexplicable mystery—all subjects close to his heart.

In the summer of 1967, the so-called Summer of Love, even as the Beatles were releasing *Sgt. Pepper's Lonely Hearts Club Band* and the hippies were gathering in San Francisco's Golden Gate Park, Bob was headed in the other direction, away from the world of fantasy and toward his roots, musical and otherwise. Gradually he disengaged from the roaring world of the previous decade. No more political songs—he was writing love songs ("I'll Be Your Baby Tonight") and songs with a religious undertone ("All Along the Watchtower"). He severed his ties with his manager, Grossman; he tried writing a novel. And he even called his old friend Larry Keegan back in Minnesota. When he told Larry about his motorcycle accident, instead of sympathy what he got from Larry was, "What kind of friend are you—I haven't heard from you in ten years." From that time on, Larry often accompanied Dylan on tour, in a special bus outfitted for his wheelchair.

On the other hand, following the motorcycle accident, Dylan appeared to lose his ability to channel the zeitgeist, to speak for the collective unconscious of his generation. Later he would say he had developed "amnesia": "One day I was half-stepping and the lights went out," he said, "and since that point, I more or less had amnesia. . . . It took me a long time to get to do consciously what I used to be able to do unconsciously." In 1967, as the hippies were gathering at his gates, Dylan retired to the basement of a big pink house in Woodstock, New York, and recorded old classic cover songs with a group called the Band. He was heading toward the *John Wesley Harding* album with its religious symbolism: "Ballad of Frankie Lee and Judas Priest," "I Shall Be Released," "Tears of Rage," "This Wheel's on Fire."

Musicians were not the only ones migrating to the West Coast in 1967. Where talent goes, promoters follow: in June of 1967, the Monterey International Pop Music Festival, a three-day concert held at the Monterey County Fairgrounds, was the first widely promoted and heavily attended rock festival on the West Coast, attracting an estimated ten thousand people. The brainchild of two Jewish producers, Benny Shapiro and Lou Adler, Monterey Pop represented a moment when large corporations found themselves marching to the drumbeat of the political times: pop music had a kind of urgency about it; it was essential. This was a time when a song would encompass a whole way of political thinking;

the song itself was "against the establishment." Also active in the festival was a young journalist, raised in a secular East Coast Jewish family, named Jann Wenner, who had just started *Rolling Stone* magazine, the first rock-and-roll journal premised on connecting the dots between the music and the counterculture. Along with many of the new bands from San Francisco, the Festival also showcased one of the greatest soul acts from the Atlantic catalog; it was a kind of coming-out party for the burgeoning California counterculture, and when it was all over, thanks to Wenner and the new rock press, the whole world knew about Otis Redding.

These West Coast rumblings were being heard in New York City—to paraphrase the words of Dylan's famous song "Ballad of a Thin Man," record execs knew that something was happening but they just didn't know what it was. Clive Davis, the lawyer who had begun his career in a standoff with Dylan, had just become president of Columbia Records—a dramatic shift in the aesthetic center of the business in which lawyers and accountants would soon replace all the promotion men and publishers who had run the industry for years. Davis knew he needed to be among the first to reach out to the West Coast phenomenon, so he contacted a San Francisco attorney named Brian Rohan, who had handled many notorious West Coast clients, including Ken Kesey and his Merry Pranksters, and Rohan agreed to shepherd Davis around Monterey Pop. In return, Rohan wound up representing many of the same musicians when they made their deals with record companies (including Columbia); if it was a conflict of interest for Rohan to work both sides of the river like this, it was a conflict that had been bridged long before he ever arrived on the scene.

Davis came back from the Monterey Pop Festival convinced that rock and roll was here to stay and that CBS needed to get into the rock-and-roll business with both feet. Up until this time, they were the last major label to commit to this music, and now he told his assistant, Walter Yetnikoff, to start letting his hair grow and act a little hipper. Yetnikoff grew sideburns and started wearing boots with zippers. Davis himself began wearing Nehru jackets and tinted glasses. It was the "psychedelic era," and he was in it to win it. He signed one of the rawest bands from Monterey, Big Brother and the Holding Company, featuring Janis Joplin; he hung her portrait prominently on the wall of his office, right alongside those of Bob Dylan and Miles Davis, like hip trophies of the wild creatures he had bagged.

During the summer of 1967, the media were in love with the image of pretty girls with paint on their faces and bearded young men smoking pot and spinning in circles under the warm California sun, and the Summer of Love was officially off and running. *Life* magazine, *Time* magazine, CBS News—the media couldn't get enough of the idea of an army of "hippies" who thought they could change the world, or at least avoid its more unpleasant aspects. "All you need is love," sang the Beatles, and the press promoted and mocked the idea at the same time. The success of Monterey Pop launched a series of large outdoor events, concerts, "be-ins," and rallies that would culminate, two years later, in the mother of them all, held in Bethel, New York, just down the road from Dylan's home: the Woodstock Festival.

Today the word "Woodstock" is synonymous with peace and love, hippies dancing in a muddy field, rock bands coming in by helicopter, thousands of people camping together and nobody getting hurt; a kind of modern utopia. For Dylan, it was anything but. Beginning with his retirement in 1966, he had been fending off wandering hippies hanging around his gate, often on some kind of vague pilgrimage, stoned out and looking for answers. Dylan himself understood he had provoked them—he later said, "If I wasn't Bob Dylan, I'd probably think that Bob Dylan has a lot of answers"—but for a man uncomfortable being a spokesperson and in the process of reevaluating his personal life, it was more than unpleasant. He felt exposed, and perhaps because he had spent his entire life hiding in plain sight, it must have been unnerving to experience this growing vulnerability on a daily basis.

Too, in the interim, while Dylan had been in seclusion, the scene around him had changed, and not for the better; every silver cloud now seemed to have its own darker lining. In the winter of 1967, just months after his major success in Monterey, and following a sold-out European tour, Otis Redding was scheduled to play in Madison, Wisconsin. On December 10, his chartered plane was coming in for a landing when it mysteriously went down in Madison's Lake Monona and the singer, along with most of his band members, perished. The opening act on the show was to have been a local band named the Grim Reapers. After the crash, they changed their name to Cheap Trick; somehow the transition from "Grim Reapers" to "Cheap Trick" seemed to speak a great deal about the tenor of the times.

I was not in Madison the day the tragedy occurred; I had moved to England that fall to study in the American Studies program at Sussex University in Brighton. I was interested in the sociology of black music in America, but in retrospect, I can see that American Studies was a perfect field of study for a young Jewish-American; Jews have always been studying America. I was also taking my place in a long line of people who had come from Europe seeking their new identity in America, and within two generations, their grandchildren were seeking their American identity in the European past. But watching American history unfold from across the ocean during the late 1960s was not only instructive but chilling.

Beginning in 1968, there began what seemed a season of death and depression, angst and anger, nihilism and self-destruction: the assassination of Martin Luther King in April of that year; the presidential campaign of Bobby Kennedy, which inspired so many blacks and young people, ending in his murder in a Los Angeles hotel corridor in June; and of course the endlessly expanding war in Vietnam, the pictures every night on the evening news of young boys being helicoptered out of the jungle, often in rubber bags. Even President

Johnson's "Great Society" programs, designed to bring racial equality to the United States, appeared to be a slippery slope. They set in place a welfare system that ultimately favored single mothers over intact families, hastening the breakup of African-American homes. More problematic, Johnson's "affirmative action" policies provoked consternation in the Jewish community. On its face, the concept of affirmative action was simple; as Johnson said, "You do not take a person who, for years, has been hobbled by chains and liberate him, bring him to the starting line of a race and then say, 'You are free to compete with all the others,' and still justly believe that you have been completely fair. This [affirmative action] is the next and the more profound stage of the battle for civil rights." Yet, asked some Jews, how different was this singling out of one ethnic group for special treatment from the singling out of another by Hitler? Either we are all equal or none of us is safe.

The issue ultimately proved to be the linchpin for one of the great tragedies of the American century: the very public and angry divide between liberal Jewish groups and a small but growing sector of the African-American community. Affirmative action drove a wedge between blacks and Jews; particularly black radical groups like the Black Panthers saw the aversion of Jews to its racial profiling as proof of their ongoing exploitation by whites, this time the Jews. Some believe affirmative action became the underlying core issue in the expansion of black anti-Semitism during the latter half of the twentieth century. In some sense, perhaps the split was inevitable: for years, blacks and Jews had been close—perhaps too close—and the problems between them in the late sixties can be seen as a kind of inevitable case of separation anxiety. Still, in the words of the author James Baldwin, "In the American context, the most ironical thing about Negro anti-Semitism is that the Negro is really condemning the Jew for having become an American white man."

This black/Jewish split came to a head at a conference in Miami in 1968 attended by African-American leaders Jesse Jackson and Coretta Scott King at which Jerry Wexler was scheduled to accept an award for his contributions to black music. However, instead of heralding Wexler's work in a spirit of unity, the agenda was hijacked by a group of black power advocates who, one after another, vilified white executives in general and called for a black takeover of all the record companies and R&B radio stations. Wexler was livid. "I'm all for it—black political power, black economic power, black ownership, but these shakedown artists had no program; it was just old-fashioned blackmail. Under the guise of righteousness, hoodlums were practicing extortion." Wexler left the conference without his award, and not long thereafter, he persuaded his partners to sell the Atlantic label, along with all the affiliate labels that pioneered soul music, to the Warner Bros. corporation, a huge conglomerate that in the end was much less sympathetic to black issues than the Atlantic operation had been. As part of corporate America, Atlantic, like all the other "major" labels, had to respond to the demands of shareholders rather than the tastes or conscience of its owners. The slippery slope was getting slicker all the time.

Both the sarcastic humor of Bob Dylan and the angry rhetoric of black separatism spoke of some deeper disturbance in the urban zeitgeist. New York City, a home to both, was itself starting to look pretty ragged around the heels—junkies in alphabet city (the Lower East Side) and Uptown too. Instead of discussion, it was all pose and counter pose (on the Lower East Side, it was mostly the pose of no pose). If the recreational drugs that are in fashion invariably tell a lot about the times (the seventies, for example, with its cocaine fixation, spoke of the frenzy in the recording business, the need to fuel the vacuousness of the disco party and to prop up the young pop stars), then the rise of heroin in New York during the sixties is a no-brainer. One could say the use of this drug was directly related to the war in Vietnam, since not only did the times appear to call for the deadening of sensibilities, especially on the hard streets of big cities, but some of the finest heroin ever to arrive on U.S. shores arrived directly from Vietnam, in the body bags of fallen soldiers.

Into this environment stepped four kids from the Jewish suburb of Forest Hills who called themselves the Ramones. Trying to pass themselves off as Puerto Ricans (their name, the Ramones, was meant to make them sound like a tough street gang), the band was conceived by Tamás Erdélyi (aka Tommy Ramone), a short Jewish kid with frizzy hair who had been born in Hungary and arrived in America as a young boy. The band was his lifeline to American society, where he couldn't shake the feeling of being an immigrant, an outsider. Most of his family had been killed in the Holocaust, and in his musical performance he appeared to exhibit symptoms of "Stockholm syndrome," occasionally found among Jews who suffered through the Shoah; like them, he often identified with the enemy and hung Nazi iconography onstage when the Ramones performed.

The neighborhood where the Ramones grew up was very Jewish, with delis on many corners and synagogues scattered throughout. In the midst of this kosher community, Tommy began palling around with an odd-looking kid with no musical experience named Jeffry Hyman (aka Joey Ramone). "He was the perfect outsider for the Andy Warhol movie I had in mind," said Tommy. To him, the band was an "art concept"; the leather jackets and blue jeans and tennis shoes were clothes that would mark them as outsiders. "Part of the whole point was that we looked like what we were, yet we were aware of doing so, of intentionally creating this image . . . it was an ironic statement about where we were from. We became a group in a uniform that we claimed was natural. We became a band." The band became the darlings of the New York music media, who, as usual, were searching for the next big thing. Yet it was Bob Dylan's own apparent lack of vocal concern and often angry pose, wrapped in a kind of ironic obscurity, that allowed the press to celebrate the Ramones: their music was beside the point.

The premier punk celebrity in sixties New York was a young man of conflicted sexual orientation who came out of Andy Warhol's "factory," the loft where Warhol painted, made films, and choreographed his bizarre happenings. A band called the Velvet Underground was an integral part of the scene, and its lead singer was a young

Jewish boy with a bad heroin habit named Lou Reed (né Louis Rabinowitz), who also affected the leather-wrapped look of a tough kid from the Lower East Side. He was in fact born into a nice Jewish family in Brooklyn and grew up in Freeport, New York. As a teenager, he had been given electroconvulsive (shock) therapy to "cure" his homosexual behavior. He once said of the experience, "They put the thing down your throat so you don't swallow your tongue, and they put electrodes on your head. The effect is that you lose your memory and become a vegetable. You can't read a book because you get to page 17 and have to go right back to page one again." It was perhaps the ultimate disconnect for a serious young Jewish boy.

Reed attended Syracuse University and studied creative writing with the noted Jewish poet Delmore Schwartz. Reed later said that his goal at the time was "to bring the sensitivities of the novel to rock music, or to write the Great American Novel in a record album." This rather delicate sensibility was clearly swamped by the environment of Warhol's factory, where the stated intention was simply to draw as much media attention to its participants as possible. Merging the concept of high art with the techniques of mass production—his silk screen process was something invented by the advertising industry—Warhol had generated enormous attention and financial success through his factory and was now promoting his personal tribe of writers, beautiful people, musicians, transvestites, street kids, and poseurs. They would, in his apocalyptic phrase, all be "famous for fifteen minutes"; everybody pretended to be somebody other than who they were or where they came from, and yet they each felt "authentic" as long as they remained under Warhol's roof. Reed himself did what he could to distance himself from his Jewishness by conking his "Jewfro" in the manner of black performers Muddy Waters and James Brown (who did it to look whiter); indeed, most of the members of the factory crowd were raised as wealthy WASPs, a life that Warhol, a working-class Catholic outsider, craved. Both Andy and Nico (the tall blond daughter of Nazi parents who fronted the Velvet Underground) were thought to be marginally anti-Semitic.

When Reed formed the Velvet Underground (with Warhol as its impresario), his musical reach was short but the New York press's reach was long, especially when it came to selling image and "authenticity" to the country at large. Just as it took white kids from London to sell the blues back to Chicago, it took the Velvet Underground to sell the style of alienation to the rest of the country. Alt-rock and punk rock, so-called radical musics that swept the disaffected youth of America and Europe in the seventies, owe more than a little of their existence to the Velvet Underground. While their first album didn't sell well, "everybody who bought it started a band." Knowledge of music was not a requirement in the world of punk bands; in fact, it was often unnecessary baggage. It was about something else entirely: Lou Reed was one of the first rock performers in American rock to wear lipstick onstage, to promote sexual androgyny (discounting Little Richard), and so gave rise to singers like David Bowie (who wound up producing Reed's hit record *Transformer*). In fact, Reed borrowed a lot of his production technique from the UK and sold it to America as their own authentic street culture.

Reed's struggle for social relevance, his in-your-face performance delivered with a hipster's skewed humor, also suggested the influence of another Jewish New Yorker, the comedian Lenny Bruce. Bruce was, in the words of comic Jerry Seinfeld, "the first guy to personalize humor; he made it about *him* . . . he made it OK to be smart." Too, one could sense the influence of Paul Krasner, the editor of *The Realist*, the first underground press periodical. *The Realist* was the product of the beat and anti-McCarthy movements; the magazine was designed with the look and feel of a normal newsstand journal, but was in fact wild, hip, and often more outrageous than anything else in print, a kind of adult successor to *Mad* magazine. The Jewish foundation of the punk movement can also be found in the many New York culture critics who helped legitimize it: Lenny Kaye, Richard Meltzer, Sandy Pearlman, Jon Landau, Paul Williams, Lisa Robinson, Greil Marcus, Nik Cohn, all helped launch punk by articulating a context in which to take it seriously, as of course did club owners like Mickey Ruskin (of Max's Kansas City) and Hillel Kristal (CBGB), who both gave it a physical place to exist.

The summer of 1969 started pleasantly enough: a rock-and-roll mud bath in upstate New York that lasted three days, attracted half a million participants, and became synonymous with the hippie philosophy "all you need is love," or, alternatively, "dope will get you through times of no money better than money will get you through times of no dope." The Woodstock Festival itself was the creation of four young Jewish entrepreneurs: John Roberts, Joel Rosenman, Artie Kornfeld, and Michael Lang. Roberts was the financial backer, only twenty-six and the heir to a drugstore and toothpaste fortune; Rosenman, a recent graduate of Yale Law School, was initially planning with Roberts to create a television show about "two pals with more money than brains and a thirst for adventure." In an effort to generate plot ideas, they placed a classified ad in *The New York Times* and *The Wall Street Journal* stating, "Young men with unlimited capital looking for interesting legitimate investment opportunities and business propositions." After receiving literally thousands of replies, they came to the realization that "we had become the characters in our own show." So they did the next obvious thing: they bagged the television show and followed their new reality to its logical conclusion.

Enter Artie Kornfeld, who at twenty-five had worked for Capitol Records and written a few pop songs, and Mike Lang, the former proprietor of the first head shop in Florida. It was Lang's idea to produce a cultural extravaganza. First, he used an old-school hustle to meet Kornfeld: he told Artie's secretary he was an old friend from the neighborhood. "My secretary said, 'There's a Michael Lang here to see you,'" remembers Kornfeld, "And I said, 'Who's Michael Lang?' And she said, 'He says he's from your old neighborhood.' And I said, 'Well, if he's from the neighborhood, tell him to come in.' Bensonhurst. It's a section of Brooklyn that's all Jewish and Italian. That's how he got to see me; by saying he was from the neighborhood.'" It was a scam, but after the two smoked some pot in Kornfeld's office, they arrived at the grand idea of a gigantic music festival somewhere in the Catskills (the location was by way of tribute to the home of Jewish summer resorts). Ultimately, they became the winners in the Rosenman/Roberts lottery, and Woodstock ("An Aquarian Festival; three days of Peace and Music") was born.

The group immediately ran head-on into the hard reality of New York's street culture, as if they were now a rival gang fighting for turf in the psychological territory of the counterculture. Rosenman recalls that when he and the other members of the Woodstock team went to the offices of *The East Village Other*, the hippie newspaper of record (hoping to persuade New York's anticapitalist community not to cause problems for the for-profit Festival), the radical Jewish agitator Abbie Hoffman (founder of the Yippies and author of *Steal This Book*) personally demanded $10,000, "or else that fucking festival you guys are planning is gonna end up around your ass."

The rest, as they say, is history. The Festival went on, but not as planned: it rained for days and hundreds of thousands of people wound up living in the muck; the security failed, and when the fences came down, the festival became a huge free event; and there were warnings from the stage about bad LSD and other chemical risks. But throughout it all, the crowd kept its sense of humor. The mood was perhaps best summed up by Country Joe and the Fish, an antiwar group from San Francisco, who brought the entire crowd of several hundred thousand people together to chant their response to the weather and the War with the "Fish Cheer" ("Gimme an F . . . Gimme a U . . . Gimme a C . . . Gimme a K"). It is tempting to see the moment as just a throwaway shout-out to the stoned thousands, but in fact it played much larger than that: as it had at rallies across the country, the "Fish Cheer" became a cathartic, taboo-breaking moment that gave the crowd a sense of its own strength, a moment as liberating as it was unifying, an "us against them" rejection of the war, brought forward by a group of antiwar Jews, even as the war itself was bringing forth a sense of Jewishness among this band and many others in the crowd.

For both of the band's founders, "Country" Joe McDonald and Barry Melton, were the children of left-wing Jewish mothers from the East Coast and non-Jewish Communist fathers from Oklahoma and Texas. Although McDonald's parents were atheists, early on his mother told him, "When the pogroms come, they will find you." "I always thought of the band as being a Jewish band," says Fish drummer Gary "Chicken" Hirsh. "People called us a rock band, but I always said, 'No, we're just a bunch of Jewish kids trying to play rock and roll.'" And it was their Jewishness, Melton believes, that enabled the band members to speak out against the war early and often. "The Jewish experience is unique in that you're able to engage in social commentary because you don't have a county. You're always ready to move. I wouldn't be here if some people hadn't been smart enough to move. . . . A reason Jews have been hated through history is because they maintained their culture. They remained in places they could be critical of and not necessarily buy into the power structure."

The Fish Cheer was a small, funny, free-form moment in a weekend of rock and roll and chaos. After it was over and the ground was nothing but a trampled field, Woodstock became just another symbol of a counterculture torn between freedom and license and a personal burden for Bob Dylan. Soon thereafter, he moved to California. "That Woodstock Festival," he said, "was the sum total of all this bullshit. And it seemed to have something to do with *me*, this Woodstock Nation, and everything it represented. So we couldn't *breathe.* I couldn't get any space for myself and my family." He did not want to be a leader or an artifact of some hippie nightmare. There had always been a misconception about who he was. He was never a radical, a protest singer, or a "spokesman of his generation." He certainly did not see himself as a part of, let alone a leader of, the hippies.

On the other hand, he had "grown pop up . . . given it brains," as writer Nik Cohn said, "and almost everything that happens now goes back to his source. He hasn't so much changed rock as he's killed off one kind and substituted another." Years later, Dylan would say, "Tin Pan Alley is gone. I put an end to it." In fact, Bob Dylan did help kill the professional songwriting industry; after him, everybody was writing their own songs. By 1968, singer-songwriters were the only thing record companies were signing; if you didn't write your own songs, you were somehow inauthentic.

How do you create your own authenticity? It's a parallel to how you pull yourself up by your own bootstraps. In the record business, it became not only an impossibility but a necessity. In a way, this very Jewish challenge became the challenge for the rest of the country too. How do you create your own authenticity if you are a Jew, now that Jews are not fixed to the book (tradition) any more? The question, of course, harkens back to the first challenge posed to Jews when they arrived in America. The fluidity and the freedom to become whoever you want fights against the sense of actually being who you are. And this tension is at the heart of the Jewish experience. "Who is a Jew in America?" is also the question that one tries to answer in regard to Bob Dylan.

By creating and recreating himself over and over again, Dylan did a very interesting thing. He developed a way to generate music that allowed him to keep changing while remaining who he was. It had to do with words; his authenticity was rooted in his mastery of the language. It was like channeling: he said that "the songs are there. They exist all by themselves, just waiting for someone to write them down. I just put them down on paper. If I didn't do it, someone else would." And that's very close to saying God exists. God exists and it is for me to hear the voice. It was a kind of faith; clearly he believed the songs came to him from somewhere and were being given to him. It's not that different from hearing a voice come out of a burning bush.

"I've written songs that I look at and they just give me a sense of awe," Bob said in 1997. "Stuff like 'It's Alright Ma,' just the alliteration in that blows me away." It is important to note that he says it was the *sound* of the words (the alliteration) that blew him away; the sound, the emotional contour of the words, not necessarily their underlying literal definition, or the cleverness of what it all "meant," but their inherent musicality. He remained firm about warning listeners against trying to attach too much meaning to his songs. "It's in *the way* you say things," he said. "It's not necessarily the things you say that make you who you are."

The *sound* of the music in the sixties was initially about caring—we know what happens without being told the details; people fall in love, they hate, they save, they spend, they live, they kill, they die—this is the story; all the rest is commentary. Dylan was like the pebble thrown in the pond, the match struck to the straw; Dave Van Ronk said that even in the beginning, everybody knew Dylan was not actually who he said he was, but they gave him a pass because of his exceptionality. And his exceptionality legitimized everybody else as well. By giving Dylan a pass they gave themselves one too.

By definition, anybody in show business is trying to escape from something and arrive somewhere else. That's what popular music is: a search for a home in the popular world; a quest to be one of the masses. By extension, the drive for stardom is a kind of extraordinary need to stand naked among your chosen people. Even Bob Dylan must stand naked sometime; he was desperate to be accepted, to be part of the mob—only it was a mob of outsiders he was interested in. He claimed he was "no leader," but he was the creator of that crowd from which, in the end, he had to seek refuge twenty-four hours a day. His early girlfriend Suze Rotolo credits Dylan's hunger for fame as the primary element that drove his transformation: "He could see these things happening to him and he wanted to make sure they would happen," she said.

In the end, Bob Dylan was a work of art that he, Bob Zimmerman, invented. It was not an act. He *became* the information. Unlike other so-called authentic rock-and-roll artists of the day, like Mick Jagger and the Rolling Stones, Dylan could put on and off different hats, could continue to change and still remain true to himself. Jagger, whose image was based on a sense of menace left over from the early days of Elvis, was revealed to be just a skinny kid in need of crowd control at the concert in Altamont; there, at the end of the Woodstock summer, while he was singing about "Sympathy for the Devil," an audience member was knifed to death by the Hell's Angels, who had—in a bravura act of fantasy—been hired by the Stones to maintain order. In Jagger's case, reality overtook the performance, completely undermining both his "demonic" pose and his authority to present himself as a tough "street fighting man." Henceforth, he would be seen as a great star perhaps but never as an authentic artist, and Jagger's performances retreated into a kind of onstage preening that resembled nothing so much as the come-hither gestures of an aging burlesque diva (one thinks of Gypsy Rose Lee's licentious act). This never happened to Dylan.

But the price he paid was obviously quite large. Was he born again? Was he a Christian? Was he a Hasid? Was he a spokesperson? Was he a loner? None of it mattered: he was an artist. As Martin Buber wrote, "When a man attached himself to God, he can allow his mouth to speak what it may speak and his ear to hear what it may hear, and he will bind the things to their higher root." Dylan did get on a speeding train, but getting off was another issue. Bloomfield's friend Nick Gravenites, the man who actually wrote the song "Born in Chicago," said "Bob Dylan was a *landsman*, which in Yiddish is a compatriot. He was a good guy. I met him a few times back in those days and he was just an ordinary, nice person. This wasn't a weird, freaky guy. It takes a little time in this business before they turn you into a fuckin' monster. A lot of times you get trapped in your persona—you're supposed to be Bob Dylan, so you're Bob Dylan, you know." In a way, Dylan paid for his life with his art—and his art with his life—because he was none of the things people said and yet he was all of those things and more. His life became a kind of grotesque parody of an authentic life.

Dylan himself said, "I don't think I'm tangible to myself. I mean, I think one thing today and I think another thing tomorrow. I change during the course of a day. I wake and I'm one person, and when I go to sleep, I know for certain I'm somebody else. I don't know *who* I am most of the time." A friend concurred, "The guy himself is, whatever we want to say, the person is in the work and I feel kind of sad for him because he's a kind of leftover from the work. Looking at his face, you can see. He looks ravaged."

If you look at the frame of pop music in the 1950s, notably the songs of the Brill Building, there were strong narrative characters, and the teenagers of the era identified with these characters and took songs like "Up on the Roof" very personally. The music had an underlying angst and an idiomatic way of talking about it. This was obviously music that was written for these young people at this particular time. But it was still within the frame of pop music, and at the end of the day, Leiber and Stoller were able to go home none the worse for the wear.

What Dylan and Bloomfield and many of these artists in the 1960s did is step out of that frame. Their music was no longer about characters within the frame of three minutes and twenty seconds. The songs were about the people who wrote them and played them. Bob Dylan *was* the theme of his songs. It is easy to see how this act exemplifies alienation in modern society, alienation from the role one is born into, the life that you've seen your parents lead: you can become, you *will* become transformed by the ideas of your time. And this was a very Jewish thing, as was his acknowledged methodology: when asked "What is your concept?" he replied, simply, "I ask questions and tell stories." Many years later, Jann Wenner summed up his own feelings about being a Jew by saying, "What can I say, I'm proud of Mike Bloomfield and Bob Dylan." Not only because of their art, one assumes, but because of the courage of their lives.

Yet if the message was transformation, it remained unclear whether one was better or worse off if and when one succeeded. Because in actually changing yourself, there is no going back and there is no sense of where you're headed. This was the real conundrum of the sixties, and is perhaps why the message of the decade—participating in a social revolution through music of conscience is good for the soul—ultimately failed to stick.

You're running away from something, trying to find something else, but in the end, you can't run away from yourself. But it would be years before we would learn that—and the whole "star" thing would degenerate into Paris Hilton showing her snatch and giggling.

You create the world you live in inasmuch as people's expectations precede you and are there to greet you when you arrive. The process becomes magnified for stars a thousand times. So how does one become authentic and succeed in show business at the same time? It is like the boy who says to his mother, "I want to grow up and be a pop star," and his mother says, "Sorry, son, you can't do both."

KING OF THE JEWS

In 1969, two recent graduates of Bard College made their way down the Hudson River Valley to New York City with the dream of becoming professional songwriters. By the time the two, Donald Fagen and Walter Becker, arrived at the storied façade of the Brill Building, however, it was no longer the musical wonderland it had been in the fifties, nor even the economic cauldron of the early sixties. In fact, there was a desperation in the air, a kind of dishabille that had nothing to do with a bohemian sensibility.

Walter got the drift: "You could tell already that this was something that was a bit down on its heels," he remembered. "The people we had contact with were clearly people who were proposing to make this sort of difficult transition from one pop-music era to another, and you could see how ridiculous it was, what they were trying to do. That reflected itself in all sorts of ways, including the way they looked and the cheesy musical stuff they were doing, trying to capture the psychedelic momentum of the day."

Walter and Donald went floor by floor, pitching their songs, office by office, but their music was out of context with the Brill Building aesthetic; instead of short, romantic playlets, or happy psychedelic ditties, the boys were writing dark postmodern narratives of love and lust in the American vernacular. "The songs we had were utterly bizarre," said Becker. "Jerry Leiber compared our music to German art music or something like that." And while they had no luck selling their creations, they did get a job playing behind a pop act named Jay and the Americans; in the year that followed, they used the group's recording studio to cut demos and get studio experience so that when they arrived in California in 1970, they were ready to record their first album as Steely Dan. Released in 1972, *Can't Buy a Thrill* contained two hit songs ("Do It Again" about addiction and "Reelin' In the Years" about aging) and a new set of pop music conventions.

Becker and Fagen had basically arrived in New York in time to turn out the lights in the Brill Building. "Suddenly," recalls songwriter Cynthia Weil, "you realized that everyone you wanted to talk to was on the West Coast: a producer, an A&R person. And New York was going through a bad period—it was at its dirtiest and crummiest." Yet, if New York in the sixties had been the context of every context—the ground in Midtown was littered with the refuse from people's attempts to define the space they occupied—at least it was about *something*; Los Angeles, the new center of the recording business, appeared to be the context of no context; it seemed to be all about itself and other trivial subjects, and these subjects were subject to change with the prevailing winds.

The big story in the Los Angles record business at the time was A&M Records, a label started by Herb Alpert (a Jewish trumpet player) and his pal Jerry Moss, a promotion man in 1962. In 1965, A&M released Herb Alpert and Tijuana Brass, *Whipped Cream and Other Delights*, which reached number one on the pop charts with the hit song "A Taste of Honey"; Alpert won the Grammy Awards that year for Record of the Year, Best Pop Arrangement, and Best Engineered Recording; not bad for an instrumental album from a relatively unknown trumpet player. In addition, *Whipped Cream and Other Delights* had a scandalous cover of a naked woman slathered in whipped cream and the music, like the photo, was a lighthearted if suggestive confection. This had been the big news on the West Coast up until the mid-sixties.

As context ultimately shapes content—that is, *where* you hear or play music is a determining factor in *what* you hear or play—this place, or lack of place, called Los Angeles inspired an entirely different kind of popular music than the East Coast. Perhaps the same thing in a different place is *a different thing*, and the music of Steely Dan—dark, cynical, hip, phantasmic, grooved, modern, noire—simply made a different kind of sense on the West Coast. What had seemed dissociative in New York City appeared postmodern in L.A. There, with the help of producer Gary Katz, Becker and Fagen became one of the most important, far-reaching pop groups of the decade. *Rolling Stone* magazine saw them as "the perfect musical antiheroes for the Seventies."

Antiheroes, certainly, because, if New York was all about the street, Los Angeles was all about the stars. Big stars. Pop stars. And in L.A., the biggest stars were the executives themselves. The Hollywood stars the audience saw were just the bounced reflection of the light from the executives; if the execs turned off the light or looked the other way for a minute, the stars dimmed. They became the dark side of the moon. So there was this panic in L.A. to stay in your light; the light of your rabbi. Except Steely Dan didn't seem to play that particular game. Their music was, in George Trow's phrase, "eclectic, reminiscent, amused, fickle, perverse." It took the "immaculate funk" of Jerry Wexler to a level never before conceived (the boys took months and dozens of session musicians to cut the tracks on their albums); their harmonies described a palette that reached from Bauhaus to bebop by way of the blues, and Fagen's voice—rough, pleading, sarcastic—was something we hadn't heard before: a world-weary embrace of contemporary decadence through a heightened historical perspective, the sound of a hip Jewish intellectual going down with the popular ship. It was anything but a star's voice.

Steely Dan, along with other seventies recording artists like Billy Joel and Randy Newman, helped to bring the keyboard to the center of modern pop music, wresting dominance from the guitar, which had made rock music so edgy, and making the music more jazz-friendly, preparing the way for both the dance craze called disco and saxophone celebrities like Kenny G (Kenny Gorelick). But perhaps Steely Dan's greatest innovation, and one that was rarely commented on, was their ability to evoke a new kind of nostalgia: a nostalgia for the future.

Fagen's world was a brilliant combination of the classic and the fantastic, of trains that ran under the Atlantic, bomb shelters where hip blondes twisted the night away, and eventually one that occasionally devolved into sadistic threesomes with teenage girls, jacked-up failed novelists, and old hipsters without the emotional strength to care; a delicious vision of thirties Berlin through the filter of our own brave new world. Whereas typical rock-and-roll nostalgia had always looked backward longingly—"Gee whiz, didn't we have fun back in the fifties with the ducktails and leather jackets and all?"—Steely Dan wrote and sang about the old days but with a kind of futuristic perspective: slick pop hooks, intellectual narratives, cool, grooved-to-the-teeth tracks built on jazz harmonies and an almost otherworldly precision. The boys were not really rock-and-roll musicians at all; their music just happened to become popular.

And like all popular acts, Steely Dan was channeling some very important themes of their day. Some of these same themes were presciently articulated by Alvin Toffler in his 1970 book *Future Shock*, in which he predicted, among other things, that as society became more materialistic, we might actually experience *fewer* choices ("The idea of choice is easily debased if one forgets that the aim is *to have chosen* successfully, not to be endlessly choosing"), and with increased technology, we might expect fewer personal freedoms and more social isolation. Predicting the future is a risky business, especially when transitioning from something as volatile as the 1960s into something as desperate as the 1970s, but of one thing Toffler was sure: "The acceleration of change in our time is, itself, an elemental force," he said, and "the *rate* of change has implications quite apart from, and sometimes more important than, the *directions* of change." As we used to say, "We don't know if we're pitching or catching but the ball is definitely changing hands." And the speed at which it was traveling was definitely increasing during the period.

Toffler continued,

> As change sweeps through the highly industrialized countries with waves of ever accelerating speed and unprecedented impact . . . it spawns in its wake all sorts of curious social flora—from psychedelic churches and "free universities" to science cities in the Arctic and wife-swapping clubs in California. It breeds odd personalities too; children who at twelve are no longer childlike; adults who at fifty are children of twelve. There are rich men who playact poverty, computer programmers who turn on with LSD. There are anarchists who, beneath their dirty denim shirts, are outrageous conformists, and conformists who, beneath their button-down collars, are outrageous anarchists. There are married priests and atheist ministers and Jewish Zen Buddhists. We have pop and op . . . amphetamines and tranquilizers . . . anger, affluence, and oblivion. Much oblivion.

Remember, this was 1970 and Toffler was already saying that in this new nostalgic future, memory itself would be forgotten, unnecessary.

There was plenty going on that people wanted to forget. For many Americans, society as they knew it seemed to be coming apart; "a youth revolution, a sexual revolution, a racial revolution, a colonial revolution, an economic revolution and the most rapid and deep-going technological revolution in history." We were "living through the general crisis of industrialism." The net result was a new "temporariness" in everyday life, a feeling of impermanence. He called it "transience," an almost tangible feeling that we live, rootless and uncertain, among shifting sands. "We develop a throw-away mentality to match our throw-away products," and if transience was the first key to understanding the new society, "novelty" was the second. The future, he predicted, would unfold as an unending succession of bizarre acts, implausible conflicts, and wildly funny dilemmas. Instead of history, there would be "public drama," in which "new faces appear daily, there is always a contest to steal the show, and almost anything can happen and often does." Through the acceleration of technological advances, we were becoming lost in our own fears and fantasies.

What psychological geography presented such a bleak landscape? First and foremost, the war in Vietnam was dragging on, generating anger among the young, frustration among their parents, and, in the population at large, a general distrust of the institutions of government. In 1968, Richard Nixon had been elected with a "secret plan to end the war." Of course there had been no plan, and the war was unwinnable. This had been spelled out in a highly classified study by the RAND Corporation, and one of the authors of that study, a former U.S. military analyst named Daniel Ellsberg, caused a national scandal in 1971 when he released the report (collectively known as the Pentagon Papers) to *The New York Times* and other newspapers. He was motivated to do so by his conscience, he said, after witnessing a young war protester proudly going to jail to stand behind his own convictions.

The Pentagon Papers revealed that the government had knowledge, early on, that the war could not be won, that continuing the war would lead to many times more casualties than was ever admitted publicly, and that high-ranking officials had a deep disregard for the loss of life that was going to be suffered by soldiers and civilians alike. Ellsberg was no nattering nabob of negativity (Vice President Spiro Agnew's term for liberals). He was a Harvard Ph.D. who also graduated first in a class of almost 1,100 lieutenants at the Marine Corps Basic School in Quantico, Virginia, and then served as an officer in the Marine Corps, deployed to Vietnam as a company commander. After his discharge, he was an aide to Defense Secretary Robert McNamara, and then landed at the conservative RAND Corporation. His wartime credentials were impeccable.

On Sunday, June 13, 1971, *The New York Times* published the first of nine excerpts and commentaries on the seven-thousand-page collection. As a response to the leaks, Nixon and his White House surrogates began a campaign to find their sources and plug them at any cost. Nixon aid John Ehrlichman supervised the creation of the "White House Plumbers," rogue agents who launched a covert operation to break into the office of Ellsberg's psychiatrist "to get a mother lode" of information about Ellsberg's mental state in order to discredit him. This is the same crew of misfits that ultimately executed the infamous Watergate burglaries only months later.

Then, in October 1973, during the holiest week in the Jewish calendar, an Arab coalition led by Egypt and Syria attacked Israel; the small nation was desperate, and Nixon immediately initiated an airlift of American arms. By the time a truce was brokered, it was clear that Israel had defeated the military might of the entire Arab world. As payback, the oil-producing cartel OPEC seized upon the opportunity of the Arabs' ignominious defeat to initiate cuts in oil production and install price hikes—as well as an embargo targeted against the United States—specifically blaming U.S. support for Israel in the Yom Kippur War for its actions. On January 2, 1974, in an attempt to save oil during the energy crisis, Nixon signed a bill that lowered the maximum U.S. speed limit to 55 miles per hour. You can do anything to Americans, but don't take away their speed.

None of the above was yet on the mind of the young man as he sped toward Los Angeles, through the roaring fires on both sides of Highway 1, past cars topping up their tanks as flames licked at the edge of the gas station, under the smoke and haze that would become all too familiar, hurtling toward his future in the music business. It was 1971, and after four years of studying the sociology of black music at a British institution, playing sessions with well-known rock and rollers in London, and writing the semi-hit song "Space Cowboy" with Steve Miller, I too was going to L.A. to get into the record business.

One day I went with a friend to Capitol Records and on the way into the studios, we stopped on the seventh floor to check in with Artie Mogull, who was now head of A&R for Capitol on the West Coast. For some reason, he was in an expansive mood. He was going to meet a friend for lunch at the Brown Derby, the restaurant shaped like a bowler hat down on Sunset Boulevard, and he invited us to join him. We walked together the few blocks down to the Derby, where we met his friend, Albert Grossman. After we were all seated and the waiter had taken the orders, Artie turned to Albert and said, "You know, Albert, there's only one girl left in this world that I want to fuck." "Who's that?" asked Albert. "The Queen of England," said Artie. "The Queen of England," said Albert, "But she's a dog. Why would anybody want to fuck the Queen of England?" "Because," said Artie, "I want to hear the Queen of England say, 'Give it to me Artie, *give it to me*.'" Albert found this enormously funny, and sitting in this restaurant shaped like a bowler hat on Sunset Boulevard, I saw my future through new eyes. I had presumed that what we were doing here was about the music, but in fact it was all about the executives. They were the stars. This was their game. The goal was to be the king and to have the queen say "Give it to me!" Musicians were just part of the court.

A few days later, when I next called Artie's office, he took the call and invited me to come in and talk. A few days after that, I had a record deal. Within two months, Artie had left the company: he had thrown me a bone on the way out the door. Before I had lunch with him, I simply didn't exist, no matter how many times we talked. But after we had lunch, once I had emerged into his social sphere, borne witness to his fantasy (his personhood), I had somehow materialized in his universe; I existed. As Groucho Marx once said, "In the halls of justice, all the justice is in the halls."

The executive as star was inevitable given the expanding size of the business and the geographic amorphousness of Los Angeles. Because there was no real center to the scene—as Gertrude Stein so famously said about Oakland in the twenties, "there was no there there"—the 1970s in L.A. was Oakland ten times over: one took freeways just to get to meetings or recording sessions, small creative enclaves popped up in various isolated valleys and canyons, and the only centers of activity were the corporate headquarters where executives held court and the restaurants they favored. Of course there was a third center of gravity in the Los Angeles music community: the recording studios. Throughout the fifties and sixties, they were populated by 350 or so first-rate studio players, all of them highly professional, able to read and write any kind of music, from rock to pop, jazz to film scores.

But by the seventies, although the studios were still busy, most of the action was from self-contained bands, usually working with a strong producer sent in by the record company to wrangle an album out of a group of novices. It took a while for the news to reach the recording industry—the engineers, studio musicians, arrangers, technicians—but the business had changed. Rock and roll was not a fad (as many had hoped) but the long-term future; no longer would professional arrangers and musicians craft three songs in three hours for an established singer or a fresh new voice. Something dramatic and fundamental had shifted; now bands with little or no recording experience (remember, prior to the mid-sixties, not even cassette recorders existed for the home user) would spend not hours, not weeks, but months in a recording studio, digging themselves deeper in debt to the record companies.

Old-guard professionals saw this as the emergence of a "cult of the primitive"—the myth of the intuitive genius or the band of beginners, launched in the previous decade by Bob Dylan and set in motion by the dozens of singer-songwriters who conjured hit records out of the chaos of the times. It was part of a larger anti-intellectualism that had taken root along with rock and roll. Rock musicians were not particularly well schooled; most couldn't read or write music, and many were distrustful of anybody who could. Often professionals had to be called in to make sense of the chaos.

"During that period of time," remembers Mike Melvoin, one of the session men in question, "I explained to one producer that if he allowed me to answer the questions that didn't interfere with the band's creativity—like is that a minor chord, is that a repeat, what are we gonna do here—if he allowed me to answer those questions on paper, that we could do three tunes a date instead of one. He understood the logic of this immediately." Carol Kaye, who played bass or guitar on hundreds of hit songs (including the Beach Boys' "Surfin' USA," "Good Vibrations," "California Girls," and "Wouldn't It Be Nice," as well as the Doors' "Light My Fire") remembers, "Very few rockers played on their own records. We [session musicians] were all very experienced, and we were able to create nice lines and make the songs groove. In the sixties, when Beach Boys fans went out to see them in concert, if the music and vocals were close enough, it was OK."

Melvoin saw this growing lack of professionalism among musicians as a logical consequence of executives ("the suits") making the creative decisions. "As people began to employ scientific demographic skills to the marketing of the music, they discovered that they could construct a bottom line product that didn't have to have any lasting value but that could be marketed rapidly and effectively. They had no loyalty to the aesthetics of it or the position in the culture of it." Too, this music "of the people"—a stance taken on by rock groups in the antiwar protest era—gave momentum to the dumbing-down of the culture in general, inasmuch as the audience demanded a kind of parity with the performers. "I think that the idea that people would be even *more* satisfied with music badly played, badly conceived, badly written, badly performed was related to the fact that the audience could then say, 'That's me. That could be me and I could be him.' And who do you get to do that? Do you get kids who really can't play very well but are performing at 100 percent of their capacity—and sound honest while doing so—or do you get a bunch of smartass professionals playing down to the audience? The choice is clear."

But below the surface of this new populism was something else: a new American "majority" just waiting for their moment in the sun. Unlike the educated East Coast (read Jewish) musicians who made up the Hollywood film music community, the typical L.A. rock musician was often from a rural or Southern environment. Starting in the sixties, musicians poured into L.A. from all over the country, from Detroit and New York, but also from New Orleans and Dallas, Nashville and Memphis, and they were arriving with blues backgrounds, rock-and-roll backgrounds, country backgrounds, strip-show backgrounds—but rarely with classical or formally educated backgrounds; this music didn't come from college-educated kids. It came from a blue-collar segment of society that had never been acknowledged in public. And they were a rising force, commercially. "They totally wiped out professional music in L.A.," said Melvoin. "You can go back to Rousseau, the noble savage—that there is something inherently better in the noble savage's art than there is in the high art—the high art is exclusionary."

It was inevitable, then, that as rock and roll became big business, creative control was often given to musicians and bands who sometimes couldn't really play their instruments (like Don Kirshner's invention, the Monkees) and whose recordings were often recorded (ghosted) by others. The authenticity was in the presentation; ultimately the sell was based on whether or not you could believe that the singer's personal experience was what you were hearing. And that was the job of the record company's marketing machine. With the consolidation of singer-songwriters and self-contained bands came the importance of what the record label could do to create the authenticity, the believability, of the artist: they had to garner radio play, hire publicists, support tours, create press releases.

"The record company became like a symphony with the president as occupying a position similar to a symphony conductor," said one observer. "With spiritual baton in hand, he must coerce and cajole disparate instruments to work together in order to have a chance at a hit record. Getting the entire record company behind you is the hardest job in the music business. The symphony direction is complicated by the number of organizational parts in a record company." The personality and aesthetics of the chief executive, then, came to define the nature of the label and the music it recorded.

Even the way the recording contracts became formalized in the seventies guaranteed that the executive was the asset and the artist was just a part of the overall transaction, as opposed to seeing the artist as something special, the creative firmament upon which the overall structure was built. The key to understanding this is the word "recoupable." According to the standard contracts, all the money spent by the record company—for producing the record, designing the packaging, even marketing the final product or helping underwrite the artist's touring—was recoupable *out of the artist's share* (usually less than 10 percent of the retail price). At the same time, the wholesale price of the record (the price the company either charged or billed their distributors) included a nice markup for the label. Hence the record label would get paid three times over before the artist would get paid once. If New York had created the climate in which the dubious ethics of the record business existed, Los Angeles now saw the refinement and institutionalization of the relationship as lawyers flocked to the executive suites. By the end of the decade, artists were struggling to get paid, even though they were selling thousands, and in some cases hundreds of thousands, of records, and the entire system was being driven by the bottomless hunger for the Hit.

What really drove the mentality of the Hit Record, however, was the creation of "branch distribution." Distribution is getting your product into the retail outlets and, hopefully, placed within the line of sight of entering customers. Traditionally, a representative from the company's wholesale outlet would visit each store, try to sell the manager on his lines (product from various labels), and check the store's back-stock for items that were selling. For years, record companies sold to privately owned points of centralized distribution, which then resold the product to one-stops (local clearinghouses for all labels), rack-jobbers (services that went into large stores and stocked entire record departments), and, in the case of large national chains such as Discount Records, directly to the retail outlets. The system of distribution placed anywhere from one to three middlemen between the record company and the customer, with each of them taking a small profit, providing a service and competing with others providing the same service.

But as profit margins narrowed, record companies felt they could service the retailers themselves, directly, by pulling the product from independent distributors and opening branch offices of their own. Branch distribution increased the company's share of the action: they collected what would otherwise go to the middlemen. It also offered people in the home office direct access to the marketplace, which could increase their ability to respond to trends. As the manager of a large Discount Records outlet reported, "Now they have much more of a thumb on the market. They get to start seeing what's selling and what's not a lot faster. They get to start pushing their albums through their distributorships, putting deals on the ones they want to sell, they can control how well an album goes just by the amount of hustle they put on it. They're controlling the market more than I am." And finally, branch distribution was only feasible if the company was billing at least $70 million in sales annually; that is, it separated the big fish from the small fry.

But branch distribution also increased the operating overhead of the record company enormously; there were ever larger payrolls and rent payments to meet each month. Large record companies became volume junkies, acquiring smaller organizations because they needed the billing just to keep their distributorships open, or they made profitless deals with major artists to keep the cash flowing. Knowing that less than 5 percent of all records released are "profitable," they developed what became known as "the Buckshot Theory of Record Releasing." Large companies were forced to produce massive amounts of product to sustain their larger corporate bodies. Huge investments were made and needed to be maintained. They needed Hits.

Too, for the executives to be the star (the asset that was permanent in the show business firmament), Hits were key; how else to prove one's genius? You couldn't quantify culture, only sales. Statistics became their instruments, and the symphony they conducted was written on spreadsheets rather than music paper. Demographics—those shared characteristics in a given population cohort that are useful to predict consumer habits—became increasingly important as statistics started to drive the industry. Since the age of marketing began, people have been segmented out by their buying choices (rather than, say, their ethnicity), which are predicated on their lifestyle accoutrements. Whereas historically, cultural history in America had been the record of great movements, the results of inquiring minds and pioneering spirits, with modern marketing techniques, history became, as Trow has written, "the lunge of demography *here* as opposed to *there*." Now, "nothing was judged—only counted." So, from the point of view of what got sold, branch distribution downplayed "art" or "esoteric" music—the jazz, pop, and cult gourmet items on the rock-and-roll shelves—and naturally promoted anything that would drive the numbers most efficiently.

Particularly among baby boomers, those born during and immediately after the Second World War, mass popularity had become the watchword for cultural importance. This cohort grew up with its own television formats (*The Mickey Mouse Club*, family sitcoms like *Ozzie and Harriet*, Westerns like *Davy Crockett*), and while they experienced a kind of charmed childhood, it was followed by what turned out to be a troubled, prolonged, and improvised adolescence (kicked off by the riotous sixties). "That it *was* improvised—mostly out of rock-and-roll music—so astounded the people who pulled it off that they quite rightly considered it [the music] the important historical event of their times and have circled around it every since." The baby boomers are still waiting to discover whether it will be possible to rock and roll all night at the old folks home.

But much like the warning not to confuse the map with the territory, one must not confuse demographics with history or what it *felt like* to be there at the time. Demographics are not history—they are simply numbers, fixed on some abstract grid, disposable with the next overlay, relevant only to other numbers; whereas history . . . well, history is what happens in the streets. During the seventies, as the size of the business grew (record sales increased almost 2,000 percent from the early fifties to the late seventies) and the dominance of professional marketers spread (accountants, advertising men, marketing geniuses, lawyers!), life's experiences, our collective memory, gradually became reduced to units sold. Quantity became quality, people voted with their dollars, and slowly what sold lived, what didn't sell disappeared without leaving a trace. (Only the infinite memory of the Internet would eventually resurrect much of this lost world.) Ultimately, we may remember what song was number one on such-and-such a date, but not necessarily where we were or what we felt like when we heard it. Upon these shifting sands is propped the celebrity culture of our times; this is the natural habitat of the "star." So for the record executive to *become* the star, he needed to make Hits happen. Only big numbers ("nothing less than super!") would do.

It wasn't just about the money; the fun of the business had long been about inner "hearing," being in touch with the public sentiment, having the common ear, being a man of the people. It is the modern analog to good *nusach*, the highest form of status in the synagogue culture. And in the record business, everybody needed to have their rabbi, a successful executive who took you under his wing. You both agreed on the *nusach*. This vestige of *yiddishkeit* had traditionally been part and parcel of what it took to be a *mensch* (a good person), to have *neshuma* (soul). Even an out-and-out gangster could be a good citizen in the record business, a man of the people, and in fact it did not disqualify him from being celebrated for his "community service." A good example would be the notoriously mob-connected Morris Levy, who received the 1973 United Jewish Appeal "Man of the Year" Award. At the award ceremony, Warner Bros.' Joe Smith, the master of ceremonies, looked around the room and said, "With the group of cutthroats on this dais, every one of you would be safer in Central Park tonight than you are in the ballroom of the Hilton Hotel," and then concluded his remarks by saying, "I take this opportunity to extend my own personal best wishes to Moishe [Levy's Yiddish name], a man I've known for many years, admired and enjoyed. And I just got word from two of his friends on the West Coast that my wife and two children have been released!" The laughter was uproarious.

By the seventies in L.A., the music business was like a private club, and the whole town (Hollywood particularly) was like an extension of the club grounds. With rapidly growing sales, there was plenty of room at the top. For example, when talent manager David Geffen put together the group Crosby, Stills, Nash and Young from the pieces of other groups, he first brought them to Ahmet Ertegun and said, "Sign them, you'll make a million dollars." Ahmet said, "I already have a million dollars; you sign them," and so in

1971, Geffen started Asylum Records, to be jointly owned by himself and Atlantic. Today Geffen is a billionaire. If the people on the streets were enjoying their prolonged "improvised adolescence," then the most powerful men in the business were those who used the power of adult competence to enforce childish agreements.

But in the end, it turned out that having the most toys was not enough. The audience may not have grown up, but many of the original record executives eventually did, discovering to their chagrin that the numbers weren't enough to justify the game they were having to play. "I wouldn't have said this two years ago," Jerry Moss said in 1975, "but I think . . . for somebody to do as we did, you know, to work in small numbers and establish some kind of growth potential is almost impossible." Artie Mogull concurred: "I have a theory," he said. "I believe that within the next five years, the president of every record company in America will either be legally or financially oriented. The record business has become too big and too complicated for the creative guy to run it anymore. I don't like it, but it's inevitable. It's like what happened to the motion picture business. It became too big for the Mayers and the Warners who created it. And I think that as the pioneer creators phase out of the business, their replacements will inevitably be legal or financial people." No more throwing the kid a bone on your way out the door; henceforth, if the numbers didn't crunch, there was no free lunch.

It is well to remember how rapidly the American record industry has grown; in 1955, the industry's total sales, all the labels combined, was $277 million. A recent estimate of revenues for just one company, Warner Music Group (WMG), was $3.491 billion. During the 1970s, Warner Bros. and Columbia (which ultimately became part of Sony Entertainment) controlled 47 percent of all the music sold in the United States. The creation of WMG and CBS/Sony, the style of their respective evolutions, the personalities of their leaders and the story of the war they fought over market share, is a good way of describing what happened with the entire music business during the crucial decade of the seventies.

Warner Bros. is by far the younger, and in many ways the more interesting, of the two organizations. Warner Bros. Records was founded in 1958 as a division of the Warner Bros. movie studio. At the time, one of its contracted actors, Tab Hunter, had recorded a hit record for Dot Records, a division of Paramount Pictures, and Warner Bros. realized they needed their own record label or they were going to miss out on a lot of future revenue. Hence Warner Bros. Records was formed. Their first hit—"Kookie, Kookie, Lend Me Your Comb," by Edd "Kookie" Byrnes—was spun off from their television show, *77 Sunset Strip*. However, the first several years of Warner Bros. Records were not profitable. Their response to the economic challenge was interesting in that, from the beginning, their A&R policy was to take chances and back talent, often looking ahead or running counter to the popular taste of the moment. For example, in 1959 they signed a rising standup comedian named Bob Newhart, who provided the label's next major commercial breakthrough. His debut album, *The Button-Down Mind of Bob Newhart*, went straight to number one in the United States, staying at the top for fourteen weeks. Comedy records may have been a long shot, but Warner Bros. later went on to record both Allan Sherman and Bill Cosby, and both sold gold. The label next scored with the Everly Brothers, whose first Warner Bros. single, "Cathy's Clown," sold more than eight million copies. But the big turning point for the label's identity and bottom line occurred in 1961 when the label signed Peter, Paul and Mary (through the friendship of Artie Mogull and Albert Grossman). Grossman's deal for the group, which included a substantial advance of $30,000 and, most significantly, the stipulation that the group would have complete creative control over the recording and packaging of their music, broke new ground for recording artists. This became the template for rock-and-roll deals for years to come, and the idea that rock-and-roll musicians should be in complete control of anything—indeed, *could* be in complete control of anything—was one that came to haunt the industry.

In 1963, Warner Bros. Pictures purchased Frank Sinatra's record company, Reprise Records, as part of a deal to acquire his services as an actor. The purchase ultimately proved very beneficial to the Warner group: Sinatra made a famous "comeback" in the late sixties and the label also secured the U.S. distribution rights to the recordings of Jimi Hendrix. But more importantly, Mo Ostin, the manager of Reprise, came along with the deal; in the end his value to Warner Bros. would dwarf that of Sinatra and Hendrix; the executive was the star.

Mo Ostin (born Moses Ostrovsky) moved with his family to California from New York when he was fourteen years old. He changed his last name after graduating from high school and went on to study accounting in college; his first job after graduating was for Sinatra's Reprise Records. Although educated in statistics, he was immediately schooled in the performing arts; in those days, Frank Sinatra and the Rat Pack were an essential part of the Hollywood culture, and Mo Ostin, as part of a core group of executives that brought this creative community together with the business community, became an immediate player.

In 1966 Ostin hired a young producer named Lenny Waronker as his A&R manager. Waronker was the son of the Liberty Records founder, Simon Waronker. He had grown up in the recording studios of Hollywood and worked as a producer for a small Los Angeles label called Autumn Records. Autumn had been founded by some of the quirkiest radio disc jockeys of the era, including Tom Donahue, the father of San Francisco free-form radio, and Sylvester Stewart, who later became famous as the R&B musician Sly Stone. Waronker had produced some of Autumn's acts, including a group that included an old family friend, pianist/composer Randy Newman, who, along with Leon Russell and Van Dyke Parks, was part of a creative circle that centered on Waronker and helped make Warner Bros. Records one of the first major rock music labels.

Warners signed some of the most irreverent and forward-looking artists on the West Coast, including—after Ostin's trip to the Monterey Pop Festival—the quintessential San Francisco group, the Grateful Dead. Some of these artists took several years to become well known (Randy Newman did not make his commercial breakthrough until the mid-1970s), but in the meantime they built Warner Bros.' reputation and credibility as the place to be for creative people. These hip artists acted as "loss leaders" that attracted more commercial acts with greater pop sales potential into the Warners fold. Bob Krasnow, who headed Warners' shortlived "black" label Loma Records, later commented that the Dead "were really the springboard. People said 'Wow, if they'll sign the Dead, they must be going in the right direction.'"

The Grateful Dead had also negotiated complete artistic control over the recording and packaging of their music. While they had a reputation for being free spirits and letting the good times roll, in truth, they were anything but confident in the recording studio. Their first album, it's true, had been recorded in just four days, but it did not sell well. Subsequently, for their second album, they embarked on a marathon series of recording sessions lasting from September 1967 to March 1968. The resultant album, *Anthem of the Sun*, proved to be even less successful than the first and put the band more than $100,000 in debt to the label. For their third album, *Aoxomoxoa*, one of the first records to be made using the new Ampex 16-track tape recorder (more room to fill up the tape with "creative ideas"; more time to fill while the clock is running at $250 an hour), they took another seven months and spent $180,000. It too sold poorly. Then, in 1969, the band presented Warner Bros. with the tapes of a live double album that they wanted to call *Skull Fuck*. Ostin pointed out to the group that they were heavily in debt to the label and would not see any royalties until this had been repaid. He further pointed out that such a provocative title would inevitably hurt sales because Sears and other major retailers would not stock it. The band changed their tune and the album was eventually released as *Skull and Roses*. It too took a long time to recoup.

In 1969, Warners purchased Atlantic Records, gaining access to their vast catalog of R&B hits, and to the business acumen of their chief executive, Ahmet Ertegun; the executive talent pool at Warners was growing deeper. Then, in 1970, the Warner Bros. roster attracted a young man by the name of Steven Ross, whose father-in-law owned a cash-rich company with a string of parking garages in Manhattan called the Kinney Corporation. Ross, another Jewish executive with a grand vision, wanted to put together a creative conglomerate, amortizing the huge investment across a larger playing field and letting the creatives (Ostin, Ertegun) steer the ship. Bigness became the solution to creativity in a growing economic environment. Ross purchased Warner Bros. Records and began buying other labels as well. Under Ross, Warner Communications (as it was now called) continued to expand: in 1970, he also bought Elektra Records and its sister label Nonesuch

Records. Eventually the whole enterprise was assembled into a group known as Warner-Elektra-Atlantic, or WEA.

While each of these investments, expansions, and absorptions broadened the company's creative base, it also ballooned the company's overhead. Fortunately for Warner Bros., the hits started coming. Aided by the growth of FM radio and the album-oriented rock format, LPs became the primary sales vehicle throughout the 1970s, and Warners was known as the champion of album-driven artists. One of Warners' first major breakthroughs in the early 1970s was Van Morrison's second solo album, *Moondance* (January 1970) which generated a couple of hits (the title track and "You'll Come Running") and established the need for serious pop artists to make albums, not singles.

When Warner Bros. Records next released albums by Fleetwood Mac and the Doobie Brothers, their reputation was fixed. These groups achieved huge sales, staggering in terms of anything in the past: whereas previously, a gold record (500,000 units sold) was considered a good showing, these groups began regularly selling platinum (one million units) and more. Ultimately, Fleetwood Mac's album *Rumours* sold more than 40 million copies. But among musicians and music fans alike, nothing established the Warner Bros. reputation for creativity like the ultimate success of Randy Newman.

In many ways, Randy Newman was not only the consummate example of Warner Bros.' A&R philosophy, but, ironically, an ultimate example of Los Angeles *yiddishkeit.* Although born into a Jewish family—his three paternal uncles, Alfred Newman, Lionel Newman, and Emil Newman, were all highly regarded Jewish Hollywood film composers—Randy claims to have had no idea what being a Jew meant until a girlfriend invited him to a dance at her country club. When her father found out, he had to call Randy and tell him that a mistake had been made, that the club was restricted and Jews were not allowed. Randy reportedly thanked the man politely, then ran to his father and asked, "Dad, what's a Jew?" And yet in many ways the music of Randy Newman is the most Jewish of all the seventies composers, particularly in his use of humor, his sense of history, his orchestral style, and his rich narratives that celebrate the wide-open American spirit, albeit in a twisted, ironic way: a very Jewish writer with no sense of being Jewish; made for L.A.

The underlying theme of Newman's songs is exposing American ignorance and prejudice without denigrating the people whence they came; typically he writes from the perspective of a character far removed from himself, only to arrive at some universal insight, delivered with a sly wink. (Perhaps this is a metaphor for the great distance between his interior Jew and the L.A. culture in which he was raised.) For example, his 1972 song "Sail Away" was written as a slave trader's sales pitch, singing, "In America you get food to eat; you don't have to run through the jungle and scuff up your feet," as if that would actually put people on a boat; yet the song draws attention to the question itself: "Why *did* people get on the boat? How did the Africans arrive here?" Similarly, "God's Song" from the same album is written from the point of view of the Deity, who brutally spells out human frailties, one of which is turning to him for answers:

> I burned down your city
> How blind you must be
> I take from you your children and you say
> How blessed are we
> You all must be crazy
> To put your faith in me
> That's why I love mankind
> You really need me
> That's why I love mankind

In Newman's cosmology, God himself has vanity and a sense of humor; how Jewish is that?

In the song "Rednecks" ("We're rednecks, we don't know our ass from a hole in the ground"), Newman begins with a description of the segregationist Lester Maddox pitted against a "smart-ass New York Jew" on a TV show, and takes aim at both Southern racism and the complacent bigotry of American Northeasterners who stereotype all Southerners as racists. Through it all, Newman writes with a kind of love, an acceptance of who we are; he is not looking for perfection in people, only self-awareness. Similarly his hit, "Short People," written from the perspective of "a lunatic" who hates the vertically challenged, is actually a song written to *reveal* the nature of prejudice: it is a song *about* bigotry.

Newman's songs are dialogues from only one side of the argument; but because he makes the argument by forcefully making the contrary argument, saying one thing and meaning the opposite, the result is a rich, textured experience. Of course saying one thing and meaning the opposite is the definition of irony, and to the extent that it is a Jewish quality, the heart of *yiddishkeit*, then Newman is a profoundly Jewish writer. Like his orchestrations, his lyrics suggest the great sweep of the American people, much as Jerome Kern did with *Show Boat* or Aaron Copland with *Appalachian Spring*. That they speak from an inauthentic perspective has been a historical criticism of Jews for years—how can Irving Berlin, a Jewish New Yorker, write about "Marie from Sunny Italy" or "Alexander's Ragtime Band"?—but Newman's approach is unique in that he somehow manages to create an authentic context through masquerade, using artifice to create the *feeling* of reality. In a free country, anybody can speak for anybody else; one simply lets the story, the narrative, do the work. His songs often seem bucolic, a dream of a dream, yet they are never without an underlying world-weary darkness; Newman is like a sardonic Stephen Foster, and if Donald Fagen makes us wonder how we fit into the narrative, Newman forces us to confront that we are all in the narrative already.

In the wide-open casino that was L.A. show business during the seventies, it was important to maintain a kind of outlaw stance, if not attitude, in order to maintain street credibility. In 1967, L.A. was not about love beads and flowers in your hair; for that you went four hundred miles to the north. L.A. was a city where, as Newman wrote, "They say money can't buy you love . . . but it will get you a half pound of cocaine and a nineteen-year-old girl in a big stretch limo on a hot September night . . . it may not be love but it's all right." Referring to his hit "I Love L.A.," a song that has been interpreted as both in favor of and against the city of Los Angeles, he explained, "There's some kind of ignorance L.A. has that I'm proud of. The open car and the redhead, the Beach Boys . . . that sounds really good to me." Randy Newman: a man of the people.

In the seventies, there were many different kinds of outlaws in L.A., some real pros working their cons. Bob Krasnow, who had been a student of philosophy at the University of Lord Buckley and Lenny Bruce, received his musical education from the hip San Francisco music mavens Bobby Dale and Tom Donahue, and earned his "street cred" as the San Francisco rep for King Records, home of James Brown and Syd Nathan. In the early sixties, Krasnow once opened his briefcase and revealed to a friend fifty 45s of James Brown's latest single and a loaded .38 pistol. "This is my office," he said.

Bob was fearless, funny, creative, and connected. Besides working for King Records, he also discovered and promoted local talent. Once, when he found a potential hit act but just couldn't break them nationally, his friend George Goldner connected him to the notorious Morris Levy in New York. Levy took on the project, sold hundreds of thousands of copies, and then never paid Krasnow. No matter how many times Krasnow called, he never got satisfaction. One day, in a fit of frustration, he flew to New York and walked, unannounced, into the office where Levy was having a meeting with a couple of his associates. Krasnow said, "I'm Bob Krasnow and I want my money!" Levy calmly opened the top drawer of his desk, pulled out a .38 of his own, and said, "I want you out of here in two minutes and I don't ever want to see your face around here again." Krasnow turned and left the office, left the building, and then, having a second thought, went back upstairs, into the office (this time knocking before entering), and said, "When you said you didn't want to see me around here again, did you mean here in New York or here in the United States?" Levy cracked up. The two men became friends.

Fearless, funny, connected. He proved the "creative" part when he finally started his own label, Blue Thumb Records, in 1968. He basically took the philosophies of free-form radio and Warner Bros.' eclecticism and expanded these to the edges of possibility. Blue Thumb had a comedy thread (the first Blue Thumb Release was a W. C. Fields collection; later the label released the National Lampoon *Lemmings* album), a British rock thread (Dave Mason, T. Rex), an urban black thread (the Crusaders, the Pointer Sisters, Ike Turner), and a thread that couldn't really be categorized (Captain Beefheart, Dan Hicks and His Hot Licks, and Ben Sidran). For some, it was, as has been said about the sixties, a case of "if you can remember it, you clearly weren't there."

The label lasted a scant six years, until 1974, and from the beginning, the operation had an outlaw mentality. One of their first ads in *Rolling Stone* read, "Are you now or have you ever been a member of Blue Thumb?"—an ironic reference to the reiterated anticommunist question of the fifties. And like Nixon's notorious enemies list, if you weren't on it, you felt you had to find out how to get there. It was no coincidence that the packaging of Blue Thumb records was a big part of the sell: Krasnow knew he had to set himself apart, so his records were often pressed on colored plastic, or his cardboard jackets were gatefolds that opened like books and seemed to suggest there was something even better inside that you couldn't see at first. The promise of a good time grabbed you even before the music.

"Bob had this wonderful way of saying to people who had a nucleus of an idea or a glimmer of light, 'Do it!,'" Don Graham, Krasnow's business partner, remembers. "Never how to do it, when to do it, how much it costs . . . just do it. If an idea had some validity, Krasnow went with it." And if the Blue Thumb Gang started as outlaws, the economic climate of the early seventies pushed them even further into the high cactus. Tommy LiPuma, Krasnow's original partner along with Graham, said, "At the time, the major record companies were paying big bucks to artists, outrageous money. And of course we didn't have the money for that. So we had to take the acts that were too far out for the major labels. They were acts that were on the fringes of the business. I don't mean the bad fringes, I mean these artists were *unique*. So we were dealing on another level. We didn't have the funds . . . but we sure had the fun."

Blue Thumb's offices were on the second floor of a small New Orleans–style building in Beverly Hills, and Krasnow's office was styled as a hip den of iniquity: the walls were painted dark gray, almost black, and one wall was dominated by a floor-to-ceiling portrait of Jimi Hendrix. Krasnow himself sat in a large comfortable chair behind the desk, and his guest would usually take the antique barber's chair across from it. "Three or four times a week," Don remembers, "me and Tommy and Bob would come together in Bob's office, sit there and look at Jim Hendrix, and talk about the future. We'd exchange ideas, get out of the barber chair, and get back to work."

One day in 1973, I was sitting in that same barber's chair when Krasnow got the news that Clive Davis had just been fired by CBS Records, allegedly over the misappropriation of corporate funds. Krasnow immediately called out to his secretary "Get Clive Davis on the phone. I want that crook to work for me!" Disreputability was not a handicap in the record business, as long as it was done with style and consequence—the size of the con had to be big enough to warrant admiration from one's peers; scandal in the business often fell into the category of "all press is good press," and ultimately, most record men survived their bouts with it.

This would be driven home several months later when Krasnow agreed to address the students in a course I was teaching called "The Social Aesthetics of Record Production." I had prepared the class for his arrival by saying, "His record label, Blue Thumb, is truly on the fringes of the industry, an artist's enclave, and Krasnow is a pioneer of the first order. He dresses in fringed leather, outhangs even the wildest artists, and is known as a man of the streets, a guy with a big Jewfro who really has his ear to the ground." That afternoon, when he arrived, Krasnow was sporting a conservative haircut and a tailored three-piece suit. Before we faced the class, I asked him about the change in his appearance, and he simply shrugged it off. Had it all been a pose then? Or was *this* a pose? What about his lust for authenticity? Was that a pose as well?

I had promoted the arrival of Jesse James and instead was walking in with the sheriff of Deadwood. The students were confused but polite. Krasnow sat at the desk, faced the class, and made a few perfunctory remarks. Then he asked, "Does everybody here agree with the philosophy of the record business?"

The students and I had been talking for weeks about just this: the philosophy that popular music was one of America's significant cultural treasures and was no longer simply "captured" in the wild but was being manufactured in the studios and shipped to the people; the implications of this on the social organization of young people in particular, but also on the society in general; the tension created by this disparity or conflict of interests that culminates in the "art" of record production. We were examining the Western conception of "art" to see whether records were an exception to the rule that art has to be separated from ordinary life, and were deep into discussions about the rarefied atmosphere of the recording studio, and I had also shared my own opinion that record production is always a statement of social commitment: "The product speaks of the process," I told them. "Production becomes a metaphor for social aesthetics. The record and its promotion become a tool to make manifest a particular worldview."

So when Krasnow asked the students if they agreed with "the philosophy" of the record business, it took a few moments for one to ask, "Excuse me, Mr. Krasnow, but what exactly *is* the philosophy of the record business?"

"Why, to make money, of course," he said. "That's the philosophy of every business." Krasnow sat there with a cat-that-ate-the-canary grin on his face: There's your authenticity. There's your reality check. The gunslinger had come in from the cold. It turned out that ABC Dunhill, a large independent record company, seeing what Steve Ross was doing with Warner Bros., had started buying up smaller labels, and Blue Thumb was one of them. Within a year, Krasnow too would be fired over the alleged misappropriation of corporate funds. The year after that, he was hired back by Warner Bros., where he signed George Benson and quickly climbed up to a corner office on the highest floor of the corporate tower, CEO of Elektra Entertainment, a position that came with a large checkbook, access to a corporate helicopter, and a retreat in Mexico.

But what had happened to Clive Davis? Here was a man credited with making many millions of dollars for CBS, single-handedly dragging the company into the rock-and-roll era. Columbia was "*his* label more than he was its president," as *Rolling Stone* put it.

Clive Davis had created a one-man company with press releases written about himself on a regular basis. There was no separation between his personal life and his business life. So when on May 30, 1973, CBS charged him with illegally spending $94,000 to decorate his New York apartment and on his son's bar mitzvah, nobody believed this was the real reason. As one executive told *Newsweek*, "CBS doesn't sue a Clive Davis for just $90,000. They're trying to get out of something fast."

There were clues to what that underlying "something" was in a column written by Jack Anderson in the *New York Post*. "We have uncovered evidence of a new payola scandal in the billion-dollar record industry," Anderson wrote. "Disk jockeys and program directors across the country are provided with free vacations, prostitutes, drugs, cash and cars as payoffs for song plugging." Wasn't Davis running CBS out of his pocket? How could he not know about this payola? Did he condone it? The story was slowly percolating when, in May and June of that year, the Watergate break-ins occurred, blowing the payola scandal off the map. Eventually, congressional hearings on Watergate were televised (when Alexander Butterfield revealed that there were actually tapes of the conversations in the Oval Office, it sent a shiver through the country: recordings!), and on television, Dan Rather and the CBS Evening News took the lead, running stories nightly about the scandal. Was there a connection between Davis and Watergate?

Simply this: corruption charges in the record industry were being used by the Nixon White House to draw attention away from the Watergate hearings, and to force CBS—which was especially vulnerable (since the television network and the record division were under the same corporate logo)—to back off. In the words of one insider, Davis was sacrificed because "CBS was very concerned about being involved in a scandal." This was reinforced in a column written by the Nixon speechwriter William Safire not long thereafter: "I'd like to hear Dan Rather cross examine an official of the Bureau of Narcotics and Dangerous Drugs about what is known so far and to watch Dan Schorr on the steps of the courthouse in Newark reporting on the latest leaks from the grand jury room on the penetration of the record industry by Mafia drug peddlers. Let the journalists of CBS News cover the story of the CBS Records in depth." Six months after the firing of Clive Davis, the Senate committee probing the payola issue did not find any evidence of widespread abuse, and of course Nixon was forced out of the White House. Daniel Ellsberg took down not only Richard Nixon, but, apparently, Clive Davis along with him. Davis resurfaced only months later as the head of Bell Records, which he then renamed Arista, after his high school honor society. Eventually, Arista artists included Barry Manilow, Whitney Houston, the Grateful Dead (when they *were* commercial), and myself. The label ultimately delivered new fortunes and mega-hits to Davis. Nixon was not so fortunate.

But Mafia drug dealers? Consider the times: in the early seventies, cocaine was everywhere, in all aspects of show business, politics, fashion, and sports. In the music business, it could be found at recording studios (where a producer might bring along a bag of the substance and leave it on the recording desk for those in need of instant inspiration), in corporate offices (where executives might indulge during the day), and at all the trendy restaurants (where it would be offered as a dessert, a little line or two served in the bathroom rather than at the table). The word on the street was that cocaine was basically benign, had little downside, and wasn't particularly addictive. (This was before the advent of crack cocaine or the multitude of young lawyers and promoters with no septum left.) "Peruvian marching powder" they called it; a little "one-and-one" helped you through the day. But, as comedian Richard Pryor pointed out, "A little 'one-and-one' and you feel like a new man; the only problem is, the new man wants a 'one-and-one.'" But it wasn't just about drugs or the misuse of funds. In the end, there was a deeper, more insidious problem in the record industry, and it was called "independent promotion."

Promotion is the art of getting songs played on the air; people do not buy pop songs they haven't heard. Independent promotion was in part a result of branch distribution. Before branch distribution, the various distributors around the country acted as the promotion men. They handled product from different labels, took on different projects, approached various radio stations; it was, in a way, well regulated.

"It was a pleasure," as Hy Weiss, the inventor of the fifty-dollar handshake, put it. "The greatest thing in the world, payola, because you didn't have to waste your time sitting with some schmuck you don't like for dinner. You could pay him off and tell him to fuck himself. You make your deal and that's the end of it. Who needs fifty thousand promotion men walking around eating your money and drinking your whiskey and fucking your broads on a company expense account when you can give it to one guy in a lump sum and save yourself a million dollars? You're done with a bunch of schmucks."

With branch distribution, the label was responsible for its own promotion, but because of the scandals in the past, they had to insulate themselves from the appearance (or the fact) of payola, so there developed a "Network," a loose confederation of "independent promotion men" who informally divided up the United States. They were guns for hire, freelance record pluggers with an uncanny knack for getting Top 40 stations to play certain songs. They sold their services to any record company that could afford them. A few were so effective that record companies kept them on retainer and paid them bonuses when they scored a station. Just as the executives at record labels were mostly Jewish, members of the Network were primarily Italian. Typical were Fred DiSipio and Joe Isgro, who both spoke Yiddish and went around with big bodyguards packing heat.

As the business expanded in the early seventies—more radio stations, more record releases, more overhead, more ways to spend your money—both radio and record companies began circling the wagons, carving out their turf, fighting for market share. Top 40 radio, for example, only wanted to play "hit" records, the songs the kids wanted, because a loss of one ratings point (a single percent of the listening population) could cost a station millions of dollars in advertising revenue. But of course airplay on the station is what would make a record a hit. No Top 40 station wanted to be the first to play a record. It became a Darwinian struggle on all sides. Radio shrank from Top 40 to Top 20; the fewer songs they played, the fewer mistakes they could make. In addition, radio stations started hiring their own outside consultants to tell them which songs would attract the listeners the station wanted (they did research, ran statistics broken out by age, race, earning power, geography, whatever you wanted.) Your local station was now most likely being programmed by people who lived nowhere near you.

By 1974, Bill Drake, a very successful Top 40 consultant, had gone exclusively into the programming of automated radio stations across the country; no humans at all. These consultants were themselves reachable only through "neutral" third parties such as the Network, somebody at arm's length from them so that if, for example, any money were to change hands, corporate hands would stay clean. In order to pierce those playlists, to get a new record into the ever tightening radio rotation, a label had to hire the Network, arm them with whatever they needed to get airplay, and hope for the best.

CBS Records had been the first label to start its own branch distribution network during the late sixties. In the early seventies, Warners too set up its own branch distribution arm, WEA. From the labels' perspective, the nice thing about the use of independent promo men (or "indies") was that small companies couldn't afford to compete. By the late 1970s, fully one-third of all albums sold in the United States came from just these two labels, CBS and Warners, a direct result of Clive Davis and Mo Ostin having recognized the potential of album rock early on and their willingness to hire the indies to work their records. With branch distribution and indie promotion, sales of albums increased enormously, but so, again, did the overhead. The major companies became hostage to their own size and success. As Isgro and DiSipio began charging more and more money for their services, radio promotion started to look like a sanctioned shakedown operation, and there was nothing the majors could do about it.

When Clive Davis was fired, his sidekick, Walter Yetnikoff, took over at CBS. Walter was initially just a run-of-the-mill Jewish lawyer from Brooklyn, with no real musical interest or experience until Clive hired him. At first, when he assumed the presidency, the CBS staff appreciated that he was so much more humble than his predecessor. But humility is no premise for leadership in the music business, where a distinctive personality is essential if one is to be a powerful label boss. Yetnikoff knew he could not be an A&R executive, a music man like Clive. Instead, Walter invented a persona based on the classic Jewish record man from the past, the streetwise hustler, the inveterate *hondler* (negotiator).

"He became wild, menacing, crude and very loud," recalls one insider. "'Nobody out-*geschreis* [hollers] me,' he boasted. He shattered glassware, spewed a mixture of Yiddish and barnyard epithets . . . His outbursts were calculated to keep people off-guard. Walter wore his ethnicity like a gabardine."

In part, Yetnikoff's act was so successful because he played right into the stereotype of the crazy (i.e. authentic) New York Jew held by the growing number of blue-collar rock artists ("you need a Jew in the business"—he was their Jew). At the same time, however, during the sixties and seventies, record executives liked to believe their artists were wild and unpredictable and needed shepherding; it was the "nature" of the rock musician to be free and out of control; this was the whole appeal of the noble savage. Walter was acting out his own stereotype of the artist, even as the artists were accepting their own stereotype of the Jew. It is a business, after all, based on mutual fantasies.

Walter saw himself as "rabbi, priest, guru, banker for sure, adviser, friend, therapist, sex counselor, soothing Michael Jackson with Talmudic wisdom and schmoozing until three with Billy Joel." He was going to be the hip Jewish father these artists never had.

Take the case of Billy Joel. His own father, Howard, was a German-Jewish Holocaust survivor and a skilled classical pianist, but had left home when Billy was just a small boy. Howard had his own issues: he had escaped the Holocaust at seventeen and, after crossing the ocean, was sent back to Germany as an American soldier, where he participated in the liberation of the Dachau concentration camp (many of his own relatives had perished in Auschwitz). After the war, Howard brought a lot of anger back home with him and some of it was directed Billy's way: "I had a Beethoven piece—one of the sonatas—and I started boogie-woogieing to it one day," said Billy. "My old man came downstairs and smacked the hell out of me." After the divorce, his father moved back to Germany and started a whole new family; Billy did not see him again for twenty years.

Billy Joel grew up in a Catholic neighborhood on Long Island and even attended Mass with his friends. At age thirteen, instead of being bar mitzvahed, his mother took him to be baptized. (The first time Billy Joel would actually wear a yarmulke was when, at forty-three years old, he visited the graves of his paternal grandparents in the Jewish cemetery in Nuremberg, Germany.) Joel grew up tough; he was a member of a neighborhood street gang that committed petty crimes, fought other gangs, and spent a lot of time hanging out, being cool. He had his own rock bands in high school, playing roadhouses and bars. When he failed to graduate, he said, "The hell with it. If I'm not going to Columbia University, I'm going to Columbia Records, and you don't need a high school diploma over there." He had some local success, made a couple of records, but at one point, out of depression, he drank a bottle of furniture polish (an attempted suicide? a plea for help?) and wound up in a mental hospital; there he realized two important things: he wasn't crazy, and he wanted to be a songwriter.

In 1971, he moved to L.A. and worked at a Hollywood club under the name of Billy Martin, an experience that gave him the raw material for his first hit song, "Piano Man." Back on the East Coast, a recording he had made for a small label had fallen into the hands of an executive from Columbia, who bought the rights to Joel's contract and in 1974 proved

Joel's prediction true: "Piano Man" was released on CBS and went Top 20, selling gold within a year. Joel became homesick for New York—he later said moving to L.A. had been the biggest mistake of his life—and decided to return to the East Coast. On the way out of town, he wrote a song called "New York State of Mind."

Joel had hoped that either Ray Charles, his early hero, or Frank Sinatra would record it. When neither of them did, it was given to an obscure singer / piano player named Ben Sidran, who became the first person to record the song; it was released in 1975 on Clive Davis' fledgling Arista label, appearing on the album *Free in America*. The song and the album received good airplay (especially in New York City) and the artist was called into Davis' office for career counseling. Unlike Krasnow's office, with its homey barber's chair, rough-hewn desk, and Jimi Hendrix mural, Davis's office was slick and modern. His desk was situated in front of a large window and appeared to be slightly elevated, so that when one sat across from him, one had to squint and look up a bit. His counsel was quick and to the point: the artist needed to form a supergroup with some famous friends ("nothing less than super" would do) to bring attention to both himself and the record. When I said that was probably the last thing I wanted to do, he said, "You don't want it bad enough. I can't work with somebody who doesn't want it bad enough." And that meeting was over.

Billy Joel's own big break came with his album *The Stranger* (1977), which included the hits "Only the Good Die Young" and "Just the Way You Are"; it won two Grammys and kicked his career into high gear. Since then, he has sold millions of albums and been nominated for the Grammy award thirty-two times, but he has lived an unsettled life; "I'm so insecure," he once said, "I sometimes don't know which the real me is." A very talented outsider who lived his life as an insider, much as Bill Paley himself did when he bought CBS and erased any signs of his own Jewishness, Joel was at the end of a long cultural line: an old-style tunesmith writing about sentimental times, often looking back at the early days of rock and roll much as the early Jewish songwriters looked back at the Swanee River, a mythical safe place for displaced Jews (in this case, Jews from the suburbs rather than from the Pale). His songs, like "Keeping the Faith" and "Only the Good Die Young," have a spiritual quality to them, while others, like "Allentown" and "We Didn't Start the Fire," reveal a strong social conscience. The latter, for example, is not just a list song, itemizing the many events of recent history—it is also a memory song. It is *about* remembering the events of the past, and in this way it is similarly very Jewish.

"The thing that fascinates me most as an artist is the human condition, the drama in life, not fiction but reality," Joel has said. "What people go through in day-to-day living is really epic to me. Just to get through a day and come home and try to keep a family together and live a decent life and be a good person is probably one of the most difficult things in the world; there are so many temptations against it. It's been a theme that's probably gone through all my songs." "We Didn't Start the Fire," then, is also about his father.

Even as Billy Joel was searching for his Jewish identity, Walter Yetnikoff had, by necessity, discovered his own. "I have to follow Clive," said Yetnikoff. "I have to develop my own image. The first thing I did was take a piece of yellow paper and write down everything everybody thought I should do. I would then go home at night, look at the yellow paper, and choose what I wanted to do. How do you forge your own image?" Walter chose to pick a fight with Warner Bros., to start a war. "I have all the troops rallying around the flag, using the excuse to go in and steal artists under the banner 'Fuck Warner Bros.' It was like I'd created a nation. Follow Walter? No one knew who I was. So unconsciously I made a war out of it. I believed in the cause and now I had an army behind me." The lawyer Elliot Goldman said, "All of a sudden, Walter had great notoriety, and it worked. So now, Walter's got to sustain the bluster. It worked because we're in the entertainment business, and people love power and the aura of power. As a result of acting that way—throwing plates across the room—Walter stirred this enormous fear. Lawyers became afraid: I can't ask Walter for that! He'll get angry at me."

Under Clive, CBS had been the A&R company. Under Walter, it became the Deal company; he ran it with the checkbook. His war was a bidding war between the two superpowers, CBS and Warners. The cost of talent, especially established talent, reached new heights; by the end of the seventies, CBS would make a deal with Paul McCartney by which they were guaranteed to lose money but, if things went well, they would gain market share. The drive for volume created more need for the services of the Network, and the Network tightened its grip around the throats of the majors. And then came disco.

Some say disco was started by a party planner in New York named David Mancuso, who, in the early seventies, threw private underground events at his loft for a mostly gay scene; he would play records, combining and mixing the various grooves to keep the crowd dancing. It was a style that had become popular in Europe at clubs like Régine's in Paris, where people were partying to endlessly repetitive grooves—collective entrainment at its most primitive—while enjoying a menu of drugs that included alcohol, marijuana, cocaine, and amyl nitrate. If the fifties was all about romance and the sixties was all about love, the seventies and disco was all about sex.

The music itself came out of James Brown by way of Motown, Sly Stone's extended funk jams mashed up with a black diva sensibility and spiced with more than a touch of transvestite; disco arrived in New York to drive a thriving gay scene, where the "party people" had their own world. Even before the advent of disco clubs like Studio 54, there were the Continental Baths on Broadway and 73rd St., a gay hangout where a Jewish diva from Honolulu named Bette Midler sang by the pool, developing her infamous "Trash with Flash and Sleaze with Ease" act. It was at the Baths in 1971 that she became "the Divine Miss M"; by the end of the decade, the Baths would morph into a place called

Plato's Retreat where more than sixty thousand people attended orgies each month, and Midler was out of there.

By 1976 there were reportedly ten thousand discos in the United States, discos for kids, for senior citizens, for roller skaters, portable discos set up in shopping malls and Holiday Inns. It was clear that discos had become an alternative to radio play for breaking new records, and the importance of club DJs increased dramatically. That year, on a regular basis, five out of ten singles on *Billboard*'s weekly charts were disco. So, by 1977, when a couple of Jewish entrepreneurs named Ian Schrager and Steve Rubell opened Studio 54 in Manhattan, it was not only the ideal environment for social voyeurs like Andy Warhol and his effete coterie, but a perfect venue for promoting the sale of records. The scene was all about music—it was music-driven—and record companies all benefited when the *National Enquirer* alerted the entire country that Bianca Jagger, wife of rock star Mick, rode into the club on a white stallion like Lady Godiva to celebrate her thirty-second birthday.

Those who gained entry into Studio 54 felt privileged; every night the velvet rope out front divided the chosen from the unwashed, and Rubell himself stood at the door and did the choosing. His criteria were not simply fashion or money (although if you had both, your odds improved). "It's all done by sight," he said. "There's a certain type of person we don't pass. People come to me and say, 'I'm a millionaire from Tucson, Arizona,' but I don't care what they are if they're not fun, if they're going to be bumps on a log and sit around. In other words, we want everybody to be fun and good-looking."

Fun and good-looking. And the music? What were the songs about? They were about themselves, the experience of no experience, about being fun and good-looking. Nile Rodgers and Bernard Edwards, creators of the group Chic, who had disco hits like "Dance, Dance, Dance," wrote their biggest song, "Le Freak," one night after they too were denied entrance to the club. "The guy at the door politely told us to fuck off. So Bernard and I went and wrote a song called 'Fuck Off.' 'Awww . . . fuck off . . . ' It sounded great, but I said we can't have a song on the radio called 'Awww . . . Fuck Off'. So I came up with 'Freak Off,' but that wasn't sexy. Then Bernard came up with 'There's that new dance everybody's doing called the Freak.' That was our version of 'Come on baby, let's do the Twist.'" The song topped the U.S. charts for six weeks and "Le Freak" became Atlantic Record's biggest-selling single ever.

Not unlike the jazz age, when people danced their lives away, during the 1970s, before AIDS, in the midst of sweeping social change, a quality of hedonism developed in America that has not been—and perhaps never will be—equaled. Just as rhythm is focused emotion, meter (repetitive, machine-driven pulse) is emotionless focus; without emotion, sexual inhibitions are relaxed. It was life lived on the surface. Don't look down. Down was where the images were flickering on television (in color!), more lifelike than ever before: the fall of Saigon, people scrambling up to the roof of the U.S. Embassy there to catch the last helicopter out of town (what had it all been for?); Phil Donahue, the daddy of the "me" decade, promoter of confessional reality television, encouraging people to reveal their inner mess in the most public way (Warhol had been right about everyone's fifteen minutes of fame); and nightly, more images of violence, more urban crime (an increase of 100 percent during the decade). In response there was a pushback from conservatives, particularly the Christian contingent; Anita Bryant challenged the rights of homosexuals to live next door to her, Jerry Falwell and Jimmy Carter both claimed to be born again; megachurches erupted across the country with millions saying they too had been born again (for Jews, once was enough).

It was a war of the raptured. One regular at Studio 54 recalls, "At one point I remember dancing, closing my eyes, and saying 'If I die tomorrow, I'd be fine—because I am so happy.'" Disco was her church, trance dancing her catechism, boogieing away the night her liturgy—many club regulars reported that it felt like "a religious experience." The church of no church; black music with the ethnicity scrubbed out of it.

This urban party was ultimately celebrated in the film *Saturday Night Fever*, based on a magazine article by Nik Cohn, who was fascinated with disco as a blue-collar phenomenon, an escape for regular kids from the outer boroughs. In the film, John Travolta played Tony Manero, a boy who dreams that his terpsichorean skills will get him out of the neighborhood. The soundtrack to the film, that included the Bee Gees' "Stayin' Alive," "Jive Talkin'," and "You Should Be Dancing," sold 25 million copies. The movie itself was a phenomenon. It drove the disco sound to new heights. The record business was in a disco fever of its own.

First of all, disco was the perfect record producer's medium. You didn't really need to put up with a temperamental artist, just find a voice that fit into the overall aural horizon and pay them scale. Secondly, everything was planned, controllable: the rhythm was dialed in exactly—some said 120 beats per minute was ideal, others liked 130 bpm—the drums were mixed up front, with the bass drum hitting all four beats of every bar: in the studios, it was called the "slave groove"; there was no escaping it. It is no accident that disco yielded few artists whose careers continued into the eighties. Disposability was the point; lack of attachment was the main means of transportation through the party culture.

In 1979, by the time the man in the street had his own double knit leisure suit and his Tony Manero moves down, it was obvious disco was over. If overkill didn't kill it, it would have died anyway. The reason was "profitless prosperity." A good example was that of Casablanca Records, run by Neil Bogart, home to disco acts Donna Summer and the Village People, a group of gay men dressed as various American "types" (a cowboy, an Indian, a fireman, a construction worker). Bogart was a Jewish promotion man who surrounded himself with other promotion men (no effete A&R types here), and he would do anything to get a record in front of an audience. "He was like the P. T. Barnum or the Mike Todd of the recording industry," said one of his minions. Bogart refined the idea that selling the product was more important than the product itself. It appeared to work.

So when Casablanca began to dominate the disco charts, it did not dawn on the industry that the company was losing vast sums of money. Sales were great but the cost of selling was greater. Disco, it turns out, was fueled by hype and by the mistaken belief that hits are bought, not born. Of course, you can buy a hit, but not always profitably. The Network really took root in the peak years of disco. It was no coincidence. Disco created the climate that made the Network possible: fast and loose money, a controlled commodity in an expanding market. But it was a bubble. After the success of the Bee Gees and *Saturday Night Fever*, the business was in a disco lather, but some labels were losing a fortune.

1979 was a disastrous year for the industry. The crash started at retail. Because every record shipped was 100 percent returnable, retailers had no inventory risk and could accept whatever the labels wanted to send them, knowing they could return any unsold albums. All the major labels had caught disco fever and were shipping vast quantities of dance and pop albums based more on fantasy and ego than on demand. In 1979, these records started to come back to them by the truckload. Disco, as they said, "shipped gold and returned platinum." The mistake made by the majors was shipping records and logging them as sales, never dreaming that the usual return estimates were way low.

By 1980, Warner Bros.' executives began to scrutinize the label's budgets and discovered that expenditures on independent promotion had reached several million dollars a year. In November of that year, the Warners labels declared a boycott of the Network. They let it be known that they were not going to pay these shakedown fees any longer. CBS decided to go along. "We weren't making money, sales were shrinking and Indie promotion remained a huge expense," said one CBS executive. In response, the Network promptly retaliated; they went to work and actually had the muscle to get Warners and CBS records pulled off the air. When artists saw their airplay fall off, they demanded the labels put the Network back on the payroll ASAP. The boycott crumbled, but not until the onus of the operation was shifted away from the executives.

Yetnikoff himself came up with the creative solution: he started paying large advances to the artists, who were then directed to spend it on indie promotion themselves. In a single stroke, he had not only handed the burden of guilt to the artists but made them liable for the expense, for in the end, the advance, under any name, was recoupable against the artists' royalties. At Epic, the money for freelance promotion was doled out under the guise of "tour support." Either way, CBS was out of the boycott, and the Network was back on the payroll. As payback, the Network raised their prices further. Now they weren't charging thousands of dollars to get a record played, they were charging hundreds of thousands of dollars. By 1982, CBS was spending at least $10 million on the Network, equal to three hundred salaries. The same year, CBS also fired three hundred employees, in a "belt-tightening measure." It was hard not to conclude that they were cannibalizing their own staff to pay the blackmail. By 1985, indie promotion accounted for almost 10 percent of the total pretax profits for both Warner Bros. and CBS.

Studio 54 stayed open until the mid-80s, although Rubell, Schrager and most of their followers were gone by 1980. Where did all the dancers go? "They went to the gym," said Nona Hendryx, one of the disco divas. "It became the new club." Instead of dance instructors like Killer Joe leading the crowd, now Jane Fonda was calling the moves on her workout tapes. Jim Fixx's bestselling book, *The Art of Running*, led to an explosion in the sport; in 1970 there were only 150 runners in the New York City Marathon; by 1979, there were 15,000. In hard economic times, cocaine was replaced with the "runner's high."

And the executives who had brought on the disco debacle? They proved, as usual, to be remarkably resilient, especially those who spoke the language of corporate largesse. By the end of the seventies, the record business was no longer one in which old-school music men like Goddard Lieberson or Jerry Wexler were likely to rise to power. Now, it was the day of the dealmaker; the top label bosses would be lawyers or moneymen who specialized in "packaging deductions" and "cross collateralization." Their peers were generally not musicians or producers but other lawyers and managers. With the executive as king, the moneymen became courtiers (albeit some with pretensions to the throne itself), and instead of music, the business was really about another art form: the art of the deal.

What was becoming clear by the early eighties was that the record business had become a much more formalized industry, built on paper rather than on stage. Instead of men like Jerry Wexler going out to the clubs to discover the talent, the musicians and songwriters now needed formal representation, advocates who could bring their case into the corporation boardrooms. Record executives (just like the radio stations who wanted a "neutral" third party to bring the music) now only wanted to talk to people they knew; if they found an artist they liked without representation, they would assign one of their favorite lawyers to "represent" the artist. Of course conflicts of interest were rampant: attorneys couldn't afford to antagonize a record label because "artists come and go but CBS is forever." A whole set of immensely powerful lawyers and managers emerged. It got to the point where artists needed managers just to go out and find an attorney to represent them to the label. So now there was a whole new class of participants, once or twice removed from the actual making of music, and most of them too came from the Jewish community.

Authenticity, if it existed, was now in the deal structure, not the music. One can see the transition in the careers of various artists, but none more clearly than that of the most overtly Jewish artist of the decade, Richard Friedman. Nicknamed "Kinky" because of his tight Jewish curls, Friedman was in the tradition of artists like Bob Dylan and Randy Newman. A teller of strange, humorous truths mixed with good-time music, he grew up on a ranch in central Texas and graduated from both high school and college in Austin; his music was all about this odd context of being a Jew in Texas. He called his band Kinky Friedman and the Texas Jewboys (an ironic turn on the great swing band of the forties,

Bob Wills and the Texas Playboys), and his slogan, "Out of the closet and into the corral," said it all; and what it didn't say, his songs like "Ride 'Em Jewboy," "We Reserve the Right to Refuse Service to You," "The Top Ten Commandments," and "They Ain't Making Jews like Jesus Anymore" filled in the blanks. (The latter even caused a bomb threat *from* the Jewish Defense League.) It was all part of Kinky's way of ridiculing prejudice in general and anti-Semitism specifically. His music required the understanding of both the Jewish and the Texas culture: Kinky once noted that cowboys and Jews were the only two groups to wear their hats indoors and "attach a certain importance to it."

His albums received good airplay at first, especially during the free-form radio days in the early seventies, and he toured successfully across the country, but his career tanked during the age of disco. In 1979, he dissolved the band and moved to New York, where he scuffled on the music scene for a while before taking up writing novels. "Very few Jewish performers are openly Jewish in their work," he mused at the time. "Bob Dylan and Paul Simon are not. I was, and I think it cost me commercially." Today he is a successful author of mystery books built around a fictional detective named Kinky Friedman. The man himself is still pushing the boundaries of the Jewish possibility; in 2008, he ran for governor of Texas, and while he did not win, he was taken seriously by the media in this new guise. Ironically, one of Kinky's biggest fan bases remains in Germany, and he has told his German audiences on more than one occasion, "The Germans are my second favorite people. My first is everybody else." This kind of candor is rare in the music business.

If in the twenties the media gave greater exposure to performers who were already well known and integrated into the popular culture (e.g. Al Jolson), and in the thirties the media began inventing performers who had no previous exposure in the popular culture but who spoke for the people nonetheless (e.g. film stars), by the seventies, the media were simply inventing performers who had no connection to the culture whatsoever. It didn't matter: it was pure hype.

After the disco debacle, for example, Casablanca Records put its chips on a rock group called Kiss that had emerged out of the darkest, most cynical recesses of the mind of Gene Simmons. Simmons, born Chaim Witz in Haifa, Israel, came to the United States at age four; his first memory of landing in New York was a picture of Santa Claus smoking a cigarette, and he knew he had found a home. He had never seen Santa Claus before—he thought it was a rabbi. In Kiss, Simmons and three other musicians each assumed a cartoon like persona through the use of elaborate face paint and bizarre costumes. Simmons himself, who sang and played bass, was styled as "the Demon" and was known to breathe fire, spit blood, and extend his strangely long tongue in a lascivious fashion at the teenage girls who came to see the band by the thousands. (Other members were fashioned as "the Starchild," "the Spaceman," and "the Catman.") With their wild theatrics, huge platform shoes, and pyrotechnics, the band was a sensation and sold over 19 million records in the United States and over 100 million albums worldwide.

It is hard to see Simmons, this young Jewish immigrant wanting to fit into America by getting onstage and painting his face, as anything other than a new form of minstrelsy; and whereas in previous times the paint was meant to make a connection to the authenticity of the African-American experience, in the case of Simmons, the paint was meant to signify the connection to Hollywood fantasy. The context of no context. Kiss was not about anything, not even music, which Simmons freely admitted.

"Music was never the point," he said. "I believe that music and inspiration and creativity are all way overvalued. Everybody who is in the arts likes to emphasize the romantic because it makes good copy. Well, I have a little bit of advice for all the new rock stars . . . I think most guys who play the guitar are unworthy of being taken seriously. About the only thing we do is while away your hours." When pushed as to why, then, he chose to pursue music, he replied, "It wasn't inspiration; it was a how-to, a paint-by-numbers. This is how you get the girls. Here's how to get the guys to think you're cool. And here's how to avoid working for a living." "Art," he concluded, "is highly overrated. Michelangelo, Mozart, Rembrandt—they were all on commission." Is this not the ultimate result of the deification of the Deal?

"You know," said Simmons, "in America, if people like what we do, that's enough. I don't think it has to mean anything. But that's the great notion of America that appeals to me—of the people, for the people, by the people. We [Kiss] have 2,500 licenses—everything from the Kiss coffin, which doubles as a Kiss cooler, to Kiss condoms. I'm starting some stuff outside of Kiss, too. There's going to be Gene Simmons *Tongue* magazine. We've already got a preorder of a million without a single word written or photo taken . . . America has been a hoot every day. I still see America as the promised land, and I still see it with an outsider's eye." He may have had an outsider's eye, but he had an insider's understanding.

In America, there is a distinction between music as popular culture and music that's popular; one is authentic, indigenous music, the other is music made not for authentic purposes but to become commercially successful. By the end of the seventies, the recording industry had stumbled on an enormous untapped pool of funds: young people were buying records in unprecedented numbers. And so even the language of the business changed: records were no longer "discs" or "platters" or "sides," they were "units." Musicians weren't entertainers or artists or players, they were "acts." And they didn't make music, they produced "product." By the late seventies, the musical idiom (jazz, pop, etc.) was not as important as the production values in terms of creating emotional states in the listener, and in eliciting certain responses. There was an exchange of feeling for construction; records became puzzles to be solved; they began to sound alike because everybody was using the same synthesizers to make them and airplay was reduced to sounding "right" for the station's format; they know you'll like a particular song because you're already listening to their station.

By the 1980s, "crossing over" didn't involve moving the music from one category to another so much as homogenizing it so that one no longer needed to have any special knowledge or taste to enjoy it—or even to hear "it." Much like fast food—where the burgers, the fries, the shakes, the pie, all taste essentially alike, as if they had all been made from the same elemental particles, just recombined in the back room by some mysterious technology—the first stage of musical digestion, the chewing, had already been done. Predigested music, designed and marketed to "feel good going down," also left one with a nervous, empty feeling. What was happening was a kind of end to history. One retailer, in order to find knowledgeable salespeople at the time, reports inventing a questionnaire to be filled out by prospective employees. In it he asked, "What are ten records you would take on a desert island?" Most applicants responded with "the last ten records they heard. . . . The idea of history is whatever they heard last week, the most recent Top Ten." The year 1945 might as well have been a hundred years ago.

If context ultimately shapes content, then the context of no context ultimately justifies no content as well. Everything becomes disposable, including ethnicity: disco was murder on ethnicity—the Village People were not ethnic types; they were lifestyle choices. And perhaps this raises one of the ultimate questions about the corporatization of popular music in America: In an age when everything is disposable, including memory—when we know the price of everything and the value of nothing at all—is ethnicity itself doomed to become just another lifestyle choice? Was this, as Toffler suggested, a harbinger that in the future, instead of history, there would only be "public drama"? And, finally, without actual history, could there be actual Jews?

YO IS
OY
BACKWARDS

One of the first things musicians notice about saxophonist Kenny G is that he appears to be smiling when he is playing. No other contemporary practitioner of the art has managed to accomplish this unusual embouchure. Born Kenneth Gorelick to a Jewish family in Seattle, Washington, he first saw the horn that would change his life being played on *the Ed Sullivan Show* and he knew then and there that that's what he wanted to do. In high school he failed to get into the jazz band ("The jazz band stands by that decision to this day," says bandleader emeritus Kwame Washington), but he did make the golf team, proving that given the right equipment, he could definitely swing.

His professional career started in 1973 when, still in college studying for a major in accounting, he was hired as a sideman for Barry White's Love Unlimited Orchestra, one of the premier fashion-plate disco bands of the era. After college, he chose music as his profession and knocked around the jazz-fusion scene as a sideman until 1982, when Clive Davis heard his version of the ABBA hit "Dancing Queen" and signed him. There, at Arista, the artistic home of romantic crooners like Barry Manilow and vocal gymnasts like Whitney Houston, Kenny G found his voice. His Arista recordings, particularly his first hit, "Songbird," virtually defined the emerging "smooth jazz" idiom—a style of playing centered on hooky chord changes, urban rhythms, and what seemed to be the same melody repeated ad infinitum.

"Smooth jazz" spawned a mini-industry of its own; at its peak, dozens of radio stations across the country were devoted to playing this placid music, a style that was designed specifically to provoke no recognizable emotion at all in the listener. In fact, the consultants that programmed the smooth jazz radio format (such as those at Broadcast Architecture) regularly tested new songs by playing them for a focus group and asking the members to press a button any time the music got their attention; not whether this attention was negative or positive (whether they hated the moment or loved it), but whether the music became a "distraction." These consultants primarily wanted to make sure the music would not interrupt the flow of the listener's thoughts, or lack thereof. If smooth jazz was designed to be aural wallpaper, Kenny G was its greatest hanger.

Since 1982, he has sold more than 75 million records, with his album *Miracles* becoming the largest-selling Christmas album ever. (Along with "White Christmas," "Silent Night," "Away in a Manger," and "The Little Drummer Boy," the album featured one Chanukah song and was thus marketed as a "holiday" album.) Kenny broke another record of sorts when, through the technique known as circular breathing, he held a single note (an E-flat) on stage for forty-five minutes and forty-seven seconds, thereby earning himself a place in the Guinness Book of World Records.

Today, Kenny G is experiencing his greatest audience growth in China, where he has recorded traditional Mandarin songs and where his recording of "Going Home" is often played at closing time in public places or the end of school. (Apparently, mass transit systems in Tianjin and Shanghai also play his songs when trains are approaching the station.) Back home in America, in the late nineties, he was pilloried for taking an iconic recording by Louis Armstrong ("What a Wonderful World") and recording his saxophone on top of it. Guitarist Pat Metheny spoke for those who considered this a sacrilege when he condemned the saxophonist "for his incredible arrogance to even consider such a thing, and as a musician, for presuming to share the stage with the single most important figure in our music." Kenny G fans, however, thought that the spot where he played along with the video of Armstrong at his concerts was a great moment of musical synergy.

When pressed about his theory as to why his music had been so successful, Kenny suggested, "I think my music gives people the opportunity to listen to their own thoughts. Tap into their imaginations. Create their own stories to songs without the limitation of words . . . plus it's a really beautiful instrument." "Smooth jazz" became the most dominant jazz radio format across the country during the eighties, and one began to hear smooth jazz in supermarkets, restaurants, and clothing stores. Along the way, its creators tossed out many historic elements of jazz, including the great American song form, relying instead on simple, cyclical harmonic patterns; to experienced jazz fans, all smooth jazz songs began sounding like variations of the same song, or lack thereof.

As an idiom, the roots of smooth jazz go back to the early seventies, when the CTI record company took traditional jazz artists like guitarist Wes Montgomery and saxophonist Stanley Turrentine and featured them with large orchestras. The success of CTI albums proved the commercial viability of orchestrated jazz, employing strings and clever rhythmic grooves to "smooth out" the traditional rough edges of the music and provide beautiful aural landscapes through which a great improviser could wander. It was highly organized and relied on the skill of the arranger to create a balance between the soloist's authenticity and the formulation of a lush sonic background. On occasion, the songs (some traditional, some original) ended with long, grooved fades that gave the featured soloist a chance to stretch out. Ultimately, these two-chord vamps proved as popular as the songs themselves and many smooth jazz tracks were reduced to nothing but the "fade," extended grooves constructed over one or two chords; in this way, smooth jazz eventually dispensed with much of the harmonic structure and rhythmic complexity of eighty years of black /Jewish musical experimentation. In the end, smooth jazz came to rely on harmonic repetition and an often overemoted melodicism that suggested caring without actually performing the act.

One of the masters of smooth jazz arranging was a brilliant Jewish pianist and film composer named Dave Grusin (*The Graduate*). He and an ex-jazz drummer turned advertising executive turned record producer named Larry Rosen formed a production company in 1972 called Grusin Rosen Productions, and their first co-production was nominated for a Grammy; by 1978 they were in a co-venture with Clive Davis at Arista, and GRP was born. By 1982, GRP had broken away from Arista and become its own operation, focusing exclusively on smooth jazz recorded through the latest digital technology.

Rosen had decided to make this commitment to digital recording a calling card, and in 1983, GRP became the first company to release every album on CD (compact disc), well before any other record company had made that commitment. His timing was prescient; a radio format called New Adult Contemporary (NAC) had just been rolled out on stations like CD101.9 in New York and the Wave in Los Angeles. NAC demanded clean sound, state-of-the-art technology, and pleasant instrumental music, and GRP was its go-to label. This launched a debate that still rages in the world of record production: what is gained and what is lost through the use of digital technology.

One small but important part of the discussion is that digital recording makes it easier to edit the music and ultimately makes it possible to move musical information around much as a word processor moves language around. Digital technology subjected music, which exists in time, to all the rules of any two-dimensional art, which exists in space. So just as a painter could keep painting over images until the vision was perfect, now record producers could "fix" anything they didn't like ad infinitum. But of course, just because one *can* fix everything doesn't mean one *should* fix everything, and the mania to make the productions perfect began to squeeze much of the musical life out of smooth jazz. Aside from the soloist and the arranger, the third star of GRP productions became digital technology.

The reduced emotional range and stripped-down structure of smooth jazz, along with digital technology, implied a clean modernism, jazz as a lifestyle; at the time, "Jazz" was also the name of a computer software program, a high-end bicycle, a fragrance for men, and a mobile phone provider in Spain. It was part of the modern buzz. Without much bother or nostalgia, smooth jazz made older jazz musicians appear retro, "classic," out of date. It also reflected a much larger trend in American popular music (think Mariah Carey or Britney Spears) wherein the goal was to simulate the experience of emotional release while keeping the questions of emotional hunger at bay. It was, as they said, "ear candy," aural calories with small nutritional value.

If jazz musicians are like the canaries in the cultural coal mine, then smooth jazz—designed not to engage the emotional center, but rather to let one's own random thoughts just burble along uninterrupted—should have been a sign to stop digging and run. Because jazz has never been about the notes; jazz has always been about the spaces between the notes, the *context* of the notes, including all the pregnant pauses in the public dialogue. It's about feeling.

Just as the opposite of love is not hate but indifference, the absence of feeling isn't serenity but just the opposite: violence. Just as pop music in the fifties was all about romance, in the sixties about love, the seventies about sex, in the eighties it was all about violence. The other end of the smooth jazz shtick—the counterbalance to music designed not to provoke any emotions at all—is "gangsta rap," music specifically designed to offend. And just as smooth jazz was not about ethnicity but rather a "lifestyle" choice, ironically, rap, too, ultimately became divorced from its authentic ethnic roots and became reduced to a lifestyle choice as well, often visible among young white kids who wore their pants around their butts as a sign of solidarity with the thug life ("prison chic"). It was no accident that these two musical forms emerged simultaneously in America when they did.

Perhaps as real life gets more universally horrific, entertainment necessarily gets more mundane, trivial, unrelated to art or real life. The amount of awfulness—not the kind—is counterbalanced by both vacuity and hollow rage. We were delivered to that place—where music either had no ethnic weight or was reduced to ethnic pose—by the same social forces that delivered the landslide victory to Ronald Reagan in 1980. The Reagan administration, relying on "trickle-down" economics, cut social services, while at the same time spending lavishly to refurbish the White House for black-tie affairs; it deregulated many key industries (transportation, communication, banking) while giving tax breaks to those who speculated in them. The message to America was clear for those who had ears to hear: the rich were about to get richer while the poor were about to get laid off. The new religion was money, god the father, god the son, and god the almighty dollar. If you didn't have some money you had better go out and get yourself some because the government was no longer in the business of helping poor folks pull themselves up by their bootstraps.

This focus on the accumulation of material wealth—what money could *buy* rather than what money could *do*—encouraged strategies in foreign and domestic policies that favored weapons systems over diplomacy and created jails instead of jobs. Ironically, the focus on materialism was something upon which both the rap culture and the smooth jazz scene could ultimately agree; for both of them, the love of material comfort seemed to be paramount (their love of "bling" was often stronger than their love of swing).

The hip-hop hustle was just the dark underside of a system that made the accumulation of wealth the highest individual priority. Beginning with the "me decade" of the late seventies, all of America was into this accumulation; at the same time, many folks were now using prescription drugs recreationally (Valium was the most frequently prescribed medication in the Western world), and the survival of the fastest was still the guiding principle. Why, then, should hip-hop artists and promoters, with their interest in money, drugs, and hustle, be left out of the game? Just as music executives during the fifties had felt unfairly singled out for a common practice, hip-hop denizens found the system unfair: when the subject had been payola in Hollywood, it was being called lobbying in Washington, D.C. This time, rap wasn't going to make that mistake; it became all about "gettin' mines." Justice would be in the spending.

There is no question about the authenticity or the deep ethnic roots of hip-hop. The music itself emerged out of the remnants of the disco scene (where there was also no aversion to ostentation) by way of Jamaican toastmasters. By the late seventies, hip-hop culture included a form of dance (later called break dancing, or b-boying), a passion for graffiti (particularly on subway cars), and parties where DJs played various musics mashed together at high volume (everything from Led Zeppelin to James Brown) while "MCs" got on the microphone and "toasted" the crowd, as in Jamaica, calling out names of neighborhoods and local celebrities in loud, rhyming doggerel.

Hip-hop originated in a seven-square-mile area of high-rise housing projects in the Bronx. These mostly African-American and Hispanic projects had been built following the construction of the Cross Bronx Expressway through what had once been nice middle-class neighborhoods. It is no small irony that the man behind these projects and the designer of the expressway itself was a powerful Jewish city planner named Robert Moses, who, by creating the high-rise ghettos, had a major hand in the creation of rap music and, by extension, its ultimate virulent anti-Semitic message.

Moses had been behind New York City's growth since the Great Depression of the thirties; he was the one who brought both the 1939 and 1964 World's Fairs to the city and was also in large part responsible for the United Nations' decision to build its headquarters in Manhattan. The Cross Bronx Expressway was part of an infrastructure Moses had designed to more efficiently deliver white-collar workers from Manhattan to the suburbs and back again. In its wake, in projects like Soundview or Bronxville or Bronx River, he built cold high-rise ghettos, concrete and brick structures with little green space and few facilities for the kids. The outdoor quad around which the towers were located was reminiscent of nothing so much as the exercise yard of a penitentiary. There, in these raw open spaces, the music that would become known as rap was born. Turntables or cassette decks were hooked up to huge loudspeakers and dragged into the quad by budding DJs, and the DJ who could make the loudest noise usually won. It was nothing but a party.

B-boy dancing first emerged in the projects in the mid-seventies. A highly aggressive form (nobody smiled when they danced), the goal was to display one's power and skills with various poses; it was style as aggression, a lot of motion and a lot of gestures indicating what one person was going to do to another, what one gang was going to do to another gang. The immediate influence on the b-boy style was James Brown, whose splits and spins became de rigueur in the early days of "the dance," and the earliest b-boy competitions emerged from regular dance parties held in one particular project: Bronxville. There, a young Jamaican boy named Clive Campbell (aka Kool Herc) took his massive sound system down to the basement rec room and held regular events that quickly became rites of passage for the kids in the Bronx. In 1974 he organized a free block party, and his style of handling the microphone—based on Jamaican toastmasters like Big Youth—took off. Just like the DJs back in Kingston, Herc had hooked up a microphone to a "Space Echo box," and during the songs, he gave loud, reverb-drenched shout-outs to the kids, making them feel important and claiming a place of importance for himself and for all the DJs to come; they controlled the flow.

But Kool Herc's greatest contribution to hip-hop was focusing on the rhythm breaks in the records he played. He had noticed that the crowds really went wild during these short instrumental sections, when the melody and chords would be suspended and it just got down to the groove. Since these sections were invariably brief, he began extending them by using two copies of the same record on two turntables and lining them up, creating a kind of primitive "loop" of just the good parts, building the groove. (In its own way, it was reminiscent of the focus on "fades" in smooth jazz.) The crowd loved it and demanded more of these "breaks" so they could display their personal styles. Herc named the result "break dancing."

The importance of the rhythm track had emerged fifteen years earlier in Jamaica, when an engineer in a primitive studio had accidentally muted the vocals and melody instruments and liked what he heard. He released the song with no vocal and scattered melodic and harmonic stabs and it was called "dub music." Soon the mixing engineer himself became the central performer—experimenting with levels, equalization, and effects to alter the feel of the rhythm, and "break free," in the words of the journalist Jeff Chang, "of the constraints of standard song form." "And quickly," Chang continues, "noise came up from the streets to fill the space—yard-centric toasts, sufferer moans, analog echoes—the sounds of people's histories, dub histories . . . a slow motion portrait of social collapse."

Over this rhythmic bed, the DJs started calling out in little rhymes, talking trash, driving the party higher. They developed followings, arrived at parties with large crews; now there were MCs to handle the microphone while the DJ programmed the music and handled the turntables. The shout-outs and rhymes grew longer, took on a greater importance. Occasionally, the events turned violent as one gang dissed another. Herc and his two main competitors divided up the turf in the Bronx according to gang boundaries: Grandmaster Flash in the South Bronx, Afrika Bambaataa and his Zulu Nation in the East, Herc in the West. Hip-hop became like a tribal ritual. In time, as the MCs, with their clever rhymes and shout-out challenges, became more important, people stopped dancing altogether, standing near the stage instead, focused on the MC. His rap became the center of attraction. (He was "representing.") By 1980, the dance aspect of hip-hop was pretty much dead in the projects; it had moved aboveground, to the suburbs, where kids could now buy special break-dancing shoes at Thom McAn or a special piece of linoleum at ToysRUs on which to practice their moves. But in the Bronx, b-boy dancing was passé. Now it was all verbal challenge and posture.

What is interesting is how quickly and earnestly the hip-hop kids, first in the Bronx and then elsewhere across America and, ultimately, around the world, attempted to turn this dance idiom into a greater frame for their lives. By the end of the eighties, one could go to virtually any spot on the globe—from Siberia to Australia, China to Peru—and hear kids rapping as if they had just stepped off a street corner in the South Bronx, trying to live the "hip-hop life." Early on, Afrika Bambaataa had developed seven "Infinity Lessons," which attempted to establish a code of conduct and give broad directives to the Zulu "way of life." These Infinity Lessons drew on the image of a glorious African past by using rhetoric gleaned from the Black Muslim Nation of Islam; much of it was just gobbledygook: "The religion of the Universal Zulu Nation is truth wherever it is." It was like *Lord of the Flies*, kids leading kids into the unknown.

The hip-hop "worldview" suggested that by expanding this notion of a gang or a tribe to include the whole world—the ultimate gang—one could achieve world peace. But of course, a gang is premised on "us against them." The "worldview" perhaps made sense so long as it was acted out in the Bronx high-rises, where cause and effect were reduced to which gang had the bigger baseball bats. Yet this need for a greater narrative is touching and frightening at the same time. It's as if, when the black culture cut loose from the Jewish narrative in 1968, they also cut loose from their historic American narrative, and now it was up to the children of violence and desperation to make one up with the shreds that they found around them: the party, the forties and the shorties (8 percent malt liquor and young women), the crazy devilspeak and anti-Semitism of Louis Farrakhan, a lot of silly wordplay (one had to "overstand" rather than "understand"), and in the end not much true knowledge of the social forces that had created the situation they were in: only one in four kids in the Bronx graduated from high school in 1980. The inherent anti-intellectualism of hip-hop, the distrust of formal education and reading books, was like a huge hole, an enormous tragic flaw, in the center of the "hip-hop life" and led those who followed it down one blind alley after another. Of course this descent into darkness had its own appeal.

On July 13, 1977, New York City experienced its second major blackout. The first one had occurred ten years before, when the loss of electricity plunged the city into a rather charming night of candlelight and ordinary folks directing traffic on Fifth Avenue; New Yorkers congratulated themselves on how civilized they all were. Ten years later, however, when New York again went dark, thousands of fires were set, particularly up in the Bronx and Harlem. There was looting and shooting, total social chaos. When it was over, New York City north of 110th Street seemed like a different country, and the hip-hop kids were calling the shots.

The first hip-hop recording to achieve hit status was "Rapper's Delight." It was like the "Rock Around the Clock" of hip-hop, a kind of polite version of the real thing that brought the music out of the hood and into the bright lights of the record business. Released in 1979 by three unknowns on a small black-owned label (Sugar Hill), it was fifteen minutes long and featured voices that were talking in rhythm (rapping), not singing. Quickly, it crossed over from black radio and raced up the Top 40 charts, at one point selling 75,000 copies a week.

Tommy Silverman, a Jewish DJ and journalist covering the dance music scene, witnessed the phenomenon. "I was there in Brooklyn on Fulton Street when they brought 'Rapper's Delight' in stores, in '79, right around Christmastime. Ten boxes came out of the truck, they went onto the floor and they opened the cardboard boxes and literally handed two copies to everybody in the store who went right to the cash register. They must've moved two million records in a month on twelve-inch vinyl just in New York. I said, 'I gotta be in this business.'" He quickly dropped out of the Ph.D. program he was registered in and started Tommy Boy Records.

Silverman signed Afrika Bambaataa and in 1981 released the album *Planet Rock*, "where the nights are hot and nature's children dance inside a trance." The record was wildly profitable; it cost $800 to make and sold 650,000 copies. At the same time, it crossed the ocean, and soon Europeans ("eurotrash") were coming to New York City, mixing with rappers, punk rockers, and b-boys at places like the Mudd Club and the Roxy; graffiti artists like Keith Haring and Jean Michel Basquiat (homeless only months before) were suddenly selling canvases for thousands of dollars. A new club scene evolved downtown, the opposite of the velvet-rope world of Studio 54. It was a raw cultural synergy of major proportions as the art world hungered for the noble savage to take on the Reagan era and the kids from uptown hungered for access to the world of money.

"The Roxy could have also been a zoo," said a b-boy named Crazy Legs. "People were able to hang out in the cage with us and feel safe from getting beat up or stuck up, as opposed to coming to the Bronx, coming to a jam. It's like they were allowed to hang out in the cage and party with the animals, you know? It was a safe haven for a lot of people. But on the flip side, it was also getting us into places that we never thought we could get into. So there was an exchange there."

How different was this from the gentlemen's rambles at the beginning of the twentieth century, when the hoi polloi came downtown to the Lower East Side to hang out with the exotic Jews? The music in both cases was modern, and the lyrics—syncopated, uniquely American—came directly from the streets. On the other hand, when Yiddish had been the metric root of lower Manhattan, when humor and irony were in play, the language had provided a platform for both the Broadway theater and Tin Pan Alley; the Jews, striving to fit in, created a kind of universal American story that accommodated everybody. Now, with the idioms of the South Bronx breaking on those same downtown streets, irony was gone, nostalgia was immaterial, and as for striving to be part of the system, well, the hip-hop world had a name for folks who wanted to fit in: "sufferers."

Despite its desire to generate a "way of life" for its followers, hip-hop had a rather limited basket of tools with which to construct any future at all. The fact is, while rap could and did spread around the world, it couldn't really change or grow. Jewish songwriters from Yip Harburg to Bob Dylan had worked hard to insert social content into their music; now with rap there was very little music to deliver the social content. Rap was primarily words, sounds, and a beat. And just as smooth jazz was contingent upon modern recording technology, rap was constructed in the studios using new digital techniques, taking snippets from older recordings, harvesting musical quotes from the sixties and seventies that were then "sampled and looped" as a musical bed. In this way, rappers and early DJs were tipping their hats to the heroes of the past, from James Brown to Led

Zeppelin, giving props to the patriarchs. But because rap is so completely self-referential (it doesn't exist outside the circumstance of its own performance; each rapper is selling himself), it has no afterlife, no way to fertilize the musical ground from which it comes. Indeed, since the underlying asset was no longer the song—it would most likely never be rerecorded—rap became about the sell; rap was selling the sell. And the sell was designed, as Silverman himself said, for thirteen-year-old black males.

Then how and why did rap come to dominate the record business in the last decades of the twentieth century? There weren't that many thirteen-year-old black kids with disposable income. Clearly, it was talking to a larger cohort. And it was being marketed by a much more sophisticated cohort as well. Phil Upchurch, the great black rhythm-and-blues guitar player, summed up the situation with perspicacity: "Rap tries to take music back to the jungle," he said. "It's nothing but a beat and a chant. Whatever happened to harmony? Whatever happened to melody?" But this is exactly why rap was so easy to sell, not only to thirteen-year-old black kids but to white kids as well. By reducing the music to the most easily understood elements, rap was designed for mass production. All over the country, bands of youngsters were quoting the latest rap single, "yo-yo-ing" each other and incorporating rap slang into their daily lives. It was doggerel designed for young minds. Soon these young minds were creating their own doggerel; you couldn't turn around at the mall without bumping into one of them.

Because rap music was marketed as fresh off the dangerous streets, it became popular precisely in those communities where the streets were completely safe: the suburbs. "When I was thirteen, I remember riding on the bus to Hebrew school," said one Jewish boy who grew up in the suburbs during the eighties, "and the best thing was knowing the words to the Coolio song 'Gangsta Paradise.' It wasn't so much to outrage your parents or whatever; it was for your peer group that you knew these words. It's like the whole rebellion thing and they're talking about things that are illegal and they're swearing and they're doing all this and that's what grabbed suburban kids."

A girl remembers, "I always went to school with these little nerdy Jewish boys and no matter what, they'd be on the side and be all rapping, right? So then the Jewish girls would like the Jewish boys who were more like thugged out. It was kind of like a cycle. If the guys liked the music, oh, well, you like the music because the guys like the music."

On the surface, this attraction to the wild side may not seem much different from the "ragtime life" in the early part of the century, the "Jazz Age" in the 1920s, or the appeal of *Blackboard Jungle* in the fifties; warm nights, fast cars, and cool girls are a staple of growing up in America. But when the mainstay elements of popular music—melody, harmony, lyricism—became marginalized, as they did in rap, it created a coarseness not just in the music but all across the public dialogue. And this coarseness too was a boon to the record industry, for as the twenty-four-hour news channels have proven, the simplest sell in America is the specter of violence and the fear that goes with it. Rap produced plenty of both: it threatened violence against women, violence against the police, against teachers, against white society, against the language itself. Whether this threat of violence was ever justifiable or part of some kind of broader cultural payback is beside the point: the specter of violence was central to the selling of rap.

Of course what first attracted the earliest rap producers and promoters was its obvious authenticity, the fact that it had the vitality and immediacy of the streets. Many rap entrepreneurs started out as hobbyists; the first among them was Rick Rubin. He was still a college student living in the NYU dorms when he began producing rap records. He was also a self-professed fan of "extreme music," including heavy metal and hard rock, and rap was operating at the furthest extremes of what was acceptable. "I like it when people take things to their limits," he said, "because I think that's the only way we find out about new things . . . I don't know; I guess I'm bored by regular stuff. Things really excite me, or else they mean nothing to me. I don't like anything that's mediocre."

Born Frederick Jay Rubin on Long Island in 1963, Rick Rubin's underlying Jewishness was perhaps not as apparent as his love for music; even as his friends were listening to Billy Joel or Led Zeppelin, he became obsessed with hip-hop. "Hip-hop was really an underground thing at the time. There weren't even albums at the time, just 12-inch singles. I'd go to clubs and hear this music and love it. Then I would, always as a fan, go out and buy the records. But the records didn't really reflect what I would hear at the clubs. So, just really as a hobby and for fun, I started making records that sounded like what I heard at the clubs—almost like a documentarian really." In one of the great moves of record business history, he borrowed $5,000 from his parents in 1983 and, while still attending NYU, recorded "It's Yours" by T. La Rock and Jazzy Jay, a 12-inch single that became a local dance hit. Rubin then invented a label, calling it Def Jam ("def" meaning great, "jam" meaning music) and running the business out of his dorm room. "The clerk at the front desk handled all the shipping."

"I saw this void and starting making those records, just because I was a fan and wanted them to exist," he said. These words could well have been spoken by Milt Gabler or Alfred Lion or Jerry Wexler: a fan, wanting to make manifest in the world what he heard in his head. Given the raw materials of your moment (and/or the lack thereof), the obligation is to *act*; Rubin was in his moment.

Then in 1984, while Rubin was visiting a club where rappers hung out, a kid named Adam Horowitz handed him a demo tape of a young rapper named LL Cool J (his name was James Smith, and his moniker stood for "Ladies Love Cool James"). "I Need a Beat" by LL was the real birth of Def Jam. Rubin did not release the track right away: he tightened up the material, editing the rhymes so they more closely resembled verses in a song—a fan of heavy metal, he was bringing some of the techniques of pop production to rap. The result was a spare, raw, drumcentric sound with industrial hard-rock overtones and a rudimentary verse-chorus structure (rather than the endless repetitions of early rap).

Rubin knew he needed some help this time around; with the last release he had had a lot of trouble getting paid. He needed a partner to give him legitimacy in the rap business. Russell Simmons was that person: an ex-gangbanger turned hip-hop producer, Simmons loved "It's Yours" when he first heard it on the radio. "I thought for sure that Rick was black," he said. They met, and Rubin asked Russell to be his partner—"by myself I was just a kid making records. He gave me credibility."

The LL Cool J album *Radio* became Def Jam's first full-length release (previously they had released only 12-inch singles); it cost $7,000 to record and eventually, following Def Jam's distribution deal with Columbia in 1985, sold 900,000 copies. It was the first time a rap label had major-league distribution, and it proved the point that this music needn't be watered down or thinned out in order to have wide appeal outside the Bronx. "I was twenty," Rubin said, "I sent a Xerox of the check to my parents. That's when this stopped being a hobby."

But it was Rubin's signing of three Jewish kids from an upscale private school in Brooklyn Heights that ultimately pushed rap music to the top of the Top 40 charts: they were called the Beastie Boys. Simmons remembers, "I met the Beasties at Manhattan's Danceteria in the mid 80s. They were wearing red sweat suits with stripes, red Pumas, and do-rags. They were assholes." Adam "MCA" Yauch of the Beasties recalls, "One time Russell put us in a limousine and sent us out to the Encore club in Queens. We were definitely the only white people for miles, and we were getting out of, like, a stretch limousine. How much more obnoxious and conspicuous could we have possibly been?" Simmons and the boys understood each other, and when they went out to Adelphi University to appear on the highly regarded radio show hosted by the nascent rapper Chuck D, the Beasties were accepted for who and what they were. "They came out to our radio show at WBAU trying to prove to the rap market that they were viable white kids," said Chuck D. "You really couldn't doubt their legitimacy, 'cause they were down with Def Jam and Run-DMC and the beats were right. And as long as they talked about white boys and beer and stuff like that, who could knock their topics?"

Instead of being defensive about their privileged upbringing, the Beastie Boys flaunted it loudly and used it as grist in their mill. Along with references to Betty Crocker, Colonel Sanders, and other white-trash commodities, shouted over musical samples of Led Zeppelin and Black Sabbath, their song "Rhymin' and Stealin'" (on the *Licensed to Ill* album) suggested that in a way, their "whiteness" was just as constructed as their "blackness." It was all at arm's length to them. "Maybe I'm weird or whatever," said Mike Diamond (Mike D), "but the whole thing is about constantly redefining identity. And to me, that's the best thing that could possibly be happening, an ongoing self and group critique."

But what of their identity as Jews, scions, even, of Jewish culture? Adam Horowitz ("Ad Roc"), the kid who had slipped Rubin the LL cassette, was the son of the famous Jewish playwright Israel Horowitz, but he had no firm connection to anything of his Jewish past. "Our Jewishness was never part of our upbringing at all," Yauch confirmed. "None of us ever really discussed Judaism. . . . All I knew was that every year or so, my mom would take me out to a seder and my Uncle Freddy would scream, 'Pass the matzoh,' and I didn't know what the fuck was going on."

In their own search for identity, the Beastie Boys represented a broad cross-section of young Americans (not just Jews) obsessed with the same question: how to figure out to whom and to what you belonged in the public dialogue. If their cultural connections were not clear, their economic impact was never in doubt. "The fact that the Beastie Boys were a white group was kind of a big deal," said Rick Rubin. "If a fourteen-year-old white girl in, oh, Alabama had brought home a Run-DMC album in those days—you know, looking at these black guys as rock'n'roll guys or sex symbols—it would not really have been OK. Whereas, as stupid and disgusting as the Beastie Boys might have been, that was OK because they were white. I think when they played the Beastie Boys on MTV, then it made it easier for MTV to play Run-DMC." In a way, the Beasties were a stalking horse for the whole business of rap.

Their first hit song was "You've Got to Fight for Your Right to Party," a clever set of hooks defending your inalienable right to feel good, most likely about yourself. In this way, it's about identity. "See, I don't think there's just a young, black male identity crisis," Yauch said. The whole fucking planet's trying to figure out who they are and why they're here. And so are we." The Beasties *Licensed to Ill* was the first rap album to go to number one on the *Billboard* chart. "And we were still in the dorms," said Rubin; he didn't want to move his office because he was getting college credits for running the company (how Jewish is that?).

In fact, Simmons himself had discovered that rap was more than a local Bronx phenomenon when, even before he teamed up with Rubin, he managed a rap crew from Queens named Run-DMC. And although Queens wasn't actual mall culture, it was much more affluent and suburban than the South Bronx. Run-DMC was a group Simmons put together around his brother, Joseph "Run" Simmons, Darryl "DMC" McDaniels, and a DJ, Jason "Jam Master Jay" Mizell. Their first record, *It's Like That*, released in 1984 on Steve Plotnicki's Profile Records, had sold 250,000 copies (distributed through Arista). Their next record on Def Jam went through the roof. Perhaps because the members of Run-DMC were from the middle-class suburbs, their raps were even more vitriolic: they needed to prove they had inner-city street cred.

When Simmons joined forces with Rubin in 1985, he brought Run-DMC with him and the two co-produced the group's *Raising Hell* album in 1986. It contained the breakout single "Walk This Way," a hip fusion of hard rock (from the group Aerosmith) and rap that ultimately sold three million copies. Sonically, there was a lot more going on in this record than on previous rap records, and Rubin's interest in hard rock—his use of its sounds, samples, musical quotes, and even the structure of pop music—set the record up as a new rap standard; but it was the video that put the song over the top. MTV couldn't stop playing the three tough rappers, all wearing dark shades and dressed in black, cavorting on the set with the glam rockers, their long hair and flamboyant silk scarves flowing, all shouting the hook: "Walk this way." It was beyond camp; it was pure show business. It was the first music video ever for Aerosmith, and although the collaboration was meant to cross the rap trio over to a larger white audience, in the end, it served to extend the pop group's longevity. Rap was the future.

Rap broke worldwide as a result of these two landmark LPs, the Beastie Boys' *Licensed to Ill* and Run-DMC's *Raising Hell.* Def Jam's success at getting these rap records played on pop radio unleashed a rap signing blitz: suddenly all the major labels realized it was not just a fad and scrambled to sign the most "authentic" rap groups; for that's how rap was being marketed (and how the obviously offensive language was being defended)—rap was "keeping it real," which led to more violence and still more offensive language as groups and labels competed to be still more "real." And out in the affluent white suburbs, the whole spectacle was a boon to white teenagers, often the offspring of liberals from the sixties, who were searching for a way to separate from their parents and establish their own credibility among their peers.

"Where I grew up," said one, "parents were more like, it's okay, you can have a party at our house, and we'll leave the liquor cabinet open and pretend we don't see it." Because their parents were so permissive, they had to reach further to do something of which their parents disapproved. It is interesting to note that whereas black music had to be tamed down to appeal to white kids in the fifties, by the eighties, it had to become even more thuggish to cross over: it was a lot more raw to try to rebel in 1987 than it was in 1957.

But it was the evolution of the notorious group Public Enemy that can serve as a kind of watershed for the rap industry. In 1986, Rubin had just finished producing the soundtrack for the film *Less than Zero*, which had done well and included a single by the all-girl pop group the Bangles. His partner Simmons, the ex-gangbanger, wanted Rubin to continue discovering and producing more white pop acts; it was good for the company's bottom line. Rubin wanted to go deeper into the world of rap, and he dragged Simmons along with him: in the end, the suburban Jew (Rubin) was more down with the street than the gangbanger from the Bronx. Rubin reassured Simmons, "We're gonna pull the mainstream in our direction simply on the basis of the integrity of the records themselves. We are going to win with no compromise."

His vehicle for "no compromise" came from three kids—Carlton (Chuck D) Ridenhour, Harold McGregor, and Bill Stephney—who had met at Adelphi College. There they had a local radio show devoted to rap and were outsiders in the fraternity and sorority scene. "We were the rebels and hip-hop was everything to us," said Stephney. "Everything, all culture, all western civilization flowed through Bam, Herc and Flash."

At the time, they were being radicalized by a professor of African-American studies named Andrei Strobert, who taught them if rap was to survive, rappers needed to control their image by "developing a theme"; they needed to attach themselves to a larger story. Through the radio program, Chuck D was developing quite a reputation as just such a rapper, and it made its way to Rubin.

Rubin had been pursuing Chuck D for months to front a new group he had in mind; eventually, he hired Bill Stephney to work radio promotion for Def Jam, and it was Stephney who got his old college friend Chuck to sign with the label. Taking the advice of their old teacher to heart, it was Bill's idea to make every track of the new project political.

"We had to create our own myth for ourselves . . . statements, manifestos, the whole nine," he said. Chuck wasn't sure at first if he could do this and still rock the crowd, but eventually, Public Enemy (the group they formed) would fashion themselves as "the Black Panthers of rap," and Chuck D would be telling black radio executives that rap was "America's TV station. Rap gives you the news on all phases of life, good and bad, pretty and ugly; drugs, sex, education, love, money, war, peace—you name it." And whereas Rubin's first hire for the company had been the black rapper Bill Stephney, Simmons's first hire was a Jew named Bill Adler, who became the company's publicist, charged with spreading the news of this new musical revolution. Clearly, Rubin and Simmons had each other's backs.

Adler began touting rap music as a new medium for desegregation and hailing Run-DMC and the Beastie Boys as important social forces. He pitched Chuck D to rock editors and writers as "the new Bob Dylan," and the rapper began sitting for what would be hundreds of interviews. He and the others began spouting a kind of rhetoric that was exactly what the kids wanted to hear: this music was not only the future but the solution. As to what, exactly, he was not too clear. Obviously, for rap to survive, it needed to expand its social context, and rappers like Chuck D began to reach back and cobble together elements from early pioneers; by merging the politics of the Panthers with the groove of James Brown, adding some flash and doodads from the world of rock and liberally sprinkling the mix with a fistful of nouns and verbs mostly taken from the world of the Black Muslims and Louis Farrakhan, they upped the rhetorical ante, thus attracting still more white kids looking to separate from their parents and giving rappers a larger vocabulary to use when they were doing all those interviews. Ironically, rap had become the stalking horse for the disaffected white middle class.

With Chuck D on board, Public Enemy expanded to include a comic character known as Flavor Flav (William Jonathan Drayton, who wore a huge clock around his neck, the Harpo to Chuck's Groucho) and Richard Griffin (aka Professor Griff), who was made the group's "Minister of Information." Griffin was the one who told reporters that the group was now drawing on the thinking of Malcolm X, Mao Zedong, the Ayatollah Khomeini, Moammar Khaddafi, Winnie and Nelson Mandela, and Minister Farrakhan. As for Chuck, he declared himself a Communist captivated by Farrakhan. The rhetoric was spinning out of control, and even Chuck's old Adelphi friend Bill Stephney, at a Howard University panel discussion in 1987, began raising warning flags: "Woe unto a community that has to rely on rappers for political leadership," he said. "Because that doesn't signify progress; that signifies default . . . you're gonna leave it up to an eighteen-year-old kid who has mad flow? That's the extent of it? If our leadership is to be determined by an eighteen-year-old without a plan, then we're in trouble. We're fucked." They were indeed, but it was not obvious until several months later. In May, 1988, Griffin, the Minister of Information, took the tribe down when he told *Melody Maker*, "If the Palestinians took up arms, went into Israel and killed all the Jews, it'd be alright." Finally even Bill Adler, the Jewish publicist of Def Jam, became concerned.

"Griff is sober, disciplined, clean and well-spoken—soft-spoken too," Adler remembers. "He's got every appearance of rationality, sobriety, and thoughtfulness and yet, in this very calm voice, he's going to say the goofiest shit in the world about how the Jews are in a conspiracy, and have been in a conspiracy forever, to destroy the black man. . . . I said to him, 'Where did you hear these things?' And he said, *The International Jew*. I said, 'The book by Henry Ford, right?' He said 'Yeah.' I said 'Griff, you know about Henry Ford. Henry Ford is a guy who established two cities for his workers on the outskirts of Detroit. One was for white folks only and it was called Dearborn and the other was for his black workers only and it was called Inkster. Understand he would as gladly have upholstered the seats of his Model T with your black hide as with my Jewish hide.' And Griff shrugged. He was absolutely unmoved. He said, 'I'm sorry, Bill. It's in the book.'" Griffin had found his story and he was sticking to it.

Next, he told a black reporter named David Mills, "Is it a coincidence that the Jews run the jewelry business, and it's named jew-elry? No coincidence. . . . I'm not saying all of them [but] the majority of them are . . . responsible for the majority of wickedness that goes on across the globe."

And so it was the language of violence and anti-Semitism that ultimately revealed the rot at the center of rap. Even though Public Enemy had been signed by Rick Rubin and were managed by Lyor Cohen, and Bill Adler was their publicist (Jews one and all), they had finally crossed a bridge too far. Adler removed himself as the group's publicist and PE went downhill, eventually disbanding. But Pandora's box had been opened and the next salvo would come from the West Coast, where a group called NWA (Niggers With Attitude) upped the ante by lowering the tone of the debate. There, just as they had in the Bronx, gangs had risen out of the ruins of the sixties in places like Compton and West L.A. and "gangsta rap" was sweeping the streets.

One of its stalwarts was a young man named Andre Brown (Dr. Dre) who had also been at Adelphi with Chuck D and the others but had apparently not learned or had discarded their professor's advice; he was not only uninterested in any larger narrative on which to hang his career, but was specifically focused on the ultimate debasement of the language. "I wanted to make people go, 'Oh shit, I can't believe he's saying that shit,'" he reported. "I wanted to go all the way left. Everybody trying to do this Black Power and shit, so I was like, let's give 'em an alternative. Nigger, niggernigger niggernigger fuck this fuck that bitch bitch bitch bitch suck my dick, all this kind of shit, you know what I'm saying?" Forget knowledge of self; this was, as the rapper Eazy-E would later put it, about "street knowledge" (although "street ignorance" was closer to the truth).

The man who managed and developed NWA, introducing gangsta rap to America, was Jerry Heller, a Jewish promoter who had grown up in the black section of Cleveland during the 1950s. "That's where all of the immigrants lived," he recalled, "and that's where the Mayfield Road Mob and Cleveland Jewish Gangsters were. I grew up in that area, so I had always been around and dealt with guys like Eazy-E. I knew guys that carried guns at eleven years old." He went to a small college on the border of West Virginia and Ohio "where people never even considered whether you were Jewish or not. It was not part of their psyche. There were twenty seven Jewish students out of five thousand. It wasn't something that crossed their minds. When I told my roommate, who was from New Jersey, that I was Jewish, I remember one night he said to me, 'Are you allowed to vote?' I grew up in an era of virulent anti-Semitism."

He claims he had no social life until he made his way to California in the late 1960s and began managing acts like soul singer Marvin Gaye, eventually rising to become one of the industry's "super agents" along with David Geffen. "I didn't get laid until I got to California," he said. "I grew up in a very Midwestern, Victorian atmosphere. And, all of a sudden, David Geffen and I are these giant agents representing everybody in the world. I'm thirty-one, thirty-two and I buy myself a new Rolls-Royce and women are all over me! I looked in the mirror one day and I said, 'Wow, you sure got handsome this year.'"

By the 1980s, Heller was managing acts on the Los Angeles hip-hop scene, including C.I.A., of which Ice Cube was a member, and the World Class Wreckin' Cru, which included Dr. Dre. In 1987, along with Eazy-E, he formed Ruthless Records, which went on to have six platinum releases in three years, one of which was NWA's *Straight Outta Compton* (1989). It marked the beginning of hip-hop's obsession with "the real," conflating the notion of "the truth" with "the unspeakable." From now on rappers would "represent" the people and places whence they came by shouting out the most objectionable language.

"That's how we sold two million," said Eazy-E. "The white kids in the Valley picked it up and they decided they wanted to live vicariously through this music. Kids were just waiting for it." Why were those white kids just waiting for it? Perhaps because in a phony world (Milli Vanilli comes to mind), rap appeared to be authentic and expressed actual emotion, often anger or frustration, but it was better to feel *something* than to feel nothing. As film director John Hughes, creator of such eighties mall-centric films as *Sixteen Candles* and *Ferris Buehler's Day Off*, once noted about modern teenagers, "At that age, it feels as good to feel bad as it does to feel good." Too, in the suburban cul-de-sac communities, posing as a "gangsta" displaced one's natural angst and confusion over the issues of intimacy: no one ever fell in love to "niggernigger fuck fuck fuck." Lest there be any doubt about the commercial value of this emotional displacement, consider the fact that to date, according to one source, "the original members of NWA have grossed somewhere in the neighborhood of $1.75 billion."

Yet even black radicals and former militants were becoming appalled by the degradation of the social dialogue. Angela Davis of the Black Panthers had a sit-down with rapper Ice Cube and attempted to show him why his "bitch, ho" lyrics might be a problem with women; his response was "It's going to be divided."

Was Rick Rubin himself ultimately disturbed by the direction rap had taken? His response was

> I believe in freedom of speech, that people should say what they want to say, whether I agree or disagree. I've put out records that have Nazi overtones and I've been a supporter of the Jewish Defense League, which is exactly the opposite. . . . It's about the extremes, and about people believing in what they believe in. I think people should be allowed to sing about what they feel, whatever that is . . . as long as what they do is good musically, which is all I really care about. It's only commentary. I don't think music can change the world. It's OK to say anything in art. Public Enemy are not politicians. All they do is try to entertain people. I don't think records can make people do anything. And I don't think there's anything people shouldn't be exposed to. I think people should be exposed to all the ideas that are out there. It's OK. If you don't like what's on TV, turn it off.

Of course, several decades earlier it had not been possible to just "turn off" the rhetoric of anti-Semitism when it got out of hand in Germany. Yet when he was pushed on whether it was all right to expose young minds to the emotional debasement of much of rap, Rubin deferred: "I think it's the parents' responsibility to teach kids values. TV, records, all these things are solely entertainment, for kids as well. . . . There are no lines. The only responsibility an artist has to his audience is to entertain"—a defense that would have served Leni Riefenstahl well. Perhaps significantly, shortly thereafter, Rubin himself sold his half of the company to Simmons and then turned his attention to producing other kinds of music, leaving the world of rap for good.

In retrospect, Rubin was not just a fan or a creative force but a kind of documentarian. He was not making nostalgic music, nor was he making music for the future. Very much a man of his time, he was trying in some way to preserve the streets as he knew them. In the process, he preserved both the wisdom and the ignorance of the streets, which was amplified as rap records sought the lowest common denominator, where the most sales existed. Because by the mid-eighties, the streets themselves were getting much more coarse: if kids in the sixties had been acting out by protesting the war and smoking pot, by the eighties young people were showing their colors by getting their bodies pierced and smoking crack.

The social arena in which they were forced to exist was an extreme one; rap caught this essential flavor and pushed the boundaries of this shattered lifestyle still further.

At bottom there was a kind of hopelessness, a deadness, in the center of America's popular music; the only alternative to the violence of rap seemed to be the equally empty provocative posturing of teenage girls (again, think Britney Spears); there was little of emotional value to hang on to and a kind of inevitable permanence to one's juvenile decisions, which was belied by the flashy commerciality of the scene (even the little jewels that young kids used in piercings to decorate their face, stomach, and tongue left permanent scars).

Ultimately, however, the central issue with rap songs was that they weren't songs at all; as an idiom, rap may have started out as a legitimate experience in a room somewhere, the sound of a voice coming out of a loudspeaker calling your name (the MC and the DJ making the party happen), but when they put the party in a recording studio, rap became an artifact—not a song (it was missing some of the most important musical elements that define a song), but an artifact plain and simple. And when rappers set out to create their myth, they sealed their fate, because a self-created myth by a couple of record business hustlers is not a backstory, nor is it a philosophy or a way of life. It is just part of a sell. This music couldn't live on because there was no way for it to survive the moment of its commodification. The artifact was itself a paradigm, a metaphor for the problem with rap: no one would ever perform this particular rap again (there were no covers—it had no direct meaning to another performer), and as there was no living moment in which it mattered more than that of the recording studio, rap was essentially dead on arrival.

Ironically, the process made perfect business sense in the short term, because there was no problem with artists, they were disposable; no problem with producers, they were replaceable; and no problem with marketing to thirteen-year-olds (the target audience for most of the records released in the late twentieth century and a cohort that is constantly regenerating); rap sold itself. If the philosophy was simply "to make money," then rap was a godsend. Even during the rough-and-tumble days of the forties and fifties, when record executives had come out of the injection molding business, there was still a greater story being told: these were men who were proud that they could "hear" the people's music, because they were *of* the people. By the early nineties, most record executives were no longer of the people; they weren't even *listening* to the "music," while, at the same time, they were scrambling to outdo each other with the violence of their releases. When Vice President Al Gore's wife Tipper publicly challenged the redeeming value of their work, they tut-tutted and cried foul over an artist's right to free speech. But this too was a feint: the issue was not about free speech, the right to shout "fire" in a crowded theater, but rather just the opposite; the right to shout "theater" in a crowded fire: rap was show business, and if it fanned the flames of civil unrest and degraded civil discourse in the process, so much the better: this only attracted more young consumers to the conflagration.

Throughout the nineties and following the turn of the twenty-first century, many millions of rap albums would be sold, and many record executives would make their bones by promoting and defending it. They would rise to positions of ultimate power in the industry: Lyor Cohen, for example, who started out managing rappers for Def Jam, would become the president of Warner Communications, and he would name Julie Greenwald, his former assistant at Def Jam, to be president of Atlantic Records. The criterion for her appointment to this lofty office, formerly held by Ahmet Ertegun, was put forth by rapper Sean "P. Diddy" Combs, whose Bad Boy Entertainment was under Atlantic's umbrella: "You gotta understand," says P. Diddy, "she grew up on tour buses with LL Cool J and Public Enemy and Run-DMC. She's one of the reasons why hip-hop is where it's at today. She's probably the coolest white Jewish girl in history."

Every day, as she enters her office in Manhattan, Greenwald passes a large framed work of art—a giant sheet of looseleaf paper designed to look like a high school homework assignment, filled from top to bottom with a single repeated sentence: "I'm still a good person. I'm still a good person . . . "

Asked to defend the sexism or violence of rappers on her label, she shrugged. "They're lyricists," she said. "They're rapping about experiences that they grew up with that are very honest. And I'm hoping at the end of the day that it sells a lot, because we want to change their lives" (presumably by making them rich and the corporation still richer). And this, along with technical innovations like digital downloading, is exactly what began the long, slow process that has evolved into a mortally wounded record industry. And while record executives continue to cry foul as kids share downloaded song files, the fact is that the record business itself lost interest in producing songs long ago; by reducing the music to, as Phil Upchurch pointed out, "a beat and a chant," and marketing it as the "real" and the "truth," the industry was already culpable, had surrendered its ultimate asset: the song. Rap pulled out the economic keystone at the core of the music business. It trivialized the music at the expense of the social content.

During the Reagan era, as large corporations were being swallowed up by even larger corporations, business executives had to generate the language that defended how they chose to operate. It's a common phenomenon: in Trow's words, as people grow older, "they *come to be responsible for what they know.* If they then continue to refer to an iconography of excrement, they have to embrace excrement as worthy of their attention, and direct the enthusiasm of their fellows to excrement—not just to the discovery of the truth about excrement but to excrement." The record executives embraced rap because they knew it was keeping them alive. They too had lost the plot. And if you forget why you make the journey, there will be nothing waiting for you when you reach the end. "The music business, as a whole, has lost its faith in content," David Geffen told *The New York Times Magazine*. "Only ten years ago, companies wanted to make records, presumably good records, and see if they sold. But panic has set in, and now it's no longer about making music, it's all about how to sell music. And there's no clear answer about how to fix that problem."

In the end, what we were left with is an image of P. Diddy pitching his personal fragrance while wearing huge diamond studs in his ears and pretending that to be rich and connected in the entertainment business is to be sophisticated and part of some important social narrative (a role he himself brilliantly parodied in the 2010 film *Get Him to the Greek*). So it is not surprising that Rubin and most of the others who invented rap are no longer actively producing the music, but have moved on—for example, as of this writing, rapper Ice T is a movie actor, Snoop Dogg and Flavor Flav are television celebrities, defanged by their own reality shows, and Rick Rubin is the copresident of CBS / Sony Records in the United States, sitting in the chair formerly occupied by Goddard Lieberson, Clive Davis, and Walter Yetnikoff. True, he refused to work in the CBS New York headquarters (known as "Black Rock"), insisting that the company outfit a more laid-back office for him in L.A., saying, "I can imagine people coming up with brilliant creative ideas here," he said, "but Sony has to agree. I'm not sure they realize that they are selling art. Right now they could be selling any product." It is difficult to know if Rubin is suggesting that the music he produced for the Beastie Boys and Public Enemy is the artistic equivalent of the music that, say, Jerry Wexler produced for Aretha Franklin and Ray Charles, or that Alfred Lion produced for Thelonious Monk and Miles Davis, or that Milt Gabler produced for Billie Holiday and Louis Armstrong; but history will decide.

THERE WAS A FIRE

And so it was into this historic moment, while "smooth jazz" and contemporary pop music were tossing out or minimizing the "authenticity of feeling," and rap music, in its pose of "keeping it real," had no need for even that small shred of melodicism, that I attempted to secure distribution for my Jewish project, *Life's a Lesson*. From both ends of the musical spectrum, the past was no longer prologue, it was simply past. *Life's a Lesson* was an attempt to keep it alive by bringing the essence of the past (the music) into the present (the sound, the technology, the musicians, the production techniques). When it was completed, in 1990, it was perhaps the first example of Hebrew liturgical music recorded in a contemporary style, not for overtly religious reasons but simply to create the musical landscape that would evoke particular emotional memories. I wanted to stand again in a room among other like-minded people and let these songs wash over me. I had, I believed, no further agenda. To accomplish this, I needed to produce a full-blown recording, no different from the other recordings I was producing at the time for Diana Ross or Van Morrison or myself; it's just that the subject of this particular one was both historic and deeply personal.

To me, the music life is a spiritual life, and what we do when we play is, I think, the same sort of thing people do when they pray: expressing the heart's deepest desire. What is the heart's deepest desire? What do you want more than anything? Why is it important to express that? What happens when you do express it? What happens when you express it in a group? What happens to you? What happens to that group? These are the kinds of questions I started to ask myself while participating in the high holy day services at the little synagogue in Madison with my young son. Each year, I encouraged him to sit next to me on the piano bench so that he would pay attention. And every year, as his feet got progressively closer to the floor, he played the music along with me, improvising at the top end of the piano while I played at the bottom. The same year that his shoes actually touched the old wooden floor, Hannah, our rabbi, asked me to include the song "Life's a Lesson" in the service. It is a song I rarely performed after I first recorded it, but she had heard me sing it quite by accident and said, "It helps me to understand the Kaddish. You can play it right before we read the prayer for the dead." What Hannah had intuited was that I had written the lyrics to "Life's a Lesson" in memory of a musician who had inexplicably, at the top of his game, shot his wife, his children, and then himself. The words simply came out of me the night I heard the shocking news:

Life's a lesson
You can fail it
You can set your spirit free
Or jail it
But setting it free is no guarantee
It's going to fly
When you sail it

The object is to ride it
But setting it free while you're sitting astride it
Isn't easy
You can learn a lot
By going crazy
You can fail it
You can set your spirit free
Or jail it
But setting it free is no guarantee
It's going to fly
When you sail it
And if you feel like you're in prison
And no one is coming to talk or to listen
Take it easy
Know that no one ever has it easy
No one ever learns to fly by freezing
Life's a lesson you can pass
Or fail.

These words say that there is a purpose to life, that it resides in the striving for freedom, that freedom is often out of our grasp but that we must strive for it anyway, that we all go a little crazy from the effort, which is part of the teaching, and the teaching is that we are not alone.

I have found that many of my generation who walked away from Judaism after their bar mitzvah eventually arrived at the point later in life when they wanted to reexamine the sense of connection to something greater, something profound, that they had felt as children, and to broaden their understanding of this connection that had, since their "coming of age," been available to them only through the music. Beginning in 1987, as I traveled around the country working in recording studios, I carried several huge reels of recording tape with me wherever I went. On them was the work in progress; songs such as "Avinu Malchenu," "Oseh Shalom," "Eliyahu," standards from the Jewish song book, all sung in Hebrew, almost like nursery rhymes to those of us recreating them now for a mature audience. There was "Ani Ma'amin," the song the Jews sang as they were taken on trains to the camps during the Holocaust: "I believe with perfect faith," the lyrics say. "Kol Nidre," "Eli Eli," each song featured one or two great jazz soloists and the soulful vocals of our "cantor" Lynette and the "Gates of Heaven children's choir" (everybody's children).

I began receiving phone calls from Jewish musicians; "I hear you're making a record of Hebrew music . . . you can't do 'Hashivenu' without me," said one, "that's my song!" Then one day I received a phone call from the great jazz musician, the vibraphonist Mike Mainieri. He said, "I hear you're making this record of Jewish music. I'd like to play on it." I said, "Mike, but it's just for the brothers, you know?" Because I knew he was raised

Catholic, and I was taking a lot of pleasure in assembling this Jewish team; even the engineer, James Farber, was wearing a yarmulke in the studios. "No," Mike said, "we've got to talk about this." And so several days later, we met at the Mayflower Hotel in New York City. Mike sat down at the table and immediately placed a large, coffee-table-sized book in front of me. It was titled *Jews in the Renaissance*, and it was opened to the biography of a painter named Danielli, Mike's distant relative, who later converted to Catholicism. Mike said many in his family had converted to avoid persecution, and his father once told him, "Don't tell anyone you're Jewish. It'll only cause problems." So of course he spent his whole life waiting to tell someone, and I was finally that someone. I said, "Okay, Mike, you're on. You can represent all those folks whose relatives converted but who still feel connected." Mike came into the studio later that week and played on the song "Life's a Lesson," which I sang as a duet with Carole King.

I've often reflected on why so many Jewish executives, subsequently and to a man, would not distribute this project, telling me, often after requesting extra copies for family members, that it was a "heroic effort." My first guess was that perhaps they were self-hating Jews, but with the passage of time, I came to appreciate the complexity of the situation they were in. On the one hand, it was all about money and the perception of failure in the music business. As Bob Krasnow had so succinctly put it years before, "Money; that's the philosophy of every business." What he didn't say at the time was that the corollary to this "philosophy" was that anything that hinted at economic risk without the possibility of substantial economic reward had become anathema to the music business. Nobody wanted to expose their bottom line, let alone their Jewishness, for a potential return of pennies on the dollar. (The same return, it should be noted, that had launched the business in the first place.) These men were all living "larger than life," in the world of superstars and mega-hits (nothing less than "super" would do), and the music we were making on *Life's a Lesson* was not larger than life: it *was* life.

Krasnow himself confirmed this. He was then the chairman of Elektra Records, where his ethnic credentials had gained him access to the top rung on the corporate ladder. "I could work for a big company like Warner Brothers," Krasnow told one reporter, "because I had all the ethnic qualities—I was white, I was Jewish, they could invite me over to their home for dinner, and I could talk to black people." Yet his decision on my Jewish project, like that of all the other executives, was not, he assured me, at all ethnically motivated. "I'm going to tell you the truth," he said. "Nobody is going to put this record out. The reason is simple. We don't believe it can sell." I said, "Bob, you put out tons of awful rap records that don't sell. Why not put out something you can be proud of?" "You don't understand," he told me. "It doesn't matter whether those records sell. It matters that I *believe* they can sell. And I don't believe this one can."

And while Krasnow was telling me the truth, it was not the whole truth, which would have to include the fact that while many Jewish executives were comfortable with guessing wrong about black music, none were comfortable with guessing wrong *as a Jew*, exposing their Jewishness to examination by others in the industry. While they were perfectly happy to be perceived as a Jew (they gladly accepted the B'nai B'rith awards, for instance) they couldn't accept the perception of failing at something Jewish; it was simply too much personal exposure. Failure is nobody's friend in the record business, but a Jewish failure was off the table. In the end, Krasnow and the others were proved wrong; *Life's a Lesson* was both profitable (it sold many thousands of copies simply by word of mouth) and a critical success. It would have stood any of them in good stead, as both a Jew and a record man. Of course, with their attention to the bottom line, their intention was to make a killing every time, while we were in it to make a living, and also to keep something very important alive within us: by making this music manifest, we were literally singing ourselves into existence.

More to the point, my approach to the music had been as traditional as my upbringing; old songs done in a new way but nonetheless connected to the European past, to the melodies sung by those immigrant men I had heard davening on Saturday mornings. That was the feeling I wanted to recreate, and it was, I think, at the core of the emotional memory for the other musicians as well. It captured who we were as Jews: the last generation of Americans who knew firsthand the European émigrés who fought to establish this fragile religious beachhead on the new American continent. Standing in a synagogue on a Saturday morning, hearing the strange language and feeling the protection of an ancient power that arrived on those haunted melodies, the sense that there is a horizon of humanity of which we are all part, that compassion is stronger than its opposite—that's what we were conjuring. And in this we shared a commonality with those record executives who needed to distance themselves from the project in order to keep their fear of failing as a Jew hidden: we all considered the Jewish "issue" to be a kind of monolith in our lives, something that had to be scaled, conquered, or denied. Specifically, it was our connection to a European past that haunted us, particularly in light of the not so distant fact of the European Holocaust: shame and pride were mixed evenly in our Jewishness. The difference was that as musicians, some of us had spent our lives training to reveal our inner selves, and so in the end, the desire to confront this withheld Jewishness was stronger than our fear of failure or exposure; we had all been waiting for the moment.

My generation is at the end of a long line—the last to know refugees from the Pale and survivors from the Holocaust. We are a bridge between the old European Jews and the new modern American Jews. I am a Jewish-American, but my son and his generation do not need that hyphen; they are Americans plain and simple, unfettered by a European past. With *Life's a Lesson*, I was trying to keep the past alive in order that some key part of myself could survive. It was perhaps an impulse as outdated as it was crucial to me. For the next generation, the "Jewish issue" was not something to be confronted, to be scaled, or to be denied; it was just another part, perhaps a key part, of their American identity. It's as if our generation was still living in the caves, sparring with shadows on the wall, while these kids were all stepping outside into the light of a new day. My generation will always be haunted by ghosts. The next generation may be entertained by ghost stories, but (with any luck) they will not know the fear firsthand.

In the past, the Jewish "problem" had revolved around dealing with the emotional and physical violence of non-Jews. In the future, in America, the question may be much more subtle: how to survive their acceptance. The Jew has made a historic profession, has raised to a high art the life of the outsider; in the process, Jews have shaped their alienation into a kind of rolling dynamic that fuels not only modernism but social progress. So it is a time of historic transition in America, a transition from a period when it was common to hear that being a Jew had "nothing to do with it" (precisely because it had everything to do with it) to a time when it is now common to hear that being a Jew has *everything* to do with it, even as this itself is becoming harder and harder to prove or experience. Those born since the 1960s find themselves in much the same situation as all the other Americans to whom ethnicity has become part of a broader menu of personal options. Ironically, as being a Jew has become less important to America, it has become more important to American Jews.

Today, one can see this transition—from having to confront or deny one's Jewishness to being able to negotiate it, and finally to choose to either promote it or forget it—in the careers of Jewish performers all across the musical spectrum, from rock and roll to jazz to rap. As an example, one might consider David Lee Roth, also known as "Diamond Dave" for his highly flamboyant stage persona, who once said, "An ounce of image is worth a pound of performance." In the 1980s, he joined forces with Eddie Van Halen, he of the high-speed guitar pyrotechnics, to create one of the most popular acts in rock and roll. In his 1997 autobiography, *Crazy from the Heat*, Roth spent an entire chapter explaining how being a Jew drove his performance. Similarly, he often advised young Jews not to view themselves as white, and to remember that like all minorities, they would have to work twice as hard to be accepted. "David Lee Roth was proof that you neither had to hide your identity, bob your nose, change your name, nor sacrifice your Borscht Belt influences to indulge in all the forbidden pleasures of rock and roll," said one biographer. "He wasn't going to let Judaism stand in the way of a good time."

About his signature stage move, the martial-arts-style kicks he incorporated into his performances, Roth said, "Every step I took on that stage was smashing some Jew-hating, lousy punk ever deeper into the deck. Every step, I jumped higher 'cause I knew there was going to be more impact when I hit those boards. And if you were even vaguely anti-Semitic, you were under my wheels. . . . That's where the lyrics came from, that's where the body language came from, that's where the humor came from. . . . All equally as important. . . . What you get from repression, and what you get from hatred, is fury, and fury was one of the main trigger points for the great Van Halen." At the same time, Roth harbored a deep love for old-time Jewish vaudeville shtick and credited Jewish legends like Harry Houdini, Al Jolson, and Eddie Cantor with being just as influential as rock legends Robert Plant and Roger Daltrey. When he finally left Van Halen and went out on his own, his first hits were remakes of "Just a Gigolo" and "I Ain't Got Nobody," songs from 1931 and 1921 respectively. Roth too was torn between the European past and the American future.

On the other hand, consider the guitarist-composer-singer Lenny Kravitz, who comes as close to the realization of Irving Berlin's dream of a self-acknowledged Jewish-American pop star as anyone. A proponent of both white rock and black funk, Lenny is a child of two cultures; his father is the Jewish TV producer Sy Kravitz and his mother the black actress Roxie Roker (who played Helen on the television series *The Jeffersons*). Kravitz grew up spending weekdays on the Upper East Side of Manhattan with his parents and weekends at his grandmother Bessie's house in the Bedford-Stuyvesant neighborhood of Brooklyn. "I was raised by a white Jew and a black Christian, on the Upper East Side and in Brooklyn, and I tend to love extremes," said Kravitz. "I like the shack and the mansion, the ghetto and the beautiful area, but I don't like the in-between." Yet it was reconciling these extremes that allowed his career to flourish.

In 1974, when Roxy landed her role on *The Jeffersons*, the Kravitz family relocated to Los Angeles. At his mother's urging, Lenny joined the California Boys Choir, where he performed a classical repertoire for three years and sang with the Metropolitan Opera. It was in Los Angeles that Kravitz was first introduced to big-time rock groups like Kiss, Aerosmith, Cream, and the Who, and in time, his musical influences stretched from Mahler to Miles Davis to Marvin Gaye, from Prince to Punk to Pink Floyd. He began his professional career as a teenager under the pseudonym "Romeo Blue," complete with straightened hair and blue contact lenses. Kravitz was told that his music wasn't "black enough" nor "white enough." "Ultimately," he said, "it got me back to myself. And when I finally did accept myself for myself, music started flowing out of me." In 1985, his father lent him the money to make his first album, and he dropped the fake name, the contact lenses, and the straightened hair. His first record, *Let Love Rule*, a synthesis of rock and funk released in 1989, was a huge success around the world.

He would later say, "When I made my first album, the Americans didn't know what to do with me. . . . Here's a black Jew, light-skinned, he's not doing hip-hop. I didn't fit in any box, because Americans are all about formats." Lenny Kravitz is one of the few black artists who have thrived in modern rock and roll, and it is interesting to note that, while in the sixties rock was made by white kids trying to sound black, Kravitz eventually made it as a black musician who was enthusiastic about playing essentially white rock. That is, his success was ultimately a result of his ability to integrate both his Jewish and black roots, as extreme as each might have appeared, rather than trying to force himself into a single ethnic "format." When he went back to his Jewish-sounding last name, he came into himself.

One also sees Jewish roots in the "jam band" movement of the 1990s. These bands were inspired by the wildly popular improvisations of the Grateful Dead, but rather than rely on country-and-western forms, as did the Dead, they were inclined toward jazz and klezmer. A case in point is the band Phish, perhaps the most successful of the jam bands. The group's bass player, Michael Gordon, had attended Solomon Schecter Day School in Boston, where he learned to speak Hebrew, and he often credited his Jewish upbringing as the core of his musical life, down to the movements he makes on stage (which, he said, came from the davening he witnessed as a child). The group's drummer, Jonathan Fishman, is also Jewish, and even though neither is religious, the band plays versions of "Avinu Malchenu" and "Jerusalem of Gold" in their sets. Their overt Jewishness is simply an accepted aspect of their personalities and performance; no big deal.

Further to the left is the band Soulfarm, a New York-based quartet that regularly draws an audience of yarmulke-wearing orthodox Jewish kids to urban clubs, and the Moshav Band, another prominent act on the Jam band scene. Like Soulfarm, the Moshav Band splits its time between Jewish events and nightclubs like the Bitter End. Both groups were followers of the late Rabbi Shlomo Carlebach, a teacher-musician who popularized traditional Hasidic melodies and Jewish mysticism during the 1960s. Carlebach's performances were folksy affairs, filled with sing-alongs and storytelling, but, today, his followers play loud rock and roll, building a sonic bridge to a younger audience. "To have Soulfarm juxtapose a Carlebach tune with the Dead's 'I Know You Rider'—that's the kind of hallmark and attitude of the jam band movement, a willingness to cross traditional boundaries," said one observer. This mix of religious orthodoxy and rock and roll may bring to mind the music coming out of born-again megachurches, but there is a dramatic difference: by and large, the jam band musicians are firmly rooted in the secular world, and they were initially surprised by the orthodoxy of their following. It simply appears that the jam band culture's "party" ethos, which reaffirms there is nothing wrong with feeling good, coincidentally fits well with the mystical Hasidic notion that trance music can be a shortcut to enlightenment. Or, as one young Hasid put it, "Once a Hasid shaves his curls, he's a hipster."

This point, where the Jewish primitive meets the avant-garde, is nowhere more apparent than in the Radical Jewish Culture movement, whose main spokesperson is the jazz saxophonist John Zorn. Zorn grew up in Flushing, New York, in the 1960s, the child of Jewish parents determined to keep him "untainted" by any Jewish background: as a boy, he was sent to a Protestant parochial school, where he was taught about Jesus and the resurrection—and teased by both his classmates and his Jewish neighbors. "My parents said that going there would give me a 'way out', but I was bullied and treated like 'the little Jew.' Of course my Jewish friends weren't much better. 'Who do you think you're fooling?'

they'd say. It was difficult. And very confusing." And so, quite naturally, this kind of isolation from one's roots only drove Zorn harder to explore those same roots, and ultimately he formed a band called Masada (named for the legendary Israeli plateau where a group of brave Jews made their last stand against the Romans) to combine avant-garde jazz with ancient Jewish melodies.

"The idea," Zorn explained, "is to put Ornette Coleman and the Jewish scales together"—perhaps a natural choice, inasmuch as Coleman's "harmelodic theory" was based on a kind of melody-driven, voice-leading approach that recalled the chanting of Jewish cantors. Coleman himself confirmed as much, recalling that once, while listening to a recording by the renowned chazan Josef Rosenblatt, he "started crying like a baby" because to him it sounded as if the cantor "was crying, singing, and praying all in the same breath."

Yet the attempt to create (or reframe) a "Radical Jewish Culture" also mirrors the failed attempt by the Israeli government during the 1940s and 1950s to create a national culture by commissioning the writing of new "folk songs." For a time it appeared the Israelis had succeeded in inventing a popular culture from the ground up, using mostly European musical forms, but ultimately they were swamped by immigrants from non-European countries who could not identify with post-1940s European culture, confirming that Jewish identity continues to evolve even as its various members try to nail it down, and that the Jewish process is stronger than the Jews themselves. Today there is even an Israeli Diaspora—unthinkable just a few years ago; Israel was the place one went *to*—and many Israeli jazz musicians have moved to New York City. For some, this too raises troubling questions, for if it was the land of Israel, the literal territory, that was promised by God to Abraham, and if now this land is no longer the driving force for Jews, what does it say about the thousands of years of Jewish longing? If Jews are no longer tied to the land of Israel, is not the original motivating covenant of Abraham itself in question?

Zorn's music, arriving as it did at a time when many jazz musicians were casting about for a new context, became a cause célèbre among critics and players alike, and eventually he was able to start his own record label, called Tzadik. Through Tzadik, many Jewish projects were realized, an array of music that drew from Jewish liturgical melodies, traditional klezmer forms, and secular Yiddish tunes.

Zorn's mission statement explained, "Just as jazz music has progressed from Dixieland to free jazz and beyond in a few short decades, and classical music went from tonality to chromaticism, noise and back again, it has occurred to me that the same kind of growth should be possible—and is perhaps essential—for Jewish music." The caveat, of course, is that Jewish music has historically been less an art form than a social statement, and so this kind of hands-on approach to its evolution becomes highly problematic; if, traditionally, music within the Jewish community has been either "table music" (designed to be sung around the dinner table) or synagogue music, with good *nusach*, or correct melody, being decided through its use by a community, how, then, can any individually created artistic expression be "authentic" to the community? And while the Jewish trumpet player David Buchbinder agrees with Zorn, saying "I think the thing jazz showed the world was how, in a hundred-year process, you could create art music out of community-embedded celebration music," this raises the question of whether it is ever possible to create "community-embedded celebration music" out of art music.

The guitarist Mark Ribot, himself a participant in Zorn's Radical Jewish Culture series, sees one of the pitfalls in trying to actively create Jewish culture in the problem of unintended consequences: the tendency by Jewish artists from jazz and rock backgrounds to define Jewish music in ways that ultimately stereotype Jews. He refers specifically to those who adopt styles out of a misplaced nostalgia for a pre-Holocaust Old World that they see themselves as helping to rebirth. Not only does this feed a "growing theology of Holocaust and redemption" (his term), but it also creates a false orthodoxy by denying the vastness of the Jewish experience prior to the Shoah, ignoring, for example, the fact that klezmer musicians of the old world incorporated a variety of styles, so there never was such a thing as "true" Jewish music in the first place.

In addition, Ribot recalls that in performances held in New York and Germany during the first year of the Radical Jewish Culture series, musicians simply showed up as themselves and played their music; by the second and third years, following the growing publicity surrounding the Radical Jewish Culture movement, they were beginning to "act Jewish," to behave as they felt one should in order to play the part of Jews as well as play the music. In other words, Radical Jewish Culture began as a way to frame what was already happening with Jewish musicians, particularly in New York, in order to focus on the Jewish aspect of their music and lives, and it wound up changing the way they played and behaved. As there is with all avant-garde movements (e.g. the avant-garde jazz movement championed by Coleman in the 1950s and '60s), there inevitably develops a new orthodoxy, one that is invariably restrictive or selective of past conventions even as it attempts to unite the past with the future.

And indeed it is this growing question of orthodoxy that continues to haunt the Jewish culture in America. After all, it was a stifling orthodoxy, in part, along with the pogroms of the czar, that propelled the Jews out of Europe in the first place. And it was the release from the pressure cooker of this orthodoxy that exploded in the nova of Jewish creativity during the first decades of the twentieth century in America. Today there are those who fear that in the not too distant future, orthodox Jews will be the only Jews left in America, and they have statistics that seem to back it up: there is a skyrocketing intermarriage rate (more than 50 percent of Jewish marriages are "out of the faith," which means that Jews who find and marry each other in America are now the exception rather than the rule) and a lower percentage of children (less than one-third) being raised Jewish.

Hence the established axis of Jewish participation in America appears to be shifting to the extremes: whereas it had previously revolved around the more centrist Reform and Conservative movements, today the fastest-growing segments of Jewish culture are the nonreligious and the ultra-orthodox; there are currently about a quarter million Hasidim in North America, and they are growing at a rate of 5 percent a year. A 5 percent annual increase translates into a doubling of population every fifteen years, which means by the year 2075 there could potentially be 8 to 10 million American Hasidim. What's more, like fundamentalist faiths across the spectrum, orthodox Jews are actively recruiting.

What drives this modern orthodoxy? In part it is the fact that as America itself becomes more "Jewish," it becomes progressively more difficult for a Jew to express one's "authentic" Jewishness. A recent article in *New York* magazine, for example, opened with the following lead: "Everyone who comes to New York City in 2008 becomes a little bit Jewish by osmosis. New Yorkers eat Thai food, buy condoms in Korean delis, and face death at the hands of insanely reckless Nigerian cabdrivers, but they inhabit a moral universe in which certainty and doubt are balanced according to a particular mathematics that is intimately familiar to Jews and not quite so familiar to other tribes." It then goes on to point out that today, everyone wants a piece of the Jewish action: "Ivy League graduates who move to New York often find themselves thinking about how their Jewish friends, co-workers, and bosses are different from their neighbors back home—less polite, more exciting, more exacting and didactic, with different ideas about pleasure and sin. . . . Today it is hard to think of a single institution in the city that doesn't open its doors wide to Jews (and not just a few token Jews, or the 'right kind' of Jews) . . . the Metropolitan Club, the Century Club, whatever. Who would want to belong to a club in New York that didn't accept Jews as members? What on earth would you do there?"

Today Jewish traditions (Jewishisms) extend way beyond the boundaries of the Jewish community. One of the most curious has been identified in the black community, where "bro mitzvahs," coming-of-age ceremonies, are occasionally being held to integrate young men into their own communities. One such was described in the *Jewish Journal*: "Decked out in a black tuxedo, a brimmed hat set fashionably on his head, Douglas LeVandia Ulmer Jr., better known as DJ, walked down the aisle to the beat of two African drummers. [His mother] knew that 16 marked a turning point in DJ's life. And while she had looked into several African rites of passage, she believed the Jewish bar mitzvah ceremony, with its emphasis on family heritage and good deeds, gave her the best blueprint to validate her son's dedication to family, school, community and church and to pass on her family's values of education, worship and social outreach." Another young black man, Yitz Jordan, pointed out that becoming a bar mitzvah is actually a universal concept, based in Genesis, which advocates against stealing and killing, "so really there is no cultural misappropriation."

On the other hand, nonreligious Jews in America are often viewed as simply "wealthy white people," and it is interesting to note that during the Bernie Madoff financial scandal, the villain's Jewishness was openly acknowledged but hardly mentioned, except to point out how his actions had devastated the Jewish philanthropic community and Jewish country clubs everywhere. This level of acceptance, akin to that of other religious denominations or ethnic groups—Methodists or Protestants, Italians or Hispanics—may ultimately have as great an impact on the Jewish culture as years of alienation and rejection. Reform Judaism (which includes one third of America's five million Jews) is currently adopting a new prayer book intended to offer something for everyone, including non-Jews (not just nonpracticing Jews). "It reflects a recognition of diversity within our community," said Rabbi Elyse Frishman, the new prayer book's editor. "We have interfaith families. We have so many visitors at b'nai mitzvah ceremonies that I could have a service on Shabbat morning where a majority of people there aren't Jewish. . . . There are even those in my community who come to Shabbat worship each week who don't believe in God. . . . How do we help them resonate with the language of prayer, which is very God-centric?" (Perhaps only the Jews would worry about all the non-Jews who want to come to *shul*.)

So to stand out *as a Jew* today requires applied effort; in America, there is so much Jewish culture around, in the very air one breathes, that being Jewish loses much of its meaning, its texture. At the same time, there is a growing "Cool Jew" movement. It first appeared in the 1990s, when one started to see an increase in Protestants using Jewish mannerisms and consciousness patterns, from the Hollywood fashionistas who studied Kabbalah to the ubiquity of Yiddish slang in our vocabulary and the traditional Jewish foods in our diet. In 2012, the most popular bagels in New York came from the H&H Bakery on Broadway, founded by Helmer Toro, a Puerto Rican businessman who grew up cutting sugarcane on his father's farm. One also finds "Cool Jews" in the popular press, in magazines such as *Heeb*, an ironic, hip, postmodern periodical (think of a Jewish *Onion*) that celebrates all things young, Jewish, and potentially shocking to your parents' generation, including an occasional ode to the ample dark armpit hair on Jewish women. Isaac Bashevis Singer once said, "The whole point of Jewishness is isolation," and the emergence of Cool Jews and Jewish rap (not just *by* Jews but *about* Jews) in the 1990s and 2000s is only further evidence that the scales of isolation have tipped in America and that the Jews, who started out here by denying their Jewish identity in the 1910s, confronting it in the 1960s, and renegotiating it in the 1980s, had finally arrived at the place where they were flaunting it.

Take for example comedian Adam Sandler, who in 1994 first performed his now famous "Hanukkah Song" on the *Saturday Night Live* television program. Built around the idea that Jewish children feel alienated during the Christmas season, the song lists Jewish celebrities (both real and fictional) who give Jewish kids some seasonal pride. It was an interesting postmodern conceit, a feint within a feint, because the fact that Sandler was performing it to great acclaim on live television was itself an indication that the issue of Jewish pride in America was already a foregone conclusion. "Its so much fun-akkah to celebrate Hanukkah," he rapped, "When you feel like the only kid in town without a x-mas tree, here's a list of / People who are Jewish, just like you and me." He then cleverly rhymed the names of dozens of Jewish, hardly Jewish and impossibly Jewish characters from American popular culture, concluding at one point, "Paul Newman's half Jewish; Goldie Hawn's half too / Put them together—what a fine lookin' Jew!"

Made up of trivial pop culture references, this song was anything but trivial. It quickly (if temporarily) achieved the status of "Rudolph the Red-Nosed-Reindeer" or "Jingle Bell Rock" as Sandler turned triviality into something caring, a song to sing Jewish kids to sleep (a spiritual song with roots of clay) and an easily accessible way for non-Jews to participate in the Jewish tradition (and perhaps as such it helps explain the Chai around Britney Spears's neck). Sandler's little Hanukkah song announced that everybody in America could now move in and out of the Jewish persona: it was on *Saturday Night Live*: it was cool to be Jewish.

Similarly, in 1998, a young man named Ross Fuller, also known as MC Remedy, pushed the boundaries of Jewish identification still further with his dramatic Holocaust rap on the album *Wu-Tang Presents the Killa Bees: The Swarm*. Produced by a member of the highly popular Wu-Tang Clan (Remedy is also known as "Jew-Tang") the song titled "Never Again" combines ancient Hebrew prayers with 'Hatikvah' and Remedy's spitfire Holocaust rap: "Never again shall we march like sheep to the slaughter / Never again leave our sons and daughters / Never again shall our children be stripped of our culture, robbed of our names / Raped of our freedom and thrown into the flames."

Fuller, who began using the name Remedy in 1987 to indicate he was part of the solution, was clearly influenced by the Beastie Boys. The success of this one track became an industry for him, and although as a child he had been afraid to admit that he was Jewish, he subsequently produced several albums of Jewish rap and made multiple trips to Israel, turning this "never again" message into a kind of hip-hop industry. Recently he was featured in a BBC documentary on the subject of "Jew Hop." Fuller said, "So many people have approached or written me over the past few years. I was hearing all types of amazing testimony from people around the world. What 'Never Again' meant to them, or how it made them feel, or where they were and what they were doing when they heard it . . . so I'm trying to document as many as I can. With the help of a publisher, we will print a book about just what 'Never Again' means and what it's done for people all over the world." Will the Holocaust too eventually become part of this "Cool Jew" movement and one day be the major attraction in a kind of theme-park version of Jewish history?

Yet the Holocaust is not the only source of memory for modern Jews, and the Passover ritual is itself creating a bridge to greater America. All across the country, Passover seders now offer a wide array of philosophical options—freedom seders, women's seders, jazz seders, heavy metal seders, even seders specifically designed for non-Jews who nonetheless want to pass around both the lore and the wine of freedom. Josh Dolgin, who records under the name DJ Socalled (he "put the Jew in jukebox") created a rap version of the Passover seder that uses a techno grammar (sound as information), various prayers, fake audio documents, hip-hop beats, and klezmer solos to tell the story of the Exodus. The project started when he stumbled upon Jewish recordings from decades past and became enthralled: "Listening to these old records, there was a whole different kind of flow, a whole way of making music that was really catchy." He hunted for more of these records, attended conferences devoted to collectors, and enlisted an eclectic group of musicians to help him craft *The Socalled Seder*, including Wu-Tang Clan's Killah Priest and clarinetist David Krakauer. In its structure, *The Socalled Seder* reminds one that Passover is built around the telling of a great adventure, designed specifically for the ears of young children using highly repetitive songs (e.g. "Who Knows One") to drill the narrative deep into the memory; it is only one of the many postmodern iterations of the Passover tradition.

Another surfaced at the White House, where, in 2009 and again in 2010, President Obama and about twenty close friends (no professional Jewish leaders or celebrities were invited) gathered for a ritual that told the story and celebrated freedom. The seder was described by one reporter thus: "In the Old Family Dining room, under sparkling chandeliers and portraits of former first ladies, the mostly Jewish and African-American guests will recite prayers and retell the biblical story of slavery and liberation. . . . If last year is any guide, Malia and Sasha Obama will take on the duties of Jewish children, asking four questions about the night's purpose—along with a few of their own—and scrambling to find matzo hidden in the gleaming antique furniture. The event was the first-ever presidential Seder, and also probably 'the first time in history that gefilte fish had been placed on White House dishware.'" Mr. Obama began the seder each year by invoking the universality of the holiday's themes of struggle and liberation; the president himself is a Cool Jew.

Cool Jews also merge with modern orthodoxy at the sold-out concerts of rapper Matthew Miller, who goes by the stagename Matisyahu. One of many young Jews who dropped out of high school in the 1990s to follow the band Phish around the country, he subsequently committed himself to the Chabad-Lubavitch sect of orthodox Judaism, a movement based in the Crown Heights section of Brooklyn. He first began performing his Hasidic reggae-style rap in New York, where he was a Jewish cult hero, but his following went mainstream after he toured as an opening act for the Dave Matthews Band and Trey Anastasio of Phish. His first solo album, *Live at Stubb's*, sold more than 100,000 copies and gave him the modern-rock hit "King Without a Crown." He wears *peyes* (sidelocks) and does beat box with his voice. His words, some in Hebrew, some in Jamaican patois, some in straight-up American English, have the flow of hip-hop and the devout spirituality of reggae. He currently plays to a thousand people or more each night, regularly encouraging ecstatic fans to sing along with the *brakhot*, the traditional prayers. According to one observer, a professor of Jewish studies, Matisyahu's popularity is a sign of the times, a response to the seemingly endless post-9/11 terrorism in Israel that makes clear a rising hatred of Jews. "I noticed," she wrote, "how Jewish students, many of them previously uninvolved in Jewish life, gravitated to my classes, seeking a kind of solace that students ten years earlier wouldn't have needed. They saw their own future at stake."

Many scholars predict that within fifty years the ethnoracial landscape of America will be drastically different. Whites will be in the minority and Asians and Latinos will increasingly compete with African-Americans, who will no longer be the archetypal "outsider" group in the USA. Whiteness itself, some predict, will lose its power and attractiveness. Will Jewish acceptance within white America hasten its dissolution or, just the opposite, will growing acceptance of Jews in America reinvigorate their desire to reassert a sense of "otherness" or specialness? Might they then begin to identify with the next wave of American minorities, say, for example, the Hispanic culture?

The Hip-hop Hoodios, a bicoastal rap group founded by the attorney turned producer Josh Norek, the "psycho-Semitic manic Hispanic," suggests this idea is not far-fetched. The name Hoodios is, of course, a play on the Spanish word for Jew (*judío*), and the group raps in Spanish, English, Hebrew, and Ladino. It was formed while Norek was a law student at Cornell, but being a bilingual kid, Norek had the concept for the Hoodios well before the band existed. When he was fourteen, his father sang in a Jewish choir, where a Ladino piece called "Ocho Kandelikas" ("Eight Candles") caught his attention. "I made a mental note—one day I will record this song. It wasn't until years later that I found the right co-conspirator." He met Abraham Velez in college, who is half Puerto Rican and half Jewish. "It was like the perfect storm. Before you knew it we had come up with our first CD and 'Ocho Kandelikas' was one of the first songs. Kind of a punk hip-hop format. We did a $400 video with girls in bagel bras and MTV played it."

The video may have been camp, but there was nothing trivial in Norek's "predisposition" to combine Latin and Jewish cultures. "I was translating John Cougar Mellencamp and Tom Petty into Spanish at age fourteen. I was always comfortable in Spanish, always interested in Jewish and Mexican culture." Aware of previous attempts at Jewish rap, Norek wanted to raise the bar: "With Jewish rap, there is a lot of kitsch, a lot of novelty," Norek says. "Two Live Jews, 50 Shekels, [these groups] take regular rap songs and 'In Da Club' becomes 'In Da Shul.' It's so lame. It's mad-libs. Take black references, replace with Jewish references, hahaha that's Jewish hip-hop." So rather than trivialize his own Jewishness by trying to insert it into black rap, he used the Spanish angle to bring it forward, employing themes of broader social justice alongside historical Jewish references: his song "Agua pa' la Gente," for example, is an exegesis of the trend in Latin America to privatize water, and in "1492," he tells the story of the expulsion of the Jews from Spain in the fifteenth century, from the Jewish point of view.

For the Hoodios, being Latino and being Jewish are both part of the same fluid conditions of a modern American identity. Norek himself has distant family ties in Colombia; Velez is of Eastern European and Puerto Rican descent. But a third member of the group, Federico Fong, is a dreadlocked Chinese-Panamanian-Jamaican-white Arkansan who identifies as Mexican. His only Jewish connection is a sister who once worked in a Jewish deli on Second Avenue. The group's fourth member, the dancer Alanna "Alannanagila" Perez (the Hoodio Honey), is the daughter of a Polish-Jewish-American mother and a Mexican father. "This [group] has made me more of what I am," she says. "I wasn't [Jewish] before I got into this band. Now all of a sudden, I'm Jewish." Perez became aware of her Jewishness by deepening her Hispanic roots, and vice versa. In the future, if the Hoodios are any indication, Jewish identity in America (much like ethnicity itself) will be created from the inside out, one person at a time.

All this is of a piece with what scholars are calling "postethnic" America, which has its legal precedent in a 1978 Supreme Court ruling (the "Bakke decision") wherein affirmative action was saved by framing it in terms of cultural diversity as opposed to ethnicity. Now in America, in fact as well as in strictly legal terms, culture is color, rather than the other way around, and one can virtually choose one's ethnicity just as one can shift one's cultural orientation. In short, we may be witnessing the beginning of the end of ethnoracial subgroups, or, alternatively, ethnoracial decisions are becoming a matter of personal choice in America; hence, as we approach a "postethnic" social order, one wonders what this means to the pursuit of an "authentic" life, either as a Jew, an American, or both. For if every American life is a self-invention, how can its authenticity ever be in question or its "Jewishness" be significant (let alone defined)? If every life is an authentic version of *that* life in *that* moment, is all American culture, then, simply part of an ongoing narrative designed to entertain during one's fifteen minutes of fame?

This sense of cultural impermanence is nowhere more apparent than in the media world—talk radio, *People*-style magazines, bit torrent downloads, Twitter, YouTube, Facebook, email, and the rest—which has become so pervasive that it is like its own world into which all Americans demand entry, and when one arrives, one surrenders any and all previous ethnicity in order to participate. American media culture in the twenty-first century is more than a new national pastime; it is, for many, the only way to live the American dream. The idea of existing in and through the media is clearly connected to our need to be a part of something larger than ourselves, and like previous communal experiences, it has developed its own mythology. Consider so-called reality television. First and foremost, it presents itself as democratic: everyone can participate if they can get past someone who pretends to be the judge or if they can do something so outrageous that they cannot be denied. Of course, these media transactions are occasionally criticized by the media themselves, but almost always in terms of their fairness: Is it fair that this one triumphs over that one, that this one has the spotlight while that one is in the shadow, that this one cheats successfully while that one languishes in honesty? The fact that the whole operation is itself artificial and dishonest rarely comes up.

A classic example can be found in the world of television advertising, where today the sponsor will often complain if the commercial "doesn't sound 'authentic' enough," which means it sounds too much like a commercial—which is exactly what it *is*, of course; but what it *is* is supposed to be exactly what it isn't. When people get involved in media transactions of this nature, it is not only their common sense that is affronted but also their very beings that are challenged. And unlike our experience with previous communal narratives, within the growing media culture we literally feel smaller as we appear to participate in something much bigger. We sense there is way too much information and not enough understanding; too much interaction and not enough connection. Will we eventually all disappear into the new "cloud" culture, where we simultaneously live singly and in great numbers, alone but in huge demographic groups, where intimacy is hard to come by and geography is irrelevant, where space no longer matters and time no longer exists, and where there is nothing but a yawning hunger at the end of the day?

By definition, technology connects us in an abstract way. It has no libido. But historically, Jews have needed a *physical* connection in order to exist; in the synagogues, everybody chants together—the voices rise to the sky—even while each person chants to his own rhythm. Doing—going forth as Abraham himself did—is what gives life context, and it is context that creates the possibility of living "authentically." In Judaism, the divine resides within the community, among people in the same room at the same time, hearing each other's voices and looking into each other's eyes. This is our context. The choices we make are made within this context; they create action, and action creates character—this is how actual drama (narrative) works and how Jews have always lived their lives. Their shared context created shared meaning. As we lose our physical connections to one another, submerge our desires into a virtual world, do we also surrender the possibility of experiencing these deeper levels of the Jewish narrative? The words may be there, but something crucial is missing: there is a basic tension between the anonymous online world and the meaning of Jewish life.

Perhaps the real problem with the new media reality is its pretense of a participatory experience and its inability to deliver. This can be discovered in details great and small: consider, for example, that the Internet provides instant access to every song that has ever been recorded, an incomprehensible panoply of choices. But when one finally makes one's way through the morass of possibility—and this too is part of the problem, the illusion of plenty and our need for someone to mediate the choices for us—and is inside the earphones to "experience" the downloaded song, there is nothing to hold in our hands; there is no "packaging." But packaging (as Alfred Lion knew with his great Blue Note art) was the material aspect of the music; the artwork, the photos, the liner notes, the handling of the album, even the historically faded cardboard cover or the pungent aroma of the attic where the object had been stored, all were part of the *experience* of the music. Packaging is part of the *intermediation*; it gives us a great deal of information—aesthetic, stylistic, tactile, literal—and anchors the experience of the music in the here-and-now of the mundane world. Music is not just "intellectual property"; without these visceral aspects we no longer have the same experience; we are missing the romance, the larger narrative, the caring, the context.

Packaging is a convenient way to understand the importance of context in any experience, and how context affects our ability to feel something; how feeling determines our ability to care about something; and how caring is what drives our communal experience. Context is memory: how we see ourselves in the greater world, how we recognize each other and our interconnectedness as social beings. In America, there is a constant struggle for context, growing more difficult every day.

Recently I attended a bar mitzvah in Southern California. It was held at a large, elegant synagogue in an affluent suburb, and the congregation enjoyed both a serious young rabbi and an enthusiastic young cantor. I recognized all the prayers from my own childhood—but something dramatic was missing: all the melodies had been changed. To me, these new melodies, which the congregation sang with enthusiasm, seemed painfully earnest, constructed like contemporary folk songs, and indeed, the cantor strummed along on a guitar as he led the congregation. After the service I asked him about the music, and he happily admitted that he had taken the liberty of writing new melodies, which he then taught to the congregation. It was, he explained, part of the "Jewish Renewal Movement," happening everywhere in America; cantors were inventing their own melodies, using the music to create a sense of "ownership" and participation among congregants. This movement, he told me, had grown out of Jewish summer camps where the singer-songwriter Debbie Friedman had become wildly popular among the children doing just this. But what about people like myself, I asked, who arrived for a service and were left in the musical dark? The songs were simple, he suggested, and could easily be picked up. As part of the new Judaism, it seems we were all being asked to maintain the beginner's mind; every twenty-five miles down the road, we might need it to reinvent our context.

What we call "Jewish" is no doubt a contextual idea that has been around a lot longer than the four thousand years or so that the Jews themselves have been a self-identified group—the Jews recognized, organized, codified, and deified something, but that something is very ancient and is probably of the same stuff that first made us human. The early Hebrews were very perceptive. They took the bedrock principles of social justice and human dignity and wrapped them in a narrative, with heroes and villains, love and death, a past and a future, so if the Jew is anywhere today, he or she is in this narrative; not in the details but in the telling; the act of people sitting around the communal fire, calling the spirit down. This is the human context, and music is not only at the heart of the experience, the spiritual glue that binds people together, but it is probably that element that makes them human in the first place.

Consider that each of us builds an infinite number of meanings from just a few sounds. Sounds are the building blocks of meaning. The first thing you learn as a child is sounds. Then some of these sounds become nouns ("dog"), others become verbs ("run"), and then, at a year and a half, we start to create something new, something magical from these sounds: sentences ("dog run"). This joining of sounds to create meaning is grammar; grammar is context, and it is what makes language a human thing. Meaning, then, comes from the ways we combine elements (again, a final nod to Wittgenstein). This is a definition of context—it takes at least two elements for there to be context, and hence meaning; the Jews who discovered how to probe the essence of things through their apparent contradictions (Talmudic reasoning) invented "us and them," "I and thou," "God and man." What we call "Jewish" is simply a way of dissecting this complicated world, a point of incision, a method of parsing our environment through shared context.

What is today's shared context? For some Jews, it is still the deep-seated conviction—nurtured through many generations and passed along on the pulse—that we are always only one social movement away from new pogroms and that at any moment there could be a knock on the door; it is why Jews have, psychologically speaking, always kept a bag packed, an onion in their pocket, and an eye on the exits. It is an essential part of the story for them, and they have taught this to their children in ways great and small—through words and silences, through actions and inactions—and it is the bedrock of their feeling (their certainty) that, as a Jew, they are different. Who is a Jew? Some would say a Jew is one who steps forward when they come for the Jews. Others will point to the fact that there is no need to step forward: *they* will always tell you who you are. And today, in Muslim nations around the world, there is widespread belief that instead of the actual 2 percent, the Jewish population in the United States is as high as 85 percent. (This among college-educated Muslims who seek to explain their sense of an undue Jewish influence around the world!) If the educated elite of sovereign nations believe that only 15 percent of us are not Jews, who are we to disagree? Perhaps they are right.

There is a Yiddish term, the *pintle,* which refers to the little Jew in all of us (the still small voice); even the most acculturated Jew (and, why not, even the non-Jew) has it, and a time will come, Jews believe, when it starts speaking to us. And so, in America, perhaps the Jewish *pintle* is also to be found in the African-American, the Hispanic, the Asian and the Caucasian, the rich and the homeless; perhaps we all carry the *pintle*. And just as the Jew is *teyku*, always in the process of becoming, always unresolved, in between polarities, so too is the American. There is in this perspective a certain acceptance of a profound alienation: we are not wholly part of anything, always in between. For each of us, then, our *pintle*, our seed of alienation, is a powerful motivation to understand others and to care about them.

The presence of the *other* within each of us forces us to care; without it, we drift. (As the late great European intellectual historian George Mosse once said, "A little alienation is not a bad thing.") In the end, caring is everything. Today, Judaism in America is part of a much larger package that includes a hundred years of work in social progress, black progress, feminist progress (seven of the nine women who wrote the book *Our Bodies, Ourselves* were Jews); the deepest part of Judaism is not throwing a shawl over your head when you pray, but rather standing up for the "other," both within and without. The Jew reminds the world that to the other guy, you *are* the other guy. The Jew makes "once upon a time" possible.

We look around and see we are standing in a long line, a line so long that Abraham once stood in it too; it goes back tens of thousands of years and stretches into an unknown future. What we call a Jew is just a recent name for an ancient phenomenon. Prayer is at the root of Jewish music just as music is at the root of Jewish prayer. How different was it in the time of Abraham, when musicians gathered at the temples in Ur, no doubt passing along the latest gossip about gigs and girls and the gods from upriver. Were they wondering, "What will become of the Jew in the music and the music in the Jew?" Or "Do you still need a Jew in this business?" It was not that long ago and probably not very different at all; in the scope of big history it is not even a whisker on the face of Father Time.

The thing that has always made us human, the reason we still write love songs (small musical narratives), the beating heart at the center of all religion, is the fact that we are all connected in some profound way, probably down to the DNA, and that it is our moral obligation to persevere, to hang in there for one another and not let the indifference overcome us. This is perhaps the greatest gift of the Jews—keeping the commitment to care for one another alive. (Perhaps the meaning of the Holocaust, if there is one, was exactly this: to survive even the greatest test of darkness and emerge into the light of caring for one another.) Certainly the natural tendency for all of us is to fall by the side of the road, to lapse into selfishness, to let the fear of the Deity turn into the deification of fear.

But therein lie hope, joy, and optimism. Without risk of failure there is no success; they are one and the same, and it requires a great leap of faith to commit oneself to the act of love, to compose a song from the heart that reaches out to the "other" and demonstrates that we are not alone here, that we are all connected, literally, through participating in this simple act. Being moved by music ("collective entrainment") is perhaps nothing more than the physical celebration of this awareness, a knowing beyond knowing, that we are here, that we are all afraid, and that there is a much larger story of which we are all a part.

Today all of us in America—not just Jews—find ourselves in much the same situation as that small Jewish community back in the Pale of Settlement who were in great danger of losing themselves; the rabbi had forgotten the special prayers and no longer knew where nor how to light the special fire, but for this small ravaged community, just the memory that there *was* a fire, "once upon a time," was sufficient, and the people were saved. Like them, we may no longer remember exactly what drove our ancestors to arrive at this particular place and time, but perhaps just the memory that there *was* a time and a place when we were all connected around a fire will again be enough and again the people will be saved.

There Was a Fire

Jews, Music and the American Dream

Ben Sidran

A tip of the yarmulke to . . .

Scott Anderson
Marv Conney
Pierre Darmon
Richard Davidson
Emily DeHuff
Jorge Drexler
Tracy Ehlers
Howard Gelman
Gill Goldstein
Bob Gottlieb
Clifford Irving
Stanley Kutler
Dan Levitin
Howard Levy
Alan Lewis
Anita Lightfoot
Tommy LiPuma
Ralph Lutrin
Elaine Markson
Pam Miller
Lorrie Moore
Rick Pepin
Lester Pines
Jon Richardson
David Ritz
Ken Robbins
Matan Rubinstein
Henry Sapoznik
Maxine Sidran
Ralph Simon
Bob Skloot
Terry Strauss
Jean Szlamovicz
and
Judy, Amanda, and Leo Sidran.

CHAPTER ONE / If God Is a Story, Who Is a Jew?

pg 3 "the meaning of a word is its use in a sentence": Ludwig Wittgenstein, *Philosophical Investigations* (Macmillan, 1953), p. 20. See also *Language in Thought and Action* by S. I. Hayakawa and the work of Alfred Korzibsky, who famously gave us the expression "The map is not the territory." And finally, see Colin Cherry, *On Human Communication* (M.I.T. Press, 1966), p.14. "Information can be received only where there is doubt; and doubt implies the existence of alternatives—where choice, selection, or discrimination is called for. . . . Now it is customary to speak of signals as 'conveying information,' as though information were a kind of commodity. But signals do not convey information as railway trucks carry coal. Rather we should say: signals have an information content by virtue of the *potential for making selections.*"

pg 5 The Jewish narrative, beginning with Abraham's covenant with God: See Thomas Cahill, *The Gift of the Jews* (New York: Anchor, 1998). See also Karen Armstrong, *A History of God*: We cannot imagine the great liberation movements of modern history without reference to the Bible. "Without the Bible," she writes, "we would never have known the abolitionist movement, the prison reform movement, the antiwar movement, the labor movement, the civil rights movement." (p. 154). Democracy grows directly out of the Israelite vision of *individuals*; there is no way that it could have been "self evident that all men are created equal" without the interventions of Jewish thought.

pg 8 while our mind-memory is inevitably inaccurate: in conversation with Professor Richard Davidson, University of Wisconsin, June, 2003: It is interesting to note that memory and emotion are not only intertwined in our experience, but anatomically intertwined in the brain as well, where the amygdala, the actual center of emotion, is literally touching the hippocampus, the reservoir of memory.

pg 8 "It's like being dead," he said: Oliver Sacks, *Musicophilia: Tales of Music and the Brain* (New York: Picador, 2008), p.189.

pg 10 the assignment of words to melody (and vice versa) was not arbitrary: Daniel Levitin, *The World In Six Songs* (New York, Dutton, 2008) pp. 173–174. "The fact that different subgroups of contemporary Jews sing different melodies suggests that there was no one magic formula for preserving the information . . . even the prosody of [each] new language [the "music" of the language] has been shown to influence the songs of that linguistic culture."

CHAPTER TWO / Where Hamburgers Come From

pg 16 "the creation of systems of courts": Karen Armstrong, *A History of God* (Ballantine Books, 1993), p. 249 "Without the Bible we would never have known the abolitionist movement, the prison reform movement, the antiwar movement, the labor movement, the civil rights movement." Democracy grows directly out of the Israelite vision of *individuals*; there is no way that it could have been "self evident that all men are created equal" without the interventions of Jewish thought.

pg 16 "The opposite of love," writes Levitin, "is not hate, but indifference": Daniel Levitin, *The World In Six Songs*, p. 235; See also p. 241.

pg 16 Perhaps it is the why of why we are here: In the beginning, all of life is music to us; there is no discrimination between what is important and what is unimportant, what is "signal" and what is "noise." We are bathed in the song of life. Development *is* discrimination; as we experience growth, we form our "self" out of how we discriminate, and how we discriminate forms the basis of our relationship to broad spiritual and social values. Thus the original bridge from the physical to the spiritual is through sound. All music can be seen as a way of preserving or recreating those first sensations of life and our connection to others: the awareness that we are here but we are not alone.

pg 16 Stuyvesant appealed to his employers back in Europe for permission to deny them permanent residency: *New York Times*, May 24, 2005. Stuyvesant had argued in a 1655 letter to the West India Company that "Jewish liberty [was] detrimental because the Christians cannot compete against them." *See also* Edward Kritzler, *Jewish Pirates of the Caribbean*, Anchor books, 2008, p. 177-179.

pg 17 comparing their flight from England to the Exodus of the Jews from Egypt: "Jews in the New Wilderness," *New York Times*, September 24, 2004. The origins of America are inseparable from currents of Judaic messianism. This is one reason that debate raged over whether the American Indians were the lost tribes of Israel. In 1641 the Pilgrim leader John Cotton proposed theocratic government based on the laws of the Hebrew Bible, and some Puritans even advocated making Hebrew the American language.

pg 17 Louis Gottschalk, whose light classical pieces were popular: See Frederick S. Starr, *Bamboula! The Life and Times of Louis Moreau Gottschalk* (New York: Oxford, 1995).

pg 17 the interpreter for Sitting Bull in the 1870s: Julius Meyer was born in Bromberg, Prussia, March 30, 1839. He emigrated to Omaha, Nebraska, in 1867 and began developing acquaintances with Plains Indians. He was reportedly able to speak six Indian languages. He served as an interpreter for Gen. George Crook and later opened an Indian curiosity shop called the Indian Wigwam at Eleventh and Farnam streets in Omaha.

pg 17 traded in rags because they were prohibited from selling new clothing: David Kertzer, *The Popes Against the Jews: The Vatican's Role in the Rise of Modern Anti-Semitism* (New York: Knopf, 2001), p. 26. Jews went into the "needle trade" because in the late 18th century, they were not allowed, among other things, to sell new clothes, only rags, and so they learned to repair them.

pg 17 The kabbalistic way of thinking, using an elaborate symbolism: Cynthia Ozick, "The Heretic: The Mythic Passions of Gershom Scholem," essay on *Gershom Scholem: A Life in Letters, 1914–1982, New Yorker*, September 2, 2002, p. 143: "The position of classical Judaism was that the essence of God is unknowable: 'Thou canst not see My Face.' The Kabbalists sought no only to define and characterize the Godhead—through a kind of spiritualized cosmogonic physics—but to experience it. Kabbalah had been shunned for its claim of ecstatic ascent to the hidden sublime; it had been scorned for its connection to folk religion and magic."

pg 18 they were already of this world, and so became transformed through the act of prayer: Henry Sapoznik, author of *Klezmer! Jewish Music from Old World to Our World* (New York: Schirmer, 1999), in conversation with the author, March, 2003.

pg 18 (they were considered *teyku*, or to be determined later): Louis Jacobs, *Teyku: the Unsolved Problem in the Babylonian Talmud* (New York, Cornwall Books) p. 14. In the Talmudic tradition the term, *teyku* dates back to Babylonian times. *Teyku* literally means that at the moment there *is no answer*. It acknowledges the duality of existence; it holds open the possibility that one day we may know; the story continues; it admits that there may well be something that we *cannot know*. It is an unresolved dilemma. As is all life. Meaning resides in the *attempt* to reconcile apparent opposites, keeping the discussion open, not in the resolution itself. To the Jews, the human condition is all about this moment of tension, putting the "quest" back in questioning, allowing the search to continue without requiring the impediment of answers. This analysis provided by Prof. Matan, Rubenstein, University of Wisconsin, in conversation with the author, October, 2004.

pg 18 The Talmud itself pours scorn on anyone "who reads without melody": Tractate Magillah, 32b.

pg 18 "laughter through the tears": Dmitri Shostakovich (as told to Solomon Volkov in *Testimony*, http://www.fuguemasters.com/prokofiev.html). "Jewish folk music has made a most powerful impression on me. It can appear to be quite happy while it is tragic. It's almost always laughter through tears. This quality of Jewish folk music is close to my ideas of what music should be. There should always be two layers in music. . . . Jews express despair in dance music."

pg 19 some of the great klezmer bands had maybe one or two Jews in them: Henry Sapoznik, *Klezmer! Jewish Music from Old World to Our World* (New York: Schirmer, 1999), p. 6.

pg 19 It had a "thin and humble sound": Ibid., p. 1.

pg 20 *Peyes* is a Hebrew word, which literally translates into English as corners, sides, or edges; in the context of Judaism, it is particularly used in relation to the head and face, denoting sidelocks, and sometimes also sideburns.

pg 20 One such city . . . was Odessa: Sapoznik, *Klezmer!*, p. 22.

pg 21 (the "blood libel" charge, which accused Jews): Max Dimont, *Jews, God and History* (Dublin: Mentor, 1964), p. 330.

pg 21 the Jews brought America's signature meal with them: Paul Kriwaczek, *Yiddish Civilization: The Rise and Fall of a Forgotten Nation* (London: Phoenix, 2005), p. 311.

pg 21 In Ireland alone, a million people died from starvation: Michael Pollan, *The Botany of Desire: A Plant's-Eye View of the World* (New York: Random House, 2001), p. 56. See also Felipe Fernandez-Armesto, *Near a Thousand Tables: A History of Food* (New York, Free Press, 2002). What saved the potato from that particular blight was resistant genes that scientists eventually found in wild potatoes growing in the Andes, the potato's own center of diversity.

pg 22 compete with blacks for jobs on the docks: John Strausbaugh, *Black Like You* (New York: Tarcher Penguin, 2006), p. 84. Blacks and Irish were auctioned off together, worked together, slept together. "They formed a large mongrel underclass, and into the 1830s, their shared class conditions, and their common mistreatment at the hands of the Anglo-American overlords could easily outweigh their racial differences. . . . Nowhere is this mongrel underclass more evident than in lower Manhattan in the early 1800s. White looking slaves shared the streets with ostensibly Black freemen."

pg 22 the first truly American form of entertainment: Jeffrey Melnick, *A Right to Sing the Blues* (Cambridge, Mass.: Harvard University Press, 1999), p. 156. James Weldon Johnson, the famous black musicologist, has called the minstrel show the "only completely original contribution America has made to the theater . . . at the heart of American entertainment, Blacks imitating and fooling whites, whites imitating and stealing from Blacks, Blacks reappropriating and transforming what has been stolen, whites making yet another foray on Black styles, and on and on . . . this is American popular culture."

pg 22 "I turn about an wheel about an do jis so": Strausbaugh, *Black Like You*, p. 60. "At a time when popular songs are mostly treacly sentimental ballads or fussily ornate imitations of highbrow concert music, this artless, silly song is like a blast of fresh air in a stuffy place. It's got pulse and a sense of humor. It's new and exciting. By way of structure it's just an endless repetition of two-line verses and a two-line chorus, verse-chorus-verse":

Come listen all you gals and boys I'm just from Tuckyhoe
I'm guine to sing a little song, my name's Jim Crow
Wheel about an turn about an do jis so
Eb'ry time I wheel about I jump Jim Crow
I went down to de river, I didn't mean to stay
But there I see so many gals I couldn't get away

Wheel about an turn about an do jis so
Eb'ry time I wheel about I jump Jim Crow
De udder gals dey 'gin to fight, I tel'd dem wait a bit
I'd hab dem all, jis one by one, as I tourt fit

pg 22 Italian commedia dell'arte performers wore makeup: Seymour Stark, *Men in Blackface: True Stories of the Minstrel Show (*Bloomington, Ind.: Xlibris, 2000) p. 25: "By their nature, clowns live on the boundary between order and chaos. The traditional European clowns worked in pairs, the whiteface who was refined and civilized and the auguste (red nose and baggy pants) who was disruptive and rude. Similarly, were disruptive but were help in check by the interlocutor. The fool often transgressed boundaries between classes or castes, a boundary that separated social order from disorder. "Within the fixed bounds of what is permitted, an experience of what is not permitted." Minstrelsy opened the door to a kind of primitivism and sensual license on stage, which began to break the Puritan taboo against sexuality. It was the beginning of a true American theater, and the beginning of the end of America's slavish turning to Victorian England for their notions of popular culture."

pg 23 "Jump Jim Crow" was his "Hound Dog": Strausbaugh, *Black Like You* (Tarcher, Penguin, 2006) p. 61.

pg 23 was greeted by a brass band playing Rice's hit: Ibid.

pg 24 Basically, they spoke black talk: See Ben Sidran, *Black Talk* (Holt, Rinehart & Winston, 1971; Cambridge, Mass.: Da Capo, 1981).

pg 25 written by no one in particular and carried on the wind: see www.pitt.edu/~amerimus/foster.htm.

pg 26 it is now the most famous river in the American South: www.pitt.edu/~amerimus/foster.htm, Foster's brother Mr. Morrison Foster gives this statement: "One day in 1851, Stephen came into my office, on the bank of the Monongahela, Pittsburg, and said to me: 'What is a good name of two syllables for a Southern river? I want to use it in this new song of "Old Folks at Home."' I asked him how Yazoo would do. 'Oh,' said he, 'that has been used before.' I then suggested Pedee. 'Oh, pshaw,' he replied, 'I won't have that.' I then took down an atlas from the top of my desk and opened the map of the United States. We both looked over it and my finger stopped at the 'Swanee,' a little river in Florida emptying into the Gulf of Mexico. 'That's it, that's it exactly,' exclaimed he, delighted, as he wrote the name down; and the song was finished, commencing, 'Way Down Upon de Swanee Ribber.' He left the office, as was his custom, abruptly, without saying another word, and I resumed my work."

pg 26 "Not a family but a whole people moved": From *Shtetl to Swing*, PBS, Great Performances, first broadcast October, 2005 (See also http://www.pbs.org/wnet/gperf/shows/shtetl/essay1.html).

pg 27 as much as $700 per day: Neal Gabler, *An Empire of Their Own: How the Jews Invented Hollywood* (New York: Anchor, 1988), p. 18.

pg 28 "No sooner did I put my foot on American soil": Ibid, quoting Adolph Zukor, p. 14.

pg 28 "this year we are slaves": Mishnah (Pesahim 10:5): "In each generation every person must act as if he or she personally had gone forth from Egypt."

pg 29 "Nothing comparable exists for blacks": Lawrence Thomas, in Jeffrey Rubin-Dorsky and Shelley Fisher Fishkin, *People of the Book: Thirty Scholars Reflect on Their Jewish Identity* (Madison: University of Wisconsin Press, 1996), pp. 169–86: "Historical narratives can be among the deepest values that individuals hold. What is more, otherwise perfect strangers who meet may have good reason to believe that they both deeply embrace the same historical narrative, and can thus display basic trust toward one another—trust being that psychological attitude which two people have toward one another without which cooperation between them is impossible. I maintain that it is precisely because there are such positive goals that Jews are able to respond so successfully in the face of a common enemy. It is one thing to know what to run from; it is quite another to know where to run to. A common enemy can yield an answer only to the former; an answer to the latter must come from values and positive goals."

pg 30 might have misspelled it, or mispronounced it: Joseph Roth, *The Wandering Jews* (New York: W. W. Norton, 1927), p. 99. "Don't be surprised at the Jews" lack of attachment to their names. They will change their names with alacrity, and the names of their fathers, even though those particular sounds, to the European sensibility, are charged with emotional weight. For Jews, their names have no value because they are not their names. Jews, Eastern Jews, have no names. They have compulsory aliases. Their true name is the one by which they are summoned to the Torah on the Sabbath, their Jewish first name and the Jewish first name of their father. . . . Does the chameleon feel any respect for the colors he continually keeps changing? In America, the Jew changes Grünbaum to Greenboom. The shift in the vowels doesn't upset him. . . . [I]n the new world, Yiddish speakers seemed to have no history . . . or to be exact, no interest in or recollection of people and places outside their own recent past . . . many didn't know the names of the east European towns from which their families had emigrated and some even forgot what their family names had been before being anglicised . . . twice dislocated, first from the European *heym* and then to the suburbs, most of the Yiddish families seemed to have abandoned their past altogether."

pg 31 Emerson himself had questions about her "Jewishness": Christopher Benfey, "The Convert," *New York Review*, February 15, 2007, p. 51.

pg 31 "Until we are all free, none of us is free": Ibid. Also see Esther Schor, *Emma Lazarus* (New York: Nextbook/Schocken, 2007 and John Hollander, *Emma Lazarus: Selected Poems* (New York: Library of America, 2007). The full text of the sonnet "The New Colossus" reads:

> Not like the brazen giant of Greek fame,
> With conquering limbs astride from land to land;
> Here at our sea-washed, sunset gates shall stand
> A mighty woman with a torch, whose flame
> Is the imprisoned lightning, and her name
> Mother of Exiles. From her beacon-hand
> Glows world-wide welcome; her mild eyes command
> The air-bridged harbor that twin cities frame.
> 'Keep ancient lands, your storied pomp!' cries she
> With silent lips. "Give me your tired, your poor,
> Your huddled masses yearning to breathe free,
> The wretched refuse of your teeming shore.
> Send these, the homeless, tempest-tost to me,
> I lift my lamp beside the golden door!"

CHAPTER THREE / *Ragtime Jews*

pg 37 365,000 pianos were sold in the United States: Thad Carhart, *The Piano Shop on the Left Bank* (New York: Random House, 2002), pp. 102–6.

pg 39 "more at home at the end of their few weeks": quoted in Stephen J. Whitfield, *In Search of American Jewish Culture* (Lebanon, N.H.: University Press of New England, 1999), p. 46.

pg 40 Jews, too, were close to the bottom: Eric Goldstein, *The Price of Whiteness* (Princeton: Princeton University Press, 2006), p. 86. The Jews were listed as a separate race in the U.S. government's *Dictionary of Races or Peoples* as late as 1911. The question of whether Jews ought to fashion themselves as a race or merely a religious denomination became one of the most hotly debated issues of early-twentieth-century Jewish communal discourse.

pg 40 "optics of pleasure": Christine Stansell, *American Moderns: Bohemian New York and the Creation of a New Century* (New York: Henry Holt, 2000) p. 19.

pg 41 "students, journalists, scholars, advanced people, socialists, anarchists, free-thinkers": Ibid. p. 22.

pg 41 "life without father": Ibid., p. 7; "a phrase of Gertrude Steins that could stand as an epitaph for a generation."

pg 41 "Baby, my heart's on fire": "Hello My Baby," words and music by Ida Emerson and Joseph E. Howard.

pg 42 "somehow we always arrived at the Thalia Theater": Harold Meyerson and Ernie Harburg, *Who Put the Rainbow in the Wizard of Oz?* (Ann Arbor: University of Michigan Press, 1995), p. 11.

pg 42 modern popular songs have generally been written music first: However, when asked which usually came first, the words or the music, Ira Gershwin famously said, "The phone call." Quoted in Paul Zollo, "Sultans of Song," *Reform Judaism*, vol. 31, no. 2, p. 15.

pg 42 the *level of sound itself*: Professor William Labov, linguist at the University of Pennsylvania, quoted by John Seabrook, "Talking the Tawk," *The New Yorker*, November 14, 2005, p. 42.

pg 43 "an instant familiarity between audience and song": Sapoznik, *Klezmer!*, p. 44 .

pg 43 "I suppose it was singing in shul": Laurence Bergreen, *As Thousands Cheer: The Life of Irving Berlin* (New York: Viking, 1990) p. 12.

pg 43 He was, he said, "sick with a sense of his own worthlessness": Ibid., p. 16.

pg 44 "Once you start singing, you start thinking of writing songs": Ibid., p. 26.

pg 44 "my vocabulary being somewhat limited through lack of education": Ibid., p. 50.

pg 44 Eventually, he stopped cowriting with others and began working with "arrangers": Alec Wilder, *American Popular Song* (Oxford: Oxford University Press, 1972), p. 93. "I heard Berlin play the piano back in vaudeville days and found his harmony notably inept. Yet Robert Russell Bennett states unequivocally that upon hearing someone's harmonization of his songs, Berlin would insist on a succession of variant chords . . . and was not satisfied until the right chord was found. I must accept the fact that though Berlin may seldom have played acceptable harmony, he nevertheless, by some mastery of his inner ear, senses it, in fact writes many of his melodies with his natural, intuitive harmonic sense at work in his head, but not in his hands."

pg 44 part of the ongoing assault on Victorianism: Ann Douglass, *Terrible Honesty* (New York: Noonday, 1995), p. 376.

pg 45 "I'm doing something they all refuse to do": Bergreen, *As Thousands Cheer*, p. 68.

pg 46 "Syncopation," he said simply, "is the soul of every American": Ibid., p. 66.

pg 46 "the secret of the song's tremendous success": Douglass, *Terrible Honesty*, p. 374.

pg 47 "When I asked Irving what was wrong": Bergreen, *As Thousands Cheer*, p. 142.

pg 47 "folks are still singing 'Swanee River'": Ibid., p. 46.

pg 49 black "Renaissance": By the late 1830s, Harlem started to develop as a residential neighborhood. The development was sparked by the opening of the New York and Harlem Railroad, which made the commute to the "city" easier for residents of Harlem. When the IRT subway was built in 1879, Harlem became a wealthy residential suburb. The real estate boom surrounding the development of Harlem as a wealthy suburb was followed by a severe real estate slump due to a nationwide economic depression. When the Depression ended, development began at a pace never before seen in New York, and just about every square inch of Harlem was covered with row houses and tenement buildings. Then the subway began to develop even further, which caused a mass exodus from Harlem to the outer boroughs and the suburbs. The exodus left many of the tenement buildings vacant for years. Eventually, the owners of the buildings rented to black people who were looking for better accommodations than could be found downtown or had been displaced by the building of Penn Station in the beginning of the century.

pg 50 if white people taught African slaves how to speak English: Strausbaugh, *Black Like You*, p. 290.

pg 50 a new "temper of mind that enriched whatever it approached": American Moderns, quoting Walter Lippmann.

pg 51 while the music of Tin Pan Alley was often assumed to be trivial: In 1909, West 28th Street between Sixth Avenue and Broadway, the district where many of the music publishers were situated, was named Tin Pan Alley by Monroe Rosenfeld in an article for the *New York Herald*. One story has him walking through the district listening to the cacophony created by pianists banging away beside open windows, vocalists belting out the hits, and composers repeating endlessly a melody or phrase, and coining the term "Tin Pan Alley" because it sounded to him like the clatter of pots and pans. Another story was floated by Harry Von Tilzer, who claimed that he was sitting at his piano composing a song and "wanted a banjo effect," so he cut up some newspapers and stuck them behind the keys next to the strings. And in came Rosenfeld. "What are you doing . . . what are those tin pans for?" asked Rosenfeld, and the rest is history.

pg 52 Kern wrote what has been called "the single most influential song": Mark Steyn, *Broadway Babies Say Goodnight: Musicals Then and Now* (London: Routledge, 1999), p. 40.

pg 53 "It evoked the same emotional response in him": Bergreen, *As Thousands Cheer*, p. 128.

pg 54 "For all of their innovation, they seem to flow": Stephen Holden, "Irving Berlin's American Landscape," *New York Times*, 1987. http://www.nytimes.com/1987/05/10/arts/pop-view-irving-berlin-s-american-landscape.html.

pg 55 "the Original Creole Orchestra—skeptical of the whole recording process": Richard M. Sudhalter, *Lost Chords* (Oxford: Oxford University Press, 1999), p. 10.

pg 55 Until then, the sound of Louis Armstrong's horn: Alex Ross, "The Record Effect; How technology has transformed the sound of music," *The New Yorker*, June 6, 2005, p. 94.

pg 56 "I learned a lot from them about how to live": Laurence Bergreen, *Louis Armstrong: An Extravagant Life* (New York: Broadway Books, 1997), p. 54.

pg 56 "They really wanted me to be something in life": Ibid., p. 58.

pg 56 "from then on, I was a mess": Ibid., p. 56.

pg 56 "it was the Jewish family who instilled in me singing from the heart": Ibid., p. 56.

pg 57 "I couldn't visualize soldiers marching to it": Bergreen, *Louis Armstrong*, p. 147.

pg 57 the most frequent last name to appear among enlistees: Jack Gottlieb, *Funny, It Doesn't Sound Jewish* (Albany, N.Y.: SUNY Press, 2004), p. 26.

CHAPTER FOUR / The New York Opera

pg 60 "Jazz Age": the term "Jazz Age" is often credited to writer F. Scott Fitzgerald; the twenties were his decade, a moment when, in his words, the nation "was going on the greatest, gaudiest spree in history."

pg 60 "a potent market force": William Howland Kenney, *Chicago Jazz* (Oxford: Oxford University Press, 1993), p. 119. Beginning in 1913, the dance craze led to the production of dance records, which quickly turned immense profits and propelled the record industry forward. As early as 1916, record companies canvassed poor urban neighborhoods, such as the South Side ghetto, to determine how many people owned phonographs. When enough inexpensive machines had been manufactured and sold—by the mid-twenties, an Artophone suitcase portable costing $13.85 became popular on the South Side—records were designed to sell to specialized urban markets. In 1919, 2,250,000 phonographs were been sold. In 1921, one American out of seventy owned a record player. In that same year, 100,000,000 records were made. Decisions to produce black jazz band music on records intended for sale in African-American neighborhoods followed earlier efforts to profit from the sale of Irish, Yiddish, German, French, Mexican, and other ethnic musics wherever these immigrant groups clustered. After World War I, black journalists referred to African-Americans as "the Race," so the choice of the term "Race Records" did not necessarily carry negative implications for those meant to buy them. Race records also sold by mail and door-to-door salesmen. Even the newsboys for the *Chicago Tribune* and the *Defender* regularly carried copies of the latest records of the week along with their newspapers; they sold the discs at $1 apiece, and for many customers, the records were as important as the news.

pg 62 Sheet music could never suffice: One of America's strongest incentives in taking the lead in post-print media development was that much of its most important, most marketable cultural legacy was fully susceptible to no other means of transmission and commodification; the conjunction of the black performance tradition and the white media was crucial.

pg 63 ("people can't seem to realize I have a Jewish soul"): Nat Hentoff, *At the Jazz Band Ball: Sixty Years on the Jazz Scene* (Berkeley: University of California Press, 2010), p. 105.

pg 63 "a myth that you actually saw come alive": Willie "the Lion" Smith and George Hoefer, *Music on My Mind: The Memoirs of an American Pianist* (Cambridge, Mass.: Da Capo, 1975)

pg 63 his parents recognized his gift and found him a serious music teacher: Edward Jablonski, *Gershwin* (Cambridge, Mass.: Da Capo, 1987), p. 8. The family bought a piano when George was 13. At first he had lessons with local teachers, but he outpaced them quickly. He started going to concerts, and by age 14 (1912) he started studied piano with Charles Hambitzer, a great teacher who taught him Liszt, Chopin, and Debussy and "made him harmony conscious." Gershwin had "an instinctive feeling for tone combinations, and many chords that sound so modern in my orchestral compositions were set down without any particular attention to their theoretical structure. He was a serious student of music from 1912 to 1916.

pg 63 immersed himself in the aural chao: "Sultans of Song," *Reform Judaism*, p. 18.

pg 63 "His rhythms had the impact of a sledge hammer": Ibid.

pg 64 Gershwin was too young, too inexperienced: Sapoznik, *Klezmer!*, p. 108.

pg 64 breaking into Yiddish theater was like "breaking into prison": legendary comic Joe Smith to Henry Sapoznik. Sapoznik relayed this anecdote to the author in the spring of 2003.

pg 64 "this very talented ofay piano player who could perform their most difficult tricks": Claudia Roth Pierpont, "Jazzbo," *The New Yorker*, January 10, 2005. "Ofay" is pig latin for "foe"—that is, "white." See http://www.newyorker.com/archive/2005/01/10/050110crat_atlarge.

pg 64 more than a hundred thousand whites left Harlem: Ann Douglass, *Terrible Honesty* (New York: Noonday, 1995), p. 72: "Harlem's Black population, a mere handful in 1900, rose to 200,000 during the 20s. In 1910, on the eve of the Great War, roughly 90% of American's Negro population still lived in the South, 78% in the countryside. 450,000 Blacks left the South between 1910 and 1920; 750,000 more in the next decade. In 1890, one in 70 people in Manhattan was a Negro; in 1930, one in 9."

pg 65 "They were like flaming arrows in my head": Rich Cohen, *Tough Jews: Fathers, Sons, and Gangster Dreams* (New York: Vintage Books, 1998), p. 42.

pg 65 "these people are the worst element": Ibid., p. 41.

pg 66 "Murder Incorporated": Ibid., p. 97. The syndicate had invented contract killing. A stranger arrives, kills, is gone. The local cops are left with nothing. By the mid-thirties the contract killer had become a national character, like the frontiersman or logger, who embodies aspects of the American personality. To some he was a kind of existential cowboy . . . the mysterious stranger of Mark Twain who carries death in his pocket. Murder, Inc. was a Jewish gang. They became the contract killers for the syndicate.

pg 66 Rothstein raised crime to a kind of economic art: Ibid. Rothstein's lawyer told him to refuse to answer questions, saying he might incriminate himself—that is, to stand on the Fifth Amendment of the U.S. Constitution. This had never before been tried, and the lawyer went clear to the Supreme Court to make it law; this alone should guarantee Rothstein tenure in any university of organized crime.

pg 66 how to turn bootlegging into a multi-million-dollar business: http://www.mail-archive.com/ctrl@listserv.aol.com/msg07875.html. Samuel Bronfman, founder of Distillers Corporation—Seagrams Ltd., and his three brothers had been in the hotel business in Canada, but they became the richest men in that country through their involvement with bootlegging. The Bronfmans formed several corporations to handle their bootlegging operation: Atlas Finance Company, Atlas Shipping Company, and Northern Export Company. The idea for this operation had originated with Arnold Rothstein. It had the advantage that, technically, no one but the final customer was breaking the law. Joseph Kennedy, the future ambassador to the Court of St. James and the father of the 35th president of the United States, is supposed to have arranged with Frank Costello to smuggle liquor into the United States during Prohibition. Before Prohibition ended, Kennedy was appointed U.S. agent for many British distillers including Haig and Haig Ltd., John Dewar and Sons Ltd., and Gordon's Dry Gin Company. Kennedy then arranged for his newly organized Somerset Importers to import and stockpile thousands of cases of liquor, the whisky coming into the United States months before Prohibition ended under "medicinal" licenses issued in Washington.

pg 67 "that's cheap; think what it would cost if I worked full time": Douglass, *Terrible Honesty*, p. 52.

pg 67 "artistic achievement and mass distribution were not yet in conflict": Ibid.

pg 69 where and how the major meets the minor: At the turn of the 20th century, when songs had long preliminary verses, there was a tradition among the Jewish-American writers to start with a long minor verse and transition into a major chorus. With the disappearance of the long introductory verse, and the formulation of the standard 32-bar song format, divided into four sections of eight bars each, the first two eight-bar sections—now called verses—often employed the minor, while the middle section, now called the bridge, likewise employed the major. This became a paradigm for many famous songs, including "Get Happy," "Crazy Rhythm," "California, Here I Come," "Bye Bye Blackbird," "Charleston," "Sweet Georgia Brown," "I Got Rhythm," and many more.

pg 69 From "Every Time We Say Goodbye":

> "Every time we say goodbye, I wonder why a little,
> There's no love song finer, but how strange the change
> From major to minor,"

pg 69 "write Jewish": Mark Steyn, *Broadway Babies Say Goodnight: Musicals Then and Now* (London: Routledge, 1999), p. 76. One day Porter told Richard Rodgers that he'd stumbled on the formula. "What is it?" asked Rodgers. "Simplicity itself," said Porter. "I'll write Jewish tunes." And he did. He was one of the few composers to routinely write in a minor key. "It is surely one of the ironies of the musical theater that, despite the abundance of Jewish composers, the one who has a written the most enduring 'Jewish' music should be an Episcopalian millionaire born on a farm in Indiana." (Richard Rodgers); see also William Hyland, *Richard Rodgers*.

pg 70 "leisure class": Not to be confused with Thorstein Veblen's *Theory of the Leisure Class*, written in 1899, in which he coined the concept of "conspicuous leisure," defined as the waste of time by people to give themselves higher status. Whereas neoclassical economics defined humans as rational, utility-seeking people who try to maximize their pleasure, Veblen recast them as completely irrational creatures who chase after social status without much regard to their own happiness.

pg 70 the third stream would be where the two met: The term "third stream" was conceived in 1957 by composer Gunther Schuller to describe a new musical genre which, he said, was "located about halfway" between classical music (the first stream) and jazz (the second stream). As a musical "form" it never took off, inasmuch as Western classical musicians were rarely adept at improvising, and, as Schuller said, by definition, there is no such thing as "third stream jazz."

pg 70 achieving the "middle way" in America involved coming to terms with African-American culture: Richard M. Sudhalter, *Lost Chords* (Oxford: Oxford University Press, 1999), p. 141. This dialogue between popular and classical music worked both ways in America. George Gershwin knew the great European composer Ravel and at one point asked him for lessons. Ravel asked Gershwin how much money he'd made that year. When Gershwin told him, Ravel said, "My friend, it is I who should be taking lessons from you."

pg 71 "It is not the few knowing ones whose opinions": See Howard Pollack, *George Gershwin: His Life and Work* (Berkeley: University of California Press, 2007).

pg 71 "I use as much energy in writing popular music": Gershwin, talking to a *Newsweek* reporter, as quoted by Gene Lees in *Jazzletter*, Vol. 24, No. 1, February 2007, p. 4.

pg 72 "the whole of New America was blossoming before me!": "Sultans of Song," *Reform Judaism*, p. 19.

pg 72 "very much what Lindbergh's flight across the Atlantic was to transportation": Edward Jablonsky, *Gershwin* (Cambridge, Mass.: Da Capo, 1998), p. 58. Paul Whiteman's "An Experiment in Modern Music" was a promotional event to further Whiteman's fortunes. In his zeal to become a musical harbinger, Whiteman conveniently overlooked jazzman James Reese Europe, who had appeared with his Clef Club Symphony Orchestra at Carnegie Hall in May 1912 and had "astounded the white critics and public who had not yet become acquainted with the sound of syncopated music" (p. 63). At the time, virtually nobody had heard of (Jewish) composer Charles Ives, who had for years been spicing up his compositions with quotations from popular songs, folks songs, even ragtime . . . " And there had been many other experiments, going back to Louis Moreau Gottschalk, who by the mid-19th century was a celebrated pianist and composer whose works evoked Creole and Afro-American songs and dances.

pg 72 "a young Jew last week went about the business of packing a suitcase": Ibid., p. 90.

pg 73 an example of Gershwin's penchant for encoding Jewish prayer: much as the opening notes of his song "It Ain't Necessarily So" have been compared to the opening notes of the well-known Jewish prayer, the *Barchu*.

pg 73 "[Lewis] made the clarinet talk": http://www.bigbandlibrary.com/tedlewis.htm.

pg 73 Kern answered, "It'll be good Jewish music, of course": Steyn, *Broadway Babies*, p. 76.

pg 74 "make NYU a white man's college": Eric Goldstein, *The Price of Whiteness* (Princeton: Princeton University Press, 2006), p. 106.

pg 74 "If she said your hands were clean, it meant that your hands were filthy": James Atlas, *Saul Bellow* (New York: Modern Library, 2002), p. 14.

pg 74 everybody was stage-obsessed: mostly controlled by Abe Erlanger, Charles Frohman, and the Shuberts.

pg 75 "regardless of the kind of music a composer is writing": Jablonsky, *Gershwin*, p. 84.

pg 76 "I would still say it takes four or five years": Ibid.

pg 76 a form that Gershwin virtually established as the model for the Great American Songbook: Deeper examination of Gershwin's harmonic devices can be found in Alec Wilder's *American Popular Song* (Oxford: Oxford University Press, 1972). Wilder points out, "The conventional A-A-B-A structure (main strain: its virtual repetition: a release, almost always new material: and finally, a literal, varied, or extended restatement of the main strain) . . . Many people . . . assume that this form goes back much further that it actually does. There were few instances of it in any type of popular music until the late teens and it didn't become the principal form until 1925" (p. 56).

pg 76 Gershwin is the jazz musician's Stephen Foster: Gene Lees, *Jazzletter,* January 2007.

pg 77 Berliner's invention totally changed the way we disseminate information: 1924–25: A year of experiments by engineers at Bell Laboratories results in the historic breakthrough of electrical recording. Instead of the acoustic process of singers and musicians performing directly into a recording horn, they are now able to record with a condenser microphone in a spacious studio. With the use of a vacuum tube amplifier and an electromagnetically powered cutting stylus, the frequency range of recorded music expands by two and a half octaves. Within a year, every major recording studio converts to the new system.

pg 77 Fred Astaire: Fred Astaire (Austerlitz) was an assimilated Jew, a descendent of an Austrian-Bohemian German-speaking Jewish family originally from Prague. His European relatives were all born Jewish, although Fred's father and the rest of his immediate family converted to Catholicism when they were living in Linz, Austria (where Fred's father, Fritz Austerlitz, was born and baptized). http://en.wikipedia.org/wiki/Fred_Astaire.

pg 78 "By that language, and only that language, could I be redeemed": Vivian Gornick, "Radiant Poison: Saul Bellow, Philip Roth, and the end of the Jew as metaphor," *Harper's* magazine, September 2008, p. 72.

pg 78 "I recognized that I did not have to do the will of others": "I Got a Scheme!" The words of Saul Bellow (*The New Yorker*, April 25, 2005), pp. 72–85. "[A]t school you were told in textbooks and by teachers that George Washington and Abraham Lincoln were *your* Presidents. You could not be excluded when the common language became your language—when you knew the National League standings, when you had learned about the Chicago gang wars. In the papers, you followed the events leading to the killing of Dion O'Banion, of the Northside bootlegging gang, and of the indictment of Al Capone for tax evasion. You knew all the facts about the death of Lingle, the *Tribune's* gang reporter, who was shot down in the Illinois Central Randolph Street tunnel. The papers informed you that Big Bill Thompson, the mayor, was in the pocket of Capone. All this was available in the dailies, when you had become familiar with the language of the historians, chronicles, and the lingo of the insiders. You didn't know the full story from sober, reliable, dependable sources. You had come to know it by mastering the language in which it was gussied up by newspapers and by magazines like *Ballyhoo, College Humor* and Henry Luce's *Times.*"

pg 78 "America offered to free us from the control of the family and of the Jewish community": Ibid. p. 80.

pg 79 "There was something in the air that whispered of big doings": Milton "Mezz" Mezzrow, *Really the Blues* (New York: Citadel Underground, 1990), p. 5.

pg 79 "Anything and everything could happen on the Northwest Side": Ibid., p. 5.

pg 79 "What I needed was the vocabulary": Ibid., p. 18.

pg 79 "I was feeling my way to music": Ibid.

pg 79 "we knew that meant us too": Ibid., p. 14.

pg 80 "They cheered me up right away and made me feel": Ibid.

pg 80 "I was going to be a musician, a Negro musician": Ibid.

pg 80 "In a country of immigrants, there was a singular need": Bellow, "I Got a Scheme, the words of Saul Bellow," *The New Yorker*, April 26, 2010, p. 60.

pg 80 Jazz, as Neil Leonard has explained, often acted in this manner as a religion: Kenney, *Chicago Jazz*, p. 91.

pg 80 "to play, to play better this minute": Sudhalter, *Lost Chords*, p. 189.

pg 80 "First to knock, first to enter": Saul Bellow, *The Adventures of Augie March* (New York: Viking, 1953), p. 1. "In the opening sentence of my work-in-progress I don't say that I am an American Jew. I simply declare that I am an American. My eldest brother was the first to point out the advantages of this. America offered to free us from the control of the family and of the Jewish community" (See Bellow, "I Got a Scheme, the words of Saul Bellow").

pg 80 to live on both sides of the tracks at once: A dangerous path, as demonstrated by one of the most notorious crimes of the mid-twenties. It was committed by Nathan Leopold and Richard Loeb, two university students whose heads were turned by the Nietzschean ideas they wildly misunderstood. Before the murder, Leopold had written to Loeb: "A superman . . . is, on account of certain superior qualities inherent in him, exempted from the ordinary laws which govern men. He is not liable for anything he may do." Their subsequent murder of 14-year-old Bobby Franks, attempted as "the perfect crime," sent shivers through all the Jewish neighborhoods of Chicago.

pg 81 "We could roam around a town for weeks": Mezzrow, *Really the Blues*, p. 61.

pg 81 there were 500 saloons, 1,000 "concert halls": Kenney, *Chicago Jazz*, p. 14.

pg 81 they could arise at 2 a.m., get dressed in their best clothes, and hit the Stroll: Ibid., p 15.

pg 81 "Armstrong virtually invented the solo form": Sudhalter, *Lost Chords*, p. 103: "Early hot jazz was basically an ensemble music: the concept of the virtuoso soloist did not yet exist . . . a few moments spent listening to the brass and woodwind parts of any Sousa march tells much about the early jazz band ensemble playing."

pg 81 "above all this, he had the swing": Kenney, *Chicago Jazz*, p. 105.

pg 82 "The music poured into us like daylight": Eddie Condon, quoted in Kenney, Ibid., p. 60.

pg 83 "the roots of the 1930s jitterbug craze": Technology and the limits thereto also influenced the dance crazes of the era, as little more than three minutes could be cut on one side and therefore record companies often had the musicians speed up the tempos to make the arrangements fit in the limited space. These speeded-up tempos in turn generated new dance crazes.

pg 83 "'Louis' recording almost drove the English language out of the Windie [*sic*] City'": Mezzrow, *Really the Blues*, p. 118.

pg 83 "But Louis never talked about this in public": Laurence Bergreen, *Louis Armstrong: An Extravagant Life* (Cambridge, Mass.: Da Capo, 1997), p. 267.

pg 84 "a nice little cute fat boy": Ibid., p. 279.

pg 84 "Now, with the heat on Capone": Kenney, *Chicago Jazz*, p. 153. In 1928, federal agents padlocked all the most prominent cafés both in and outside the Loop. Most of the places decided alcohol was too risky and turned to gambling. By early 1929, most of the clubs using small orchestras had been closed on account of Prohibition violations. With the Depression, those small neighborhood speakeasies that survived resorted to single piano players, which furthered the development of "boogie-woogie" with pianists Jimmy Yancey, Albert Ammons, "Pine Top" Smith, Meade Lux Lewis, Clarence Lofton, Cow Cow Davenport, Montana Taylor, and others . . . boogie-woogie featured a pulsing left hand that kept the customers dancing.

pg 84 "My education was completed . . . and I became a Negro": Mezzrow, *Really the Blues*, p. 206.

pg 85 Samson Raphaelson's short story "Day of Atonement": Seymour Stark, *Men in Blackface: True Stories of the Minstrel Show* (Bloomington, Ind.: Xlibris, 2000), p. 102. Samson Raphaelson, a Jewish New York writer, was inspired by Jolson's performance on Broadway—he said Jolson's voice "reminded him of the chazans [cantors] I'd heard as a boy." Jolson was born in Seredzius, Lithuania, a crossroads village of mud paths and log houses. His father headed the village synagogue as rabbi and cantor. When Jolson was four, his father emigrated to America, leaving behind the mother and four children. Jolson was eight when they joined the father. They settled in Washington, D.C., where, nine months later, Jolson's mother died. Jolson's signature song "Mammy" is thus connected with his early loss. The personal tragedy was a key to his singing career. For Jolson, the religious Jew who could be easily recognized—by accent, dress, mannerisms, food—was a throwback to Russia.

pg 85 "first talking picture": Pioneered by Warner Bros., the Vitaphone system synchronized sound recorded on an oversize disc to be played in tandem with a running movie.

pg 86 "He is located nowhere but in his own imagination": Michael Alexander, *Jazz Age Jews* (Princeton: Princeton University Press, 2001), p. 177.

CHAPTER FIVE / Over the Rainbow

pg 92 the Aryan ideal: Other parallels from Nietszche's 1883 book *Thus Spoke Zarathustra* include the concept of the "art and power of forgetting," a kind of radical editing or blocking out of consciousness everything that doesn't serve the present purpose. A man seized by a "vehement passion" will be blind and deaf to all but that passion. Everything he does perceive, however, he will perceive as he has never perceived anything before: "All is so palpable, close, highly colored, resounding, as though he apprehended it with all his senses at once." Boethius, the sixth-century Neoplatonist, said the goal of our spiritual striving was "to hold and possess the whole fullness of life in one moment, here and now, past and present and to come." Likewise in the Eastern tradition: "Awakening to this present instant," a Zen master has written, "we realize the infinite is in the finite of each instant." Michael Pollan, *The Botany of Desire: A Plant's-Eye View of the World* (New York: Random House, 2001), p. 164. Yet we can't get there from here without first forgetting. There is another parallel here to what Mezz Mezzrow said was the goal of the Chicago jazzman's existence, to "live your whole life in one day": it was as if Jews, in coming to the New World, were forgetting their past in order to experience the present in a profound new way. It is also interesting to note that in 1924, two young Chicago

Jews, Nathan Leopold and Richard Loeb, wealthy University of Chicago students, read this same Nietzsche text and were motivated to commit the "perfect crime," murdering 14-year-old Bobby Franks to prove their own superiority.

pg 92 "Superman is the ultimate immigrant": James Wolcott, *Vanity Fair*, March 2002, p. 132. See also Michael Chabon, *The Amazing Adventures of Kavalier and Clay* (New York: Random House, 2000).

pg 93 "When we get through with the Jews in America, they'll think the treatment they received in Germany was nothing": William Manchester, *The Glory and the Dream* (New York: Bantam, 1974), p. 176.

pg 93 "at American corporations, Jewish employees were often nonexistent": Stark, Men in Blackface, p. 112. In one famous showdown between Harry Warner of Warner Bros. and the Western Electric Corporation, Warner, who was suing Western for monopolistic practices, said, "I will withdraw all our suits if you'll do one thing; if you'll give me the name of one Jew who works for your company." The suit was not withdrawn. Stark, p. 112.

pg 93 Eugenics was "the study of, or belief in, the possibility of improving the qualities of the human species": Dictionary.com Unabridged (v 1.1), Random House. Eugenics as first formulated by Sir Francis Galton.

pg 94 "to the present day we cannot forget our own slavery in Egypt": Eric Goldstein, *The Price of Whiteness* (Princeton: Princeton University Press, 2006), p. 153.

pg 94 the Scottsboro Boys (nine African-American youngsters falsely accused): See http://www.loc.gov/exhibits/treasures/trr114.html. On March 25, 1931, nine African-American males were arrested and charged with the rape of two white women. Within twelve days, all of the men were tried and convicted in a Scottsboro, Alabama, courthouse. As a result of the courageous writings of some newspaper editors and other famous writers, the U.S. Supreme Court ordered a second trial on the grounds that the men had not received adequate legal counsel in a capital case. The Communist Party moved aggressively to defend the men by hiring Samuel Leibowitz as their legal counsel. One of the plaintiffs, Ruby Bates, admitted during the second trial that the story was fabricated and that no crime had been committed, but the men were again found guilty. Subsequently, there were successful appeals and reconvictions. Although justice was never rendered, all of the Scottsboro defendants eventually found their way out of Alabama.

pg 94 "the shock troops of the revolution": Goldstein, *Price of Whiteness*, pp. 128 and 153.

pg 94 "Jews in America could be Americans first and foremost": See Mordecai Kaplan, *Judaism as a Civilization: Toward a Reconstruction of American-Jewish Life* (Philadelphia: Jewish Publication Society of America, 1981)

pg 94 *Strike Up the Band* (1930), *Of Thee I Sing*: Unlike most Broadway musicals of the 1920s, the score for *Of Thee I Sing* was not salted with hoped-for hit songs. Instead, the Gershwins wrote long-form libretto music, searching for another way to push the Broadway musical form. The result has been compared to the Gilbert and Sullivan operettas, and Gershwin even quotes from *The Pirates of Penzance* (the "Pirates' Chorus," known better today as "Hail, Hail, the Gang's All Here") in his overture. *Strike Up the Band* is in the mode of the satirical Gershwin-Kaufman-Ryskind musicals to follow. But *Let 'Em Eat Cake* (1933) has a hard-edged political thrust even by today's Broadway standards. The story concerns a Babbitt-like tycoon who protects his monopoly on the American cheese market by manipulating the United States into a war in Switzerland. The authors shoot to kill at such satirical targets as presidential cronies, red-baiting "patriots," and sanctimonious warmongers of all demagogic stripes. The cheese war is fought exclusively to fatten the wealthy, whose profiteering extends even to the auctioning of book and movie rights to the carnage. The soldiers who actually do the fighting are mere pawns of the powerful: "We don't know what we're fighting for," goes their verse in the title song. "The book's acerbic point of view holds up amazingly well—it's the writing that does not. Kaufman's lines are funnier in principle than in practice. . . . There are few such difficulties with the score. Along with the unbeatable standards ('The Man I Love,' 'Soon,' 'I've Got a Crush on You'), there are some wicked comic ditties that both hark back to Gilbert and Sullivan and anticipate Brecht and Weill: 'A Typical Self-Made American,' 'Yankee Doodle Rhythm,' and, four decades ahead of Joan Littlewood's time, an item titled 'Whoops! What a Lovely War.'" Frank Rich in *The New York Times*, http://www.nytimes.com/1984/07/11/arts/theater-a-reworking-of-strike-up-the-band.html.

pg 95 a mood somewhere between the cantorial and the blues: Howard Levy, from a lecture at the University of Wisconsin, February 5, 2003: "So on the way from major to major, you step through minor. And that's a lot of what these composers are doing, shifting up and down tonal centers, very cleverly using minor in a major context. Perhaps the most famous example of this, whether people know it or not, is from Gershwin's *Porgy and Bess*, which is 'Summertime.' And 'Summertime' really sounds like Jewish music to a lot of people. One of the reasons is because it pretends to be a totally minor experience. 'Summertime, when the living is easy . . .' It's very minor. But then the resolution. . . . And it gets positive right at the end. It pretends to be a blues, but it's not a blues. It pretends to be minor, but it's not minor. And it leaves you with the impression of a sad song but something happens within it that is upbeat, major. Even if you don't know theory, you know something interesting happens. It's still the same notes being used in the melody but [the underlying harmonic structure] gives it a totally different meaning. One has sort of a darker shading to it and the other one, it's lighter, brighter. . . . It's like a hope: 'Hush little baby, don't you cry . . .' It's like the new morning is going to break and there's an optimism. . . . It's an optimistic song, even though it's sad, which is where the major chord comes in."

pg 95 Gershwin would endow Heyward's Porgy with a "mythic immortality": Edward Jablonski, *Gershwin* (Cambridge, Mass.: Da Capo, 1987), p. 253.

pg 95 "I wrote my own spirituals and folksongs": Claudia Roth Pierpont, "Jazzbo," *The New Yorker*, January 10, 2005

pg 96 "flows on a stream of song and chant": Jablonski, *Gershwin*, p. 253.

pg 97 "I was crying. I was weeping": http://www.classical.net/music/comp.lst/works/gershwin/porgy&bess.php.

pg 97 "stole the show from their champion shouter": Jablonski, *Gershwin*, p. 276.

pg 97 "'we go around with practically nothing on'": Ibid.

pg 97 "never wavered in the conviction that he had produced a work of art": Ibid., p. 290.

pg 97 "depressing moments, too, when talk of Hitler and his gang": Ibid., p. 312.

pg 99 "more than 60 percent of the major film composers were Jews": Lees, *Jazzletter*, vol. 24, no. 1, p. 8.

pg 100 in boxing, Barney Ross: Barney Ross, born Dov-Ber Rasofsky, was a rabbinical student who, after his father died in his arms, a victim of a random robbery, lost his faith in God and, abandoning his studies, became a street brawler. He worked for Al Capone and quickly transformed himself into the first three weight-class champion in boxing history. In World War II, he became a leader for the Jewish people and all Americans in the battle against Hitler and Nazism when he gave up boxing and insisted on fighting as a Marine in Guadalcanal, where at the age of 33 he single-handedly killed 22 Japanese soldiers. Ross was perhaps the first Jewish-American person ever to have a ticker tape parade held in his honor, and likely the first to be celebrated by a president, Franklin D. Roosevelt, in a Rose Garden ceremony after his war heroics. See http://www.jewishvirtuallibrary.org/jsource/biography/ross.html.

pg 100 Yip: Harold Meyerson and Ernie Harburg, *Who Put the Rainbow in the Wizard of Oz?* (Ann Arbor: University of Michigan Press, 1995), p. 10. "*Yipsl* was the Yiddish term for a squirrel and evidently I was quite a flighty kid. I moved fast and went from one thing to another and I clowned a lot and I sort of was a maverick in the family. They were all frightened people. I tried to lift them up all the time with games and fun and running . . . so I was *yipsl* to the kids around the block."

pg 101 Gershwin insisting that Duncan was more Jewish than he: Jablonsky, *Gershwin*, p. 276.

pg 101 "'the chill of poverty which never leaves your bones'": Ibid., Yip, quoting George Bernard Shaw.

pg 101 "Parents were very proud of children who spoke English": Ibid., p. 8.

pg 101 "Jewish socialism": Irving Howe, *World of Our Fathers: The Journey of the East European Jews to America and the Life They Found and Made* (New York: Galahad Books, 1976), p. 519.

pg 102 "I don't think I could live with myself if I weren't honest about that": Meyerson and Harburg, *Who Put the Rainbow*, p. 14.

pg 102 "I was dumbfounded, staggered. Gilbert & Sullivan tied Ira to me for life": Ibid., p. 25.

pg 102 "when I lost my possessions, I found my creativity": Ibid., p. 15.

pg 103 "he raised me from a couplet": Ibid., p. 15.

pg 103 "a way to combine street smarts with book learning": Ibid.

pg 103 "internal rhyme is often a function of melodic": Ibid., p. 43.

pg 103 "Brother, Can You Spare A Dime?" Lyric by E.Y. "Yip" Harburg, Music by Jay Gorney © 1932 (Renewed) Glocca Morra Music and Gorney Music All Rights Administered by Next Decade Entertainment, Inc. All Rights Reserved.Used by Permission. Reprinted by Permission of Hal Leonard Corporation

pg 103 "The system fell apart. This was a good country": Ibid., p. 49.

pg 104 "couldn't stop crying . . . I write with what they call in Yiddish *gederim*": Yip Harburg at a speech at the 92nd Street Y, New York City, see http://www.answers.com/topic/yip-harburg

pg 104 "a great composer brings out the best in a lyricist": Stephen Whitfield, *In Search of American Jewish Culture* (Hanover, N.H., University Press of New England, 1999), p. 69.

pg 105 "an almost supernatural belief in inspiration": Meyerson and Harburg, *Who Put the Rainbow*, p. 36. See also Edward Jablonski, *Harold Arlen: Rhythm, Rainbows and Blues* (Boston: Northeastern University Press, 1996), p. 80. Gershwin said Arlen would never "approach the simplest musical requirement or idea without first calling upon 'the fellow up there'"—jabbing his finger at the ceiling.

pg 105 "the most delicious improviser I ever heard": "Sultans of Song," *Reform Judaism*, p. 20.

pg 106 many of these bands expanded: A convention pioneered by Jimmy Lunceford and Ferde Grofé on the West Coast and brought East by Fletcher Henderson, among others.

pg 107 "one of the few writers I can think of who have any emotional kinship with the jazz musician": Wilder, American Popular Song, p. 255.

pg 107 "You take a rousing song like 'Get Happy'": Jablonski, *Gershwin*, p. 81.

pg 107 "I was singing the story of my misery and confusion": Ibid., p. 51.

pg 108 "And I never gave it a thought": Ibid., p. 51.

pg 108 "He simply didn't equate quality with sales": Ibid., p. 254.

pg 108 "we'd hang around George's piano, playing our latest songs": Meyerson and Harburg, *Who Put the Rainbow*, p. 68.

pg 108 as competitive as rappers in Los Angeles today: Stephen Holden, "The Man That Got Away: The Gershwin Brother Who Treasured His Dictionary," the *New York Times*, May 11, 2009, p. C4.

pg 110 "it cannot be emphasized too much that jazz music was seen initially by the mass American audience as dance music": Barry Kernfeld, *The New Grove Dictionary of Jazz* (New York: Grove Press, 1994).

pg 110 "When they were tired, we'd end the piece": Richard M. Sudhalter, Lost Chords (Oxford: Oxford University Press, 1999), p. 330.

pg 111 "So I discovered the secret of solid drumming": Ibid., p. 35.

pg 111 The device, which he called a sock cymbal: Ibid., p. 139.

pg 111 "And all of a sudden, jazz, which was almost a cult music": www.pbs.org/jazz/about/pdfs/Maher.pdf, March 21, 1996.

pg 112 "Why don't you get a Harlem book?": Ibid.

pg 112 "This is our guy": Ibid.

pg 112 "That was the most incredible playing I've ever heard": "Sultans of Song," *Reform Judaism*, p. 19.

pg 113 "That was a wonderful band . . . a listening thrill": Whitfield, *In Search of American Jewish Culture*, p. 158.

pg 114 changing the way Americans could hear both recorded music and radio broadcasts: The ribbon or "velocity" microphone was introduced by RCA in 1931, as the model 44A, and became one of the most widely used microphones in vocal recording, to be followed in 1933 with the 77A cardioid-pattern dual-ribbon microphone.

pg 115 "He had started his Music Corporation of America in Chicago": Guy Lombardo, *Auld Acquaintance* (New York: Doubleday, 1975), p. 153.

pg 115 "I drew into a little shell, a coat of armor": Artie Shaw, *The Trouble with Cinderella* (McKinleyville, Calif.: Fithian Press, 1992), p. 25.

pg 116 "I was a Jew, whatever that meant": Ibid., p. 33.

pg 116 "I was 'different' from other kids, a strange kind of creature called 'Jew'": Ibid., p. 25.

pg 116 "Which intensified my self hatred": Ibid., p. 138.

pg 116 "in a vortex of exhibitionism": Lees, *Jazzletter*, vol. 23, no. 6. p. 5.

pg 117 "knelt down on one knee (looking sharp as a tack . . .)": Ibid.

pg 117 "I was ashamed of being a Jew": Shaw, *Trouble with Cinderella*, p. 91.

pg 118 "I didn't have to try to make a good impression on the Gentiles": Amos Oz, *A Tale of Love and Darkness*, Harcourt, 2003, p. 197.

pg 118 "there was always an underlying sense of guilt": Ibid.

pg 118 "so subtle that it could never possibly have had a lot of communicative meaning to anyone but another musician": Lees, *Jazzletter*.

pg 118 "Had Louis Armstrong never lived, I suppose there would be a jazz": Lees, *Jazzletter*, vol. 23, no. 6.

pg 119 "No clarinet player has ever created such an aura of command": Ibid.

pg 119 "I found my way to Harlem. . . . There I found temporary haven": Shaw, *Trouble with Cinderella*, p. 224.

pg 119 "I used to wish I could actually *be* a Negro": Ibid., p. 228.

pg 119 "I felt trapped, helpless, bitter, desperate, enraged": Ibid., p. 240.

pg 119 "this was for me by far the more important life": Ibid., p. 43.

pg 120 "As when you look into a clear pool of water and see the sand at the very bottom of the pool": Ibid., p. 331.

pg 120 "In spite of the recording manager": Ibid., p. 333.

pg 121 "I believe I was about as utterly miserable": Ibid., p. 346.

pg 121 "Far more so than the man who regards music as a strictly business matter": Ibid., p. 380.

pg 121 "a sideshow freak, gaped at and stared at": Sudhalter, *Lost Chords*, p. 588.

pg 121 "Any commentary that might occur to us would be lost": Ibid.

pg 122 "unworthy, undesirable, unacceptable": Shaw, *Trouble with Cinderella*, p. 288.

pg 122 "I think he enjoyed the attention he got from disdaining fame": Lees, *Jazzletter*, Vol. 23, No. 7, p. 4.

pg 122 "Artie was ashamed of being a clarinet player": Ibid.

pg 122 "I prefer to invert the old phrase": Ibid. p. 7.

pg 123 "Eugene O'Neill took five hours to say": Meyerson and Harburg, *Who Put the Rainbow*, p. 68.

pg 123 "I devised the satiric and cynical idea of the Wizard handing out symbols": Ibid., p. 153.

pg 124 the medium through which plot unfolded: Ibid., p. 122.

pg 124 "I loved the idea of having the freedom to do lyrics": Ibid., p. 140.

pg 124 "Give me time and let me think the thing out musically and lyrically": Ibid., p. 125.

pg 125 "with such symphonic sweep and bravura that my first reaction was, 'Oh, no, not for little Dorothy!'": Jablonsky, *Gershwin*, p. 131.

pg 125 "So the song went back in the picture": Meyerson and Harburg, *Who Put the Rainbow*, p. 156.

pg 126 If Congress hadn't voted a few years earlier: See http://americanhistory.si.edu/starspangledbanner/ The national anthem of the United States was written by Francis Scott Key, a lawyer, after watching the British attack Fort McHenry, Maryland, in 1814, during the War of 1812. The melody was taken from a drinking song of the Anacreontic Society (of London) that was written by the British composer John Stafford Smith. Key's words were first published in a broadside in 1814 under the title "Defence of Fort M'Henry." The song's title was changed when it appeared in sheet music form later the same year. After a century of general use, the four-stanza song was officially adopted as the national anthem by act of Congress in 1931.

pg 126 "If you want to know what's wrong with the grammar of the television news writers and announcers": Lees, *Jazzletter*, vol. 21, no. 3, p. 5.

CHAPTER SIX / Strange Fruit

pg 130 "I wanted a club where blacks and whites worked together": John Wilson, "Strange Fruit," *New York Times*, Friday, September 30, 1988 (http://www.nytimes.com/1988/09/30/obituaries/barney-josephson-owner-of-cafe-society-jazz-club-is-dead-at-86.html).

pg 130 "Why can't the nightclub business be legitimate, like shoes?": Ibid.

pg 130 "I told them," Barney said, "I was going to open a political cabaret": Ibid.

pg 130 "Betty Comden and Adolph Green were a regular feature": Max Gordon, *Live at the Village Vanguard* (Cambridge, Mass.: Da Capo, 1980), p. 35.

pg 130 "He treated musicians honestly and was always there to hear us play": Steven Holden, "Jazz Musicians Honor Max Gordon, Impresario And Father Figure," *The New York Times*, March 12, 1988,http://www.nytimes.com/1988/03/12/arts/jazz-musicians-honor-max-gordon-impresario-and-father-figure.html?src=pm pg 130 "Because of that, [the club] was intimate": Ibid.

pg 131 a poem entitled "Bitter Fruit": in the January 1937 issue of *The New York Teacher*, a union publication.

pg 132 "Sometimes singing a song can be a reaffirmation of a feeling": "Extended Interview Section: Pete Seeger," *Strange Fruit*, DVD, written and directed by Joel Katz, California Newsreel, 57 minutes, 2002.

pg 133 "jam-packed with exciting material, photos": Billy Crystal, DVD, *Billy Crystal presents the Milt Gabler Story*, © 2005 Verve Music Group.

pg 133 "So that's part of his character": Ibid.

pg 133 "The marvel and mystery of great jazz": Jerry Wexler, *Rhythm and the Blues* (New York: St. Martin's Press, 1993), p. 24.

pg 133 "Just as Picasso signed his name": Ibid., p. 37.

pg 134 "weaving a spell over the smoky Sunday afternoon": Ibid., p. 44.

pg 134 "For God's sake, when are you going to put the hole in the middle?": Lees *Jazzletter*, vol. 23, nos. 8, 9 & 10, 2007.

pg 136 these songs went on to become bestsellers: CD booklet, *Frank Sinatra: The Columbia Years: 1943–1952*, The Complete Recordings, vol. 1, 1993.

pg 137 "When Frank hit that screaming bunch of kids": Jeffry Ward and Ken Burns, *Jazz: A History of America's Music* (New York: Knopf, 2000), p. 311.

pg 138 "Gone, perished, vanished from the face of the earth": Wexler, *Rhythm*, p. 183.

pg 138 As early as 1911, the *Forward* noted that: Eric Goldstein, *The Price of Whiteness* (Princeton: Princeton University Press, 2006), p. 75.

pg 138 "We used to bring twenty different bands in": Hy Weiss, from a rare interview done in the late 1960s for Jerry Wexler of Atlantic Records, tape provided to the author by Mr. Wexler.

pg 138 "These were the artists who made my career": Wexler, *Rhythm*, p. 83.

pg 140 "My job was throwing out whiskey heads": Hy Weiss tape.

pg 140 "[They] only sold three labels: RCA, Columbia and Decca": Ibid.

pg 140 "Then when you walked downtown [to the franchise stores], they wouldn't even let you in": Ibid. .

pg 140 "And they never were able to get back into the rhythm-and-blues field": Ibid..

pg 141 "Everybody in this business thinks they're an artist": Bob Krasnow to the author.

pg 141 How *authentic* was Irving Berlin writing "White Christmas": "Sultans of Song," *Reform Judaism* magazine, p. 15.

pg 143 "made for hire": a term that appears on copyright forms as well as many industry contracts, indicating that the composition and/or performance was bought and paid for at the moment of conception by a third party.

pg 144 "I always admired Mr. Glaser. . . . He was a crude sonofabitch, but he loved me and my music": Laurence Bergreen, Louis Armstrong: An Extravagant Life (New York: Broadway, 1997), p. 279.

pg 144 "It is an essential paradox of the vernacular arts": Tom Piazza, "Pop View: The Little Record Labels That Could (and They Did)," *New York Times*, November 6, 1994.

pg 145 without the white college audiences, bebop . . . couldn't have survived: Dizzy Gillespie, in conversation with the author, Chicago, 1976.

pg 146 pumping out local dance music, jazz, hot blues and boogie-woogie: Piazza, "Pop View."

pg 146 "reel-to-reel magnetic recording tape": Nick Tosches, "Who Killed the Hit Machine?" *Vanity Fair* Magazine, November 2002: "The Magnetophon recording device was originally invented in Nazi Germany by AEG, which later was acquired by Daimler Benz. The plastic-based electromagnetic tape itself was invented by BASF, a part of I. G. Farben, the manufacturer of Zyklon B, the death gas used in concentration camps. So vastly superior was the lifelike fidelity of the technology that it allowed Hitler to address the nation by radio while confounding the Allied forces, who could not determine his location by tracing the sources of these time-delayed broadcasts. When the war ended, the United States commissioned the new Ampex Corporation of California to further develop this Nazi technology. By the spring of 1949 high-fidelity magnetic-tape recording had become the standard of the music business, and the first high-fidelity phonographs and records—vinyl 33 1/3 rpm long-playing microgroove records, then vinyl 45 rpm singles—had been introduced to the market."

pg 147 "Why can't we sell a few more while we're there? So we got in the race business": This Syd Nathan quote comes from a rare interview done in the late 1960s for Jerry Wexler of Atlantic Records; provided to the author by Mr. Wexler.

pg 147 "There are no geniuses": Ibid.

pg 147 "And brother if you don't believe that people in business are tight with their money": Ibid.

pg 148 Wabash Avenue, a white neighborhood with a sizable Jewish population that bordered on an expanding black neighborhood: Nadine Cohodas, *Spinning Blues into Gold: The Chess Brothers and the Legendary Chess Records* (New York: St. Martin's Press, 2000), p. 20.

pg 148 sustained in part by keeping some of the traditions from home intact: Ibid.

pg 149 "a marriage of commerce and culture": Ibid., p. 35.

pg 149 "You got a hit record there," the owner said: Ibid., p. 39.

pg 149 "because he was around black people all his life": singer Paul Gayten, New Orleans; See www.discogs.com/artist/Paul+Gayten.

pg 149 "Here was a guy who had blind faith": Ibid.

pg 151 "It was the beat and it got into my boots": Alfred Lion, *Blueprints of Jazz: Blue Note at 60.* EMI press release, 1999.

pg 152 "Now Is the Time," which itself became the template: Paul Williams released "Hucklebuck" in 1949 on Savoy, and it was number one on the R&B charts for 14 weeks; a shuffle blues instrumental built around the sound of a furiously honking saxophone, it helped give impetus to the raucous variant of R&B that evolved into rock and roll. Williams was an alto player, a jazz musician, from Detroit, where Herman Lubinsky of Savoy heard him and sent Teddy Reig in to produce him. Reig told him to honk; "He kept telling me not to play a whole lot of notes. He kept saying 'Honk! Honk! Honk!'"

pg 153 "he's recognizable and he's unique": Rudy Van Gelder to the author.

pg 153 "Some of this music moved me so much": Art Rupe, *The Specialty Story*, box set liner notes.

pg 153 "I had studied records . . . I did it with a stop watch": Ibid.

pg 154 "On Jordan, we used a perfectly balanced rhythm section": "Milt Gabler and the Commodore Records Story," National Public Radio, *Riverwalk*, broadcast the week of October 11, 2001.

CHAPTER SEVEN / Up on the Roof

pg 158 a simple love story represents the possibility of Jewish assimilation: see Andrea Most, *Making Americans: Jews and the Broadway Musical* (Cambridge, Mass.: Harvard University Press, 2004).

pg 158 "All parties are passing the buck": Saul Bellow in a letter to Cynthia Ozick, July 19, 1987, quoted in *The New Yorker*, April 26, 2010, p. 60.

pg 160 "And if everything is loud and at the same level": Mark Steyn, Broadway Babies Say Goodnight (London: Routledge, 1999), p. 218.

pg 161 Shortly thereafter, he was leading the group through six hours of a hammering, monotonous cycle of major chords: author's experience.

pg 162 "What we were doing was presiding at a happening starring Ray Charles": Jerry Wexler in conversation with author.

pg 162 "cat music": When Leonard Chess first got into the South, he found people who believed in him. He made friends with the disc jockeys, with the manufacturers, and with the suppliers. The South was really his prime territory. This is an interesting contrast with the Jewish "Southern experience" from the period around 1911–12, when Irving Berlin wrote "Alexander's Ragtime Band." Then Jews were totally focused on the South as well, but they had never been there and didn't know anything about it. Now the Jews were going to the South and they were learning more about it than anyone ever knew. This was the South for real. This was the real America. This wasn't some mythical "Way Down Upon the Swanee River" and "Old Folks at Home" South. When the Jews eventually figured out the Southern market, they were able to totally transform the record business.

pg 166 "Music was everywhere. Music was running through my head" Jerry Leiber and Mike Stoller with David Ritz, *Hound Dog: The Leiber and Stoller Autobiography* (New York: Simon & Schuster, 2009), p. 7.

pg 166 "I was trusted and therefore untouchable," he remembers: Scott Benarde, *Stars of David* (Waltham, Mass.: Brandeis University Press, 2003), p. 19.

THERE WAS A FIRE: JEWS, MUSIC AND THE AMERICAN DREAM

pg 167 "The doors had opened. I had entered his world": Ritz, *Hound Dog*, p. 25.

pg 167 "It was the late forties," he remembered: Ibid., p. 12.

pg 167 "and our notion of fun was rooted in authenticity": Ibid., p. 34.

pg 168 "We knew they felt authentically black": Ibid., p. 37.

pg 169 "he de-sexed it but it was enough that it freaked out the white folks": Michael Billig, *Rock and Roll Jews* (Syracuse: Syracuse University Press, 2000), p. 37.

pg 169 "When the music was sung by one of their own": Ibid., p. 37.

pg 170 "black life was being presented as a mirror": Ibid., p. 52.

pg 170 "The best way to cross boundaries is the promise of a good time": John Pareles, obituary of Ahmet Ertegun in *The New York Times*, December 15, 2006.

pg 172 "On Broadway" Words and Music by Barry Mann, Cynthia Weil, Mike Stoller and Jerry Leiber (c) 1962, 1963 (Renewed 1990, 1991) SCREEN GEMS-EMI MUSIC INC. All Rights Reserved. International Copyright Secured. Used by Permission Reprinted by Permission of Hal Leonard Corporation.

pg 173 "Most people spend their lives trying to get out of the slums": David Kamp, "The Brill Building," *Vanity Fair*, November 2001, p. 248.

pg 173 Carole King and Jerry Goffin's hit song, "Up on the Roof"; lyrics available on many websites including www.oldielyrics.com.

pg 174 "we knew they'd be writing their asses off": Kamp, "Brill Building." p. 250.

pg 174 "I got this kid. He's talented": Ibid.

pg 175 "No hint of the personal tragedy was audible": Billig, Rock and Roll Jews, p. 104.

pg 175 What this story doesn't tell us about Spector's emotional compass: On April 14, 2009, after 30 hours of deliberation, a jury convicted Phil Spector of second-degree murder in the death of actress Lana Clarkson. Spector showed no reaction as the verdict was announced. Superior Court Judge Larry Paul Fidler declined to allow Spector to remain free on bail pending sentencing, citing Spector's years-long "pattern of violence" involving firearms. "This was not an isolated incident," Fidler said, noting Spector's two previous firearm-related convictions from the 1970s. "The taking of an innocent human life, it doesn't get any more serious than that." Clarkson, 40, was found dead, slumped in a chair in the foyer of Spector's Alhambra, California, mansion with a gunshot wound through the roof of her mouth in February 2003. See http://www.cnn.com/2009/CRIME/04/13/phil.spector.verdict/index.html.

pg 175 "They knew nothing about the record": Billig, Rock and Roll Jews, p. 105.

pg 176 "He took on Senator Joseph McCarthy as surely and seriously in the pages of *Mad* as Edward R. Murrow did on television": Steven Heller, *New York Times Book Review*, August 9, 2009; see also Denis Kitchen and Paul Buhle, *The Art of Harvey Kurtzman: The Mad Genius of Comics* (New York: Abrams Comic Arts, 2009).

pg 176 "Payola," a word combining the words "pay" and "victrola": Cohodas, *Spinning Blues into* Gold, p. 174: "Payola had been going on for a century. It was not thought of as illegal and no one had ever been punished for it. In 1863, the composer of 'Tenting Tonight on the Old Camp Ground' gave the leader of a famous singing group a share of the song's earnings to make sure the group would sing the song at well-attended concerts. By 1905 music publishers on Tin Pan Alley were paying out five hundred thousand dollars a year to get stage stars to sing certain songs. *Variety* first used 'payola' in public in an editorial in 1916 condemning the 'direct payment evil.' By the 1920s, 'song plugging' was a recognized profession where vaudeville performers or band leaders were persuaded to perform a tune. The emergence of the phonograph record combined with commercial radio broadcasting reduced the influence of plugging songs for live performances. Now the focus was on broadcasters. In the beginning it wasn't so much getting a record played—it was not yet clear whether air play would boost sales—but rather broadcasting the live performances of bands at hotels and ballrooms around the country. By the late 1940s and early 1950s, it was clear that radio play was important in creating a hit."

pg 178 "He knew it meant 'fucking' in the black community": Hy Weiss interview.

pg 178 "Had Freed been a Methodist, it is hard to imagine Richard praising 'the little Methodist boy'": Cohodas, *Spinning Blues into Gold*, p. 110.

pg 178 "I wasn't identifying down; I *was* down": Wexler to author.

pg 179 the name "Bo Diddley" popped into his head: Cohodas, *Spinning Blues into Gold*, p. 104.

pg 179 "They wouldn't have sat down like Leonard did": Ibid., p. 105.

pg 179 "the integration of chart categories": Ibid., p. 106.

pg 180 "At the same time record people were being thrown in jail": Ibid., p. 182.

pg 180 "the whole game was: Can I get the sounds in my head on tape?": Alec Wilkinson, "The Gift: Paul Simon's search for the next song," *The New Yorker*, November 25, 2002, pp. 64–76.

pg 182 "Dust Bowl Troubadour": See http://xroads.virginia.edu/~1930s/RADIO/woody/ah.html.

pg 182 "He put himself in the camp," Nora said: Michael Hill, "Jewish Songs Show New Side of Guthrie," Associated Press, 2003.

pg 182 "Jack sounds more like me than I do": www.newportfolkfest.net/lineup/ramblin-jack-elliott.

pg 184 "there would be a little group around them": Dave Van Ronk, *The Mayor of MacDougal Street* (Cambridge, Mass.: Da Capo, 2005), p. 42.

pg 184 "that rush to assimilate was not limited to Jews": Ibid, p. 29.

pg 184 "Now, Ladies and Gentlemen, I would like to present the three Jews from New York": Ibid., p. 30.

pg 185 "Any music is the music of its time": Ibid, p. 162.

CHAPTER EIGHT / Hiding in Plain Sight

pg 189 Her response was to develop the demeanor of a star: James Spada, *Streisand* (New York: Crown, 1995), p. 166: "The allure of Barbra's glitzy success was especially inspiring to youngsters who didn't fit into the WASPish mold of cheerleader or captain of the football team. If she could turn homely into exotic and a prominent 'schnoz' into a classic profile and make the cover of *Vogue* in the bargain, maybe they could too."

pg 189 "I felt like I was chosen": Ibid., p. 166.

pg 189 "Why can't you be more like other domestic girls?": Ibid.

pg 189 "I knew what she was feeling": Ibid.

pg 191 "The first guy that picked me up asked me": *Playboy*, February 1966. See http://nymag.com/daily/entertainment/2007/10/the_ten_most_incomprehensible.html.

pg 191 "I'll let you be in my dream if I can be in yours": "Talkin' World War III Blues."

pg 192 "it wasn't an ideology, it was a mood": Van Ronk, *Mayor of MacDougal Street*, p. 200.

pg 192 "bears in the pine forests": Howard Sounes, *Down the Highway: The Life of Bob Dylan* (New York: Grove, 2001), p. 16.

pg 192 "you can have some amazing hallucinogenic experiences": Ibid., p. 17.

pg 192 "I think it's the land. The streams, the forests": interview with Bill Flanagan, Huffington Post, April 15, 2009.

pg 193 "Because frankly, if it hadn't": Sounes, *Down the Highway*, p. 17.

pg 193 not disenfranchised but focused, smart, funny: Lauterbach interview.

pg 193 "those who are not busy being born are busy dying": "It's Alright Ma (I'm Only Bleeding)."

pg 193 "I become speechless unto myself": Sounes, *Down the Highway*, p. 16.

pg 194 "The stuff *off the main road*": Flanagan interview.

pg 194 "spacey little guy, you know": Sounes, *Down the Highway*, p. 43.

pg 194 "I would run into him at seven in the morning": author's interview.

pg 195 "I went out and traded my electric guitar and amplifier for an acoustical guitar": Sounes, *Down the Highway*, p. 44.

pg 195 "a vessel waiting and wanting to be filled": Ibid., p. 44.

pg 195 It was not that he was ashamed of being Jewish: Ibid., p. 44.

pg 195 "He had a sense that fortune had put her hand": Ibid.

pg 195 "He was definitely one of the most noticeable people around": Ibid.

pg 195 "Really nice and clear and had bite to them": Clinton Heylin, *Bob Dylan: Behind the Shades* (New York: HarperCollins, 1999), p. 41.

pg 196 "If you didn't call him Woody": Ibid., p. 46.

pg 196 "a voice in my head said, 'So this is the game.'": Louis Menand, "Bob on Bob," p. 129 Also see Bob Dylan, *Chronicles: Volume One* (New York: Simon & Schuster, 2004).

pg 197 "I have a very strong memory of his sitting on that mattress": author's interview with Ann Lauterbach.

pg 197 "he was extremely attractive in his mysteriousness": Ibid.

pg 197 "He didn't come there for that": Ibid.

pg 197 "He was an avatar of this kind of troubadour energy": Ibid.

pg 197 "He had this notion of being inside of a time": Ibid.

pg 198 "That's the thing about his work": Ibid.

pg 198 "I'm here to pay tribute to Woody Guthrie": Sounes, *Down the Highway*, p. 83. Guthrie's second wife was Jewish, and his kids (Nora and Arlo) had the same kind of hair and looks as Bob. The kids were home watching television and they let him in. Eventually, Marjorie (Woody's ex-wife) befriended him in part because (in Nora's words) "I think my mother responded to the Jewish part of him. I think that was endearing to her."

pg 199 "He had to reinvent the wheel all the time": Van Ronk, *Mayor of MacDougal Street*, p. 84.

pg 199 "He fed right into that romantic myth": Ibid.

pg 199 "I remember he solemnly gave us a demonstration of Indian sign language": Ibid., p. 83.

pg 199 "This is what he did": Lauterbach interview.

pg 201 "Everything about that movie I identified with": Van Ronk, *Mayor of MacDougal Street*, p. 85.

pg 201 Dylan emerged from seeing *The Threepenny Opera*: *The New Yorker*, May 1, 2006, p. 94.

pg 201 "the spectator adopts an attitude of smoking-and-watching": Ibid.

pg 201 "It was the form, the free verse association": Ibid.

pg 202 "I pitied the people who had to work with him": Sounes, *Down the Highway*, p. 103.

pg 202 "To be on the side of people who are struggling": Heylin, Bob Dylan, p. 95.

pg 203 "the songs were the most powerful thing in our arsenal": "Joan Baez: How Sweet the Sound," PBS, October 14, 2009.

pg 204 Dylan's lyrics too were deceptively simple:

> How many roads must a man walk down
> before you call him a man?
> Yes, 'n' how many seas must a white dove sail
> before she sleeps in the sand?
> Yes, 'n' how many times must the cannon balls fly
> before they're forever banned?
> The answer, my friend,
> is blowin' in the wind,
> The answer is blowin' in the wind.

pg 204 "He was driven, and obviously enlightened": Sounes, *Down the Highway*, p. 121.

pg 204 "It roared through him the way paint roared through Van Gogh": Ibid.

pg 205 "Line after line after line trying to capture the feeling of nothingness": Heylin, Bob Dylan, p. 102.

pg 205 "that unswerving understanding of who he was": Ibid., p. 84.

pg 205 "those dumb guys . . . but then these words came out": Ibid., p. 115.

pg 205 knowledgeable A&R men like John Hammond: Lieberson, a Jewish bon vivant who mingled with royalty, was president of CBS in 1956. He had joined Columbia as an A&R man in 1939 and built up the roster of classics and pop. In addition, he signed Vladimir Horowitz and Leonard Bernstein to CBS and produced the original cast album of *My Fair Lady*—which sold 5 million copies worldwide in 1957, more than any previous LP ever. And because Goddard had persuaded CBS to financially back the show, the company made another $32 million. His employees loved him, he was tall and distinguished, wore custom-made clothes, and had, as his friend Walter Cronkite said, "impeccable taste in all things. He was perfectly tailored for Bill Paley's 'Tiffany' network." (Paley, a Jew, bought Columbia Records in 1938 for $700,000). Leiberson employed a core of senior executives that shared his breath of cultural vision, that it was the obligation of a major American corporation to develop classical music, and as cultural engineers, to be able to develop Broadway as a musical tradition, to develop sound tracks for movies as a cultural tradition, and to develop popular music, particularly in the area of rock and roll where a whole counter culture was starting to seep into the firmament.

pg 207 "polite, studious and eager to please—college boys": Alec Wilkinson, "The Gift: Paul Simon's Search for the Next Song," *The New Yorker*, November 25, 2002, p. 69.

pg 207 When the interviewer pressed him: Ibid.

CHAPTER NINE / Sorry, Son, You Can't Do Both

pg 212 Jerry Wexler "was at the beginning": Al Bell in an interview provided by Wexler, done in 1986 for KKSU student radio at Kansas State by Dave MacFarland, associate professor of radio/television.

pg 212 "he [Wexler] doesn't draw the line, he erases it": Ibid.

pg 212 "Jerry Wexler always turned that element up": Jim Dickinson, quoted in Alex Halberstadt, "Jerry Wexler," Salon.com, September 5, 2000 (see http://entertainment.salon.com/2000/09/05/wexler_2/).

pg 213 "brought the depth of literature to a music": Ibid.

pg 213 "That kind of gritty earth-driven music": Jan Wolkin and Bill Keenom, *Michael Bloomfield: If You Love These Blues* (San Francisco: Miller Freeman Books, 2000), p. 3.

pg 213 "just a fat kid. Bad at school, bad at sports": Ibid., p. 3.

pg 214 "Sit over there and don't tell anybody you're my son": Ibid., p. 8.

pg 214 "If you didn't have the ability to add and calculate quickly": Ibid., p. 9.

pg 214 "Get a real job. Go into business": Ibid., p. 13.

pg 214 "I saw myself, in my mind, as this lanky hillbilly": Ibid., p. 10.

pg 214 "The maids were cool, hip, sophisticated people": Ibid., p. 12.

pg 215 "You can play whatever the tune is, but you can't do any type of encore": Ibid., p. 15.

pg 215 "So that proved to us even more that these white people we knew were really stupid": Ibid., p. 16.

pg 215 "He wanted me to be a jock and he wanted me to be a good student": Ibid., p. 17.

pg 215 "Michael would bring his guitar and amp into his father's bedroom": Ibid., p. 18.

pg 215 "I couldn't play it. All I could do was play rock and roll": Ibid.

pg 216 "Here was this other world that was totally unimaginable": Ibid., p. 21.

pg 216 "I don't think Michael wanted to distance himself from the money": Ibid., p. 48.

pg 217 "Everything was so awful back then for everybody": Ibid., p. 52.

pg 217 "Sometimes a cat would be up there, and the groove'd be so strong": Ibid., p. 22.

pg 217 "I'd be tremblin'. I'd be like a dog in heat": Ibid., p. 25.

pg 218 "And then we'd go downstairs to where Spann lived": Ibid., p. 27.

pg 218 "What I learned from them was invaluable": Ibid., p. 27.

pg 219 "These were times when the culture was saying": Ibid., p. 33.

pg 219 "You had to be a man up there": Ibid., p. 36.

pg 220 "Anyway, we jammed that day,": Ibid., p. 99.

pg 220 "There was no concept. No one knew what they wanted to play": Ibid., p. 100.

pg 220 "went into the control room and sat there pretending to be a reporter": Al Kooper, *Backstage Passes and Backstabbing Bastards* (New York: Billboard Books, 1998), p. 35.

pg 221 "Hey, you don't even play the organ": Ibid.

pg 221 "The best I could manage was to play hesitantly by sight": Ibid., p. 36.

pg 221 "Like a Rolling Stone" went to number one: Ibid.

pg 222 "It's that thin, that wild mercury sound. . . . crack of dawn": from the 1978 Ron Rosenbaum interview for *Playboy*, quoted by Louis Menand, "Bob on Bob," p. 130.

pg 222 "I knew I was listening to the toughest voice I ever heard": Sounes, *Down the Highway*, p. 180.

pg 222 "a generation that I was supposed to be the voice of": Bob Dylan, *Chronicles: Volume One* (New York: Simon & Schuster, 2004), p. 115.

pg 223 "Bob was like a warrior": Wolkin and Keenom, *Michael Bloomfield*, p. 107.

pg 223 "He said we'd go on and be stars and everything": Kooper, *Backstage Passes*, p. 41.

pg 224 "Everybody wound up going to San Francisco": Wolkin and Keenom, *Michael Bloomfield*, p. 142.

pg 224 "Michael, I think, was the guy, *the* guy, that got a lot of the black blues bands playing in the major venues": Ibid., p. 124.

pg 224 "Bloomfield and Graham, they're both like funky Jews": Ibid., p. 123.

pg 224 "as great a guitar player as Michael was, he was really a teacher": Ibid., p. 125.

pg 225 "We were hula hoops. We were skateboards": Ibid., p. 192.

pg 225 "Dylan was physically vibrating . . . there was a yawning chasm between him and any kind of human activity": Johnny Byrne quoted in *Bob Dylan: Behind the Shades Revisted*, Clinton Heylin (New York, HarperCollins, 2001), p. 258.

pg 226 "He was also reading the stories of Isaac Bashevis Singer": Sounes, *Down the Highway*, p. 231.

pg 226 "From that time on, Larry often accompanied Dylan on tour": author's interview with Bob Cohen.

pg 226 "It took me a long time to get to do consciously what I used to be able to do unconsciously": http://en.wikipedia.org/wiki/John_Wesley_Harding_(album).

pg 228 "If I wasn't Bob Dylan, I'd probably think that Bob Dylan has a lot of answers": Louis Menand, "Bob on Bob," *The New Yorker*, September 4, 2006, p. 126.

pg 229 "This [affirmative action] is the next and the more profound stage of the battle for civil rights": See www.infoplease.com/spot/affirmative1.html.

pg 229 "In the American context, the most ironical thing about Negro anti-Semitism": Eric Goldstein, The Price of Whiteness (Princeton: Princeton University Press, 2006), p. 219.

pg 229 "Under the guise of righteousness, hoodlums were practicing extortion": Wexler, *Rhythm*, p. 227.

pg 230 "We became a group in a uniform": Steven Lee Beeber, *The Heebie-Jeebies at CBGB's: A Secret History of Jewish Punk* (Chicago: Chicago Review Press, 2006), p. 118.

pg 231 "You can't read a book because you get to page 17": Ibid., p. 13.

pg 232 "the first guy to personalize humor": Robert Klein interviewed by Anderson Cooper, "Jerry Seinfeld; the Comedian Award," HBO special, April, 2007. (also see http://www.thenation.com/article/fear-and-laughing-las-vegas).

pg 232 "dope will get you through times of no money": Gilbert Shelton, *The Collected Adventures of the Fabulous Furry Freak Brothers* (San Francisco; Rip Off Press).

pg 232 "That's how he got to see me": Joel Makower, Woodstock: The Oral History (Albany, N.Y.: SUNY Press, 2009; originally published New York: Doubleday, 1989), p. 25.

pg 233 "that fucking festival you guys are planning": Rosenman, Roberts, Pilpel ("Buying Off the Underground"), *Young Men With Unlimited Capital: The Story of Woodstock* (New York, self-published, 1974) p. 102.

pg 233 "No, we're just a bunch of Jewish kids trying to play rock and roll": Scott Benarde, *Stars of David* (Waltham, Mass.: Brandeis University Press, 2003), p. 124.

pg 233 "They remained in places they could be critical of": Ibid., p. 126.

pg 234 "I couldn't get any space for myself and my family": Howard Sounes, *Down the Highway*, p. 208.

pg 234 "He hasn't so much changed rock as he's killed off one kind and substituted another": Louis Menand, "Bob on Bob, Dylan talks," *The New Yorker*, September 4, 2006, http://www.newyorker.com/archive/2006/09/04/060904crbo_books#ixzz1SSpr8V1e.

pg 234 "Tin Pan Alley is gone. I put an end to it": Sounes, *Down the Highway*, p. 180.

pg 234 "I just put them down on paper": Heylin, *Bob Dylan*, p. 82.

pg 234 "Stuff like 'It's Alright Ma'": Sounes, *Down the Highway*, p. 167.

pg 235 "It's in *the way* you say things": Louis Menand, "Bob on Bob, Dylan talks."

pg 235 "He could see these things happening to him": Heylin, *Bob Dylan*, p. 150.

pg 235 "When a man attached himself to God": Martin Buber, *The Legend of the Baal-Shem* (Princeton: Princeton University Press, 1955), p. 39.

pg 236 "A lot of times you get trapped in your persona": Wolkin and Keenom, *Michael Bloomfield*, p. 110.

pg 236 "I wake and I'm one person": David Gates, "Dylan Revisited," *Newsweek*, October 6, 1997, p. 64.

pg 236 "He looks ravaged": Lauterbach interview.

pg 236 "I ask questions and tell stories": Heylin, *Bob Dylan*, p. 179.

pg 236 "What can I say, I'm proud of Mike Bloomfield and Bob Dylan": author's interview, 2006.

CHAPTER TEN / It's Good to Be King

pg 240 "That reflected itself in all sorts of ways": David Kamp, "The Brill Building," *Vanity Fair*, November 2001, p. 248.

pg 240 "The songs we had were utterly bizarre," said Becker: Ibid.

pg 240 "you realized that everyone you wanted to talk to was on the West Coast": Ibid.

pg 240 the context of no context: See George W. S. Trow, *Within the Context of No Context* (New York: Little, Brown, 1978).

pg 241 "the perfect musical antiheroes for the Seventies": http://rockhall.com/inductees/steely-dan.

pg 241 "eclectic, reminiscent, amused, fickle, perverse": Trow, *Within the Context*, p. 99.

pg 242 "The idea of choice is easily debased": Trow, *Within the Context*, p. 60.

pg 242 "The acceleration of change in our time": Alvin Toffler, *Future Shock*, (New York, Random House, 1970), p. 3.

pg 242 "We have pop and op . . . amphetamines and tranquilizers": Ibid., p. 11.

pg 242 We were "living through the general crisis of industrialism": Ibid., p. 166.

pg 243 "We develop a throw-away mentality": Ibid., p. 50.

pg 243 "a covert operation to break into the office of Ellsberg's psychiatrist": Egil Krogh (June 30, 2007), "The Break-In That History Forgot," *New York Times*, http://www.nytimes.com/2007/06/30/opinion/30krogh.html.

pg 245 "He understood the logic of this immediately": Mike Melvoin, interview with author.

pg 245 "In the sixties, when Beach Boys fans went out to see them in concert": Scott Benarde, Stars of David (Waltham, Mass.: Brandeis University Press, 2003), p. 27.

pg 246 "Do you get kids who really can't play very well": Melvoin interview.

pg 246 "You can go back to Rousseau, the noble savage": Ibid.

pg 246 "The record company became like a symphony": R. Serge Denisoff, *Solid Gold: The Popular Record Industry* (New Brunswick, N.J.: Transaction Books, 1975), p. 146.

pg 248 they developed what became known as "the Buckshot Theory": Ibid., p. 97.

pg 248 "the lunge of demography *here* as opposed to *there*": Trow, *Within the Context*, p. 56.

pg 248 "That it *was* improvised—mostly out of rock and roll music": Ibid., p. 56.

pg 249 "The laughter was uproarious": Fredric Dannen, *Hit Men* (New York: Random House, 1990), p. 53.

pg 250 the most powerful men in the business: Trow, *Within the Context*, p. 4.

pg 250 "And I think that as the pioneer creators phase out of the business": Ben Sidran, "Tightening the Hand-Tooled, Turquoise-Encrusted Belt," *Rolling Stone*, May 22, 1975.

pg 252 "Wow, if they'll sign the Dead": Bob Thomas, *Clown Prince of Hollywood: The Antic Life and Times of Jack L. Warner* (New York: McGraw-Hill, 1990), p. 62.

pg 253 "Dad, what's a Jew?": Benarde, *Stars of David*, p. 159.

pg 253 "God's Song (That's Why I Love Man Kind)"

> I burned down your city
> How blind you must be
> I take from you your children and you say
> How blessed are we
> You all must be crazy
> To put your faith in me
> That's why I love mankind
> You really need me
> That's why I love mankind

pg 255 "They say money can't buy you love . . . but it will get you a half pound of cocaine": from the song "It's Money That I Love."

pg 255 "There's some kind of ignorance L.A. has that I'm proud of": See http://en.wikipedia.org/wiki/Randy_Newman.

pg 255 "This is my office": Tommy LiPuma, interview with author, 2002.

pg 255 "When you said you didn't want to see me around here again, did you mean here in New York or here in the United States?": Ibid.

pg 256 "Never how to do it, when to do it, how much it costs": Don Graham, interview with author, 2002.

pg 256 "We didn't have the funds . . . but we sure had the fun": author's interview, 2002.

pg 256 "We'd exchange ideas, get out of the barber chair and get back to work": Graham interview.

pg 258 "CBS doesn't sue a Clive Davis for just $90,000": "The Spector of Payola," *Newsweek*, June 11, 1973, p. 79.

pg 258 "We have uncovered evidence of a new payola scandal": *New York Post*, March 31, 1972.

pg 258 "Let the journalists of CBS News cover the story": William Safire, "The Drugola Scandal," *New York Times*, June 21, 1973, p. 39.

pg 259 "You're done with a bunch of schmucks": Hy Weiss interview.

pg 260 radio promotion started to look like a sanctioned shakedown operation: Fredric Dannen, *Hit Men: Power Brokers and Fast Money Inside the Music Business* (New York: Random House, 1990), p. 16. By 1979, CBS was spending $10 million a year on Indie promo. That meant the industry as a whole was spending at least $40 million. How much was being used to bribe radio stations? It was becoming "institutionalized payola." . . . It was driven in part by the realization at large record companies that if radio airplay were not free, it would mean a major competitive advantage for them. The threat of RICO liability—following the '60s "payola" scandals—created an incentive for record companies to retain independent contractors for record promotion in order to insulate themselves from criminal liability. . . . By 1985, Indie promo was costing as much as $80 million a year and a label was spending up to $300,000 to promote one record. The record industry was spending at least 30% of its pretax profits on indie promotion."

pg 260 "Walter wore his ethnicity like a gabardine": Ibid., p. 22.

pg 261 Walter saw himself as "rabbi, priest, guru, banker for sure": Ibid., p. 23.

pg 261 "I had a Beethoven piece—one of the sonatas–and I started boogie-woogieing to it one day": Debbie Geller and Tom Hibbert, *Billy Joel* (New York: McGraw-Hill, 1985), p. 8.

pg 261 "If I'm not going to Columbia University, I'm going to Columbia Records": Hank Bordowitz, *Billy Joel: The Life and Times of an Angry Young Man* (New York: Billboard Books, 2006), p. 22.

pg 262 "You don't want it bad enough": On the way out of the building, I ran into Steve Backer, the man who actually ran the jazz program at Arista. I told him about my meeting and he told me, "Don't blame the messenger for the message."

pg 262 others, like "Allentown" and "We Didn't Start the Fire": lyrics can be found on many web sites including www.metrolyrics.com

pg 262 "It's been a theme that's probably gone through all my songs": Geller and Hibbert, p. 226. See also http://www.thevillager.com/villager_12/billyjoel.html. Billy Joel grapples with the Past, Jerry Talmer.

pg 263 "So unconsciously I made a war out of it": Dannen, *Hit Men*, p. 120.

pg 263 "Lawyers became afraid: I can't ask Walter for that!": Ibid., p. 126.

pg 264 "In other words, we want everybody to be fun and good-looking": See http://everything2.com/title/Studio+54.

pg 264 "That was our version of 'Come on baby, let's do the Twist'": "History of Disco," *Vanity Fair*, February 2010, pp 133.

pg 265 "At one point I remember dancing, closing my eyes": Bethann Hardison quoted in "History of Disco," p. 134.

pg 265 "He was like the P. T. Barnum or the Mike Todd of the recording industry": Dannen, *Hit Men*, p. 168.

pg 266 "We weren't making money, sales were shrinking": Ibid., p. 211.

pg 267 "It became the new club": "History of Disco," p. 140.

pg 268 "Very few Jewish performers are openly Jewish in their work": Benarde, *Stars of David*, p. 207.

pg 268 "The Germans are my second favorite people": Ibid., p. 208.

pg 268 "a picture of Santa Claus smoking a cigarette": Questions for Gene Simmons by John Glassie, December 2, 2001, http://www.glassie.com/_questions_for_gene_simmons__13366.htm.

pg 269 "Art . . . is highly overrated. Michelangelo, Mozart, Rembrandt": Ibid.

pg 269 "I still see America as the promised land": Ibid.

pg 270 1945 might as well have been a hundred years ago: author interview with Morgan Usadel, Champaign, Il., 2004.

CHAPTER ELEVEN / Yo Is Oy Backwards

pg 274 (The jazz band stands by that decision to this day): Jaime Diaz, December 2006 http://www.golfdigest.com/golf-tours-news/2006-12/kennyg.

pg 274 "earning himself a place in the Guinness Book of World Records": Bruce Haring (1997-12-02), "Kenny G. Blows," at http://music.yahoo.com/read/news/12037787.

pg 275 "for his incredible arrogance to even consider such a thing": Pat Metheny on Kenny G, http://www.JazzOasis.com.

pg 275 "Create their own stories to songs": See www.youtube.com/watch?v=iaOg6kkheu4.

pg 275 "Grusin Rosen Productions, and their first co-production was nominated for a Grammy": the album was *Rashida* for the artist Jon Lucien.

pg 275 "by 1978, they were in a co-venture with Clive Davis": See http://www.grusin.net/first_grusin_rosen_production.htm.

pg 277 Beginning with the "me decade" of the late seventies: The term "me decade" was coined by novelist Tom Wolfe in *New York* magazine in August 1976.

pg 278 a lot of motion and a lot of gestures: See Zora Neale Hurston, "Characteristics of Negro Expression," in *Folklore, Memoirs and Other Writings* (New York: Library of America, 1995), p. 835.

pg 279 "the sounds of people's histories, dub histories": Jeff Chang, *Can't Stop Won't Stop: A History of the Hip-Hop Generation* (New York: Picador, 2005), p. 30.

pg 281 "I said, 'I gotta be in this business'": Ibid., p. 131.

pg 281 "But on the flip side, it was also getting us into places": Ibid., p. 177.

pg 282 "It's nothing but a beat and a chant": Phil Upchurch, interview with author, Los Angeles, 2004.

pg 282 "the best thing was knowing the words to the Coolio song 'Gangsta's Paradise'": interview with author, 2003.

pg 282 "I always went to school with these nerdy little Jewish boys": author's interview, 2003.

pg 283 "I don't like anything that's mediocre": interview of Rick Rubin by Lisa Johnson and Joy Williams (http://www.artistwd.com/joyzine/music/rubin/rubin.php).

pg 283 "I started making records that sounded like what I heard at the clubs": Lisa Roy, *Confessions of a Professional Fan: the Rick Rubin Story*, EQMag, online, December 31, 2001.

pg 283 "I saw this void and starting making those records": Lynn Hirschberg, "The Music Man: Can Rick Rubin Save the Record Business?" *New York Times Magazine*, September 2, 2007, pp. 28–50.

pg 284 "by myself I was just a kid making records": Johnson interview of Rick Rubin.

pg 284 "I sent a Xerox of the check to my parents": Hirschberg, "The Music Man," http://www.nytimes.com/2007/09/02/magazine/02rubin.t.html

pg 284 "They were wearing red sweat suits with stripes": Alan Light, "The Story of Yo", *Spin* magazine, September 1998 http://www.spin.com/search/search.php?q=15th+anniversary+issue.

pg 284 "How much more obnoxious and conspicuous could we have possibly been?": Ibid.

pg 284 "And as long as they talked about white boys and beer and stuff like that": Ibid.

pg 284 "an ongoing self and group critique": Ibid.

pg 285 "I didn't know what the fuck was going on": Ibid.

pg 285 "I think when they played the Beastie Boys on MTV": Ibid.

pg 285 "The whole fucking planet's trying to figure out who they are": Ibid.

pg 285 "And we were still in the dorms": Ibid.

pg 286 "you can have a party at our house": author's interview, 2003.

pg 286 "We are going to win with no compromise": Chang, *Can't Stop Won't Stop*, p. 244.

pg 286 "Everything, all culture, all western civilization flowed through Bam, Herc and Flash": Ibid., p. 24.

pg 287 Public Enemy (the group they formed) would fashion themselves as "the Black Panthers of rap": Ibid., p. 246.

pg 287 "Rap gives you the news on all phases of life": Harry Allen, "Public Enemy: Leading a Radio Rebellion," *Black Radio Exclusive*, February 26, 1988, p. 38.

pg 287 "Griffin was the one who told reporters that the group was now drawing on the thinking of Malcolm X": Paul Cruickshank, "Public Enemy: The Complete Rap," *Valley Regional*, November 1988.

pg 288 "If our leadership is to be determined by an eighteen-year-old without a plan": Chang, *Can't Stop Won't Stop*, p. 275.

pg 288 "If the Palestinians took up arms, went into Israel": The Stud Brothers, "Black Power," *Melody Maker*, May 28, 1988.

pg 288 "He was absolutely unmoved. He said, 'I'm sorry, Bill'": Chang, *Can't Stop Won't Stop*, p. 284.

pg 288 "I'm not saying all of them [but] the majority": Ibid., p. 285.

pg 289 "Nigger, niggernigger niggernigger fuck this fuck that bitch bitch": Brian Cross, *It's Not About a Salary: Rap, Race and Resistance in Los Angeles* (New York: Verso, 1993), p. 197.

pg 289 "I remember one night he said to me, 'Are you allowed to vote?'": http://heebmagazine.com/jerry-heller-2/1215.

pg 289 "I looked in the mirror one day and I said, 'Wow, you sure got handsome this year'": Ibid.

pg 289 "The white kids in the Valley picked it up": Lynn Hirschberg, "The Music Man."

pg 289 "At that age, it feels as good to feel bad": David Kamp, "Sweet Bard of Youth," *Vanity Fair*, March 2010, p. 262.

pg 290 "the original members of NWA have grossed somewhere in the neighborhood of $1.75 billion": *See* http://www/imdb.com/name/nm1060397/bio.

pg 290 "If you don't like what's on TV, turn it off": Lisa Roy, *Confessions of a Professional Fan*, EQMag, online December 31, 2001, 04:47:00:000 p.m.

pg 290 "I think it's the parents' responsibility to teach kids values": Ibid.

pg 292 "She's one of the reasons why hip-hop is where it's at today": Karen Schoemer, "Women in Music: Record Breaker," *Elle*, June 26, 2009, p. 122.

pg 292 "I'm still a good person. I'm still a good person": Ibid.

pg 292 "And I'm hoping at the end of the day that it sells a lot": Ibid.

pg 292 "they *come to be responsible for what they know*": George W. S. Trow, *Within the Context of No Context* (New York: Little Brown, 1978), p. 58.

pg 293 "And there's no clear answer about how to fix that problem": Lynn Hirschberg, "The Music Man."

pg 293 "I can imagine people coming up with brilliant creative ideas here": Ibid.

CHAPTER TWELVE / There Was a Fire

pg 296 Life's a Lesson, © 1980 Ben Sidran, Bulldog Music.

pg 298 "I was white, I was Jewish": Dorothy Wade and Justine Picardie, *Music Man* (New York: W. W. Norton, 1990), p. 58.

pg 300 "An ounce of image is worth a pound of performance": interview on CBS Television, January 4, 1984.

pg 300 Roth spent an entire chapter explaining how being a Jew drove his performance: See David Lee Roth, *Crazy from the Heat* (New York: Hyperion, 1997).

pg 300 "He wasn't going to let Judaism stand in the way of a good time": Scott Benarde, *Stars of David* (Waltham, Mass.: Brandeis University Press, 2003), p. 257.

pg 300 "What you get from repression . . . is fury": Ibid.

pg 301 "I like the shack and the mansion": "Lenny Kravitz, Profile in Style," *International Herald Tribune*, November 20, 2010, p. 62.

pg 301 "And when I finally did accept myself for myself": See www.mtv.com/bands/az/kravitz_lenny/bio.jhtml.

pg 301 "Here's a black Jew, light-skinned, he's not doing hip-hop": Tim Murphy, *New York Magazine*, October 9, 2009 (http://nymag.com/news/intelligencer/encounter/59892/).

pg 302 The band plays versions of "Avinu Malchenu": Bernard, *Stars of David*, p. 341.

pg 302 "To have Soulfarm juxtapose a Carlebach tune to the Dead's 'I Know You Rider'": Michael Endelman, "Pop Bands Whose Beat Is Orthodox and Hip," *New York Times*, July 10, 2003 (http://www.nytimes.com/2003/07/10/arts/pop-bands-whose-beat-is-orthodox-and-hip.html).

pg 302 "Or, as one young Hasid put it, 'Once a Hasid shaves his curls, he's a hipster'": Baruch Herzfeld, quoted by Michael Idov, "Hipsters, Hasids and the Williamsburg Street," *New York*, April 19, 2010, p. 49.

pg 302 "Of course my Jewish friends weren't much better": Steven Beeber, *The Heebie-Jeebies at CBGB'S*, (Chicago Review Press, 2006), p. 214.

pg 303 "The idea is to put Ornette Coleman and the Jewish scales together": Quoted in "Beyond Tradition," *Jazziz*, Winter, 2009 p. 70.

pg 303 he "started crying like a baby": Ibid.

pg 303 "Just as jazz music has progressed from Dixieland": Quoted in "Fine Jewish Cuisine," Radical Jewish Culture series on John Zorn's Tzadik label, *Jazziz*, November 2008.

pg 304 "I think the thing jazz showed the world": Neil Tesser "Beyond Tradition, "*Jazziz*, Winter 2009, p. 73.

pg 304 there never was such a thing as "true" Jewish music: Beeber, p. 222.

pg 305 "a particular mathematics that is intimately familiar to Jews": David Samuels, "Assimilation and its Discontents," *New York*, October 6, 2008, p. 206.

pg 305 "Who would want to belong to a club in New York that didn't accept Jews as members?": Ibid.

pg 305 "the best blueprint to validate her son's dedication": Jane Ulman, *Jewish Journal*, Friday March 13, 2008 (http://www.jewishjournal.com/bar_and_bat_mitzvahs/article/will_bro_mitzvah_find_roots_in_african_american_community_20080314/).

pg 306 "How do we help them resonate with the language of prayer": Laurie Goodstein, "In New Prayer Book Signs of Broad Change," *New York Times*, September 3, 2007 (http://www.nytimes.com/2007/09/03/us/03prayerbook.html).

pg 306 complete lyrics from Sandler's Hanukkah song, at http://www.asandler.com/lyrics.

pg 307 "tidal wave of vivid, chilling, overpowering imagery and poetry": Benarde, *Stars of David*, p. 364.

pg 307 "So many people have approached or written me": See http://wu-international.com/misc_albums/Interviews/Remedy%20Interview.htm.

pg 308 "Listening to these old records, there was a whole different kind of flow": See http://www.mcgill.ca/news/2006/summer/rock/.

pg 308 "The event was the first-ever presidential Seder": Jodi Kantor, "Next Year in the White House: A Seder Tradition," *New York Times*, March 27, 2010 (http://www.nytimes.com/2010/03/28/us/politics/28seder.html?partner=rss&emc=rss).

pg 309 "They saw their own future at stake": Dara Horn, "Commentary Young Jews, Unvanishing," *Hadassah Magazine*, May, 2007 http://www.hadassahmagazine.org/site/c.twI6LmN7IzF/b.576694/k.1BD4/May_2007_Vol_88_No_9.htm.

pg 309 "Whites will be in the minority": *New York Times*, May 6, 2010, p. A18. "The percentage of babies born to non-Hispanic white women declined to 53 percent of all births in 2008—only slightly more than half—compared with 65 percent in 1990."

pg 309 "Kind of a punk hip-hop format": author's interview, 2010.

pg 309 "It's so lame. It's mad-libs. Take Black references": Teresa Wiltz, *Washington Post*, Saturday, June 11, 2005, p. C01.

pg 310 "I wasn't [Jewish] before I got into this band": Ibid.

pg 311 "what it *is* is supposed to be exactly what it isn't": author's interview with Leo Sidran, March 6, 2010.

pg 311 When people get involved in media transactions of this nature: George W. S. Trow, *Within the Context of No Context* (New York: Little Brown, 1978), p. 60.

pg 311 "among people in the same room at the same time": Rabbi Gerald C. Skolnik of the Forest Hills Jewish Center in Queens, *New York Times*, Sunday, July 5, 2009, p. 4.

pg 314 the deepest part of Judaism is not throwing a shawl over your head: Yet it is important to note, as does the Dali Lama in his book *Toward a True Kinship of Faiths*, that Jewish ritual, especially in the context of exile and diaspora, is "a particular form of continuity and connection that allows great pluralism of views and beliefs" (p. 95).

pg 314 The Jew reminds the world that to the other guy, you *are* the other guy: See Howard Becker, *Outsiders: Studies in the Sociology of Deviance* (New York: Free Press, 1963).

SELECTED BIBLIOGRAPHY

Alexander, Michael. *Jazz Age Jews.* Princeton: Princeton University Press, 2001.

Armstrong, Karen. *A History of God.* New York: Ballantine, 1993.

Atlas, James. Saul Bellow. New York: Modern Library, 2002.

Becker, Howard. *Outsiders: Studies in the Sociology of Deviance.* New York: Free Press, 1963.

Bergreen, Laurence. *As Thousands Cheer: The Life of Irving Berlin.* New York: Viking, 1990.

———. *Louis Armstrong: An Extravagant Life.* New York: Broadway, 1997.

Benarde, Scott. *Stars of David.* Waltham, Mass.: Brandeis University Press, 2003.

Billig, Michael. *Rock and Roll Jews.* Syracuse: Syracuse University Press, 2000.

Bordowitz, Hank. *Billy Joel: The Life and Times of an Angry Young Man.* New York: Billboard, 2006.

Buber, Martin. *The Legend of the Baal-Shem.* Princeton: Princeton University Press, 1955.

Cahill, Thomas. *The Gift of the Jews.* New York: Anchor Books, 1998.

Carhart, Thad. *The Piano Shop on the Left Bank.* New York: Random House, 2002.

Chang, Jeff. *Can't Stop Won't Stop: A History of the Hip-Hop Generation.* New York: Picador, 2005.

Chatwin, Bruce. *Songlines.* New York: Picador, 1998.

Cherry, Colin. *On Human Communication.* Cambridge, Mass.: MIT Press, 1957.

Cohen, Rich. *Tough Jews: Fathers, Sons, and Gangster Dreams.* New York: Vintage, 1998.

Cohodas, Nadine. *Spinning Blues into Gold: The Chess Brothers and the Legendary Chess Records.* New York: St. Martin's Press, 2000.

Cross, Brian, *It's Not About a Salary: Rap, Race and Resistance in Los Angeles.* New York: Verso, 1993.

Dannen, Fredric. *Hit Men: Power Brokers and Fast Money Inside the Music Business.* New York: Random House, 1990.

Denisoff, R. Serge. *Solid Gold: The Popular Record Industry.* New Brunswick, N.J.: Transaction, 1975.

Dimont, Max. *Jews, God and History.* Dublin: Mentor, 1964.

Douglass, Ann. *Terrible Honesty.* New York: Noonday, 1995.

Drachsler, Julius. *Democracy and Assimilation: The Blending of Immigrant Heritages in America.* New York: Macmillan, 1920.

Dylan, Bob. *Chronicles: Volume One.* New York: Simon & Schuster, 2004.

Fiedler, Leslie. "Come Back to the Raft Ag'in, Huck Honey!" from *The New Fiedler Reader.* Amherst, N.Y.: Prometheus Books, 1999.

Foer, Jonathan Safran. *Everything Is Illuminated.* New York: Houghton Mifflin, 2005.

Gabler, Neal. *An Empire of Their Own: How the Jews Invented Hollywood.* New York: Anchor, 1988.

Geller, Debbie, and Tom Hibbert. *Billy Joel.* New York: McGraw-Hill, 1985.

Goldstein, Eric. *The Price of Whiteness.* Princeton: Princeton University Press, 2006.

Gordon, Max. *Live at the Village Vanguard.* Cambridge, Mass.: Da Capo, 1980.

Hayakawa, S. I. *Language in Thought and Action.* San Diego: Harcourt Brace Jovanovich, 1990.

Heller, Joseph. *God Knows.* New York: Scribner, 1984.

Hentoff, Nat. *At the Jazz Band Ball: Sixty Years on the Jazz Scene.* Berkeley: University of California Press, 2010.

Heylin, Clinton. *Bob Dylan: Behind the Shades.* New York: HarperCollins, 1999.

Hollander, John. *Emma Lazarus: Selected Poems.* New York: Library of America, 2007.

Howe, Irving. *World of Our Fathers: The Journey of the East European Jews to America and the Life They Found and Made.* New York: Galahad, 1976.

Hurston, Zora Neale. "Characteristics of Negro Expression," in *Folklore, Memoirs and Other Writings.* New York: Library of America, 1995.

Jablonski, Edward. *Gershwin.* Cambridge, Mass.: Da Capo, 1987.

———. *Harold Arlen: Rhythm, Rainbows and Blues.* Boston: Northeastern University Press, 1996.

Kamenetz, Roger. *The Jew in the Lotus: A Poet's Rediscovery of Jewish Identity in Buddhist India.* New York: HarperCollins, 1994.

Kaplan, Mordecai. *Judaism as a Civilization: Toward a Reconstruction of American-Jewish Life.* Philadelphia: Jewish Publication Society of America, 1981.

Kenney, William Howland. *Chicago Jazz.* Oxford: Oxford University Press, 1993.

Kernfeld, Barry. *The New Grove Dictionary of Jazz.* New York: Grove, 1994.

Kertzer, David. *The Popes Against the Jews: The Vatican's Role in the Rise of Modern Anti-Semitism.* New York: Knopf, 2001.

Kirsch, Jonathan. *King David: The Real Life of the Man Who Ruled Israel.* New York: Ballantine, 2000.

Kitchen, Denis, and Paul Buhle. *The Art of Harvey Kurtzman: The Mad Genius of Comics.* New York: Abrams Comic Arts, 2009.

Kooper, Al. *Backstage Passes & Backstabbing Bastards.* Milwaukee: Backbeat, 1998.

Kriwaczek, Paul. *Yiddish Civilization: The Rise and Fall of a Forgotten Nation.* London: Phoenix, 2005.

Lehrer, Jonah. *How We Decide.* Boston: Mariner, 2009.

Leiber, Jerry, and Mike Stoller, with David Ritz. *Hound Dog: The Leiber and Stoller Autobiography.* New York: Simon & Schuster, 2009.

Levitin, Daniel. *The World in Six Songs.* New York: Dutton, 2008.

———. *This Is Your Brain on Music.* New York: Dutton, 2006.

Lombardo, Guy. *Auld Acquaintance.* New York: Doubleday, 1975.

Makower, Joel. *Woodstock: The Oral History.* New York: Doubleday, 1989.

Manchester, William. *The Glory and the Dream.* New York: Bantam, 1974.

Melnick, Jeffrey. *A Right to Sing the Blues.* Cambridge, Mass.: Harvard University Press, 2001.

Meyerson, Harold, and Ernie Harburg. *Who Put the Rainbow in the Wizard of Oz?* Ann Arbor: University of Michigan Press, 1995.

Mezzrow, Milton "Mezz," and Bernard Wolfe. *Really the Blues.* New York: Citadel Underground, 1990.

Mithen, Steve. *The Singing Neanderthals.* Cambridge, Mass.: Harvard University Press, 2006.

Most, Andrea. *Making Americans: Jews and the Broadway Musical.* Cambridge, Mass.: Harvard University Press, 2004.

Palmer, Christopher. *The Composer in Hollywood.* London: Marion Boyars, 1993.

Pollack, Howard. *George Gershwin: His Life and Work.* Berkeley: University of California Press, 2007.

Pollan, Michael. *The Botany of Desire: A Plant's-Eye View of the World.* New York: Random House, 2001.

Roth, David Lee. *Crazy from the Heat.* New York: Hyperion, 1997.

Roth, Joseph. *The Wandering Jews.* New York: W. W. Norton, 1927.

Roth, Philip. *Operation Shylock*. New York: Vintage, 1994.

Sacks, Oliver. *Musicophilia: Tales of Music and the Brain*. New York: Picador, 2008.

Sapoznik, Henry. *Klezmer! Jewish Music from Old World to Our World*. New York: Schirmer, 1999.

Schor, Esther. Emma Lazarus. Nextbook/Schocken, 2007.

Shaw, Artie. *The Trouble with Cinderella*. McKinleyville, Calif.: Fithian, 1992.

Shorto, Russell. *Island at the Center of the World*. New York: Doubleday, 2004.

Sidran, Ben. *Black Talk*. New York: Holt, Rinehart & Winston, 1971; Cambridge, Mass.: Da Capo, 1981.

Smith, Willie "the Lion," and George Hoefer. *Music on My Mind: The Memoirs of an American Pianist*. Cambridge, Mass.: Da Capo, 1975.

Sounes, Howard. *Down the Highway: The Life of Bob Dylan*. New York: Grove, 2001.

Spada, James. *Streisand*. New York: Crown, 1995.

Stansell, Christine. *American Moderns: Bohemian New York and the Creation of a New Century*. New York: Henry Holt, 2000.

Stark, Seymour. *Men in Blackface: True Stories of the Minstrel Show*. Bloomington, Ind.: Xlibris, 2000.

Starr, S. Frederick. *Bamboula! The Life and Times of Louis Moreau Gottschalk*. Oxford: Oxford University Press, 1995.

Stearns, Marshall. *The Story of Jazz*. Oxford: Oxford University Press, 1956.

Steyn, Mark. *Broadway Babies Say Goodnight*. London: Routledge, 1999.

Strausbaugh, John. *Black Like You*. New York: Tarcher Penguin, 2006.

Sudhalter, Richard M. *Lost Chords*. Oxford: Oxford University Press, 1999.

Thomas, Bob. *Clown Prince of Hollywood: The Antic Life and Times of Jack L. Warner*. New York: McGraw-Hill, 1990.

Thomas, Lawrence, in Jeffrey Rubin-Dorsky and Shelley Fisher Fishkin. *People of the Book: Thirty Scholars Reflect on Their Jewish Identity*. Madison: University of Wisconsin Press, 1996.

Toffler, Alvin. *Future Shock*. New York: Random House, 1970.

Trow, George W. S. *Within the Context of No Context*. New York: Little, Brown, 1978.

Van Ronk, Dave. *The Mayor of MacDougal Street*. Cambridge, Mass.: Da Capo, 2006.

Wade, Dorothy, and Justine Picardie. *Music Man*. New York: W. W. Norton, 1990.

Ward, Geoffrey C., and Ken Burns. *Jazz: A History of America's Music*. New York: Knopf, 2000.

Wexler, Jerry. *Rhythm and the Blues*. New York: St. Martin's Press, 1993.

Whitfield, Stephen J. *In Search of American Jewish Culture*. Lebanon, N.H.: University Press of New England, 1999.

Wilder, Alec. *American Popular Song*. Oxford: Oxford University Press, 1972.

Wittgenstein, Ludwig. *Philosophical Investigations*. London: Macmillan, 1953.

Wolkin, Jan, and Bill Keenom. *Michael Bloomfield: If You Love These Blues*. San Francisco: Miller Freeman, 2000.

INDEX

INDEX

CPSIA information can be obtained at www.ICGtesting.com
Printed in the USA
LVOW11s2041020616

490959LV00002B/367/P